D1035549

# My Friend, the Enemy

## The Author

Born 10 September 1923, in Beckum, Germany, Uri Avnery emigrated to Palestine in 1933, became a member of the Irgun from 1938 to 1942, and fought with the Haganah in 1948, being wounded in December of that year. He has served three terms in the Israeli Knesset, and is Co-Chairman of the Progressive List for Peace, as well as being a founding member of the Israeli Council for Israeli–Palestinian Peace. Today he is Publisher and Editor-in-Chief of the prestigious weekly news magazine, *Haolem Hazeh* (This World). In addition to four books in Hebrew, his most recent book, *Israel without Zionists*, was published in English in 1968 and has since been translated into Hebrew, French, Italian, German, Danish, Dutch and Spanish. Uri Avnery has campaigned unceasingly for peace between Jews and Palestinians based on mutual acceptance and recognition, withdrawal by Israel to the pre-1967 borders, and coexistence of Israel and Palestine as two independent friendly states.

# My Friend, the Enemy

URI AVNERY

Westport, Connecticut

*My Friend, The Enemy* was first published by Zed Books Ltd.,
57 Caledonian Road, London N1 9BU, UK, in 1986



Avnery, Uri, 1923-
My friend, the enemy.

1. Jewish-Arab relations—1973- . 2. Palestinian Arabs—Interviews. 3. Hammami, Said—Interviews. 4. Sartawi, Issam—Interviews. 4. Sartawi, Issam—Interviews. 5. Arafat, Yasir, 1929- —Interviews. 6. Lebanon—History—Israeli intervention, 1982- 7. Avnery, Uri, 1923- —Journeys—Lebanon. I. Title.
DS119.7.A92 1986 956'.04 86-82531
ISBN 0-88208-212-4
ISBN 0-88208-213-2 (pbk.)

Published in the United States by
Lawrence Hill & Company, Publishers, Inc.
520 Riverside Avenue, Westport, Connecticut 06880

Printed in the United States of America

# Contents

To

**Khalida**
widow of Said Hammami

**Waddad**
widow of Issam Sartawi

and to

**Rachel**
my wife, who has spent so many hours of anxiety

Will they ever meet?

The Friend and the Enemy, Beirut, 3 July 1982

# PART I

# Beirut

# 1

*Suddenly, it is all very scary.*

*We are in the middle of a huge traffic jam, between the two parts of war-torn Beirut. We have crossed the lines of three armies — the Israelis, the Phalangists and the regular Lebanese Army. No one has asked us any questions, perhaps because we have attached ourselves to the car of a German television crew, whose chief is just waving his Lebanese credentials. My blue eyes and northern appearance must have convinced the Lebanese that we too belong to this outfit.*

*We are a part of a sea of cars inching forward at a snail's pace. Many Lebanese who have found refuge from the war in the eastern, Christian part of the city, still have business and families in the western, Muslim part and use every lull in the fighting for a quick dash there and back. Since the early hours of today, there has been no bombardment, just sporadic machine gun fire.*

*It is very, very hot.*

*The three of us — the reporter, Sarit Yishai, and the photographer, Anat Saragusti, both members of the staff of my magazine, and myself — are in a Lebanese taxi, which we have hired for the occasion, not daring to use our own car with its Israeli licence plates. Suddenly we realize that there is no way back. We are hemmed in on all sides by the mass of cars crawling forward.*

*To the right of us, there is the building of the Lebanese Parliament, guarded by some Lebanese gendarmes, and to the left of us, the bulk of the famous museum. We are blissfully unaware that inside this building there is a hidden outpost of the PLO forces.*

*And there, in front of us, 50 yards ahead, is a big mound of earth blocking the road. On top of it — some wild-looking, khaki-clad figures, brandishing Kalashnikoff assault rifles.*

*We see them for the first time in our lives: the terrible enemy, the 'terrorists', the guerillas, the Fedayeen, the PLO Army.*

*What is going to happen? Have they been told? How will they react when they see for the first time the enemy, the Zionists, the Israelis?*

*I look at the two girls with me. The colour of the skin of their faces has changed, paled, become greenish. 'I am scared!' says Sarit.*

*The first thing which comes to my mind is a joke I heard many years ago. To quiet their nerves, I tell it to them:*

*A rich American comes to Shanghai. He sees a Catholic nun tending a group of lepers.*

*'Gosh, I would not do this for a million dollars!' says the rich man.*

*'Neither would I', says the nun.*

# 2

I didn't see him come in.

We had been sitting for some time in the apartment of Imad Shakur, Arafat's assistant for Israeli affairs and a former employee of my magazine, making conversation, making the time pass. Children were rushing around, relatives were coming in and out. We were waiting, not really believing that the incredible was about to happen.

Suddenly he was there. I realized it when there was a sudden quickening of the tension, a commotion near the entrance.

He came in quickly, embraced some of his people. Then he came towards me, a big smile on his face, embraced me and kissed me on both of my cheeks, a gesture I still find a little embarrassing.

He was exactly as I had seen him so many times on television, and also very, very different. I have seen in my life many political leaders and international celebrities, but never one whose public image is so different from his real self as Yassir Arafat.

He was taller than I had expected. The first thing that I noticed was that he had a well-kept beard, not the odd three days' stubble which has become his trademark. That was an optical illusion. His beard is grey laced irregularly with black. The camera does not see the grey, and that is how the unkempt appearance is created.

The second thing one notices is his eyes. On the television screen they appear fanatic, even a little bit crazy. In reality, they are very warm, brown eyes, liquid, doe-like. They give him a soft look. So does his mouth with its fleshy, soft lips. The two girls with me also noticed his small, white, delicately-shaped hands. He was dressed in well-pressed khaki battle dress and wore his famous khaki army cap.

He sat down on the sofa, between my correspondent Sarit Yishai and me, and from that point on it all became very natural, two people meeting and talking, sometimes joking, sometimes arguing. His English was good, not perfect, and from time to time he asked his people to translate a word from the Arabic.

At one point, he was trying to find the English word 'conspiracy'. He said it in Arabic, the Palestinian poet Mahmud Darwish translated it into Hebrew, I translated it from Hebrew into English; we all laughed.

At another point Sarit asked him if he knows any Hebrew. Laughing, he said in Hebrew: 'I love you. How are you?'

'You see', joked Darwish, 'he is a bachelor. Why don't you marry him?'

'No, no!' exclaimed Arafat, 'that's too much!' But after a second: 'But if this would bring a solution, why not?'

One could easily forget for a moment that we were in the middle of a war, in the middle of a battle. Arafat believed at that moment, as did I, as did practically everybody, that Ariel Sharon was set to attack West Beirut, to destroy the PLO forces there, to kill Arafat. Hundreds of Phalangists and Israeli agents were surely looking for him in West Beirut at this very moment. There was a kind of euphoria in the air, the kind people have when they know that they may die any day, that their chances of survival are slim, that anyhow it's out of their hands and in the hands of Allah, or God, or plain chance. I felt it sometimes when I was a combat soldier in 1948.

It was a deadly serious meeting, and a deadly serious discussion, even if it had its lighter moments. We felt that we were making history.

Yet, 24 hours before, I hardly dared dream of this meeting.

* * *

I had come to Beirut two days earlier, accompanied by an officer of the Israeli Army Spokesman's Office, as I had already done several times since the outbreak of the war. I had asked the spokesman to be left there alone, with my two assistants, because I wanted to interview political figures. This was contrary to the spokesman's routine at that time, but permission was granted.

Upon arriving at the Israeli Army command post in Beirut, I met some foreign journalists who were staying in the city. One of them, a German television cameraman who had once interviewed me in Tel Aviv, volunteered to give me the telephone number of the important politicians, Bashir Jumayil, Camille Shamoun and others. 'Do you also want the telephone number of Arafat?' he asked.

I was amazed. 'Can one call him?'

This is how I learned an astounding fact: In spite of the war and the siege of West Beirut, telephone communications between the two parts of the city were intact. The switching station was located in the western part.

I wrote down the numbers and during the day tried several times to establish contact. There was no answer. I had been warned that the PLO offices in West Beirut were changing their location daily, in order to forestall the kind of commando raid for which the Israeli Army is renowned.

After some time, I gave up. Instead, we travelled around the country — those parts which were controlled by the Israeli Army or the Phalangists. We went to Jubail, the biblical Byblos, on the way to Tripoli. I believe we were the first Israelis there. In the evening, we were invited to a party of some rich Maronites in Junia. Somebody was having a birthday, we ate and drank a lot and had a highly civilized conversation in English and French with a group of cultured people, merchants and artists. No one paid any attention to the thunder of shells and bombs in nearby Beirut.

At the height of the festivities, one of my hosts, a well-to-do Maronite merchant, in an advanced stage of intoxication, asked me: 'What are you people waiting for? You have to go into West Beirut!'

'What for?'

'Why, to kill all of them, every single Palestinian!'

'Women and children too?' I asked.

'Everyone of them!'

For a moment I thought this was a kind of joke. But the man was quite serious.

It was a crazy country.

On the way back, around midnight, I had an inspiration. We were staying at the Hotel Alexandre in East Beirut, near the front line, which was the mecca of all journalists in the East, not because of its luxury — there certainly was none — but because it was the only hotel in that part of the town, and also because its roof provided a front seat for the night's entertainment. Every night, around midnight, the Israeli Air Force would come over West Beirut, to drop flares and bombs. Some of them fell only a few hundred yards from the hotel.

But that night I did not go up to the roof. I went to the switchboard of the hotel and called Paris. I knew the number by heart, because I had called it hundreds of times during the last few years: I called the office of Issam Sartawi, the man who had been appointed by Arafat to conduct the secret contacts with Israeli peace activists, and who had become a close friend of mine.

During those days, the telephone was manned around the clock, because Sartawi's office had become the main link between Arafat, in beleagured Beirut, and the Western world. He answered immediately, I told him that I was calling from East Beirut, and that I was trying to contact Arafat's office in the western part of the city. He gave me the telephone number of the present location, and also promised me to call Arafat's office himself in order to help arrange a meeting.

By now it was two o'clock in the morning. I went up to my little room and called the number. A very Arabic voice answered after the first ring. 'I am Uri Avnery, from Israel', I said in English, 'I am in East Beirut and I would like to meet the Chairman.'

'Where are you staying?' the voice asked. I told him.

'I will ask and call back,' the voice said.

I went to sleep, without much hope. About an hour later, I was awakened by the ring of the phone. Half asleep I took the receiver.

'Are you Uri Avnery?' another voice asked.

'Yes.'

'Do you want to speak English or Hebrew?'

'Either.'

The voice continued in Hebrew, with an Arabic accent. 'The Chairman will receive you today. What time suits you?'

With a jolt, I was wide awake. I did not believe my ears. Was it really happening?

I was desperately trying to collect my wits. 'Would 10 o'clock be all right?' I asked.

'Yes. Where do you want to cross?'

'I haven't the slightest idea. What do you suggest?'

'Come to the museum crossing. At our checkpoint ask for Ahmed. He will be waiting at 10 o'clock.'

I put the receiver back. So that was that. I went back to sleep. I learned in the army to sleep in all situations, and I did now. But I slept fitfully. All kinds of questions roamed in my mind. What would the repercussions be? How dangerous would the crossing be? How to go about it?

The telephone rang again. It was Issam from Paris. He wanted to know what had transpired. When I told him he sounded anxious. 'Look', he said, 'I'll call our people there and try to make sure as much as I can that there will be no hitch.'

At about 6 o'clock in the morning, I had another inspiration. I knew that my friend Gerholt Arentz, the German cameraman, knew the ropes in Beirut. He had been covering the war for some time. I called him at his home and told him that I was going to meet Yassir Arafat that day. How would he advise me to get there?

'Better take a Lebanese taxi. Try not to be recognized by the Israelis and tell the Lebanese that you are German', he said.

I went back to sleep and the phone rang again. It was Gerholt. 'I was sleeping when I talked with you!' he exclaimed. 'Look, this is a world scoop! I want to be in on it. Can I join you?'

This was, of course, an ideal solution. He had been in Beirut for a long time and had credentials both from the Lebanese government and the Phalangists. It would be much easier to pass the checkpoints in his company. So it was settled.

There was another problem — the two girls.

I needed Anat, the photographer. She is a little slip of a girl, very tough, totally without fear, or so at least it seemed. I had been with her in combat situations in Lebanon during our prior visits. She was single and had no responsibilities. But the correspondent, Sarit, was a different story; she had a little girl back home, and I could manage without her.

I called them both to my room. 'I am not going to compel either of you to come', I told them. 'If you do join me, you come as volunteers. Think it over. I think it is reasonably safe, but the risk is there.'

Anat agreed immediately to come. Sarit was torn by conflicting emotions — the terrific scoop on one side, the responsibility for her daughter on the other. But she is a journalist; she came along.

* * *

'Are you afraid, too?' Sarit asked me when we were sitting in the Lebanese taxi, in the huge traffic jam between the lines.

'Not really. But tense.' I said. I have had this sensation many times in war. A complete absence of fear while the action was going on. But a certain tenseness, a controlled excitement, which does not prevent you from functioning, but rather helps you. An animal reaction in danger.

It was hard to sit still. And the heat made it even harder. Was 'Ahmed' there, near the earthern mound in front of us?

I got out of the taxi and with Gerholt approached the checkpoint on foot. Near it I stopped in the shade of a tree and asked him to walk up to the PLO fighters and ask him about 'Ahmed'. After a few minutes, he came back. No one knew anything about a person called Ahmed.

I looked at the watch. It was still a few minutes before 10. And anyhow, in the Middle East, time is relative.

We went back to our cars. I tried to talk with the girls, ease the tension. After ten minutes. Gerhold and I walked back towards the checkpoint. In the meantine, the cars had crawled forward not more than 20 yards.

Again Gerholt went up and walked to the earthern mound. A few minutes of suspense, and then I saw a sight which made my heart jump with joy.

It was Ghazi, a PLO official I had known for many years, from the early days of our contacts in Europe. He rushed out towards me and we embraced. Never in my life have I been so glad to see anyone.

From there on it was easy. We dispensed with our Lebanese taxi, still stuck in the jam, and walked past the checkpoint. The wild-looking fighters looked at us with some curiosity. A group of people were standing on the side. One was the man who, I discovered, I had spoken with the night before, Imad Shakur. I realized also that I knew him: he had been working years ago on my staff in Tel Aviv, when we were publishing an Arabic edition of the magazine. He had disappeared — crossing the frontier at night, joining the PLO forces, like many other young Palestinians who were Israeli citizens. He had studied at the Hebrew University in Jerusalem, and his Hebrew was perfect.

Another person in the group was uniformed, mustachioed, very stiff, very correct. He was, it transpired, Arafat's chief personal bodyguard. He also was the first honest to goodness PLO Army Officer I had met in my life. During the day, he loosened up and in the end we became quite friendly. He was in charge of my security.

His name was Major Fathi.

The Chairman had not only sent his bodyguard but also his armoured Mercedes. I was asked to enter.

'What about the two ladies?' I asked.

'They will follow in another car', the Major said. I was about to enter the car when I saw the look of sheer panic on the faces of the two girls. 'We can't do that', I said, 'they must come with me.'

After a moment's hesitation, my hosts relented. We all entered the big limousine, and together with two other cars, one in front and one behind, full of armed bodyguards, we were on our way. Somebody was taking very great care to protect us.

Even if I had known West Beirut, it would have been difficult for me to follow the road. We were taken in a criss-cross pattern through the town, perhaps to make sure we did not know exactly where we were. I was rather surprised at what I saw. After three weeks of siege, shelling and bombardment, the town was living. Children were playing in the street and in the schoolyards. Here and there PLO fighters, some of them in their early youth, were digging trenches, laying mines. A thought crossed my mind: These were mines laid for a battle against my own people, my friends, my relatives.

Morale seemed quite high. The fighters reminded me of my own early ially came into being, r stage and not yet a when I had a chance to te of fatalistic euphoria, possibly survive, trusting

partment building, with a ned upstairs, in a knot of . It appeared that this was there, his wife, his children, ficer, and his family.

, coffee was served, cigarettes ense, especially between the

he told me his side of the story. He pected, the guests of the Chairman host. She had rebelled, and only after at for the sake of the cause she had to do ed very politely until the point in the where she came from, and she replied that was I!' Anat happily exclaimed. That was too ould not stand the idea that Jews were born ned into the kitchen, and it took some more again.

* * *

leader by the way his people treat him.

aides were about to leave the room, assuming that Arafat nt to talk privately. But the two girls again sent me imploring d not taken all those risks in order to trade pleasantries with ans and their wives in another room, and I needed Anat for the he was crouching at our feet, clicking away happily.

was also another consideration. I was not sure that I would not be ted upon my return, under the article of the law which makes act with the enemy' a serious crime, equal to espionage. I wanted e two witnesses present during the whole conversation. I also took down ery word on tape. (These tapes did, indeed, serve as evidence when a criminal investigation was opened against me by order of the Israeli cabinet.)

So we were all seated in a haphazard fashion around the room, Arafat between Sarit and me on the sofa, Anat on the floor, three or four Palestinian officials on chairs all around. People butted in from time to time, everyone interrupted Arafat when he saw fit; in between, some official would submit to the Chairman some urgent papers to sign. It was all very informal, hardly the way a European or American would imagine a meeting with the supreme leader of a nation.

Yet, I soon understood why Arafat was the leader. Everyone treated him

with the utmost respect. It is a unique quality of th
believe, this esteem. He has a quick mind, a rapid
is highly intelligent, but not intellectual. What c
foremost, is the pathos of the Palestinian experi
somehow personifies the tragedy of the Palestinian p
the voice of the Palestinian people.

To this one must add the remarkable fact that Araf
war was no surprise to any Palestinian in Lebanon. It
6 long days to reach the outskirts of Beirut. Arafat had
for Tripoli, Damascus or anywhere else in the Arab wo
the besieged city, and for seventy-nine days and nights
and deprivations of his fighters, knowing that perhaps th
war aim of Ariel Sharon was to liquidate him personally.
this feat a year later, during the siege of Tripoli.

The personal courage and integrity of a leader are respon
part of the respect he commands. This is true everywhere, mo
in the Arab world than in other nations.

There was nothing pretentious about him. He was qu
Throughout the two-hour-long conversation, the children of t
all over him, climbing on him, embracing him, trying to attract h
They seemed to be used to him. It did not seem to bother Arafat,
children of his own. I have seen this tolerance towards the antic
children many times among Arabs.

When I later published the pictures of Arafat hugging the ch
aroused great indignation in Israel. Arafat, the terrorist, the lead
organization which had committed so many violent acts in which c
had perished — how could anyone dare show him as the benevolent
of children? Yet I was simply stating a fact, there was this relatio
between the man and the children.

(Palestinians, of course, were just as indignant when they saw pict
showing Menachem Begin, whose warplanes were bombing refugee cam
hugging little children. No one likes to see his enemy as a hum
being.)

* * *

I had not come for the pleasantries, nor for the adventure, not even for the scoop. I wanted to convey a message.

I had been in contact with Yassir Arafat for many years, but indirectly. I had spent thousands of hours talking, arguing, exchanging insights with Palestinian officials, like Said Hammami and Issam Sartawi, knowing that everything would be reported to the Chairman. Indeed, this was one of the main reasons for the meetings. From time to time, sometimes on the advice of my Palestinian friends, I had also sent him letters, either private ones or open letters published in my magazine, analysing a current situation and suggesting policy decisions.

But for years, I had looked forward to this opportunity to say the things face to face. I have been often surprised by the power of the written word to reach out across borders and front lines and plant seeds in the minds of people you have never seen. This has certainly happened with some of the articles I have written to change the minds of Palestinians, as they told me much later. Right at the beginning of our conversation, Arafat told me that he had read every word I had addressed to him during the years.

But a million written words don't equal one minute of face-to-face conversation, when you look into the eyes of the man opposite you, register his facial expressions, his glances, his body language, while he unconsciously watches yours. This has become an article of faith with me: There is no alternative to dialogue; straight, direct, face-to-face dialogue.

But the dialogue is not always easy. Different people, different peoples, have different languages, not just in the linguistic sense, but also in the sense of style. Arafat is a Palestinian, an Arab. He can be extremely irritating to American journalists, who ask short questions and expect crisp, direct answers that lend themselves to quotation. Arafat never gives a direct answer to any question, if a long, indirect and meandering one will serve. Our tape-recorded conversation shows many examples.

That very day, 3 July, a huge demonstration was about to take place in the centre of Tel Aviv. When the war broke out, nearly four weeks earlier, those of us who had protested against it were a small bunch, lonely voices crying in the wilderness. A year before, I had interviewed the new Defence Minister, Ariel Sharon, and he had held forth at great length about his plan to invade Lebanon and the aims of this operation. In the intervening months, I had written several articles warning against this adventure, trying to convince people that the aims — and especially the aim of destroying the Palestinian national movement by military means — were illusory. But the enthusiasm of the first days of the war — of any war — made these warnings ring hollow. This changed quickly after the first week, when the winds of disillusionment began to blow from the north, especially from the Syrian front. On the third Saturday of the war, a new anti-war group called for a demonstration. Instead of the few hundred expected, 20,000 showed up. Encouraged by this, the bigger Peace Now movement had called for a demonstration on the same spot a week later, and this was the day.

I asked Arafat: 'If you were addressing today the mass demonstration of the peace movement in Tel Aviv, the people there who are dedicated to peace and against the war, what would you tell them?'

*Arafat*: 'We are human beings, and we have the right to live!'

'What do you think they should do?'

*Arafat*: 'To see that the United Nations resolutions will be implemented. We are not asking for the moon!'

A little later, I said: 'I have been waiting for this meeting with you for many years, for this is exactly what we wanted to tell you: the real problem is that a great number of Israelis really believe these stories about the Palestinians never being ready to recognize the State of Israel, even in the context of peace based on the coexistence of the State of Israel and the State of Palestine. This is one thing which has to be made clear in a way that any man in the street can understand: that what we want is a peace solution based on mutual understanding, mutual respect, mutual recognition.'

And again: 'You see, the situation in Israel is like this, and has been so for a long time: You have a minority in Israel which would support Begin and Sharon always, they want to destroy the national identity of the Palestinian people and to annex the West Bank, but this is a minority. On the other side, there is a minority which is against the war and understands the Palestinian problem. In the middle you have the great mass of the people who can be influenced this way or that, and our job is to influence them in the direction of peace.'*

What I was trying to say, what I have been trying to say to my Palestinian counterparts for years, was that Israeli public opinion could be changed, but that is was absolutely necessary for us to have a clear-cut, unequivocal statement by the highest Palestinian authority that the repartition of the country along the pre-1967 lines would mean peace, final and absolute peace. But, this was exactly what the other side found extremely difficult to provide, for reasons which I hope to explain in this book. What came through instead were statements which were clear to experts practised in the deciphering of coded political texts, but quite useless in a mass meeting in Tel Aviv.

For example, I was saying: 'The great majority of Israelis, who, I think, are basically peace-loving people, have become convinced by our official propaganda that the PLO does not really want peace.'

*Arafat*: 'The PLO?'

*Avnery*: 'How to convince them . . .'

*Arafat*: 'The PLO? You know it is not so! We have declared our approval of the American-Soviet Communiqué of October 1977. We have declared our approval! [This communiqué included the "legitimate right of the Palestinian people" and "measures for insuring security of the borders between Israel and the neighbouring Arab states."] You see, when we have said okay to this initiative, this means that we accepted all its parts. We said that it is a good platform for a peaceful settlement, for a just settlement, for a peaceful solution in the Middle East. And you remember that I, myself, have declared that the Fahd proposals are a very good platform for a solution in the Middle East. [The proposals of King Fahd of Saudia Arabia later became the basis for the peace plan adopted at the summit of Arab heads of state in Fez, Morocco.] So we gave many signals that we are looking for peace. But I am sorry to say that this military Israeli junta are acting in an arrogant way.'

These were clear statements — for diplomats, but not for ordinary people. I came back to this near the end of the conversation: 'Mr. Arafat, if the Israeli government would come today and say: Okay, we had a war, you have fought very bravely, our people have fought very bravely . . .'

*Arafat*: 'Definitely fought bravely, we know that.'

*Avnery*: '. . . Let's make peace now, based on mutual respect of the people who have been fighting, you should have a Palestinian State, we have the State of Israel, we shall live peacefully together. What would you say?'

---

* All quotations are taken from the tape-recorded, unedited text of the conversation.

*Arafat*: 'You see, we have given a positive answer, but nobody has offered it to us!'

One of the aides (Mahmoud Labadi, who a year later joined the extremist, pro-Syrian rejectionist faction): 'I was in Berlin in 1970, when I was still a student, and I heard there a lecture by Mr. Avnery about his book, in which he proposed a federation of Semitic peoples, a Semitic union.'

*Arafat*: 'Inshallah!' (If God so wills.)

*Avnery*: 'You see, I believe that in the end, after everything is finished, there should be an Israeli State and a Palestinian State, with its capital in East Jerusalem, and there should be a general regional organization unifying all the Arab States and Israel in one economic and political union.'

By that time I remembered the poor German television crew, which had been shepherded to another place and told to wait. I asked Arafat, as a favour, to let the crew shoot for a few minutes. He agreed, and when the camera started to roll, there was a subtle change in his expression. The camera saw the Arafat it was used to seeing. Not the real person I had been talking with for two hours.

Perhaps the main difference is in the smile. On the TV screen, Arafat's perpetual smile looks arrogant, even irritating. In reality it is a smile of shyness, a rather pathetic smile, a smile of a people telling the world: 'You can bury us one hundred times, but we are still alive and shall go on living.'

When this crossed my mind, I was struck, not for the first time, by the growing similarity between the Palestinians and the Jews.

It was long past noon when Arafat got up and excused himself. He had to see the former Lebanese Prime Minister, who was mediating between the PLO and the Christian faction. Before he was whisked away by his bodyguards, he produced a big volume of old drawings of Palestinian landscapes and presented it to me with his signature.

The next few hours were dedicated to an inspection of the horrors of war. We collected some papers of dead Israeli soldiers, saw hundreds of destroyed houses, went to a bombed-out home for retarded children and a hospital shelled from the sea. In one half-destroyed street, there was something which looked from afar like the stall of a fruit vendor in a market. When we came close, we saw it was an exhibition of cluster bombs, phosphorus shells and other fruits of modern mass destruction, which had been raining on the city. We also inspected the Sabra and Shatilla refugee camps, not dreaming that they were destined to become, two months later, household words.

As a special favour, we were allowed to meet with the sole Israeli prisoner at that time in Beirut, an Israeli pilot shot down over South Lebanon. He was guarded by the PLO forces like a jewel, and had become extremely friendly with his guards. As usual when Israelis and Palestinians meet, mutual curiosity plays a big part in their relationship.

It was already late afternoon when we were brought back to the museum checkpoint by the same people who had met us there. As I was taking leave of Major Fathi, the commander of the checkpoint warned me: 'Look over there behind that building, there is an Israeli tank. Take care!'

It was a curious remark, an enemy soldier warning me against my own army. But it was a fact. That very same day the Israeli Army had taken up positions along the line around West Beirut, from sea to sea.

When we came to West Beirut, we crossed the lines of four armies — the Phalangists, the Lebanese Army, the PLO forces, and the remnants of the Syrian Army in the city. On our way out, we had to cross the lines of five.

It was easy. The Israeli soldiers in the tank did not dream that there were Israelis in the car of the German television crew.

This changed an hour later. We were racing back to Israel, in our own car, to tell the news. While passing Sidon, we were astounded by the news coming over the radio from Jerusalem: The PLO spokesman in Beirut had announced our meeting with Yassir Arafat.

In Israel, all hell broke loose. We were near Tyre when we heard that three cabinet ministers were demanding that I be tried for high treason, and a spokesman announced that the matter would be discussed at the next meeting of the Israeli cabinet. We could not be certain that we would not be arrested at the border checkpoint.

Suddenly I remembered something silly. A Lebanese fellow, whom we had given a ride the night before from Junia to Beirut, had left a packet of hashish in my car. Perhaps it was an oversight, perhaps it was intended as a present to new-found Israeli friends. Now it came back to my mind. How awful if somebody found hashish in our car after such a meeting! There was no choice. We did something many a hashish lover would consider an intolerable crime: we opened the window and threw it out.

Months later, when I was appearing with Issam Sartawi in a meeting in Holland, just before his assassination, he told the audience: 'Let me tell you what was the longest day in my life. It was the day that Uri Avnery crossed the lines in Beirut and met with Chairman Arafat. After I had helped to arrange the meeting during the night, I was waiting for a call from Beirut or from Tel Aviv telling me that Avnery had come out of Beirut alive and happy. The call never came. The most awful ideas crossed my mind. If anything had happened to Avnery in these circumstances, while under our protection, the consequences would have been irreparable. Then an international news agency called me to ask about the meeting, and I knew it was all right. My God, how I cursed that day!'

# 3

*It's a meeting somewhere. Perhaps Amsterdam, perhaps Copenhagen. A few hundred concerned faces look up at me.*

*It's question time. 'How would you define your philosophy?' somebody asks. The chairman gives me a discreet sign that we must finish. It's already late.*

*I have an idea. 'One of the great Jewish sages of all times, Rabbi Hillel the Elder, was asked two thousand years ago to define Judaism while standing on one leg. He answered: 'Do not do unto others what is hateful to you'.*

*I raise one leg. 'I believe that the Palestinian people have the same rights as I have. I have the right to live in a state of my own, under my own flag, to hold my own passport, to elect my own government, good, bad or very bad. The Palestinians must have the right to live in their own state, under their own flag, to hold their own passport, to elect their own government – hopefully a good one.'*

*I put my leg down.*

# 4

One day, when I am old, I shall want to write a book about the history of our country.

By that time, I hope, peace will reign supreme. The two states of Israel and Palestine will live together, side by side. People will pass to and fro across the open border, which will be merely a line on the map. Young people from both sides will meet and deliberate various forms of a common future, joint enterprises will do business all over a flourishing Middle East.

One thing will be missing: a history book to instruct the children of both states. A picture of the history of our joint homeland with which the young people, both Israeli and Palestinian, can identify.

The idea came to me one day when I was glancing through a history book for British children. A question occurred to me: What do British children learn about the Battle of Hastings? With whom do they learn to identify – with the Saxons, who lost the battle and their freedom, or with the Normans, the foreign invaders, who later played such a big role in English history? I found that the author had solved the problem very simply: he taught the children to identify with both. The modern British nation, today's British culture, is the result of Saxon and Norman influences. The modern English language is a mixture of Germanic Anglo-Saxon and French Norman speech. William the Conqueror and King Harold are both fathers of the British nation.

* * *

The story could begin thousands of years ago, when the inhabitants of what was then called Canaan created a Semitic culture resembling that of their neighbours. Other Semitic tribes, later called Sons of Israel, infiltrated into the country, as happened before and after. They were not strong enough to conquer the fortified Canaanite towns, a fact admitted by their chroniclers in the first chapter of the Book of Judges, so they settled in the open countryside, especially on the hilly, difficult to cultivate lands. In the course of many generations, these tribes merged with the former inhabitants, until the nation we know as Israel emerged and created that unique chapter in the story of human genius, the religion of Israel.

Many misfortunes befell the kingdoms of Israel and Judea. At different times, the upper classes of the two kingdoms were exiled. Some of their members returned later to found the new Jewish nation and added another chapter to the history of culture and religion. But the simple people, the peasants tilling their soil, the shepherds tending their flocks, never left the country. They stayed behind when the second Jewish commonwealth was destroyed by the Romans. A few remained Jews, others joined the Jewish heresy called Christianity. When the country was conquered by the triumphant followers of Mohammed, the founder of yet another Semitic religion, they gradually adopted Islam and the Arab language. They became what are today called the Palestinians, while those who went into exile, together with masses of converts, became what are today called Jews. Viewed historically, they are two branches of the same family, locked today in mortal battle.

The glory of our country, the small slice of territory called at various times Canaan, Israel, Palestine and many other names, is an endless procession of cultures, peoples, conquerors, religious and cultural geniuses. Wherever you move in this country, you find the traces of Canaanites and Israelites, Jews and Christians, Muslims and Crusaders, Mameluks and Ottomans and many, many others. Trying to obliterate the traces of any of them is like taking out stones from a beautiful mosaic, pulling out the threads from a wonderful tapestry, scraping off a colour from a painting by Michelangelo. Yet this is what each of the warring factions is trying to do. Many Palestinians view the history of the country as if it started with the Muslim conquest thirteen centuries ago, while history as taught in most Israeli schools is a moving caravan, concentrating on the land of Israel for the fourteen centuries preceding the rebellion of Bar Kochba eighteen centuries ago, then roving through those parts of the world where Jews lived, and returning to the country with the first Zionist settlers.

But the history of our country, in which every Israeli and Palestinian child should take pride, includes all of it: Canaanite kings, Israelite judges, Moses and King David, Jesaia and Jeremiah, Cyrus and Alexander the Great, the Hasmoneans and King Herod, the Romans and Byzantines, the Calif Omar and Godfrey the Crusader, Saladin and Richard the Lionhearted, Baibars and Suleiman the Magnificent, Zionist pioneers and their Arab enemies, Ben-Gurion and Arafat. All this belongs to our country, a unique and many-splendoured story which will go on after all of us, with our hopes and our battles, are things of the past.

* * *

But the most controversial chapter of this yet unwritten book will concern, of course, the history of the last hundred years.

During the many hundreds of hours I spent in conversation with Palestinian militants, parts of this history invariably cropped up. I tried to avoid this, but I was also intrigued by the way Israel's enemies see this chapter of our common history, which was very, very different from the way we Israelis see it. As a general rule, I requested them to avoid this argument. 'We cannot agree on anything that belongs to the past,' I told them, 'so let's concentrate on the future and agree to disagree about what happened.' This was a useful rule, and we generally adhered to it.

But this is a temporary expedient. Sooner or later we shall have to come to grips with this history, which unites and divides us. The next generation will have to learn to view it in a manner acceptable to both sides, much as Germans and Frenchmen will have to learn to view their centuries-long history of antagonism in a way acceptable to both peoples living now within a joint European framework.

How did this conflict come about? Who was right? Who was wrong?

* * *

One of the best descriptions of the Israeli-Palestinian conflict was given by the historian Isaac Deutscher. He told the story of a man whose apartment has caught fire. Trying to save his life, he jumps from the window and falls on top of an innocent passerby, who is grievously injured. The man is convinced of his absolute justness: he only saved his life, he didn't intend to hurt anyone – he didn't even know anyone was underneath. But the passerby is not interested in what happened in the burning apartment. He only knows a terrible injustice has been done him through no fault of his own.

Like every story which tries to simplify an incredibly complex conflict, this one has many shortcomings. But it may serve to explain the roots of the Israeli-Palestinian conflict.

A different way of looking at the origins of the conflict may be to liken the Zionists to a man faced with mortal danger in his own house. Fleeing these dangers, he enters another house, believing it uninhabited. When he finds this is not so, he pleads for the right to live in one room, citing the fact that many, many years ago his ancestors lived there. The inhabitants of the house naturally object to this invasion, and try to evict the man by force. Faced with this new danger, the man becomes violent, fights for the room and, in the course of the melée, takes over more and more rooms of the house, until the original inhabitants are in danger of being thrown out altogether.

Zionism was a Jewish movement born in faraway Europe at the end of the last century. Basically, it was an endeavour to save the Jews before the gathering gloom turned into total darkness, though none of the founding fathers could have imagined a catastrophe so terrible as that which befell their people a few decades later. But many of them were haunted by terrible fears. They wanted to take the Jews out of the threatened ghettos, away from the pogroms, the discrimination, the growing anti-Semitic terror, to some country where they could create a new national home. Some of them did not care very much where this home would be. It was the situation in the old homelands which was uppermost in their minds, not the situation in the homeland-to-be.

The history of modern political Zionism starts with a little book by the bearded Viennese journalist, Theodor Herzl, now officially venerated as The Seer of the state. It is a detailed account of the Jewish state which he had in mind, containing chapters about 'Workers' Dwellings,' 'Purchase of Land,' 'Unskilled Labourers.' It describes what the future flag would look like (it does not), details how the project was to be financed and deals with many other topics.

But the book did not contain one single reference to the fact that Palestine was inhabited by Arabs. In fact, the word 'Arab' does not appear in the book at all. Strange as it may seem, there was a reason for this: when Herzl dreamed about his state-to-be, he did not think about it in terms of any particular country. His was a blueprint for a national home that could be set up anywhere – in Argentina, in Canada, in Uganda. Only during the last phase of writing his book did Herzl become convinced that the idea of Palestine might give the project of creating a Jewish state the necessary emotional thrust. Because of this he inserted a small passage into his book, saying that Palestine might be the best of the potential sites for the new Jewish state. In this passage, which sounds rather like an afterthought, he said that a Jewish state in Palestine would constitute 'a part of the rampart of Europe against Asia,' adding, 'We would serve as an outpost of culture against barbarism.' These words, put down perhaps without much thought, are highly significant. Herzl at that time had obviously thought very little about Palestine as a concrete entity. Probably he knew very little about it, about its inhabitants and geopolitical significance. The phrases he used were simply unconscious echoes of the spirit of the times.

At the 1931 Zionist Congress, an interesting description of the evolution of Herzl's thought was given by Chaim Weizmann – later to become the first president of Israel – in a speech opposing demands to set the 'final aim' of Zionism as a Jewish state. 'In all of Herzl's declarations', said Weizmann, 'the idea of the Jewish State appears only in his book, *Der Judenstaat*. When he wrote this book, Herzl was far from certain that Palestine was the land where his plan would probably be realized.'

On the contrary, contended Weizmann, 'Herzl thought about the Palestinian plan as something academic, as a pious wish not meriting serious consideration. There is no certainty whatsoever that his vision of a Jewish state applied to Palestine. The whole style of his book makes it probable that while writing it he was thinking about another land [Argentina], and that he added the passage about Palestine later on, just to make his Zionist friends feel good.'

The First Zionist Congress, convened in Basel, Switzerland, in 1897, finally fixed the location of the future Jewish state in Palestine. Yet of all the Jewish activists assembled at that solemn occasion, only a handful had ever been to Palestine or had the slightest idea what the country looked like. The Palestine they knew was the country of the Bible, the picture in their mind's eye was the land of milk and honey depicted in the pages of the Holy Book. The countries they knew were in Europe, and the situation they were acquainted with was the one they were trying to escape. For them, Palestine was an empty country. If there were any people there at all, they were non-people by the standards of Europe at the end of the last century – Asiatics, barbarians, people of no account.

These good people assembled in Basel had no idea that while they were creating a movement destined to change the fate of their people, another, quite different movement was being born in the very country they were thinking about. At the end of the century, all over the Arab world, in Palestine and around it, the new spirit of nationalism was taking hold in the minds of young intellectuals, Arab officers in the Turkish Army, poets and merchants. The aim, at first vague and undelineated, sharpened over the years into a very clear idea: the renaissance of the Arab Nation, autonomy, freedom, independence. Palestine, then a minor province of the Turkish Empire, was a part of Syria, which was a part of the Arab world, which was a part of the great expanse of territory of Asia and Africa, which was just about to shake off the yoke of empire and cross the threshold of national freedom. The Palestinians and their neighbours were part of this great historic movement.

While Herzl's spiritual predecessors, contemporaries and heirs were creating Zionist theory and forming their ideas, Arab thinkers and poets, in Palestine and the surrounding countries, were laying the groundwork for Arab nationalism.

The young Arab army officers creating secret cells in the Turkish Army and the young poets calling for an Arab awakening could not have imagined in their worst nightmares that somewhere, in some little hall in some little town in some little country in central Europe, a congress was taking place which was to change their lives, the lives of their families, and the life of their country, bringing upon them untold miseries. The few Jews they knew – there were about 24,000 Jews in Palestine in 1881, when the first new immigrants arrived, living with half a million Arabs – were not particularly different from the other inhabitants, for there were Jewish Arabs, as there were Muslim and Christian Arabs in Palestine.

This, then, was the beginning of the tragedy. Two great historical movements were born roughly at the same time, each one with the most praiseworthy aims and ideals – national and human salvation, freedom, cultural and social renaissance – both striving to realize these aims in the very same small territory, each completely ignorant of the other.*

* * *

Whenever I think about the beginning of the conflict, a picture forms in my mind. It is taken from an old American movie about robber barons battling for control of the railways. In the movie, two trains, each carrying a load of mercenaries for one of the feuding corporations, steam towards each other on the same single track. The mercenaries don't know what's in store for them, but the audience knows that they will soon crash and give bloody battle. This is what happened in our country.

Once the Zionist movement was created, it started to move settlers into Palestine. Aided by the Jewish plight in Europe, the trickle grew to a great flood. Imbued with the loftiest ideals, some of the immigrants set out to create the most just and beautiful society ever created – kibbutzim, moshavim and other experiments in utopian living. They were astonished, and then furious, when their new neighbours did not perceive the beauty of it all. Had they not bought the land with good money? Had they not turned shopkeepers and stock exchange brokers into manual labourers, who now

* The author has dealt with the roots of the conflict at greater length in his book, *Israel Without Zionists* (Macmillan 1968).

tilled the soil? Had they not brought their neighbours the benefits of modern medicine? Had they not offered them concerts of Beethoven and Brahms, indubitably preferable to the ugly and monotonous Arabic songs?

To the Arabs, of course, the whole thing looked quite different. Here was a bunch of foreigners, coming from who knows where, claiming that the country was theirs because some relatives had lived there two thousand years ago, buying the land from rich absentee landowners and chasing away the fellahin who had tilled it for generations, creating colonies in which no Arab was allowed to live, persecuting any Jew who dared employ Arab workers instead of the new Zionist shopkeepers turned labourers.

It is a moot question to ask if things could have worked out differently had the Zionists understood the problem and faced it squarely, heeding the warnings of the very few prophets who foresaw what was going to happen. The fact is that being what they were, coming from where they came from, imbued with the ideas and prejudices of nineteenth-century Europeans, they probably could not have behaved otherwise. Nor could the Palestinians have reacted differently. Indeed, it was the most extreme Zionist leader, Vladimir (Zeev) Jabotinsky, who, in the twenties, wrote that the Palestinian Arabs were reacting to Zionism as any normal people would react to white settlers trying to take over their country. Because of this, Jabotinsky, the mentor of the modern Herut Party, proposed setting up an Iron Wall to protect the Jews from the inevitable Arab reaction.

Who was right? Who was wrong? Each side was totally convinced that it was right. Progressive Zionists, like Chaim Weizmann, managed to bring themselves to say that it was not a question of right against wrong, but rather of right against right. But even this may be a convenient oversimplification.

* * *

In the beginning, there were small incidents between neighbours, some kibbutzniks here, some Arab shepherds who let their flocks graze among the hard-worked fields there. Sticks were raised, people were wounded, the quarrel was patched up in a traditional Arab *sulkha* (reconciliation) ceremony. Then there were skirmishes, and shots rang out. Jewish watchmen wearing exotic dress were idolized by the Zionists, while local Arab strongmen formed bands to raid Jewish villages. After the pistols came rifles, then machine guns. With the creation of the State of Israel came tanks and fighter planes. And then came the rumours about nuclear bombs and other forms of mass annihilation.

When I was 13 years old, a guerrilla war began, called 'disturbances' by the British government, 'the Arab rebellion' by the Arabs, 'riots' by the Jews. Three years later I was training with pistols without bullets, then I was a soldier carrying a machine gun. Now the most sophisticated weapons are employed. The conflict between neighbours in Turkish Palestine turned into a battle between two peoples under the British Mandate. The whole Arab world and the whole Jewish diaspora were drawn into the war in 1948. Now political scientists, playing at simulating the Third World War, assume that it will all start with a battle over Jerusalem.

There can be no doubt that if things continue along their present course, more wars will be fought for this country, leading towards the destabilization of the whole region, perhaps to global confrontation. The employment of nuclear arms may become inevitable, with consequences too gruesome to contemplate.

Is there a solution to this conflict? Can it be brought to an end before it ends us?

Can these two highly intelligent peoples, the most dynamic peoples in the Middle East, who have both tasted the bitter experiences of exile and tragedy, be brought to live together peacefully in the country they both claim as their homeland and to which both are now indissolubly attached?

Many years ago, Eric Rouleau, the French journalist, arranged a meeting between a well-known Egyptian left-wing leader and me. After midnight we were sitting in La Coupole, the fashionable Paris restaurant, arguing about possible solutions. Using the paper cloth covering the table, a bit soiled after the meal, we drew up a list of theoretical solutions. There were five: either one people annihilates the other, or one people subjugates the other, or one people drives the other out, or both people live together in one state, or the country is partitioned.

After that we went about analysing each possibility. We agreed that annihilation is out of the question, not only for moral but for practical reasons. In a war between nations, in this day and age, before a state is eradicated it will use weapons of mass destruction, thus turning the whole area into a graveyard.

The subjugation of one people by another is much more likely. As a matter of fact, after that conversation, Israel conquered all of Palestine, and is quickly turning into a Middle Eastern South Africa. But even if it were possible for Israel to hold millions of Palestinians, an ever-growing minority, in total subjugation, denying them all national and most human rights, what kind of Israel would it be? It would be a very far cry indeed from the ideal commonwealth envisioned by Herzl in his second book. *Altneuland*, the one he prefaced with the motto 'If You Will It, It Is No Legend'.

The idea of driving out all the Palestinians from Greater Israel – an idea which is becoming more and more popular in certain Israeli circles – is the only way of combining the ideas of a Greater Israel and the Jewish State, but is even more preposterous. Even if it were possible to evict the Palestinians, it would lead to an eternal war between Israel and the whole Arab world, thus reverting to possibility number one. Israel cannot throw the Palestinians into the desert, just as the Palestinians cannot throw the Israelis into the sea.

The idea of living together peacefully in one state may be more attractive, but not more practical. No one can foresee how the relations between the two peoples will develop once peace comes about. The whole world may change, and we with it. Someday new forms of social existence may supersede nationalism, but we are still far from that time. The Israelis and the Palestinians are both intensely nationalistic peoples, traumatized by their experiences, the Israelis by the Holocaust and their national history of suffering, the Palestinians by the humiliation of colonialism and later by expulsion. After a total war lasting now for four generations, no total peace can come about overnight. No one can really believe that Israelis would enjoy equality in a Greater Palestine, nor that Palestinians could enjoy equality in Greater Israel. The idea of a democratic secular state in which Israelis and Palestinians would live peacefully together is at best premature, at worst a camouflage for quite different designs.

Thus, by a process of elimination, both of us, at our Paris table, reached the inescapable conclusion that there is no other solution than the one envisaged by the unusually intelligent resolution of the United Nations in 1947, even if history has changed the borders drawn then. When two peoples claim a country as their exclusive homeland, and each wants to express its personality in a state of its own, each living under its own flag and its own government, partition is the only viable solution. It is also a good solution.

## 5

*'Have you ever met Gamal Abd-al-Nasser?' a Palestinian asks me.*

*'Oh yes!' I reply, 'we had lunch together!'*

*Seeing his surprised look, I tell him a joke.*

*'Do you know Pedro?' somebody asks Juan. And Juan replies: 'Why, we had lunch together!'*

*'How's that? You and Petro?'*

*'It was like this: I am riding on my horse in the pampas, when Pedro pops up from behind a bush. He points his pistol at me and says: 'Juan, get down from the horse.' He has a pistol, I have no pistol, so I get down from the horse. Pedro says: 'Juan, eat the horseshit.' He has a pistol, I have no pistol, so I eat the horseshit. Suddenly I see Pedro is looking away, so I give him a big kick and grab the pistol. I say: 'Pedro, eat the horseshit.' I have the pistol, he has no pistol, so he eats the horseshit. That is how we had lunch together.'*

*For six months, Gamal Abd-al-Nasser and I fought on the same front. Reading his memoirs, I realized that we took part in dozens of the same engagements. He was wounded in a battle for which my company got a collective decoration. He was decorated for a battle in which I was wounded. Nearly all these battles were fought at night, so we must have been very close to each other, only yards apart.*

*But we were never properly introduced.*

# 6

I don't remember when I started to get involved with the Palestinian problem.

I grew up in a street which was the official boundary between Tel Aviv and Jaffa. Both sides of the street were Jewish, but a few blocks away Jaffa proper — the Arab town — started. The two towns, the Jewish and the Arab, were actually two boroughs of one city, but they were further apart than two cities in different continents. An ordinary Jew in Tel Aviv could go for weeks without seeing an Arab. Very few Jews visited the Arab town, and then only on such business as existed between Jews and Arabs. The only exceptions were on Pesach, the Jewish Passover, when masses of Jewish Tel Avivians would descend on Jaffa to buy bread, which was unobtainable in Tel Aviv; and on Yom Kippur, when some Jews went to Jaffa to eat.

At the age of fourteen I left school and started to work for a lawyer in Tel Aviv. Some of the courts and government offices were located in Jaffa, and every few days I would spend some hours there, meeting Arab officials, talking with Arab colleagues, strolling in the streets, smelling the Oriental smells, eating Arab sweets, listening to the strange language. I liked them.

Since then, what later became known as the Palestinian Problem was never an abstract thing to me. It meant people, people I knew, superficially at least, as a teenager; sounds and smells which belonged to the landscape of my youth. Unlike most Israelis of today, I don't have to read books and manifestos to know that two peoples are living in this country and that they have lived here side-by-side for a long time.

* * *

Before my fifteenth birthday, I joined the *Irgun Tsvai Leumi* (the National Military Organization, commonly known as the Irgun), which was at that time the only Jewish nationalist underground organization. I joined it because I believed that the British colonial regime had no business governing our country. In 1938, the British authorities hanged a young Jew, Shlomo Ben-Yosef, for throwing a bomb at an Arab bus, in retaliation against some Arab outrage against Jews. It was at the height of the disturbances which the Palestinians call the Arab Rebellion, and which the Jews call The Events.

Like other young boys in Israel, I decided to join the underground in protest against the hanging. One day, after a talk with a colleague who was a member of the Irgun, I was called to face a reception committee. In the evening, at exactly the proper time, I approached a school building which seemed empty, no lights showing from any window. In the dark corridor, two figures lurked. I uttered the password — Samson and Delilah — which had been given to me. After some time I was told to enter a room and sit down on a chair. A strong projector was aimed at my face and blinded me. I could just make out three figures, two men and a woman, behind the projector.

The interrogation began. Questions were thrown at me. What were my motives, my feelings, my opinions? Did I hate the British?

'I don't hate anyone', I replied.

For a minute, incredulous silence. If I didn't hate the British, why did I volunteer to fight them? I tried to explain, rather haltingly, that I wanted to fight for freedom, and that I didn't believe one had to hate anyone to do this.

But did I hate the Arabs? No, I said, I did not hate them at all.

This time the silence was thunderous. How was it possible for a young Jew not to hate the Arabs, after more than two years of Arab outrages against his people?

To the three underground officers facing me, I must have sounded like a very mixed-up kid. The Irgun had very clear-cut ideas: we had to throw the British out and suppress the Arabs in order to turn our country, Eretz Israel — all of it — into a Jewish state. When I left the dark building, which still looked totally deserted, I was quite sure I had flunked the examination.

Yet the committee must have decided that I was not beyond redemption, for a few weeks later I was notified that I had been admitted to the Irgun.

For three glorious years I was a member of the underground. I lived for the Irgun. Everything else — family, work, girls — was unimportant. I learned to shoot pistols, run errands, distribute leaflets — some of them announcing Irgun actions against Arabs, such as putting bombs in crowded Arab markets. I clashed with the British police in illegal demonstrations, burned government offices (the same I had visited as a lawyer's clerk). My home served as my company's arsenal, a crime punishable at the time by death. I carried guns to training exercises. Danger was intoxicating. I was a terrorist by British standards, a freedom fighter by our own definition. Since then I have never forgotten this lesson: a terrorist is a freedom fighter in his own eyes, a freedom fighter is a terrorist in the eyes of his enemy.

I left the Irgun in 1941, a year before Menachem Begin, who eventually took command of the organisation, arrived in Palestine. By that time I was seventeen years old, and it had become increasingly impossible for me to support the right-wing, reactionary and anti-Arab stance of the Irgun.

My years in the Irgun had been important to me in many ways. Today they help me understand what is going on in the minds of young Palestinians who join the Fedayeen organizations. Whenever I ask myself how young Palestinians will react in certain situations in the territories occupied by us, I try to imagine myself as I was when I was sixteen years old. How would I have felt? What would I have done?

Five years later, in 1946, I created a new group. We called it Young Palestine (*Eretz Israel Hatzeira*, in Hebrew), but it was commonly called the

Struggle Group, because that was the name of the publication we issued. We proclaimed a new creed, which was quite revolutionary at the time: that we Jews in Palestine constituted a new Hebrew nation linked to the Jewish people but separate from it, that we belonged to the Third World, that our own nationalism and the Arab national movements should combine in a common 'Semitic' front to fight colonialism and to create a new, free and progressive Middle East (which we called the Semitic Region).

The fight for Palestine had by that time become more and more bitter. Jews, Arabs and British were killing each other. The days of the British Mandate in Palestine were drawing to a close. The United Nations decision to partition the country into Jewish and Arab states was the signal for the outbreak of a full-fledged war between the two peoples of Palestine.

A few weeks before the outbreak of the war, I published a booklet entitled *War or Peace in the Semitic Region* in which I outlined a plan for a Semitic federation in the Middle East and for the cooperation of Hebrews and Palestinians in Palestine. We sent an English synopsis of this Hebrew booklet to Arab newspapers throughout the Middle East, and it was quoted by some of them.

I visited Jaffa — Arab Jaffa — for the last time before the war broke out, to give copies of the booklet to the Arab newpapers there. The atmosphere was tense and sombre. War was in the air. Very few Jews were still to be seen in the Arab town. It was already too late.

Many years later, when I met and came to like Said Hammami, we spent many hours talking about old Jaffa, where he was born and which he left at the age of seven, during the war of 1948. It crossed my mind that I may have passed him in the street during that last, sad visit of mine to the doomed town.

* * *

When the war broke out, I joined the Haganah army, which became, in the middle of the war, the Israeli Defence Army. For a year, until I was wounded, I was a combat soldier.

As a member of Samson's Foxes, a commando unit mounted on jeeps, I entered dozens of Arab villages in the south of the country. Many of them had been abandoned by their inhabitants only a few minutes before. Ovens were still hot, in some houses food was still on the table. I became obsessed by the human tragedy of war. I would gather snapshots of the inhabitants, which were left behind like all other personal belongings. I still have some of them — photos of children, women, old men. Whenever I hear about the problem of the Palestinian refugees, these pictures come to mind. When I visited the refugee camps of Sabra and Shatilla, that day in July 1982, it crossed my mind that some of the inhabitants may have come from those villages, that some of the children whose snapshots I still keep are by now old refugees in the camps. For me, refugees are people — some of whom may have been evicted by my machine gun — not just a Problem.

Throughout the war, I came across the Palestinian Problem in its human shape: wounded villagers, whom we would take to the field dressing station; civilian prisoners, whom we combat soldiers would try to shield from tough intelligence officers who came to interrogate them; old fellahin who infiltrated back through our lines and who were sometimes shot to death by my comrades at close range. Some of these scenes are still imprinted in my mind. I've only to close my eyes to see them again, terrible reminders of what the war was all about.

I was wounded during the last days of the fighting, by Egyptian machine-gun fire. Lying in the hospital, after the operation, unable to sleep for many days and nights, I thought about the new Palestinian Problem, trying to rearrange my ideas. I was convinced, and I have remained convinced ever since, that there can be no peace without taking into account the fact that two peoples live in this country, and that each of them must have a state of their own to live in.

I was still wearing a uniform, on sick leave, suffering from my wounds, when a friend asked me if I would like to meet some young Arabs who had remained in the territory of what was now the State of Israel. I agreed eagerly. One day, in the spring of 1949, a meeting took place in Haifa, at the home of Rustum Bastoni, a young nationalist Arab who later became a member of the Knesset. We talked about the future. We both agreed: the Palestinians are a people, they must have a state of their own alongside Israel, it is in the interest of Israel to help the Palestinians create this state, there will be no peace without it.

Even before this, while still in the hospital, I wrote an article for the *Haaretz* newspaper. It was published on 28 January 1949, under the headline 'Pax Semitica'. It outlined the idea of the new State of Israel taking part in a regional organization to be set up together with the Arab states, to help them to get rid of the last vestiges of colonialism, cooperating within the framework of a Middle Eastern political community, common market, defence union and development scheme. It must have made some impression on the editors, because I was invited by them to join their staff upon discharge from the army and to write editorials. Our cooperation was short and stormy. I was very much concerned with the government policy of expropriating the lands of the Arab villages left in Israel, relocating villagers and destroying hundreds of villages abandoned by their inhabitants in the course of the fighting. When I was not allowed to voice my protest in the editorials of *Haaretz*, I resigned. In April 1950, I acquired a weekly magazine called *Haolam Hazeh*, meaning This World. It had been founded in 1937 as a nice, innocuous family magazine. When I took it over it quickly became, and remains to this day, the main voice of dissent in Israel.

During the early years, a great part of our writing was concerned with the struggle against the David Ben-Gurion policy of discrimination against the Arabs in Israel. Arab citizens, of which about two hundred thousand had remained in Israel after the mass exodus, were subjected to a military government which deprived them of their civil rights. Ours was a long and arduous fight, culminating in the abolition of the military government a short time before the Six Day War, after which a different kind of military government was imposed on the Palestinians in the newly-occupied territories.

Until then, the main cause of conflict between Israel and the Palestinian people was the terrible tragedy of the Palestinian refugees. Hundreds of thousands of them languished in abject conditions in refugee camps in the Arab countries around Israel, despised and persecuted by most Arab governments. Year after year the United Nations reiterated its demand that the Israeli government offer them a free choice between repatriation or compensation. David Ben-Gurion adamantly refused to accede to this. It was quite clear to me that we were not only perpetuating the misery of the refugees, but were virtually launching an unending and ever-widening war between Israel and the Arab world.

Every single refugee was not only an island of misery, but also a carrier of hatred and revenge.

On 17 August 1954, *Haolam Hazeh* published a plan called Operation Ismael, a detailed blueprint for the solution of the refugee problem as the main lever for the achievement of peace. It called for the repatriation of some of the refugees, in ten yearly instalments, and the creation of a gigantic plan for compensation and resettlement of the others — something along the lines of the German restitution scheme for Jewish refugees, which at that time payed a great part in healing the terrible wounds of hatred created by the Holocaust.

Yet I was sure that no permanent solution was possible without the creation of a national state in which the Palestinians could gain their independence and regain their dignity. At that time, those parts of Palestine which were not incorporated into Israel were annexed to Jordan or occupied by Egypt. During one of the periodic outbreaks of the smouldering Palestinian rebellion against the Jordanian regime in the West Bank, on 29 December 1955, *Haolam Hazeh* called upon the government of Israel to do something which sounded crazy: to support the Palestinians with arms and money to facilitate their revolutionary movement, which would enable them to throw off the Jordanian yoke in the West Bank and Egyptian rule in the Gaza Strip and to set up their own state. The policy of Ben-Gurion, as well as his successors', was, of course, to do the exact opposite: to guarantee the continued existence of the Hashemite regime in Jordan, and to help it suppress the Palestinians.

Two years later we went a step further. On 2 June 1957, I published in *Haolam Hazeh* a detailed plan, complete with maps, for the creation of a Palestinian state in the West Bank and the Gaza Strip, coupled with a proposal to set up a confederation of the two states, Israel and Palestine.

Sometime before that, in the aftermath of the Sinai War of October 1956 — to which we objected violently — I created, together with a group of like-minded friends, a new movement called Semitic Action. In September 1958, this group published a document which, I believe, will someday be considered of historical significance. The Hebrew Manifesto was a daring attempt to redefine the basic tenets of Israel as a secular, democratic, liberal state, devoted to the ideals of equality and humanism, identifying itself with the Third World, ready to play its part in a great Semitic Confederation. One chapter of this document was devoted to the idea of a Palestinian state in the West Bank and the Gaza Strip, to be created with the active support of Israel.

* * *

One night, in the late 1950s, I nearly had an accident. It was after midnight, and a friend of mine was driving me in his little Volkswagen through the almost-deserted streets of Paris. At the Etoile we narrowly missed another car; fortunately my friend swerved aside at the very last moment.

Fortunately, indeed, because our little car was full of FLN leaflets. My friend, the driver, was one of the leaders of the FLN underground in France. An accident would have brought the police to the scene.

It was the heyday of the Algerian War of Liberation, led by the FLN — the National Liberation Front.

I had established contact with the FLN some time earlier. At the time, the Israeli government supported the French government to the hilt against the Algerians. I believed that the real, long-term interests of Israel demanded the very opposite — that we should support the Algerian freedom fighters in their hour of need, forge the first links of friendship between Israel and an Arab national movement, and eventually ask the Algerians to pave our way to Cairo and the Palestinians.

I never believed that we could make peace with the Palestinians without integrating Israel into the general pattern of the region, and this meant, of course, supporting all Arab liberation movements. Because of this, *Haolam Hazeh* was, in 1952, the only Israeli voice which wholeheartedly supported the revolution of the Free Officers in Egypt. While the Israeli government was urging Britain, in 1954, not to evacuate the Suez Canal zone, the last remnant of the British occupation of Egypt, we took the opposite line, demanding that Israel support the Egyptian demand for total freedom.

It was therefore quite natural for me to seek contact with the FLN. They welcomed me warmly, even gratefully, knowing that I took some risks meeting them on French soil. The man who established the contact, Henri Curiel, a unique personality, will play an important role later in this narrative.

When I asked them what we could do for them as Israelis, they presented quite a list. First of all, could we send them some veteran underground fighters, experts in electric and chemical sabotage devices, to train their men in Yugoslavia or Tunisia? Secondly, could I set up an Israeli body to support openly the Algerian revolution? The idea was that such a body might have some influence on the masses of Algerian Jews who were supporting the most obnoxious colonialist organizations, such as the infamous OAS.

We set up the Israeli Committee for a Free Algeria. One of its prominent members was Natan Yallin-mor, the ex-leader of the Lehi underground (commonly known as the Stern Group). We published statements and propounded our views, and the FLN saw to it that they were published in Europe and known in Algeria. But we never succeeded in sending those demolition experts.

Some time after that, at the United Nations in New York, I met the new FLN observer Abd-al-Kader Chanderli, with whom I had many discussions about the future of the Israeli-Arab relations. One day he asked me, 'Why don't you come to a reception that the other Arabs at the UN are giving me?' Of course I went. It was quite an experience: here I was, a lone Israeli in a hall full of Arab diplomats and dignitaries, including some Palestinians, striking up acquaintances left and right. I believe my presence created quite a stir. Many of those present had never talked with a real live Israeli. On my way home, I wondered how our security people would take this affair. After all, this was Contact with the Enemy, a major crime in Israel. However, nothing happened.

When the Algerian Provisional Government was formed, we established official contacts with it. One of my colleagues met openly with several of the new ministers, who agreed readily to be photographed in his company. We published the picture on the cover of *Haolam Hazeh*.

However, all that time Golda Meir, then foreign minister, was busy poisoning the well. She supported the most extreme French elements, even when Charles de Gaulle began calling for the Peace of the Brave. When peace came to Algeria, a new leadership took over. They remembered Golda. They did not know us.

For the same motives, we supported the Iraqi revolution of 1958, publicly calling upon the Israeli government to express its solidarity with it. Soon after, again at the UN, I had several long conversations with Hashem Hawad, who became, a few days later, the foreign minister of Iraq. He was a wonderful person and expressed his heartfelt belief in Israeli-Arab peace and the eventual integration of Israel into a regional community. Our meetings took place in the great hall of the Delegates' Lounge at the UN Headquarters. I shall never forget the expression on the faces of Abba Eban, then head of the Israeli delegation, and his Egyptian opponent when they passed us time and again, hardly believing their eyes.

On my way back from those meetings, I was received by Jean-Paul Sartre in Paris. Amos Kenan, the Israeli writer, was with me. When I told Sartre about the meetings and our ideas, he said a memorable thing: 'You take a stone off my heart. All my life I have supported Zionism. Now I must be silent. I cannot support the policy of the Israeli government. And I do not want to raise my voice against it, because then I would find myself in the same camp as the people I detest, the anti-Semites.' He asked me to write an article about my ideas in *Les Temps Modernes*, and it was duly published.

As my views became more widely known, quite a number of people in Europe and the US volunteered to arrange meetings between me and Arab leaders and intellectuals. During the early 60s, I went every year to Florence, where the mayor, the 'little professor' Giorgio La Pira, held 'Mediterranean' conferences, the real purpose of which was to get Israelis and Arabs to meet. My presence proved increasingly annoying to Golda Meir, and she took the quite unprecedented step of instructing the Israeli ambassador in Rome to protest on official embassy stationery against the invitation extended to me. During the last Florence conference, in the summer of 1965, Golda Meir sent a functionary of her establishment, David Hacohen, chairman of the Knesset committee for foreign and military affairs, to warn the participants about me. At the height of the discussion, when the Arabs and I had put forward a joint draft resolution, Hacohen shouted in great excitement: 'Avnery represents nothing. Not even a fraction of a fraction of the Israeli public!'

Then and there, I decided to put this to the test. A few weeks later, on the eve of elections for the sixth Knesset, I issued a call for the creation of a party, the first really new party to come into being since the birth of the State of Israel. Using the name and prestige of our magazine, we called it the Haolam Hazeh — New Force Movement. Its main purpose was to fight for the twin ideas which had crystallized in my mind during all those years of contacts and deliberations: Israel's integration into a new community of states in the Semitic region, and the creation of a Palestinian state, to exist side-by-side with our own.

Greatly helped by a new law enacted by the Knesset on the request of the government, quite openly aimed at silencing Haolam Hazeh, I won a seat in parliament, to the surprise of everyone, perhaps even myself. I held this seat for eight consecutive years, and returned to it later, making at least a thousand speeches in the Knesset Plenum. Several hundreds of them were devoted to a single issue: the Israeli-Arab conflict.

* * *

On 5 June 1967, the Israeli Army crashed across the frontier. On the fourth day of the war it was clear that all the territory of Palestine west of the Jordan river had been captured.

The Israelis were in a state of exhilaration, perhaps intoxication. The Arabs were in a state of shock. The war was still going on.

That day we sat in the editorial office of *Haolam Hazeh* in Tel Aviv trying to assess the new situation. Most of the members of our staff were in the army, fighting. The few of us who remained behind were working round the clock, feverishly producing a newspaper which we had decided to publish daily for the duration of the war and its aftermath, in order to have a more direct influence on the quickly-moving events.

Yet in the midst of the whirl of events, fatigued as we were, it was quite clear to us what had to be done. A moment of historical importance had arrived. A dramatic opportunity was staring us in the face. The historical homeland of the Palestinian people was in our hands. All barriers between us and the Palestinians had come down. We could address them directly, talk to them face to face, offer them the thing most precious to every people on earth: a national state of their own.

In a flurry of activity, I wrote an Open Letter to the prime minister, Levi Eshkol, with whom I had friendly relations. It was published in our daily paper, *Daff*, on the fifth day of the war, 9 June 1967, and in greater detail in the weekly *Haolam Hazeh* on 14 June.

After congratulating the prime minister on the victory, I wrote: 'Now, Mr. Prime Minister, all our thoughts must be devoted to the achievement of a permanent peace, which will safeguard for generations the independence, security, and development of the State of Israel. The wisdom of the politicians must reap the harvest sown by the blood of the soldiers . . . I take the liberty of submitting to you, for your consideration, the following plan for the establishment of peace: 1) Within three months the inhabitants of the

Gaza Strip and the West Bank will be invited to take part in a plebiscite. In this referendum they will be called upon to determine their future in a democratic way. 2) The voters will be asked to vote yes or no on the principle of the establishment of a free and independent Palestinian state, which will include the West Bank and Gaza.'

The sections of the plan that followed dealt with federative arrangements between the Palestinian state and Israel, the status of Jerusalem, UN supervision of the referendum, the return of the refugees, the links between the Palestinian state and the Arab world (parallel to the links between Israel and the Jewish world), and the attainment of peace treaties between Israel and the Arab states.

I suggested that Eshkol make a dramatic gesture at this very moment of turmoil and disorientation, when all established ideas had come crashing down, when mental patterns were disintegrating and there was a chance for the creation of totally new ones.

There was, of course, no reaction from Levi Eshkol. I shall try, in a later chapter of this narrative, to explain how the official Israeli policy towards the Palestinian problem and the occupied territories evolved from that day onwards. But during those first few days, no one in official circles had any clear idea what to do. The tendering of my initiative must have looked to them suspiciously quick. How could anyone come forward with a complete plan on the spur of the moment? But of course there was nothing improvised about it. I had been thinking about this solution for many years. It was easy for me to recognize the opportunity the moment it arrived.

During those hectic first days, when I was racing to and fro from the Knesset to the editorial office, I dealt mainly with another tragic aspect of the war. Friends in the army sent us reports of what was happening — the town of Qalqilya was being systematically destroyed, villages near Latroun were being obliterated, refugees coming back from the other side of the Jordan, who were crossing the shallow river at night, were being murdered in great numbers. I appealed to the chief of staff, Itzhak Rabin, to the prime minister and other cabinet ministers, including Menachem Begin, who had entered the National Unity cabinet on the eve of the war. The destruction of Qalqilya, the Arab town nearest the old border on the coastal plain, was halted. The houses were rebuilt, and the inhabitants, who had been deported to Nablus, were allowed to return. It was too late to save the villages near Latroun, which had been eradicated from the face of the earth; this area is now a national park, called Canada. The wholesale slaughter along the river was stopped.

During the next six years, until the Yom Kippur War which cost me my seat in parliament, I made innumerable speeches in the Knesset and outside about the Palestinian solution. I saw with an aching heart how a unique opportunity was being missed. I approached Levi Eshkol several times in private, and tried to convince him that he had the chance to imprint his personality upon the course of history, as David Ben-Gurion had done when he proclaimed the establishment of Israel. He was always polite, even friendly, but totally unresponsive. I was trying to explain a beautiful picture to a colourblind person.

I submitted dozens of draft resolutions to the Knesset, proposing that the government make the historic offer to the Palestinians, that it give political freedom to the people in the occupied territories and allow them to develop their ideas and choose their leaders. Time after time I raised my hand for these resolutions, remaining in splendid isolation, one against 119. Even the communists were at that time resolutely against the idea of a Palestinian state, following as usual the dictates of Moscow, which was then still demanding the return of the West Bank to King Hussein — a unique demonstration of communist monarchism.

One sentence, uttered in the excitement of a debate by a member of the Knesset, sticks in my memory: 'Uri Avnery and the Mufti have invented the Palestinian people!' The Mufti was Hadj Amin al-Husseini, the foremost leader of the Palestinians between the two world wars, the favourite hate object of the Israelis.

There were some members of the Knesset who used to approach me after such debates in the corridors, shake my hand and say quietly: 'I would have voted for your resolution, but you know, party discipline . . .'

One incident may shed some light on the situation then prevailing. During a debate I had said that all prominent West Bank leaders had told me privately that they favoured the creation of an independent Palestinian state. In summing up the debate, Eshkol hotly denied this. Yet a few hours later his adviser for the occupied territories, Moshe Sasson, called and asked me for a meeting, saying that he had been instructed by the Prime Minister to examine my information in detail. The meeting took place on 19 November 1968. In the protocol which he submitted to me for confirmation, he said that he agreed with my assessment of the West Bank leaders' attitudes: they did indeed favour the creation of a national Palestinian state. Sasson continued: 'Without going into the question whether a Palestinian state is desirable or not, the question is whether the Arabs want such a state if it does not include Jerusalem. As we [meaning the government of Israel] are not ready to give back Arab Jerusalem — and as I do not know one single Arab who is interested in a Palestinian state without Jerusalem — the debate about a Palestinian state becomes abstract and useless . . . Neither I nor Mr. Avnery could point out one single leader in the West Bank who is ready to support the idea of the Palestinian state without Jerusalem. Answering my question, Mr. Avnery explained that his formula relating to Jerusalem is at this stage intentionally a general one: united Jerusalem will be the capital of Israel, the capital of the joint institutions and the capital of the Palestinian state.'

* * *

In the autumn of 1967 I wrote a book outlining the history of the Israeli-Palestinian conflict and the proposed two-state solution I had in mind. The book, *Israel Without Zionists*, was published in the United States in 1968. Some time afterwards I made the rounds in Washington, D.C., trying to sell the idea. I talked with Lord Caradon, the chief of the British delegation at the UN and the father of Resolution 242; Joseph Sisco at the State Department; Harold Saunders in the White House; Charles Yost, the chief of the US delegation at the UN; Senator William Fulbright, chairman of the Foreign Relations Committee; and many others. The results were depressing. Most of the people I talked with were adamantly against a Palestinian state. They neither recognized, nor did they want to see, the existence of the Palestinian people.

Yet my book had a curious result. Early in 1971, the Research Centre of the Palestine Liberation Organization in Beirut published, in Arabic, a book called *Uri Avnery or Neo-Zionism*. Soon afterwards the same book was published in Beirut in French. The author was one Camille Mansour. He rejected what he called the 'Avnery Plan' for the creation of a Palestinian state alongside Israel, calling it a Zionist plot to end the Palestinian revolution and induce the Palestinians to settle down in a state of their own and recognize Israel.

I wondered why anyone in the Palestinian leadership would take the trouble to publish the book in Arabic and to debate an idea put forward by an Israeli opposition member of the Knesset. What was the sense of it? There could be only one logical answer: the debate was not with me but with other leaders of the PLO, who had arrived at the same solution.

From then on I waited for some sign from the other side. Who were the anonymous people in the PLO who secretly advocated the creation of a Palestinian state in the West Bank and Gaza? What were they doing?

* * *

With the Yom Kippur War, in October 1973, events took another dramatic turn. The first Geneva Conference was convened, without, of course, the participation of the Palestinians. Israel was occupied with 'the war of the generals' (also nicknamed 'the Jewish wars'), an acrimonious debate between the chiefs of the army who blamed each other for the mistakes committed before and during the war.

In the tumult, a little article which appeared in the *The Times* of London on 16 November 1973, was practically ignored. It included the sentences:

> Many Palestinians believe that a Palestinian state on the Gaza Strip and the West Bank, including al-Hammah region, is a necessary part of any peace package. Such a Palestinian state would lead to the emptying and closing down of the refugee camps, thereby drawing out the poison at the heart of Arab-Israeli enmity. It is no small thing for a people who have been wronged as we have to take the first step towards reconciliation for the sake of a just peace that should satisfy all parties.

The article was signed by Said Hammami, the representative of the PLO in London. The editor prefaced the article with a remark saying '. . . (Hammami) explains his personal view of the issue. Since he is known to be very close to the PLO chairman, Mr. Yasser Arafat, his decision to make his views public is of considerable significance.'

On 17 December Hammami published another article in *The Times*. It said, among other things:

> The October war could create a new map of the Middle East with a new state of Palestine joining the comity of nations . . . The Palestinian Arabs and the Israeli Jews were and still are the principal parties of the conflict . . . these two parties — and only these two parties — can lay the foundation stone for a peaceful future in the Middle East . . . I believe that the first step towards that should be a mutual recognition for the two respective parties. The Israeli Jews and the Palestinian Arabs should recognize one another as peoples, with all the rights to which a people is entitled. This recognition should be followed by the realization of the Palestinian Arab entity through a Palestinian state, an independent, fully-fledged member state of the United Nations.

It was clear to me that no official representative of the PLO could publicly express such views without the full support of Yassir Arafat and a significant group in the PLO leadership. Here was the signal I had been waiting for. Our Palestinian counterpart had surfaced.

At the Geneva Conference in December 1973, I met Edward Mortimer, the Middle East expert of *The Times*. I asked him about Hammami. Who was he? What was he like? Would he consent to meet me, if necessary, in deepest secrecy? Mortimer promised to find out. He was destined to play a small but highly important role in what followed.

From that moment on, I had only one objective: to meet that man, Said Hammami.

# PART II

# Hammami

# 7

*I am giving a lecture in a kibbutz in the south. I am talking about peace, about an Israel integrated into a flourishing and united Middle East, devoting its resources to the creation of a highly-developed technological industry rather than to war.*

*The kibbutzniks listen politely, attentively, sceptically. This is all science fiction to them. They don't know what peace is, can't even imagine it. For them, war is the normal state of affairs; they know what to do in war, how to cope, it doesn't frighten them. But peace is something else, something out of their ken, something bewildering, perhaps even intimidating, like everything unknown.*

*At question time, a young kibbutznik who looks like a tank commander in the reserves, asks a hard-headed question: 'You want us to give up a lot of territory, the oil wealth of Sinai, strategic depth and a lot of other things. What shall we get in return? A scrap of paper?'*

*I look desperately for an answer which will appeal to this pragmatic no-nonsense person. How does one describe peace in concrete terms?*

*'Look,' I say, 'at this moment, in hundreds of thousands of classrooms all over the Arab world, from Casablanca in Morocco to Mossul in Iraq, there hang maps of the Middle East. On all these maps the territory of Israel is either left blank, or is labelled Filastin al-Mukhtalla, Occupied Palestine. All we want in return for the things you mention is one little thing: that on all those maps this territory be marked Israel.'*

## 8

There was a soft knock on the door.

I hesitated for a moment before opening it.

The man looked younger than I expected, about 34. He had soft dark eyes, black hair, a rather round face. He was conservatively dressed, the English way. He did not look at all like a dangerous terrorist.

I said *ahalan we-sahalan* in Arabic. Welcome.

He came into the room, looked quickly around, saw that I was alone.

We looked at each other, two people in a London hotel room. I think we liked each other.

We were enemies.

* * *

It was a dangerous meeting. Both of us had taken risks.

He knew my name and what I stood for. But he could not be sure that the whole thing was not a trap by the Mossad. Israeli intelligence had already killed several officials of the PLO, an organization considered by the Israeli government to be its mortal enemy. Some had been killed by bombs in the streets of Beirut. Some had been surprised and killed by Israeli commandos at their homes in the Lebanese capital. Some had been shot or bombed in Europe. He could not be certain that the Mossad had not used me or my name to lay an ambush for him.

There was another risk for him. He was the first PLO officer ever to intentionally meet an Israeli, a Zionist. For many Palestinians, this was an act of treason, punishable by death. This threat hovered like a cloud over all the meetings to come, up to the tragic end.

I was not sure either. Here was a good chance for some terrorist outfit to kidnap a well-known Israeli, recently a member of the Knesset, who could be exchanged for Palestinian prisoners.

Neither of us could be quite certain that on the other side of the door people were not waiting with loaded guns.

As for me, I stood on very shaky legal ground. Under Israeli law, meeting an enemy agent is a major crime, tantamount to espionage, unless there are 'valid reasons' for such a meeting, and if there is no 'intent to hurt the security of the state'. It is up to the judge to decide whether the defendant's reasons are valid, and what his intentions were. There was no test case. It was up to the Security Service, the famous Shin Bet, to decide whether to arrest me upon my return.

We had both decided to take these risks. And now we were here, looking at each other with unashamed curiosity, as at strange animals.

* * *

Edward Mortimer had done his job well. He had approached Hammami and told him of my request to meet him. Preparations had taken many months. It was obvious that Hammami had referred my proposal to Beirut, and that it took some time for Yassir Arafat and his colleagues to make up their minds. I suppose that they had wondered whether I could be trusted to keep the contact a secret. After all, I was not only a politician but a journalist — two species not known for their ability to keep secrets. (Indeed, many years afterwards I indirectly received a compliment from Yassir Arafat. He told a friend: 'More than anything else I respect Avnery for the fact that he had so many journalistic scoops, and didn't betray any secrets.')

I confided in no one except my closest friend, adviser and legal counsel, Amnon Zichroni, a brilliant young lawyer who had been at my side during my eight years in parliament. We decided to run the risk of keeping the initiative secret — which increased the danger of criminal prosecution — so as not to risk the destruction of this unique chance by government interference.

At long last I received a positive answer. Mr. Hammami was ready to see me in London. Both sides agreed to maintain total secrecy about the contacts, unless both agreed to change this policy.

On my arrival in London, Mortimer gave me Hammami's private phone number. I called and identified myself. A very cold female voice, with an Arab accent, answered — Hammami's wife Khalida who, I later learned, was a refugee from Jerusalem.

For her I felt I was the Enemy, the hated Zionist, who had driven her people out.

A moment later, Hammami himself was on the phone. Where was I staying? I gave him the name of the hotel, Mount Royal on Oxford Street, and my room number. Would I be in my room in the late afternoon? Yes, I would. He promised to call me again to fix a time and place for our meeting. There was just a hint of conspiracy in his arrangements, reminding me of the old Irgun days.

My wife, Rachel, who was with me, had bought tickets for the theatre for that evening. Ten minutes before we were supposed to leave, the phone rang. It was Hammami. He told me that he would come to my room in a few minutes. It was a matter-of-fact and sensible precaution.

Rachel went to the theatre alone. I remained behind, feeling that if all the world was a stage and all the men and women merely players, having their exits and their entrances, in this little hotel room a new scene was about to unfold.

The date was 27 January 1975.

* * *

So here he was.

A scene from a long-forgotten book flashed before my eyes. During the Napoleonic wars, two warships, one English, one French, had to seek refuge in the same harbour on a neutral island. At the ball given by the governor, the officers of the two ships, resplendent in white uniforms and gold braid, met, coldly exchanged courtesies, and flirted and danced with the same girls. Here and there a human message, a look of sympathy, may have passed between two enemy officers, but they all knew that the next day they would leave the island and start again trying to kill each other. In theory that was what our situation was, too. The Mossad had killed his colleagues in Europe, and might kill him tomorrow. Back home, my life was threatened by Fedayeen attacks, like that of everyone else. My plane could be hijacked by his people on the way home. We were at war.

Yet at the same time we were comrades in another battle, a battle for Israeli-Palestinian peace. This created, from the very beginning, a vague sense of camaraderie. The ambivalence of this dualism would put its mark on all our meetings throughout the following years. Quite often we would have to remind ourselves, consciously, that no, we were not friends, we were enemies.

Nearly three years later, the last time I saw him alive, Hammami himself would remind me: 'We made a mistake. We told our people in Beirut Uri Avnery is a good man, we must talk with him. That is not true. We must not talk with you because you are nice people who understand us. We must talk with you because you are our enemies, because we must make peace. One does not make peace with friends, one makes peace with enemies.'

* * *

I didn't take notes, of course. Later, after he was gone, I jotted down some of the things I remembered.

What do two enemies talk about when they meet for the first time?

The first emotion, overriding all others, is curiosity, sheer, overwhelming curiosity. Who is he? What is he like? Where does he come from? How does his mind work? What makes him tick?

I think the first thing we talked about was his home, the home in Jaffa he had left behind at the age of seven. Where was it? He tried to describe the building, somewhere near the Muslim cemetery. Where exactly? What is the street called now? He didn't know. What was it called then? He didn't remember. I took a piece of paper and tried to draw a rough map of the neighbourhood. He mentioned a nearby Jewish suburb, Bayit we-Gan, a name I had long forgotten, because its name was changed many years ago to Bat Yam. For a few minutes we were lost in memories, memories of his childhood, my youth.

And between us, unmentioned, there stood the stark tragedy of the Palestinian refugee.

I promised him to look for the house upon my return, have one of my photographers photograph it and send him the picture. I did, a few days later. But it was the wrong house. I repeated this after each of our meetings. I never found the right one. I sent him many pictures of houses. I have spent many hours looking for it, questioning old Arabs in Jaffa, who looked at me with bottomless suspicion, fearing the sinister motives of this Jew who asked for the house of the well-known PLO officer. I never found the house of Adel Hammami, former deputy mayor of Jaffa, the birthplace of my friend, my enemy.

* * *

I wanted to know: How many like him were there? Who shared his beliefs? On behalf of whom was he speaking? What was happening within the PLO? He answered and asked, I answered and asked. There was so much to talk about, so much to learn, so much we needed to know!

After the initial awkwardness had been overcome, we settled down to business — the business of peace. As an introduction, Said Hammami outlined his approach to our problem. It went, more or less, like this:

The two peoples, the Palestinian and the Israeli, exist.

He did not like the way the new Israeli nation in Palestine came into being. He rejected Zionism. But he accepted the fact that the Israeli nation does exist.

Since the Israeli nation exists it has the right to national self-determination, much as the Palestinians have this right. At present, the only realistic solution is to allow each of the two peoples to have a state of its own.

He did not like Itzhak Rabin and understood that the Israelis did not have to like Yassir Arafat. Each people must accept the leaders chosen by the other side.

We must make peace without the intervention of either of the superpowers. Peace must come from the peoples in the region itself.

These were sensational views, coming from a senior PLO officer. Yet to me they were commonplace. They were almost exactly my own, stated as I had stated them myself many times. The idea struck me: here we are, two enemies meeting for the first time, and we have nothing to quarrel about. If I had opened the discussion myself, my opening remarks would have been more or less the same as his.

For how long had he held these views? He said that he had believed in the partition of the country since the end of the '60s.

Did Yassir Arafat notice? Yes. He had listened to his views without rejecting them. Knowing his views, Arafat had supported his appointment as PLO representative in London. He had also supported him when he published his views for the first time in *The Times*, after the Yom Kippur War. The radicals, such as the Popular Front of Georges Habash, had attacked him violently. But here he was, more then a year later, still representing the PLO in an official capacity — a clear proof that he had the support of the top leadership.

Did the leadership know about our meeting? Of course they did. He said it several times: 'I am not here as a private person. I am the representative of the PLO.'

Arafat was moderate. 'If he were to be killed, the next Arafat will be more extreme.'

Hammami was quite bitter about the killings. They were so senseless. For example, the Mossad had killed the PLO representative in Rome, Zueiter. Yet Zueiter was a moderate. After he was killed, he became the hero of Fatah. His family, an important one in Nablus, which had supported King

Hussein until then, became Fatah supporters. Even from the Israeli point of view, what was the sense of it?

* * *

He wanted to know what we could do, how many Israelis would follow us on this path.

I told him: That depends on you.

I gave him the message, which became the leitmotif of all the conversations I had from then on with PLO leaders, each and every one of them. It was this:

Israel is a democracy, at least as far as its Jewish citizens are concerned.

In a democracy, government policy responds to public opinion. If there is a gap between the two, it will be filled sooner or later either by new elections or by changes in the leadership.

If one wants to change government policy, one has to change public opinion. That is the main point. Everything else is immaterial.

One does not change public opinion by words, statements, diplomatic formulas. One changes public opinion with the impact of dramatic events, which speak directly to the heart of everyone, events which a person can see with his own eyes on television, hear on the radio, read in the headlines of his paper.

Israeli attitudes towards the Arabs are the result of deeply-rooted mental patterns. As long as these patterns are predominant in the conscious and unconscious minds of the average Israeli, any passing news story which conforms to them will be absorbed and reinforce them, any item which does not conform will be ignored, rejected or explained away, not just by the reader, but also by the writer and the editor.

Therefore, the basic mental pattern has to be shattered, destroyed. There is only one way to do this: to create new mental patterns to replace the old ones. New patterns are created by events so big, so shattering that the old ideas have to yield to them.

Earthquakes can change a landscape, erecting mountains where there were valleys, creating valleys where there were mountains. We need events which are earthquakes. Wars can be such events. If one wants to wage peace one has to create the dramatics of peace.

I have repeated this message many, many times over the years, sometimes feeling like a parrot. I gave it to Hammami at that meeting, trying to put into my words all the powers of persuasion I could muster.

What did I suggest? As this conversation took place nearly three years before the dramatic visit of Anwar al-Sadat to Jerusalem, I could not give it as an example, as I did later on. But I had prepared a list of possibilities, big and small. The biggest was: have Arafat invite me to Beirut and meet me publicly. Would I dare go? Yes, I would. Would I be arrested and put on trial upon my return? Probably. But such a trial would become, in itself, a powerful instrument for addressing public opinion in Israel and the Arab world and in conveying new ideas.

I knew this was a utopian suggestion; at least it was wildly premature. Therefore I had prepared some more modest proposals. Why not have Arafat reply to a set of written questions, to be published in Israel? Why not have some PLO people meet with a group of Israelis, publicly, somewhere in Europe, to discuss the future? And so on and so forth, all the various ideas I had been turning over in my mind for a long time.

He hastened to dampen my enthusiasm. Things take time, they have to ripen, it was a process. Things which might be possible tomorrow were not possible today. 'It would be easier if you were a member of the Israeli government.'

It looked like a perfect vicious circle. We needed manifest signs of PLO moderation in order to gain credibility and strength in Israel. They needed proof of our strength in order to override their own radicals and gain support for a policy of moderation. It was a basic contradiction which was to haunt all our contacts for many years and still does to this very day.

In the meantime, we had to set up a framework for continued contacts. I would come from time to time to London to meet him. If anything urgent cropped up, I could phone him at his home in London, or he would phone me in Tel Aviv. He would identify himself as Sam. I would send him *Haolam Hazeh* regularly, and he would get the relevant parts translated.

For the time being, we would keep our contacts absolutely secret. He would report, of course, to his leaders. I was allowed to report to anyone I saw fit, including members of the Israeli government, but would not publish anything at all. If there were any leaks, I was neither to confirm nor to deny.

Our first meeting must have lasted two or three hours. It seemed much longer. When he disappeared down the long corridor of the hotel, after quickly looking around, it seemed incredible to me that we had only known each other for a few hours.

## 9

*I am sitting in my apartment, talking with Talik.*

*Talik is General Israel Tal, the legendary tank commander, who is considered the best strategic brain in the Israeli Army. He is busy constructing the Merkava tank, which he proudly considers superior to any tank in the world.*

*We talk about the lessons of the Yom Kippur War. Suddenly the phone rings.*

*I conduct a long conversation in English. No, there are no real chances of Abba Eban returning to the cabinet. Yes, Itzhak Rabin has said this or that. And so on.*

*'Who was that?' the general asks, curious, when I finally put down the receiver.*

*'That was Said Hammami, the PLO representative in London', I answer.*

*The general is floored. 'Impossible!' he exclaims.*

*And so it is.*

# 10

During our many meetings, whenever I talked with Hammami, the conversation inevitably turned towards himself. It was quite impossible to separate his own story from the story of the PLO, or indeed from the story of his people.

Meeting him in hotel rooms in Oxford Street, having lunch with him in a Turkish restaurant near Edgware Road, walking with him in the streets of London, I bombarded him with questions about his life, his experiences, his feelings. Thus, slowly, I pieced together the story of his life. A typical story of a Palestinian refugee, militant, political activist and, finally, martyr.

* * *

His whole life was overshadowed by one black day. He did not even remember the exact date. At the time he was only seven years old. But he remembered the month: May 1948.

For Israelis, this month has a special meaning. On 14 May 1948, the state of Israel officially came into being. I, his elder by seventeen years, was fighting along the Jerusalem Road, and later that month along the coastal road by which the Egyptians tried to advance upon Tel Aviv. For Said Hammami that month meant tragedy.

Arab Jaffa fell. On the 13th, the Emergency Committee governing the besieged town signed the document of surrender. Many thousands of its inhabitants, led by the rich, had already fled by land or sea before the town was finally surrounded by Haganah and Irgun forces.

Adel Hammami had not fled. He was a respected citizen, a member of the municipal council, the owner of a large house in the Jebaliya quarter and of other properties. He decided to stay on.

One morning a squad of Haganah soldiers appeared at the door. The leader announced that the Hammami family, as well as other inhabitants of the neighbourhood, had to clear out immediately.

In the memory of Said, the boy of seven, the event was inscribed with an iron pen. The Haganah truck waiting outside, the family dragging along some belongings, the truck carrying them to Beth Dagan, a village some eight miles to the east, now called, in Hebrew, Beth Dagon. They were told to get off. 'Find some Arab bus to take you to Gaza!' the Haganah man told them.

What remained with Said Hammami? A vague picture of Jaffa, an enchanted town seen through the veil of childhood memories. Jebaliya. The adjacent Muslim cemetery, a place he spoke about frequently. A big house he never saw again, but which he saw clearly in his mind's eye. The nearby seashore. The smell of orange groves near the street then called Jaffa-Tel Aviv Road. The nearby Jewish suburb then called Beit we-Gan.

Jaffa. Paradise lost. 'I dream of our house every night', he once told me. It was not an ideological declaration, just a simple human statement.

I could understand him. I left the house in which I grew up when I was ten years old and did not see it again for thirty years.

Once, when I asked him, 'When did you leave Jaffa?' he answered vehemently: 'I did not leave! I was expelled!'

In the following years, when I met scores of PLO people, big and small, I heard many stories like this. In my mind they recreated the map of old Palestine, with its towns and villages, many of which have been razed from the face of the country. They exist in the mind of the people who remember them, a different kind of reality, but still a formidable one. Listening to the stories told by the conquered people, I, a member of the conquering nation, a soldier of that war, felt the full weight of the tragedy which had become an abyss between us, an abyss we were trying to bridge.

* * *

What is the fate of a refugee? How does he spend the formative years of his youth? Said Hammami did not grow up in a refugee camp, like so many others. He did not go hungry. His family was wealthy and had relatives in the neighbouring countries. But the wounds of the mind are often worse than those of the body. He told me many stories of humiliation.

As a boy of sixteen in Syria, before the short-lived union with Egypt and the creation of the Baath ('resurrection') party dictatorship, the young Hammami, like many young Palestinian refugees, embraced the ideas of the Baath — a pan-Arab revolution, the birth of a great Arab state. For the Palestinians, deprived of their national identity, their homeland, their sense of belonging, even of a passport, this looked like the solution to their problem. They thought they could merge with a new, great, all-embracing Arab nation.

One day Said Hammami was arrested by the Syrian secret police, together with a group of his comrades; all the others were Syrians. Everyone was released after a short interrogation, except Said, the Palestinian boy.

He was roughed up, beaten, cursed. 'You dirty Palestinian!' the Syrian policeman shouted at him, between blows. 'You have sold your country to the Jews, and now you come here to ruin ours?'

Hammami never forgot this incident. It left a lasting mark, not because he was physically tortured, but because he was humiliated. That day he made a final decision: I am a Palestinian. Not a Syrian. Not a Jordanian. Not a Lebanese. A Palestinian.

It also left behind an abiding hatred for the Syrians.

Incidents like this are burnt into the soul of many Palestinians. In a famous story by Ghassan Kanafani, the great Palestinian writer who was killed by Israeli agents in Beirut, a Lebanese policeman confronts a

Palestinian in similar language. A whole generation of Palestinians grew up feeling they were outcasts, accursed. And long before the events in Lebanon, they nursed, like Hammami, a special hatred for the Syrian regime.

Another incident, of a different kind, branded the young Hammami. He had finished his studies and had to start working. What could a young Palestinian, an intellectual, do for a living? He could become a teacher among his people in the West Bank.

His uncle was a respected sheikh, a graduate of the famous al-Azhar College in Cairo, a centre of Muslim studies. He arranged for the young man to be received by an exalted personage: the Jordanian minister of education, Sheikh Ahmed Muhammed al-Jaabari, the Mayor of Hebron, the man who appointed every teacher in the kingdom.

The young man presented himself to the bearded sheikh. Two generations of Palestinians looked at each other: the old politician and the young rebel. Hammami remembered the meeting thus:

'Do you believe in Allah, my son?' the old sheikh asked.

'I respect the tradition of Islam', Hammami replied evasively, not being religious.

'Are you a communist?'

'No, oh sheikh!'

'Are you a Nasserite?'

Hammami explained that he was an Arab nationalist.

'Are you loyal to our master?' the sheikh asked, meaning King Hussein.

It seems that the young man's answers did not satisfy the wily old fox. Out of respect for the uncle, though, he had to offer him a job. But instead of appointing him to a school in Palestine proper, in the West Bank, he appointed him to one in a remote corner east of the Jordan: in Ma'an, on the road to Aqaba.

Hammami refused.

Sometime later, al-Jaabari chanced to meet the young rebel again, in a public place. Trying to be jovial and to show the people around him how generous he was, he called Hammami to his side and addressed him in a fatherly tone.

Hammami happened to be smoking. 'Take the cigarette out of your mouth!' one of the sheikh's bodyguards shouted at him.

Hammami could not control his rage. He hurled a terrible Arab curse at the sheikh, and disappeared into the shocked crowd.

After the occupation I met al-Jaabari many times. He became friendly with Moshe Dayan, and was considered a staunch supporter of the Hashemite regime. But in private he told me that he was all for the creation of a Palestinian state. Recounting the history of the 1948 War, as seen through Palestinian eyes, he described the role of Egypt and the other Arab states in the most scathing terms. Once, taking leave of him, I expressed my hope that one day I would greet him as the president of the Palestinian republic. He seemed deeply gratified.

But, of course, he belonged to a dying generation. The good old days, when a Jordanian minister of education would accept fifty dinars as a matter of course for the appointment of a teacher, were gone and reviled by a new generation, of which Hammami was a representative.

* * *

Hammami was seven years old when he was deported from Jaffa. He was 22 years old when the second revolution in his life occurred. He remembered the date exactly: 17 July 1963.

The union of Egypt and Syria had already broken up. The young Palestinians had despaired of the Baath party. They sympathized with Gamal Abd-al-Nasser, who was violently attacked by the new Baath regimes both in Damascus and Baghdad.

On that day, units of the Palestine Liberation Army rebelled in Damascus. These units belonged nominally to the new PLO, but were in reality subservient to the armies of the various Arab states. A Syrian officer called Jassim Aluan had attacked the new Baath regime which had just come into power. He was a Nasserite and the Palestinian units joined him. Like him, they adored Abd-al-Nasser, on whom the Palestinians at that time pinned their hopes.

The Palestinians had stormed and occupied the headquarters of the general staff in Damascus. The regime counterattacked and won. Mass executions of Palestinian soldiers followed.

This bloodbath finally disabused the young Palestinians of any hope of one, all-embracing Arab nation. Between them and the Arab countries there opened an abyss which has never been bridged since.

For the young Hammami this was another shattering trauma. He told me about this incident several times as a central event in the life of the Palestinian nation, a statement questioned by Palestinians who had lived at the time in other Arab countries. When I later asked Israeli experts on Arab affairs, I found that this event had left no mark at all in Israel.

Hammami joined the Fatah movement, which had been founded some years earlier by Yassir Arafat and his colleagues. One of the main tenets of Fatah was the rejection of the 'guardianship' of the Palestinian cause by any Arab state. The time had come for the Palestinians to make their own decisions.

Curiously enough, Hammami never told me that he had been a Fatah fighter. 'I am neither a soldier nor a hero', he once told me, 'I don't even know how to handle a pistol.' But I later learned from other PLO officers that Hammami had been, in fact, a commander in the military arm of Fatah, al-Assifah, and a very respected one at that. For some time he was the commander of a camp near Damascus.

Another fateful date in his life was 21 March 1968.

On that day, the Israeli army mounted a major attack against Karameh, a village east of the Jordan, which had become a major Palestinian guerrilla base. At the time, Yassir Arafat and many of the Fatah leaders were in the village. Among them was Said Hammami and also, curiously enough, Issam Sartawi, who did not know him yet.

This is how Hammami told me about it: 'I was sleeping, when I was suddenly awoken by the cry: The Jews are coming! I was shivering from fear. I did not know what to do, I decided to flee towards the Jordan River and hide. I looked through the window and saw that it was too late. An Israeli armoured car was advancing in our direction on the main road. For the first time since 1948, I saw Israelis. Suddenly, some of our fighters opened fire on the armoured car. I saw the Israeli soldiers jumping out, abandoning the car and their weapons and fleeing. I told myself: they are only human. They are not supermen. You can fight them and win.'

When I told the story to General Shmuel Gonen, one of the commanders of this action, he said that this description could not be exact. 'No Israeli unit fled. Actually no fire was exchanged at all inside the village, all the fighting occurred outside.' It is a classic case of different people in a battle seeing different things.

The battle of Karameh became the turning point in Palestinian consciousness. In concert with the Jordanian Army, the Palestinians had inflicted a defeat on the invincible Israelis. For the Palestinians it was a baptism of fire.

* * *

In 1972, Hammami was appointed PLO representative in London. Until then he had been one of the many bright young men serving in the Fatah army and other services. In his new job his quick intelligence caught the eye of Yassir Arafat, and he became one of the 'bright young men of Abu-Amar'. Abu-Amar is the *nom de guerre* by which Arafat is generally known to Palestinians.

He told me that he had accompanied Arafat on several missions. Hammami would sit quietly in a corner and give his opinion afterwards, when asked.

He told me about a dramatic meeting between Sadat and Arafat in 1972. Arafat came with a Palestinian delegation, prepared for a showdown with the Egyptian president. Had not Sadat promised to launch a war against Israel during the 'Year of Decision', unless Israel retreated from the occupied territories? Had not Arafat been one of the first Arab leaders to support Sadat against his domestic enemies, when Sadat was in dire need of such support?

The discussion became more and more heated, with Arafat accusing Egypt of cowardice and treachery. Sadat defended himself, arguing that his army was still insufficiently armed and ill-prepared. Arafat rejected this contemptuously.

Suddenly Sadat stopped in mid-sentence, went to a little cupboard and took out his personal Koran. 'You know I believe in God. I swear to you on this book that I shall fight!' he declared. 'I shall fight when I am ready, but I shall decide myself when. Trust me!'

With tears in his eyes, choking with emotion, Arafat embraced the Egyptian leader. On the tenth of Ramadan, 1973, Sadat fulfilled his promise.

Hammami told me many stories like this. I was never quite sure whether they were eyewitness accounts or apocryphal tales. He wanted me to understand the Arab scene. He thought it would help me to do my part for Israeli-Palestinian peace.

* * *

Within a short time, Hammami became surprisingly popular in the British capital. Journalists and politicians were attracted by the serious young man with the dark complexion and the brown eyes, who was so soft-spoken and so dedicated to his cause. They liked him because he represented the underdog. They liked him the more because he remained at his post after his colleagues in Rome and Paris were killed by Israeli agents. But most of all they liked him because of his sensible ideas.

Long before coming to London, while he was still active in Fatah in Jordan, Hammami started to follow a new line of thought. He studied Israeli realities and examined with growing curiosity the history of the state which had expelled him from his home. He came to the conclusion that Israel is a reality which could not be abolished without paying a terrible price.

Reality, for Hammami, meant that two national entities now existed in the country: the Jewish-Israeli and the Arab-Palestinian ones. Neither had a choice but to recognize the other. A settlement had to be reached between the two, without foreign interference. Such a settlement could only be based on the coexistence of two national states, Israel and Palestine, side by side.

At the same time, Hammami discovered that there were people in Israel who harboured similar ideas. He told me: 'One day, while visiting a Jordanian government office, I came across a copy of *Hazah al-Alam* (an Arabic edition of *Haolam Hazeh*, which appeared for a time). This issue contained your open letter to Yassir Arafat. I was amazed to see that there are Israelis who advocate negotiations with the PLO in order to achieve peace.'

Thus, without my knowing, my dialogue with Said Hammami, and indeed my dialogue with Arafat, had started long ago. My letter to Arafat had appeared in *Haolam Hazeh* in May 1969, under the headline 'A Letter to an Enemy,' and thirteen years later the addressee told me himself that he had read it.

When I received the book published in Beirut condemning my ideas, I knew there were people out there arguing along the same lines as I. Without knowing Hammami, I knew he was there. Like men in a dense fog, we sensed rather than saw each other.

When Menachem Begin and others threw at me, during heated Knesset debates, the ironic question, 'Where are the Arab Avnerys?' — a question which became a refrain — I answered: 'They exist!' But I could not mention names.

* * *

When Said Hammami finally surfaced, in his two articles in *The Times* of London, I felt like a skipper catching the first glimpse of a submarine with which he had had sonar contact for some time.

Throughout 1974 the PLO was quickly gaining international recognition. By a brilliant manoeuvre, it achieved a resolution at the Rabat Summit Conference of Arab kings and presidents, which recognized it as the sole representative of the Palestinian people. More than 100 governments recognized it one way or another. The United Nations followed suit and invited Arafat to address the General Assembly on 13 November 1974.

The next great date in the life of Hammami was 20 March 1975. This time it was he himself who created the event. On that day, at a seminar in London, he delivered a speech entitled 'A Palestinian Strategy for Peaceful Coexistence — on the Future of Palestine'. It was a carefully-worded statement, each word of which was approved in advance by Yassir Arafat, after many exchanges between London and Beirut. I have no doubt that my first meetings with Hammami, two months earlier, exerted some influence on its contents.

The speech, which was widely distributed in print by the PLO, was a clear call for the setting up of a Palestinian state alongside Israel, in the framework of a peace settlement which would guarantee peaceful coexistence between the two states. Hammami tried to reconcile this practical solution with official PLO ideology, which called for the eventual reunification of the country in a 'democratic non-sectarian state' (sometimes rendered as 'democratic secular state', which is not quite the same), by expressing his hope that eventually, 'perhaps not in our lifetime', the two peoples would decide of their own free will to merge their two states 'through cantonal arrangements'. Hammami also took great care to denounce Zionism and the 'racialist' character of Israel.

It was the practical solution envisaged in the speech which constituted the revolutionary breakthrough. Never had anything like it been openly said by a leading Palestinian, or indeed Arab, functionary — with the possible exception of President Habib Bourguiba of Tunisia in 1965, and before that by King Hassan II of Morocco.

Hammami suggested 'a nonviolent, evolutionary Palestinian approach to a tolerable form of coexistence between Israeli Jews and Palestinian Arabs, following on the establishment of a limited or partial peace settlement'. He called for the cessation of violent action against Israel, saying: 'The practical question for our Palestinian leadership in the context of possible peace negotiations is whether a continuation of the armed struggle against Israel is the most effective method to be pursued. In particular, if we assume that a probable outcome of any peace settlement is likely to be the establishment of some kind of Palestinian state on territory recovered from Israel.'

After outlining the practical problems facing the future Palestinian state, he said: 'We would aim to open and maintain a continuous and developing dialogue with any elements within Israel who were prepared to meet and talk with Palestinians regarding the form of a mutually acceptable coexistence which might in time be developed between the two peoples living in the country to which they both lay claim. We have our own ideas on this subject, of course, but we wouild approach the dialogue with open minds, ready to listen to what Israelis have to suggest as well as to put forward our own suggestions.

'To promote confidence and a frank and realistic exchange of ideas, consideration could be given to the maintenance of open frontiers between Israel and the Palestinian state and to permitting, even encouraging, a mutual inter-penetration of commerce, industry and cultural activities. Within reasonable limits and having regard to the need to provide for the in-gathering of the exiled Palestinians, one need not even exclude the idea of allowing Israeli Jews to live in the Palestinian state (not, of course, in paramilitary settlements like the existing *nahals*, but as peaceful private individuals prepared to live in harmony with their neighbours) provided they accepted Palestinian citizenship and provided a corresponding concession were made to enable Palestinians to go and live in Israel. In the Middle East of today, these ideas may sound like a dream. But this is the Palestine of tomorrow which the Palestinians dream of, as Yassir Arafat said at the UN.'

Hinting at our meetings, Hammami added: 'Already a growing number of Israelis are alive to the need for a new and more constructive attitude towards the Palestinians . . . We shall be offering to anyone who cares to listen in Israel the chance to sit down and talk with us like sensible human beings about our future, on the basis not of conflict but of peaceful and mutually advantageous coexistence.'

Implied in the speech was the hope that the PLO would be invited to a reconvened Geneva Peace Conference, and that such a conference would endorse his proposal. As he told me, he went to Beirut three times for the specific purpose of checking the proposed text. Actually it was initially supposed to be printed as an article in *The Times*, but for some reason the newspaper did not agree to publish it, perhaps because it had come under fire from Jewish circles after the publication of the previous Hammami articles. It was then decided, again with the approval of Arafat, to use the seminar in the National Liberal Club for this purpose.

After ten years this speech still stands out as a Palestinian manifesto for peace. It contained all the elements needed.

After sounding this clarion call, Hammami and his superiors in Beirut sat back and waited for the Israeli response which they were sure would follow such a revolutionary new departure. None came.

Israeli papers mentioned the speech in a few sentences, if at all. No daily newspaper printed it either in full, or even major excerpts. The Israeli establishment, under Prime Minister Itzhak Rabin and the Labour Party government, ignored the speech altogether. It was left to us, at *Haolam Haseh*, to call attention to it.

I believe that this disappointment was a major setback for Hammami and his supporters in the PLO. Arafat had allowed him to make a statement in order to see what would come out of it. If there had been any positive reaction by official Israel, even a cautious or secret one, Hammami would have become, overnight, a leading figure in PLO councils, and his new approach could have been openly endorsed and adopted by Arafat. The Israeli government prevented this by maintaining a stony silence — on purpose, as we shall see.

This non-reaction by the Israeli establishment cast its shadow over my next meetings with Hammami. We both knew now that our task would be much harder than either of us had, perhaps, feared.

## 11

*I am eating breakfast, hoping to be left alone, when somebody comes up, asks me if I am Uri Avnery, and introduces himself. He had recognized my face, and when he introduces himself I recognize his name. He is Mohammed Abu Tarbush, a Palestinian and a banker, who sometimes writes articles in the* International Herald Tribune.

*As usual, in such encounters, I ask him about his origins. He was a tiny boy when his family had to leave Beit Natif, an Arab village south of Jerusalem, in territory occupied by Israel during the war of 1948. Near this village, a unit of Haganah fighters was ambushed and destroyed. After the Arab village was razed to the ground, the kibbutz set up there was named in memory of the thirty-five fallen fighters, nativ halamed-hay*, The Way of the Thirty-Five.

*We talk about the situation and then he says: 'You Israelis and we Palestinians are the two most intelligent and dynamic peoples in the Middle East. We are crazy to fight each other. If we could combine our talents, we would be a regional power!'*

# 12

Perhaps the most exciting part of my first meeting with Hammami was the lecture he gave me about the movement to which he belonged. During this and following conversations with him and others, I slowly pieced together the story of the PLO, as seen through the eyes of its own militants.

It was the other side of the hill. As an Israeli, I had been very much involved in nearly all the events which had given birth to this movement. But I saw them through Israeli eyes.

In Israel at that time, the PLO was referred to, officially, as 'the organization of murderers' or *ha-mehablim* — a Hebrew word specially coined for them meaning the saboteurs. There is another Hebrew word for saboteurs, *ha-hablanim*, but this belongs to the honourable estate of army demolition experts. After it was used for some time as a name for PLO 'terrorists', army officers decided it was improper, and the new word was invented. In the beginning it was applied to Fedayeen crossing into Israeli territory, but later it became the official Israeli name for the PLO, and still later it was applied generally to all Palestinians. The name played a major role in the dehumanization and the demonization of the Palestinians, providing justification for the perpetration of any kind of atrocity. The Israeli Air Force was not bombing refugee camps in Lebanon, but 'nests of saboteurs'. It was not women and children who were being killed, but saboteurs. One of the aims of the Lebanon War of 1982 was not to destroy the political base of the Palestinian leadership, but to annihilate the 'substructure of the saboteurs'. If 'life and death are in the hands of the tongue', as an ancient Hebrew proverb says, this word killed more people than any gun.

Fatah was a name used to frighten children or incite hatred. The name evoked immediate associations with atrocities in which dozens of Israelis, among them many women and children, were indiscriminately killed. When my opponents in the Knesset tried to shout me down, whenever I talked about the rights of the Palestinians, the worst epitaph they used was 'Fatah agent!'

Listening that evening to Hammami, I tried to see this organization as he saw it, using my own experience as an ex-terrorist. It needed an effort of imagination and dispassionate objectivity. Yet I felt that if I was to talk with The Enemy, the saboteurs, I needed to understand his self-image.

Several good books have been written about the history of the PLO, and I do not intend to add another. Rather, I shall try to portray the developments in the PLO which led up to our contacts as Hammami and his colleagues saw them.

* * *

After the 1948 War, David Ben-Gurion and the entire Israeli leadership believed that the Palestinian people had ceased to exist. The name Palestine had ceased to exist on the map. Israel had annexed the greater part of it. Most of the rest, the so-called West Bank (of the Jordan River) was annexed by the Jordanian dynasty. The coastal area next to Egypt, the so-called Gaza Strip, was occupied by the Egyptians but not officially annexed to Egypt.

There was one little episode immediately after the war which has remained nearly unnoticed. A reconciliation committee was set up by the UN and held hearings in Lausanne, Switzerland. There appeared before it a delegation officially representing the Palestinian refugees but which was actually a kind of unofficial Palestinian negotiating team. This group, which included the Ramallah lawyer Aziz Shihadeh, approached the Israeli delegate, Eliahu Sasson, and told him that the Palestinians were ready to make peace with Israel. After consulting his government, Sasson rebuffed them bluntly. The government of Israel was not interested in dealing with people who did not represent any government. He would deal with the king of Jordan only.

Later on I shall try to explain this Israeli obsession with the Hashemite regime in Amman, which still plays a major role in Israeli thinking and diplomacy. At the time, it was clear why Ben-Gurion took this line. He believed that the Palestinian national identity could be obliterated, which would make it easier for Israel to fulfill its aims as he saw them. The Palestinians had refused to accept the UN partition plan of 1947 and had started a war to frustrate its implementation. They lost the war. Therefore, in Ben-Gurion's way of thinking, they did not exist any more. It was a naive belief.

For several years, however, it seemed that he was right. Very few of us in Israel insisted at that time that this was an illusion, and a dangerous one. The Palestinians were dispersed. Those left in Israel — about 200,000 of them, many of whom were transferred to Israel by King Abdallah after the fighting, according to the armistice agreement of 1949 — were not considered by the Palestinians themselves as part of their people, but as traitors who had opted for the Zionist Enemy.

Hundreds of thousands of Palestinian refugees, who had fled from Israeli-held territory or been forcibly thrown out,* were vegetating in refugee camps in abject misery all over the Middle East. In the West Bank and Gaza Strip, the Palestinian population was subject to a merciless dictatorship.

These were the years of Palestinian despair. Only the Jordanian kingdom gave them citizenship, in order to consolidate the annexation imposed after some notables assembled in Jericho had been forced to agree. Everywhere

* The author has tried to solve the riddle of how the Palestinian refugee problem came into being in his book *Israel Without Zionists*.

else the Palestinians were stateless, deprived of any civil and, indeed, human rights. They were subject to arbitrary rule by secret police officers, who could deport troublemakers across the nearest border, arrest, torture, deprive them of their livelihood. Many stories have been written about this Palestinian condition, especially by Ghassan Kanafani.

While denying the Palestinians the minimal conditions for human existence, the Arab regimes used the Palestinian cause to further their own interests. It was easy for the Israeli government to pretend that the Palestinians were but an invention of various Arab dictators.

But, like the ghost of Hamlet's father, the Palestinians were haunting the Middle East.

During the 1950s, the Arab world was torn between two contradictory concepts — the idea of *kaum*, or an all-embracing Arab nation, and the idea of *wotan*, which emphasizes the individuality of each Arab people. The Palestinians, naturally, embraced with enthusiasm the *kaumi* concept, propounded by the Baathists, and later by Gamal Abd-al-Nasser. They had nothing to lose but their misery. In a large Arab nation and state they could become the equals of other Arabs. As early as the 1940s, Palestinians like Georges Habash had played a part in creating, together with others in the American University in Beirut, the Movement of Arab Nationalists, which later gave birth to the Popular Front for the Liberation of Palestine.

During the first years of Israel, Palestinians often crossed the borders. At first these were villagers returning at night to gather some of their crops, perhaps believing that they could return to their villages, hundreds of which were standing abandoned in what had now become Israel. Soon these villages were levelled to the ground by Israeli bulldozers, so that not even a trace remained of most of them. Still the infiltrators would come in, killing here and there, operating mostly under the auspices of Egyptian or Jordanian intelligence officers. Now they were called Fedayeen — those who sacrifice themselves for the holy cause — a term deeply embedded in Arab history.

During the Sinai War of 1956, when Israel occupied the Gaza Strip, an attempt was made by the Palestinians there to organize a guerrilla war. The commander of the Strip at that time was an Israeli officer named Mattitiyahu Peled, who will play a major role in this narrative. It was there that he was confronted with the Palestinian problem and decided to study Arabic.

Soon Gaza, together with the Sinai, reverted to Egyptian rule, putting an end to the dream of a Palestinian guerrilla war there. Abd-al-Nasser, who had vanquished Britain, France and Israel and got all the territory back without firing a single shot, became the idol of the Arab masses, and especially of the Palestinians. When the United Arab Republic of Egypt and Syria was formed, it seemed that the dream of the pan-Arab state was starting to be realized.

But it soon fizzled out. On 28 September 1961, the Egyptian and Syrian union broke up. The Syrians remembered their own separate identity and kicked the Egyptians out of their country. The Baath party came to power both in Syria and in Iraq, and a violent propaganda war between those two countries and Egypt ensued. The Palestinian nationalists despaired of the Baath. The demise of the pan-Arab dream brought back to them their own national aspirations. When the waves of pan-Arab nationalism receded, the Palestinians were again left stranded. All other Arabs had their own identity, their own state and passport, or were soon to get them. Only they were without any of these trappings of modern existence, without which there is no human existence even for individuals, as Jews know better than anyone else. Even Georges Habash, one of the first to renew the Palestinian movement, turned towards Nasser.

This was the background of the uprising of the Palestinian units attached to the Syrian Army, which made such a deep impression on Hammami. Syrian and Palestinian units rebelled against the Baathist regime and failed. The ensuing massacre of the Palestinians left them with an abiding hatred for the Syrian regime. It fortified the new Palestinian consciousness and provided a great number of martyrs. When the struggle between Cairo, Damascus, and Baghdad flared up, each of the protagonists tried to exploit the Palestinian issue for his own ends. Abd-al-Karim Kassem, who had come to power in Baghdad during the 1958 revolution, declared that not only Israel but also the Arab states had robbed the Palestinians of their rights. He started to set up Palestinian institutions under his aegis. The Syrians, for their part, saw the Palestinian cause as a convenient instrument with which to embarrass Nasser and to prove to the Arab world that he was a show-off and a coward. They tried to heat up the Arab-Israeli conflict, using the Israeli schemes for diverting the Jordan waters as a pretext. They requested a meeting of the Arab heads of state, to talk about common military action against Israel.

Nasser saw the danger. It was clear to him that his army was unable to confront Israeli forces. He wanted to avoid war at any cost and looked for an elegant way to do so that would steal the thunder of the Syrians and the Iraqis. He prepared a trap for them.

He did not object to an Arab summit. On the contrary, he welcomed it. But he posed a question: How could one discuss a problem which concerns the Palestinians without the participation of the Palestinians themselves? Indeed, how could the heads of Arab states, the kings and the presidents, meet without a leader of the Palestinian people taking his seat among them, symbolizing the existence of the Palestinian nation?

The Egyptian president was quite sure this ploy would postpone the summit for years. After all, there was no Palestinian body, and haggling over its situation and composition would drag on for a long time. In the meantime, he hoped, the Jordan issue would disappear, war would be avoided, and the Syrians would shut up, *inshallah* (God willing). But Abd-al-Nasser walked into his own trap, as he did again on the eve of the Six Day War.

Looking for a Palestinian politician who would become his stooge, he chose one Ahmed Shukairy, a refugee from Acre, a lawyer and politician endowed with great rhetorical talents, who had served as the Saudi representative at the UN. He was detested by the Israelis as much as the Grand Mufti of Jerusalem, Hadj Amin al-Husseini, before him. Nasser told

Shukairy to find some formula for Palestinian representation in an Arab summit conference.

Nasser was not prepared for the results. The Palestinian cause was only a stratagem for him. Like his successor, Anwar Sadat, he was not aware of the depth of the Palestinians' emotions. As happened many times before and after, the dynamism of the Palestinian cause, which has a life of its own, confounded all those who tried to play with it, not least the Israelis.

Shukairy did not delay. He rushed to Gaza and proclaimed enthusiastically that the president of Egypt had recognized the Palestinian entity. Local reaction was stupendous. A tide of excitement engulfed the population of the Gaza Strip, about 350,000 at the time, who were vegetating in a pressure cooker, controlled by the Egyptians but nearly shut off from Egypt. Intoxicated by this response, Shukairy proclaimed the creation of the Palestinian Liberation Organization.*

Nasser was presented with a fait accompli. He had no choice but to accept it with good grace. He became the patron of the PLO, and Shukairy became his handyman. The result was the very opposite of what Nasser had had in mind when he helped to release the Palestinian genie from its bottle.

He had not wanted to convene an Arab summit to discuss the Jordan water conflict, lest it bring about another war. Instead he now had to agree to a summit devoted to a much more explosive issue — the liberation of Palestine.

The Arab summit conference was convened in Alexandria in January 1964, and decided upon the establishment of the Palestine Liberation Organization and a Palestine Liberation Army, regular units to be attached to the armies of the Arab states. The PLO was officially founded a few months later, in May 1964, at a conference in East Jerusalem.

* * *

In the meantime, far from the manoeuvres of the Arab governments another chain of events of even greater importance was taking place.

In the oil states of the Persian Gulf, where the Palestinian intelligentsia had congregated, a group of young Palestinians had founded an organization, Fatah. Among them was a young engineer named Abd-al-Raouf al-Qudwah, soon to become known as Yassir Arafat.

The PLO was a non-party, quasi-governmental body. Fatah was a political movement, a fighting party with a military wing. It provided the Palestinian movement with a dynamic force. Later on, many rumours concerning the beginnings of Fatah and the political and even physical origin of Arafat were spread. It was said that he came from the Muslim Brotherhood. According to Hammami, all this was nonsense. Some people saw a religious, fanatical Muslim significance in the very name of Fatah,

* The name is usually rendered, mistakenly, as Palestine Liberation Organization. There is a subtle difference.

which means, literally, religious conquest. But the real name of the movement is *Harakat Tahrir Falastin*, Movement for the Liberation of Palestine. Fatah is the reverse Arabic acronym of the full name. It was not invented by Arafat but by one of his early associates, who has since died.

What made Arafat exceptional was his determination to start military action without regard to chances of success or to the smallness of his forces. His gospel was quite simple: The Palestinians have to start fighting in order to prove their independent existence in the area and to prevent a compromise between Israel and the Arab regimes which would exclude the Palestinians.

Some of the atrocities committed by Fatah were horrible. But they certainly achieved the two objectives outlined by Arafat. Confirmation of this came years later from none other than that great expert on terrorism, Itzhak Shamir, then Prime Minister of Israel. Asked by a British historian about the effectiveness of terror as employed by the Stern Group, Shamir justified his actions by citing the example of the PLO, saying that the PLO would not have achieved anything without employing terror.

The very starting point of Arafat's policy was a profound distrust of the Arab governments, a sentiment mixed with a deep bitterness, which is one of the basic components of the new Palestinian consciousness. I remember that this bitterness, which underlay everything Hammami said, was a great revelation to me. Even today most Israeli leaders are quite unaware of this basic fact of the Palestinian condition. It is no exaggeration to say that Fatah was founded not only to act against Israel but also against all Arab governments and their obnoxious pretence to be the guardians of the dispossessed Palestinians.

When Arafat and his associates first propounded their idea of armed struggle, many Palestinians argued that it was 'not logical', a comment never forgotten by the founders of Fatah. Arafat's opponents proposed to create first a network of cells throughout the Palestinian diaspora, in order to prepare the struggle properly. Arafat's answer was: 'If we set up cells in Nablus and al-Halil (Hebron), the Israelis will come and conquer those places.'

In January 1965, the Fedayeen offensive against Israel started. The first Fedai was captured near Beth Govrin. His name was Mahmoud al-Hedjazi, and he became a hero of the movement. He was sentenced to death by a military court, his sentence was commuted, and he was later exchanged for an Israeli prisoner of Fatah.

With the beginning of the Fatah action, the breach between the Palestinians and the Syrians was repaired — for the time being. The Syrians understood that it was worthwhile to support Fatah, in order to drag Abd-al-Nasser into the war he did not want. The cooperation between Fatah and the Syrian army expanded between 1965 and 1967, and the number of Fatah attacks planned in Syria grew steadily and created mounting tension all along Israel's northern and eastern borders. Damascus proclaimed a national war of liberation, Prime Minister Eshkol and his chief of staff, Itzhak Rabin, publicly warned Syria and threatened to overthrow the

Syrian regime by military force. Everything proceeded according to Arafat's plan.

Fatah could penetrate places where Shukairy's PLO could not act. As a lackey of Abd-al-Nasser and Egyptian policy, Shukairy was boycotted by Syria, and for other reasons by Jordan. Algeria was close to him because there Houari Boumedienne had come to power, a man who hated Nasser because the Egyptians had supported his enemy, Ahmed Ben Bella.

In June 1967, Arafat achieved his aim. Fatah activity brought the tension between Israel and Syria to a climax. Israel seemed to be on the verge of invading Syria. In order to prevent this, Abd-al-Nasser concentrated his army in Sinai, evicted the UN forces stationed there and announced the closing of the Straits of Tiran. Israel went to war, in the course of which it occupied all the remaining parts of Palestine, as well as the Golan Heights and Sinai.*

After that war, Israel missed the historic chance to make peace with the Palestinian people, as previously described. A new phase of the war between Israel and the Palestinian people had begun.

The Six Day War had two important consequences which were at the time ignored in Israel. First, for the first time since 1948 all the territories of Palestine were united under one government — the Israeli. Three branches of the Palestinian family — the Arabs of the West Bank, the Gaza Strip and Israel proper — were reunited. Secondly, the Fatah movement was the only Arab force not tarnished by the shame of defeat. The prestige of the armies of Egypt, Jordan and Syria was in tatters. Only the Fatah guerrillas (or terrorists, according to the Israelis) were continuing to fight. To many Arabs it seemed that only they upheld Arab honour. Honour and shame, as has so often been said, play a great role in Arab consciousness and tradition, much as innocence and guilt do in European culture.

The battle of Karameh, in March 1968, raised the prestige of Fatah even higher. To Israelis, this was just another sally, and a rather unsuccessful one. But to the Arabs it looked like a major battle, in which the Palestinian forces had gained a great victory over the Israelis. After the shame of the six days, this was a great boost to Arab morale, and it did wonders for the Palestinians, especially those who were there, such as Arafat himself, Hammami and Sartawi. In Fatah rhetoric, the victory of Karameh was mentioned in the same breath as the battle of the Yarmuk (in 636, the victory of the Muslim forces over the Byzantine army which opened the gates of Palestine to the Arabs), the battle of the horns of Hittin (1187, near Tiberias, where the great Saladin vanquished the Crusader Kingdom of Jerusalem) and the battle of Ain Jalut (1260, near today's Kibbutz Ein Harod, where the Egyptian army defeated the Mongol hordes, thereby saving the whole Middle East from a Mongol conquest).

'It is no coincidence', Hammami remarked, 'that all these four victories

* The events leading up to the war were described in detail by the author in his book *Israel Without Zionists*.

were won a few miles from the Jordan River.' It was also no coincidence that they became names of Palestine Liberation Army brigades, and that the Israeli Army encountered them in the Lebanon War.

* * *

The new prestige of Fatah turned it into the dominant force within the Palestinian people. It inevitably led to its taking over the PLO.

The grandiloquent Shukairy, who had (or had not) promised on the eve of the Six Day War to throw the Israelis into the sea (in his conversation with me. Arafat denied that this remark was ever made) was dismissed. After a caretaker regime, Fatah and its supporters gained a majority in the fourth session of the Palestinian National Council, which was convened in July 1968 in Cairo. Soon afterwards Arafat became chairman of the PLO executive, in addition to his position as leader of Fatah and commander-in-chief of all Palestinian forces.

But Arafat never became a dictator, nor was the new PLO a homogeneous or monolithic organization. These are central facts of the Palestinian situation and have to be well understood.

Palestinians are apt to state with pride that Israel and the PLO are the only true democracies in the Middle East. This is quite true. It may be partly explained by the Palestinian character, partly by necessity.In this respect, as in many others, there is a certain parallel between Zionist and Palestinian experiences. Israeli democracy was formed in the Zionist movement, long before the state of Israel came into being. The Zionist congresses, parliaments in exile, created a democratic tradition. The Zionist movement had no individual members: its members were the various Zionist parties. Some kinds of elections, rather dubious ones, were conducted before each congress. The right to vote was purchased together with the Zionist shekel, as the one-time membership payment was called. The tradition thus created took hold in Israel. To some this looks like a miracle, considering that nearly all new immigrants came from dictatorial regimes, both eastern and western, or had grown up under the colonial dictatorship of the British Mandate in Palestine.

The PLO is composed of member organizations. These appoint the delegates to the Palestinian National Council. Their membership is dispersed throughout the Middle East. Apart from individuals living in the West, no one of the four and a half million Palestinians lives in a free country, is free to vote, conduct an untrammelled political debate, or form free associations.

Apart from the short-lived mini-state in South Lebanon, there was no place where the PLO could exercise political authority. No Palestinian leader can impose his will on the Palestinians, such as Arab dictators do in many countries, nor does he have at his disposal a police force, prisons, or a fettered, subservient press.

This means that decisions can be made only with some kind of consensus. This is a long and cumbersome process. Policies have to be explained to vast numbers of people in many different countries, under the eyes of mutually hostile regimes and their secret police forces. This process comes to its climax at the session of the National Council, whose members come from widely-dispersed 'constituencies', far apart both geographically and politically. The positive side of all this is that the PLO does indeed function as a kind of democracy, with good chances that this democracy will take hold in the future in the Palestinian state, as it did in Israel. The negative side is that it is extremely difficult to innovate, to adopt new resolutions, and once they are adopted, to change them. Like adopting amendments to the American constitution, it is a long, long process.

This would have been difficult enough if the PLO had been one homogeneous organization, like Fatah. But the Palestinian condition and Arab reality presented a constant temptation to every Arab government to meddle in the affairs of the PLO, to install its own agents and create its own Fedayeen organization, to gain influence over PLO decision-making in order to further its own interests. One of the main objects of Fatah became to attain 'independence of decision', the ability of the PLO to make its own decisions, according to Palestinian interests only, without being coerced or threatened by the various Arab governments, each of which uses the Palestinians in its land as hostages.

When I started the contacts with Hammami, I was only vaguely conscious of these facts. Israeli ignorance of Palestinian affairs was abysmal, and even I, who had already devoted many years to dealing with the Palestinian question, knew precious little about the interior workings of the PLO, an organization still shrouded in mystery. It took us many years to gain a better understanding of the problems of the PLO, and we could have saved ourselves many disappointments if our knowledge had been better.

* * *

The development of Palestinian consciousness may be compared to a long march. The marchers set out at the same time from the same place, but as the march goes on the line becomes attenuated, some striding ahead with resolute steps, others lagging behind and becoming stragglers, while in between, the mass of the marchers walking on, each finding his own pace. Some near the finishing line, while others seem hardly to have budged from the start. Moreover, the march does not follow a straight line. Like a river striving towards the sea, it follows a zig-zag course, circumvents obstacles, going left and right, sometimes even seeming to go backwards to find a new avenue. To the interested onlooker, this may all be very frustrating, but that is the way great historical movements proceed, the Palestinian national movement perhaps more so than others.

* * *

The starting point of the long march was the Palestinian national charter, first adopted at the first session of the Palestinian National Council in May 1964, and amended in the fourth session of the council in July 1968. No document ever did greater harm to those who wrote it than this unfortunate instrument, which has become and still is the main propaganda weapon of the Israeli government. It helped the Israeli establishment more than an army of tanks and a fleet of warplanes ever could.

The covenant reiterated the basic tenets of the Palestinian national movement since its very beginning, which may be placed in the early days of the British occupation of Palestine — assuming that before the Balfour Declaration Palestinian nationalism was but a part of Greater Syrian or pan-Arab nationalism. It objected to political Zionism, to the influx of Zionist settlers whose obvious aim was to create in Palestine a new Jewish nation and a Jewish state. It argued that the Balfour Declaration was illegal, because it was given by an imperial power without the consent of the people living in the country, that Palestine had been an Arab country for thirteen centuries. Jund Filistin, the military district of Palestine, was established by the Muslim conquerors immediately upon their taking possession of Byzantine Palestine in the seventh century.

The covenant denies the existence of the Jewish nation, and, of course, any Jewish rights to Palestine. It demands the creation of a Palestinian state in all of Palestine, and the expulsion of all Jews who had come to Palestine 'after the Zionist invasion' — generally assumed to mean the Balfour Declaration of 1917.

Innumerable words have been written about this document. Many PLO leaders have tried to explain it away, either by pretending that the document does not mean what it says or by saying that it has been superseded by later resolutions of the Palestinian National Council. These were generally adopted unanimously, and the Charter says in Article 33 that it can be amended by a majority of two-thirds of the total membership of the national congress.

The real argument against the demand for an official abrogation of the Charter is that it is not a usual procedure in political life to abrogate any document. The usual way to put an end to a document is to adopt a new document. American agreement to detente with the Soviet Union was not based on a demand that the Soviet leadership officially abrogate the Communist Manifesto. A paragraph in any future Israeli-Palestinian peace agreement to the effect that all contrary prior statements and resolutions are hereby null and void should satisfy this demand and put the Charter to rest once and for all.

The right way to look at the Charter is in its historical context. It embodied the beliefs and attitudes to which the Palestinian people have clung for two generations: that all of Palestine was their country, and theirs only, that the Jewish settlement was an invasion by strangers and that whatever happens, the Palestinian people in adversity must uphold this position as their main source of strength and cohesion, an immovable object facing an invincible force.

The Charter should be viewed as an expression of the Palestinian consensus prevailing at the time it was written, between 1964 and 1968, when Palestinian fortunes were at their lowest ebb. It was divorced from reality, when reality was too black to face.

Yet even at the time of its formulation it was obsolete. Israel had become a reality, the existence of a new Jewish nation in Israel was a fact which could not be wished away, the idea that the Arab world would unite to fight for the Palestinians was sheer utopia. By no stretch of the imagination could any reasonable Palestinian expect to obliterate Israel by force of arms. Violent action could only serve to draw the world's attention to the plight of the Palestinians and convince the powers that be that the Palestinians and their aspirations have to be reckoned with.

Soon after the final version of the Charter was adopted, the long march got under way. The first station was the idea of the so-called Palestinian democratic and secular (or non-sectarian) state, in which Muslims, Jews and Christians would live together in equality.

Israelis generally fail to understand why this was a big step forward. To them it was just another formulation of the basic idea of the Charter: the destruction of the State of Israel. The creation of such a state in all of Palestine would of course entail the dismantling of Israel.

As a practical idea, the democratic secular state is as utopian as anything previously adopted by the Palestinians. It would mean that a state of total war, which has existed now for three generations, would be turned overnight into a state of total peace, such as does not exist anywhere else in the world. Moreover, by putting the Jews in the same category as Muslims and Christians, this formulation denies Jewish or Israeli nationhood, defining the Jews as a religious community only.

But looked at from the Palestinian side, the new idea included a very important step in the development of Palestinian consciousness. No more were the Israelis viewed as strangers who must be sent back where they came from. It implied that all Jews in the country would become members of the new society on an equal footing with Muslims and Christians. This was expressed explicitly later on by Arafat and others. In this roundabout way the PLO recognized the right of the Jews to live in the country, if not their status as a nation with a right to national self-determination. It was a station on the march to reality, even if Israelis, understandably, did not perceive it as such.

It would be easy to say that this idea had died when the next step was made, but this is not quite so. It lives on, but it has been relegated to the status of a dream for the remote future. Loath to give up the idea that the country between the sea and the Jordan River is one unit, Palestinians still frequently bring up the idea of the democratic secular state as something which will be realized by future generations. This made it easier for them to take the next step forward; it eased the pain of making the decisive break with the past.

The next phase was ushered in by the October 1973 War. In the meantime the PLO had suffered the setback of 'Black September' — the onslaught of the Jordanian regime on what was the quickly becoming a PLO mini-state in Jordan. The PLO then established itself in Beirut and recreated its mini-state there.

The Yom Kippur War gave a big push to the process. The victory of Egyptian and Syrian arms at the beginning and the success of the Israeli counter-offensive on both fronts finally put an end to any dream of militarily defeating Israel in the foreseeable future. The interim agreement between Israel, Egypt and Syria, and the American effort to bring about an interim agreement between Israel and Jordan created the fear that parts of the West Bank would be turned over to King Hussein, preempting a Palestinian solution. This was only prevented by the timidity of the new Rabin government. Golda Meir had promised to hold elections before an inch of West Bank territory would be given back to the Arabs. When Foreign Minister Yigal Allon informed Prime Minister Rabin that Henry Kissinger proposed to turn Jericho over to King Hussein, so that the Jordanian flag could be hoisted on West Bank soil and the continued adherence of the West Bank to the Hashemite kingdom demonstrated, Rabin is supposed to have answered: 'I will not hold elections because of Jericho!'

The new reality established by the Yom Kippur War made thoughtful Palestinians realize that now was a time to set their sights on realistic goals. Said Hammami got a green light from Arafat to make a statement in *The Times*, coming to terms for the first time with the existence of Israel as a permanent fact in the Middle East and defining the Palestinian aim as the setting up of 'a new state of Palestine joining the comity of nations'. More than this, in his second article Hammami recognized not only the State of Israel but also Israeli nationality, by saying: 'I believe that the first step towards that should be a mutual recognition for the two respective parties. The Israeli Jews and the Palestinian Arabs should recognize one another as peoples, with all the rights to which a people is entitled.' This means of course the right to self-determination and to a state, the very rights the Palestinians now claim for themselves, and by implication, therefore, must concede to the Israelis.

How far did Hammami at that time reflect the attitude of the PLO? There can be no doubt that Hammami was acting under the auspices of the supreme Fatah leadership, especially Yassir Arafat, Khalil al-Wazir ('Abu Jihad') and Mahmoud Abbas ('Abu Maazen'). It was to the latter, a very central figure in Fatah and the PLO, but generally unknown abroad, to whom Hammami reported directly.

Hammami could not have published his statements and remained the official representative of the PLO in London if he had not enjoyed the full support of Arafat. But this does not mean that the Palestinian leadership at that time was ready to stand officially and unequivocally behind his statements. Like Sartawi afterwards, Hammami was a pioneer, marching ahead, supported by his superiors but also taking steps on his own initiative. A lot had to be done to turn those ideas into a general consensus supported by the whole movement, or at least by the great majority. The mass of the people still lagged behind, and had to be brought forward.

In June 1974, the Palestinian National Council was convened in Cairo and adopted a ten-point programme. As usual when the PLO takes a big step forward, the operative part of the new resolution was obfuscated by revolutionary phrases, and great pains were taken to pretend that nothing new had happened and that the new resolutions were but a continuation of older ones. This was necessary in order to adopt a resolution by unanimous consensus, with the agreement of the radical, rejectionist elements in the

PLO who were acting on behalf of the radical Arab regimes. Unfortunately, it had the effect of deadening the impact on Israeli public opinion, making the resolutions practically useless as a means of convincing Israeli public opinion that the PLO was moving towards peace. This was a problem we came up against time and again, which formed a subject of many of my conversations with Hammami. Like Arafat himself, he could not perceive that such a supposedly sophisticated and intelligent people as the Israelis would fail to notice the big step taken.

The operative sentence in the ten-point programme of June 1974, a veritable landmark in the evolution of the PLO, was Paragraph 2: 'The PLO will struggle by every means, the foremost of which is armed struggle, to liberate Palestinian land and to establish the people's national, independent and fighting authority on every part of Palestinian land to be liberated.'

To be understood, this sentence had to be decoded.

The words 'national authority' were chosen in order to avoid the term national state, which means a clear acceptance of the partition of Palestine, an idea rejected by the Palestinian leadership in 1947 when the territory allotted to the Palestinians was far larger. National authority means the same, but is less explicit and therefore easier to swallow by many still reluctant to accept what they knew had to be accepted.

During the thirteenth session of the Palestinian National Council, in 1977, the next step was taken. Paragraph 11 of its resolutions stated clearly: 'The Council resolves to pursue the struggle to recover our people's national rights and, first and foremost their right to return, to exercise self-determination and to establish their independent national state on their own land.' This was acceptance of partition, plain and simple.

The words 'every part of Palestinian land to be liberated' was repeatedly rephrased by Arafat himself as 'every part of Palestine from which the Israelis will withdraw.'

At this stage, it was obvious to every Palestinian that the repartition of Palestine and the creation of a Palestinian state could only occur with the agreement of Israel. Such an agreement could only come about if international pressure, meaning in practice US pressure, could compel Israel to accept this solution involuntarily, or if Israeli public opinion itself changed.

Two other developments took place at the same time. The summit of Arab heads of state in Rabat recognized the PLO as the sole legitimate representative of the Palestinian people, and the United Nations accorded to the PLO similar recognition. The world saw Yassir Arafat addressing the UN General Assembly, and heard him say that he carried an olive branch in one hand and a gun in the other.

This, then, was the setting for the first meeting between a Palestinian official and a Zionist Israeli — the meeting between Hammami and myself. The PLO had taken another great step forward on its long march; it was our task to make sure that this step would receive a response from Israel.

# 13

*'I'm just back from Beirut,' says Hammami. 'I've been there for several weeks, and I've done nothing but argue about you. Some say that you are a son of a bitch, others say that you are a true friend of the Palestinians. In the end I was so fed up that I told them: By God, let's kill the man and be done with it!'*

# 14

'Well, here we two old terrorists are again!' Said Hammami said, walking into my room at the Mount Royal.

'Neither of us seems to have been killed in the meantime!' I replied in the same vein.

This constant joking about getting killed was becoming a regular feature of our conversations. It was, I suppose, an unconscious way of dealing with the dangers involved in our meetings. Yet I never quite realized how big the danger was for Said. He never told me about the flak he was getting in his own organization. Only much later, in the light of what I learned from Sartawi, did I come to understand the ups and downs of his moods.

It was 14 October 1975, and we were starting a new round of meetings. They took place at the Mount Royal again. The hotel is immense, a warren of hundreds of rooms. The service was lousy and no one gave a damn whether the guests were alive or dead. It was a good place to meet without drawing attention.

* * *

In the preceding months we had been in constant contact by phone. I never ceased to be amazed by the miracle of the international telephone. The phone would ring, I would lift the receiver, and the familiar voice of the enemy would talk, as if calling from the next street. Sometimes he would say 'This is Sam', sometimes he would not bother to introduce himself at all.

Much later in this narrative, I would receive telephone calls from besieged Beirut, from Aden in South Yemen, from Tunisia. But by that time I had become much more blasé.

The main topic of our conversations, during this time, was the Israeli reaction to the historic speech which he had delivered in March. Or, rather, the absence of any reaction.

The PLO leadership had sanctioned the speech, at least as a trial balloon. Hammami told me that he had gone to Beirut three times in order to have every word ratified by Yassir Arafat himself. The leadership group was obviously shocked by this total failure of the Israeli establishment to reply to it in any way. Here was a high-ranking PLO diplomat proposing, for the first time, a far-reaching peace plan, and no official person in Israel had even acknowledged it, much less answered in any way. Hammami was obviously worried that this non-reaction would discourage the moderate wing of the PLO. The rejectionists could say: 'You see, you are giving away our cards, and get nothing in return. The more moderate we become, the more expansionist the Israelis will be.' It was an argument I was to come up against many, many times. I believe it was deliberately encouraged by the Israeli government, in order to destroy any sign of moderation in the PLO that would create international pressure on Israel to negotiate about the West Bank and the Gaza Strip.

At this juncture it became obvious to me that there was an urgent need to create in Israel a body that could act instead of the establishment, and respond in some way to the signs of moderation in the PLO, thus providing our counterparts with the ammunition they needed in their battle to win the confidence of their people.

I should add here that I use the term 'moderate' as it is understood by the Western reader. Hammami, Sartawi and their friends always objected to this term, which they found misleading and quite unsuited to their temperament, as it is to mine. They were not moderate in their demand for Palestinian independence and national rights. If they believed that these could be achieved only through peace and reconciliation, this was a realistic appraisal. In their own eyes, they were the realists, not the moderates.

* * *

Throughout the first months of 1975, a series of meetings took place in Tel Aviv to debate the Palestinian question. It was one of the periodic attempts to unify various elements of the peace camp, on a platform advocating recognition of the Palestinians' right to self-determination and the necessity of dealing with the PLO.

The debate was endless. All the mental blocks, which even peace camp activists have about the Palestinian issue, and especially about the PLO, came to the fore. After several meetings, which led to nothing but further debates, I was fed up. Everybody talked; each of those present had a different idea; nearly everybody objected to the participation of somebody else. The sole result was a renewed feeling of impotence.

I decided on a different tack: to have a very small group of like-minded people take the decisive step, publish an unequivocal statement, and then call upon others to join. This way a lot of futile discussions could be avoided.

Amos Kenan, one of Israel's most talented writers, who was as disgusted as I was with the interminable squabbles of the various peace groups, was abroad. We had cooperated in the past in setting up a shortlived Association for an Israeli-Palestinian Federation. This was immediately after the Six Day War, during which Kenan had given me a moving eyewitness account of the destruction of the Arab villages in the Latroun sector. This description, later published, is one of the important documents of that time. Before going abroad he had told me: 'You can use my name for any purpose you see fit.'

At the right moment, Yossi Amitai happened to visit me in my office. He, too, was upset by the lack of any reaction to Hammami's speech. Yossi is a young expert for Arabic affairs, the secretary of a kibbutz in the Negev, one of the best examples of the sabra pioneering spirit. I told him about my phone conversations with Hammami and proposed that he join Kenan and me in setting up a new body, whose main function would be to propagate the idea of Israeli-Palestinian peace. He agreed on the spot.

Then and there Yossi and I drew up the founding manifesto of 'The Israeli Council for Israel-Palestine Peace', which consisted of thirteen points. The English version was published in the *Jerusalem Post* on 10 June 1975, under the headline 'A Statement by Uri Avnery, Yossi Amitai and Amos Kenan.' It read:

> We believe: one, that this country is the homeland of two peoples — the Jewish and the Palestinian peoples. Two, that the core of the conflict between the Jewish people and the Arab world lies in the historical confrontation between the two peoples of this country, which is so precious to both of them. Three, that the only road to peace is through the coexistence of two sovereign states, each of which will be the national home of its people — the state of Israel and the state of Palestine. Four, that the establishment of the sovereign state of Palestine alongside the state of Israel will be the outcome of negotiations between the government of Israel and the Palestine Liberation Organization, as the recognized national representative of the Palestinian people.

Other points of the manifesto dealt with boundaries, the status of Jerusalem, the refugee problem, mutual security arrangements, links with the Arab world and the Jewish people, and an overall regional organization.

It ended with the following words:

> We call upon all Israelis who regard the above principles as the best way to consolidate the sovereignty, integrity, security and prosperity of the state of Israel to join us in establishing The Israeli Council for Israel-Palestine Peace. This council will explain, in Israel and throughout the world, the vital need for coexistence between Israel and Palestine, and take part in a dialogue with all Palestinian elements who are ready to promote contacts between the two peoples of this country.

We used the words 'this country' in order to circumvent a major psychological obstacle: the fact that the same country is called in Hebrew Eretz Israel and in Arabic Falastin (or Filistin) two names with profound emotional and political import.

Never was a far-reaching manifesto drawn up in less time. We both knew what we wanted, and the Israeli-Arab sensibilities that had to be taken into account. It took us less than two hours. The full text was first published in Hebrew in *Haaretz*, on 9 June. On 11 June, the Israeli press published a report about a press conference held by Amitai and myself, announcing the aim of the new council. At the conference I mentioned Hammami's peace initiative and said that I had met in Europe 'PLO representatives', without, however, specifying that I had met Hammami himself. I had agreed with him on this formula.

The creation of the Council received wide publicity throughout the world. Obviously, many well-meaning people had been waiting for such a voice to come from Israel. Not only did *Le Monde* in Paris and *The Times* in London announce our initiative, but also Arab papers in Europe and in the Arab countries themselves.

* * *

When Hammami and I met again after these developments, the main topic was, of course, the attitude of the Israeli government. Why had it ignored Hammami's statement? Why was there no echo in the Israeli press?

I told him that insufficient communications between us were at least partly to blame. Why had he not sent me the text of his speech in advance? It had taken us quite a while to obtain the full text, and then it was too late for the daily papers to print it as news, even if they had been inclined to do so. But, of course, the main reasons for the negative attitude in Israel were much more profound, and I shall go into them soon. The prime minister, Itzhak Rabin, objected adamantly to any accommodation with the Palestinians. The vast majority of Israelis took the same stand. There was not much we could do about it if the PLO did not give us ammunition for our fight.

What ammunition? I reiterated what I had said at our first meetings, in January: In order to effect a change in official policy, we had to change public opinion. We could do this only if dramatic events helped us to overcome the old fears and prejudices. We must demonstrate that the PLO had changed, that the Charter had become inoperative, that the Palestinians were now ready for a peaceful solution of the conflict. Cautious diplomatic texts, coded statements and speeches were not enough. We must create events which could be seen by everyone, which were unequivocal, which television could bring into the living room of every Israeli.

The trouble was, Hammami said, that it was very difficult for the PLO leadership to do anything dramatic along those lines, after the failure of the Israeli government to respond to Hammami's daring speech. It was the old vicious circle all over again. The lack of Israeli response was weakening the moderate wing of the PLO, and because of this the PLO was unable to provide us with the response we needed to strengthen our own credibility in Israel. Lacking this, how could we change the climate in Israel and compel our government to change its line?

We talked for three days. I did not have to convince him, but I tried to provide him with the arguments he would need to convince his people in Beirut. He in turn tried to provide me with the arguments I might need to encourage my friends in Israel to take bolder action. We were partners, somewhere between the enemy lines. Sometimes we forgot how exposed we were to fire from both sides.

What could be done now? I drew up a list of possible events, big and small — a kind of political menu from which one could choose the dish easiest to digest at the moment.

My biggest project was a conference of Palestinian and Israeli personalities to work out a detailed draft peace agreement between Israel and the PLO. Who could convene such a conference, making it possible for Yassir Arafat to give his approval and for Israelis from the peace camp to attend? Perhaps some academic body in Oxford? Perhaps Lord Caradon, the father of Security Council Resolution 242, whom both of us knew well and respected?

I had had a long conversation with Caradon during his visit to Jerusalem a few weeks earlier. An incorrigible Anglophile, I enjoyed his typical upper-class British humour. He called himself a colonial governor who had run out of colonies. When I first met him five years earlier in New York, while he was chief of the British delegation to the UN, he was still an ardent advocate of the Jordanian solution, but in the meantime he had become convinced that peace could be achieved only through a solution providing for the establishment of a Palestinian state.

Another possibility I proposed was that Hammami and I publish a joint communiqué, thereby making our meetings public, and demonstrating the beginning of direct cooperation between the peace elements of both sides.

There were several other ideas. I could interview Hammami for *Haolam Hazeh*, thus demonstrating that the PLO was ready to address the Israeli public directly. I could try to arrange an interview with him by Israeli television. He could send a message of support to our council. We could appear together on a BBC television programme, which would create a worldwide sensation and was certain to be rebroadcast by Israeli TV.

Hammami was sceptical. Although a daring visionary, he was in practice a cautious man, with a sound appreciation of what was politically possible at any given moment. In spite of the fact that he was seventeen years younger than I, I always seemed the more impatient, the more enthusiastic partner. This was a feature of all our contacts, indeed of all the contacts between Palestinians and Israelis later on.

'Later, later! It's too early! You must be patient!' he would object.

He did agree, however, to submit the whole list of proposals to Yassir Arafat. We agreed that I should send, in the meantime, a letter to Lord Caradon, who happened to be out of England, and ask him discreetly whether he might be ready to invite the parties to such a conference. I sent the letter from Tel Aviv on 2 November.

Finally we agreed to try to do something to resurrect Hammami's March speech as a news event. Our council would send him a long list of questions, ostensibly to clarify several points in his peace plan. If permitted by his superiors, he would reply to the questions in a letter addressed to the Israeli Council. Such a letter would constitute a *de facto* recognition of an Israeli body by the PLO, and would enable us to concentrate public attention in Israel on the new line of the PLO. I drew up this questionnaire a few days later and sent it to him through Edward Hodgkin, a senior editor of *The Times* and a good friend of mine, who was visiting the veteran Palestinian leader, Mussa Alami, in his children's village near Jericho. Hodgkin, who had been in charge of a British Army radio station in Jaffa during the Second World War and had met and married his wife there, was one of the many foreigners who discreetly helped our contacts throughout the years, for purely idealistic reasons.

* * *

We talked, we walked, we joked, exhilarated by our contact and perhaps, unconsciously, by the dangers which cast their shadow over our meetings.

Said never approved of my way of looking at beautiful girls in the street. He was extremely conservative on this point, saying that he could not look at other women when he was in love with Khalida, his Jerusalem-born wife. Once we met to have lunch at some Oriental restaurant. In some shop on the way he joked with Jewish salesmen, who knew him, and introduced me as 'one of your compatriots from Israel'. They were speechless. He left with a jaunty 'shalom!'

Over a Turkish hoummas and kabab we talked about the history of Palestine, Zionism, the climate of Tel Aviv and the present state of affairs. Inevitably the conversation turned to his old home in Jaffa, which I had still failed to locate. On a page in my notebook, we drew up a map of the neighbourhood, in order to facilitate my search. I still have this page, a touching souvenir of this meeting.

I have others. One is the menu of the coffee shop of the Mount Royal Hotel, on which I jotted down points from our conversation, a few minutes after he left. I never took notes in his presence, fearing that it would dampen the spontaneity of the conversation. The menu contains parts of his personal biography, his remarks about the worsening situation in Lebanon, his assessment of the relative strengths of the various currents in the PLO.

Another souvenir is the only personal note I have in his handwriting. We were supposed to meet at ten o'clock in the morning in my hotel. I thought that we had agreed that he would phone me first to confirm this, and when he didn't, I went out. He did come, however, and left me a note on the hotel stationary: 'Uri, I came at ten to see you. You were not there. Good boy, you are up early, Please ring me. I am at the office. All the best. Sam.'

On some of my pages there is his handwriting in Arabic. When he mentioned Arab names, I would ask him to write them down, so I could get the spelling right and transcribe them correctly into Hebrew.

Yet, in spite of occasional humorous intermezzos, neither of us was particularly optimistic. We were both acutely aware of the fact that time was passing by, and that the PLO was wasting an opportunity which might not return for a long time. 1975 was a year of great possibilities. It had started just after the PLO had won international recognition, first at the Rabat Arab Summit conference, and later in the UN. After addressing the General Assembly, Arafat was stronger than ever. He could go further than before.

Hammami explained to me why Arafat did not go as far as I wanted him to. But I sometimes had a lurking suspicion that he himself was impatient. It was on one of these occasions that he said to me: 'I told him: If a hundred nations recognize us and Israel does not — what have we gained?' A prophetic question indeed.

* * *

But how to get Israel to recognize the PLO?

While Hammami was trying to explain the problems of the PLO leadership to me, I reciprocated by explaining to him the psychology of Itzhak Rabin and his colleagues in the Israeli cabinet. Quite naturally the question arose: Why not try to get Arafat and Rabin together?

At first this seemed an impossible proposition. The leader of the Fedayeen, the chairman of an organization officially decried in Israel as a Gang of Murderers, and the former chief of staff of the Israeli army and present prime minister?

But then, why not? If it could be arranged secretly somewhere on neutral ground — Romania for example, or on a boat in the Mediterranean, or on the Lebanese frontier?

Hammami was certain that Arafat would come, if I could set up such a meeting. I was much less certain that Rabin would take to the idea, but I decided to try to convince him as soon as I was back in Israel. (Much later, when I talked with Sartawi about this conversation, he maintained that it would have been quite impossible at that point for Arafat to agree to such a meeting.)

At the time, Arafat was engaged in a bitter propaganda war with President Sadat, who had just concluded his interim agreement with Rabin. I asked Hammami why Arafat had reacted so violently, in a way bound to strengthen his intransigent image in Israel. In reply, he told me a story about the behind-the-scenes relations of the two leaders.

According to him, at the beginning of the negotiations between Kissinger, Sadat and Rabin, the Egyptian president had sent a special emissary to Arafat to show him a draft agreement containing a paragraph reaffirming the right of the Palestinians to self-determination and to a state of their own. Because of this, Arafat had ordered the PLO to refrain from attacking Sadat during the negotiations. However, just before the conclusion of the agreement, Sadat had to surrender this point, and in the final text there was no mention at all of the Palestinian cause. Arafat felt misled and double-crossed. His furious denunciation of the agreement was caused as much by this betrayal as by the agreement itself. However, Hammami believed that in the end the Egyptian-PLO alliance was bound to reassert itself, while the temporary rapprochement between the PLO and Syria would give way to the basic enmity between the two. This story was to repeat itself during the historic peace initiative of Sadat.

* * *

At one point I asked him: 'Why don't you come home?'

'What do you mean?' he asked, uncomprehending.

'Jaffa, of course. Would you come if I get Rabin to invite you quietly?'

'Of course I would!' he exclaimed, 'I want to see my house again!'

I was flying back the next morning. I decided to ask immediately for an appointment with Itzhak Rabin.

## 15

*The day I am to leave London, we take a taxi together. I drop him off near his office in Mayfair.*

*It is a typical London day, drizzling, grey, cold.*

*'You are going home, and I am staying here,' he says.*

*It is a simple statement of fact. But in his voice I hear the longing, forlorn plaint of the refugee.*

# 16

'No,' said Itzhak Rabin, 'I do not intend to meet Yassir Arafat!'

He was sitting behind the big writing desk in the Prime Minister's office in Jerusalem, a square, rather ugly new building, not far from the Knesset. The desk was completely bare. Not a single object or piece of paper lay upon it, not even an office calendar or a pen.

'By the way,' he added, 'you're not the first person to suggest I should meet him. Several international personalities have approached me with the same idea.'

* * *

A few days after my return from London, I had written to the prime minister, asking to meet him.

In my letter, dated 19 October 1975 and marked 'secret', I wrote:

> During my visit to London last week I had long talks with Mr. Said Hammami, the official representative of the PLO in London and one of the central personalities in the political leadership of the organization.
>
> At the beginning of the year, after a previous talk with me, Hammami published a detailed statement proposing the setting up of a Palestinian state alongside Israel, mutual recognition, negotiations and the cessation of terrorism.
>
> He informed me of the developments since then, the thinking of the top leadership of the PLO and Fatah, etc.
>
> At his request, we agreed not publish our meetings.
>
> Knowing your extremely negative attitude towards the idea of a Palestinian state and a dialogue with the PLO, I still believe that you should hear these things with your own ears from someone who has direct contact, if only in order to reexamine your position and to bring it up to date in light of changing circumstances.
>
> I would like to ask you, therefore, to give me an opportunity to tell you about my meetings on a personal and absolutely informal basis, and of course without any publicity.

The next day the prime minister's secretary, Eli Misrachi, called and invited me to see Rabin on 28 October, at 3.00 p.m.

Perhaps I should explain here my peculiar relationship with Itzhak Rabin, one which went back a few years.

In the spring of 1969, Prime Minister Levi Eshkol had died. Under Israeli law, the president of the state is obliged to consult with the leaders of all factions in the Knesset before calling upon a member of the Knesset to form a new government.

In spite of the fact that I was at that time the sole representative of my party in the Knesset, I had the status of the leader of a faction — a one-man faction, as it were — and president Zalman Shazar invited me to present my views. It was, of course, a mere formality. But it was a unique opportunity to voice a dissident point of view with maximum public impact. Every word said on such an occasion is news for the media.

By that time it was already clear that the next prime minister was going to be Golda Meir, a woman whom I frankly detested — a mutual sentiment, I might add. I knew her as an opinionated, obstinate person, primitive in her outlook, rigid in her attitudes, with a genius for reaching and exploiting the deepest fears and prejudices of the Jewish masses. I was certain that with her as prime minister, all peace efforts would come to a total standstill.

There was nothing I could do to prevent her appointment, but at least I could warn against it. The best way was to suggest to the president, and indirectly to the Israeli public, a candidate representing different qualities. He had, of course, to come from the ranks of the ruling Labour party.

Looking for such a person, I decided upon Rabin, who was then ambassador in Washington. I did not believe in Abba Eban, a dove of many words, in many languages, who did not have the courage of his convictions — if, indeed, he had any convictions at all. Nor did I believe in Yigal Allon, the author of a famous plan for far-reaching annexations.

After the Six Day War, in which he had commanded the armed forces, Rabin had made a surprisingly humane speech on the occasion of receiving an honorary doctorate from the Hebrew University. In newspaper interviews, he came through as a dove who preferred peace to the annexation of territories.

When I officially proposed Rabin as the next prime minister, the president was amazed, and not only because such a nomination would have necessitated changing the law. (Rabin was not at that time a member of parliament, as the law required.) No one had ever proposed Rabin as a prime minister before. But I had made my point.

A year later I had my first serious talk with Rabin, at the embassy in Washington. He reaffirmed my opinion about him by saying: 'I don't care a damn where the borders will be, as long as they are open. Only open borders are safe borders.' In Hebrew, safe is *batuah*, open is *patuah*. A few days later I wrote him a letter explaining that only if Israel's neighbour was a Palestinian state would there be any assurance that the border would stay open, first because the Palestinian state would comprise two separate parts, the West Bank and Gaza, divided by Israeli territory, and second because the Palestinians themselves would insist on this, because the unity of the country was a sacred dogma to them.

But even at that meeting, Rabin was extreme in his opposition to the very idea of a Palestinian state. I found this difficult to comprehend. There seemed to be no logical correlation between his general outlook and his opinions about this particular subject. I had the feeling that a mental block was confounding his logic at this point, and I tried — then and later — to remove it. I had great respect for his logical mind and I gave up hope only after many efforts.

Five years after I had first proposed him for the job, Rabin did become prime minister through a singular set of circumstances. After the Yom Kippur War, both Golda Meir and Moshe Dayan had to go, in the face of a spontaneous outburst of public indignation. Eban and Allon, as members of the government responsible for the lack of preparedness on Yom Kippur, were also implicated. The people wanted a new man, a knight in shining armour, unblemised by the recent past. As Ezer Weizmann, his enemy and a man renowned for his vituperative and uncontrollable tongue, remarked: 'The only qualification for a prime minister at this moment is that he was not present in Israel on Yom Kippur.'

Thus, to his own great surprise, Rabin was swept into power. He was hailed as the standard bearer of the sabra revolution, the first Israeli-born leader to assume supreme executive power. It was the beginning of a new era. Everything would be reexamined. Everything would be changed.

Or so we hoped.

* * *

After my first meetings with Hammami, I asked myself to whom I should report in order to create the beginning of a pro-Palestinian lobby within the Israeli cabinet. I chose Yigal Allon, the new foreign minister, with whom I had been friendly for many years. In 1948 I had fought on the Egyptian front under his command, and since then I had had many conversations with him, mostly confidential.

On 4 February 1975, I had written him a letter telling him about my meeting in London and offering to meet him to tell him more about them. A strange silence ensued. After a week his secretary called. The foreign minister was, unfortunately, extremely busy. He could not possibly find the time to meet me — to his greatest regret. But if I wanted to convey any information to him, his secretary would be only to happy to talk with me.

I politely declined.

I knew what the trouble was. Apart from being charming and intelligent, Yigal Allon was also a moral coward. It was this weakness which doomed his career. Several times, when a smiling Goddess of Fortune extended her hand to him, he was too afraid to grasp it. Now he was obviously afraid that he might be contaminated by my PLO contacts, the legality of which was still in doubt.

At that stage, I did not want to approach Rabin himself. I wanted to wait until I had more concrete suggestions to make. Instead, I asked for a meeting with the man whom I considered to be the most intelligent person in the cabinet — the minister of justice, Haim Tsadock. I met him on 14 February, in his Tel Aviv office. The subject was quite new to him, and he was keenly interested. I told him as much as I could and asked him to inform the prime minister. All this was within the framework of my agreement with Hammami: I might inform, in secret, anyone I saw fit, in order to facilitate our common task.

A few months later I reported to Rabin in writing about some talks with Soviet representatives whom I had met during an abortive conference, which had taken place, mainly under communist auspices, in Rome, in July. He had sent me a cordial acknowledgement.

He was therefore in the picture. When I wrote to him, after my second series of meetings with Hammami, asking for a meeting, the response was immediate and positive.

* * *

Itzhak Rabin is an introvert, more introverted than any politician I have ever come across. He has no social graces, and is acutely aware of the fact. His mind is sharp and logical, but pedestrian. He lacks that touch of imagination, of art, which enables a politician to transcend the boundaries of existing realities and create something new. He is usually credited with having an 'analytical mind', but, as Abba Eban once told me in a rather malicious way, 'analysis means taking things apart, not putting them together'.

Rabin makes no small talk. When I was ushered into his room, where he was already waiting, he plunged immediately into a serious discussion. It was an intellectual pleasure, which went on for nearly two hours.

From the outset he made clear what the basis of our meeting should be. I was not 'reporting' to him, because that would mean I was on an official or semi-official mission. I was acting solely as a private citizen. But if, as a private citizen, I met interesting people and thought the prime minister should hear what transpired in those meetings, it was quite proper for me to tell him, and he was always ready to listen. He did not approve of the meetings, but he had no objection to my conducting them and, indeed, thought they might prove of some value.

That was fair enough. It automatically made my meetings legal, according to the vague language of the law. It also gave me a chance to continue my endeavours to change his mind about the Palestinian solution.

He explained his refusal to consider a meeting with Arafat or to conduct any kind of negotiations, or even dialogue, with the PLO. On the face of it, his reasoning made sense. If one took the first step on this road, one must be ready to accept the inevitable, ultimate goal: a Palestinian state. If one did not want to reach this objective — and he certainly did not — it was foolish to take even the first step.

Thus, very early in the discussion, we reached the crux of the matter. Was the creation of a Palestinian state good or bad for the long-term interests of Israel?

I brought up all the arguments I could muster. A peace which ignored the collective will of four million Palestinians could not possibly last. From the point of view of security, peace with the Palestinian people would be safer than peace with a basically unstable dictatorial regime in Amman.

Rabin insisted that the Palestinians would never make peace with Israel, that any Palestinian who said otherwise was only pretending. By advocating negotiations with them, I was helping them gain legitimacy in the international arena. It was an argument I was to hear frequently.

Rabin had no illusions about the allegiance of the Palestinians. Unlike many other Israeli politicians, he admitted in private that the PLO was in fact accepted by the bulk of the Palestinian people as their leadership. He did not believe in trying to set up any kind of quisling leadership on the West Bank. He did not even believe that King Hussein would survive for long. 'We need him to sign a peace treaty with us. He will be the first Arab ruler to do this. What happens to him after that is not important.'

'Allow me to analyse what you are saying', I answered. 'Let us assume, as a hypothesis, that King Hussein will indeed sign a peace treaty with you, and that you will give back to him the bulk of the West Bank. Of course I don't believe in this for a minute. King Hussein cannot possibly give up East Jerusalem or an inch of the West Bank, because he is so vulnerable to accusations that he is a Zionist imperialist stooge. Arafat can afford to be much more flexible than Hussein. But let's assume that Hussein could sign such a treaty. What would happen?

'You yourself say that he is likely to fall sooner or later. Let's say he is overthrown in five years. The new regime will probably be a radical Palestinian force, because the Palestinians will constitute three quarters of the population of the kingdom. The new regime will denounce the king as a Zionist agent and abolish the peace treaty as an act of treason committed by him.

'In practice, therefore, you are going to have after five years a Palestinian state as your neighbour, but it will not be the Palestinian state which I propose. It will stretch from the outskirts of Netanya to the outskirts of Baghdad. It will have common borders with Syria, Iraq and Saudi Arabia, and could become the staging point for four Arab armies. Its leadership will have no commitment at all to peace with Israel. On the contrary, it will be committed to the slogans of non-recognition and war. What is the sense in that?'

I thought it was a pretty good argument, to which there was no sound answer. Even Rabin's famous analytical mind did not find any. But it did not shake his convictions. Only once, during the long and friendly debate, did I feel that I might be penetrating his armour. It was when I said: 'The Americans are realists, they may try again to destroy the PLO, probably by organizing another Black September in Lebanon. But sooner or later they will realize that they will have to deal with the PLO, if only to avoid a general destabilization of the Middle East. They will offer the PLO a Palestinian state, in one way or another, as a prize for leaving the Soviet camp and joining the American one. After my conversation with Hammami, I am quite convinced that the PLO leadership will jump at such a chance. They are no communists. As you have often said, you believe Israeli interests are identical with US interests in the Middle East. If the Americans recognize the PLO and make a deal with them, you will have to follow suit. So why wait? Why not take the initiative and get everything we can from the PLO, instead of paying a huge political commission to the Americans tomorrow for arranging a deal between the Palestinians and Israel?'

I had the feeling — it was only a feeling — that this was the only argument which struck home. Rabin was more pro-American than any other Israeli politician. Even more than his colleagues, he was profoundly sceptical of any possibility of real peace. He was, therefore, convinced that the security of Israel, perhaps for generations to come, was totally dependent on the US. He believed that every American success was automatically an Israeli victory, and every American setback automatically a defeat for Israel.

* * *

Rabin's attitude towards the Palestinians typifies that of the vast majority of Israelis of all shades of opinion.

There are many ways to explain this.

I have already described my conversations with Levi Eshkol immediately after the Six Day War. His was, so it seemed, the pragmatic approach. If you have to negotiate about the West Bank and Gaza, try to offer as little as possible and get as much as you can, buy cheaply and sell dearly, the traditional trader's approach. For such an approach, King Hussein looked the ideal trading partner. For King Hussein, the West Bank was only a part of his kingdom. He could give away some of it in order to get back the other part. And, most important of all, as his capital is in Amman, he could give up Jerusalem, and this seemed at the time the most important concession desired by Israel.

Of course this was a complete misconception. Not only was King Hussein in no position to give up anything, being vulnerable to accusations by Arab nationalists, but he also had a deep commitment to Jerusalem. The Hashemites are the family of the Prophet. Hussein considers himself a direct descendant of Mohammed, and it would be inconceivable for him to give up one of the three holiest places of Islam — the al-Aqsa Mosque on the Temple Mount in the Old City of Jerusalem.

There is a story that before meeting Yigal Allon for the first time after the Six Day War, Hussein asked for the support of Gamal Abd-al-Nasser. The Egyptian leader is said to have told him: 'Go and meet them, but remember that if you give up Jerusalem, Arab history will never forgive you.'

During that meeting with Allon, Hussein is said to have told him: 'I can be the first Arab leader to make peace with Israel, and I can give up some part of Arab territory — but I cannot do both.'

Since then, the so-called Jordanian option, the illusion of peace with Hussein, persists in many quarters in Israel, and has even been used from time to time by Likud propagandists. But this has become nothing but a subterfuge. The Jordanian option is used as a ploy to avoid the only option that really exists, peace with the Palestinians. While the Likud and many other Israelis do not want to give up the West Bank and the Gaza Strip under any circumstances, for reasons of ideology or simple greed, decorated with security slogans, others pretend they are ready to give back some of it, but only to those who are not able to take it back. This is the traditional stance of the Labour party.

The Jordanian option has haunted the Israeli establishment for a long time. During the Second World War, when King Hussein's Hashemite cousin was kicked out of Baghdad by pro-German Iraqi nationalists, the Iraqi Hashemites who came to Palestine received all possible support from the Zionist institutions, including a secret radio station on Mount

Carmel. Many years later one of the people involved, Eliahu Sasson, complained to me about the ingratitude of the Hashemites. After being reinstated in Baghdad by the British, they immediately attacked Zionism. During that operation the commander of the Irgun, David Raziel, who was cooperating with the British, lost his life. Prior to the 1948 War and during that war, David Ben-Gurion and his colleagues, among them Golda Meir, had many contacts with King Abdallah of Jordan. It seems certain now that Ben-Gurion conducted his strategy throughout the war in such a way as to enable King Abdallah to take over the West Bank and annex it to his kingdom. The few battles between the new Israeli Army and Abdallah's Arab Legion were in places not covered by this secret agreement.

Because of this obvious cooperation with Israel, Abdallah was assassinated on the steps of the al-Aqsa Mosque, in the presence of his young grandson, Hussein. It is a lesson Hussein has never forgotten.

One of the reasons cited for the continued support given to the Hashemite regime in Jordan by the Israeli government was that this was in line with Israeli orientation on the major Western power in the region, first Britain and then the US. I myself was connected with a curious episode in the early fifties. A group of Iraqi nationalists, who were planning a coup d'etat against the Hashemites in Baghdad and their British overlords, had approached a young Iraqi Jew and sent him to Israel. Their idea was that the Israelis, having shaken off the British yoke in an underground war the Iraqi nationalists much admired, would help their revolution in Iraq, in return for Iraqi recognition of Israel. The emissary came to Israel and after many attempts was allowed to meet Ben-Gurion, who listened to him noncommittally and sent him to Reuven Shiloah, his expert on Arab affairs and secret service chief. Shiloah gave him the runaround for some time,and when an Israeli intervened and asked Shiloah why he did not take up such an attractive offer. Shiloah exclaimed in exasperation: 'Are you crazy? We are allied with the British, why should we cooperate with those who want to kick the British out?'

Until the Six Day War, it was official Israeli policy that 'any change of the status quo in Jordan would be a *casus belli* for Israel'. Thus, the Israeli threat upheld the Jordanian regime during the height of Nasser's pan Arab wave. Ariel Sharon told me that during 'Black September' he was the only person in the General Staff forum of the Israeli Army to advocate support for the Palestinians against the Jordanian Army, the exact opposite of the official Israeli line, which threatened an Israeli invasion of Jordan in case the Syrian army entered in support of the PLO forces. Without knowing about the debate in the General Staff, I also called, in parliament, on the Israeli government to support the Palestinians.

Underlying all these Israeli government actions was and still is the basic belief that with the help of the Jordanians, Israel could avoid facing the Palestinian issue. The wish to do this may stem from the unwillingness to give back the West Bank and the Gaza Strip, or from a basic disbelief in the possibility of a reconciliation with the Palestinians, or from both.

The perfect representative of this double attitude was Moshe Dayan. In a famous speech made on the grave of a friend killed on the Gaza Strip border a few months before the Sinai War of 1956, Dayan, who that day had turned 41, said: 'Let us not today fling accusations at the murderers. Who are we that we should argue against their hatred? For eight years now, they sit in their refugee camps in Gaza, and before their very eyes we turn into our homestead the land and the villages in which they and their forefathers have lived. . . . We are a generation of settlers, and without the steel helmet and the cannon we cannot plant a tree and build a house.

'Let us not shrink back when we see the hatred fermenting and filling the lives of hundreds of thousands of Arabs, who sit all around us. Let us not avert our eyes, so that our hand shall not slip. This is the fate of our generation, the choice of our life — to be prepared and armed, strong and tough — or otherwise, the sword will slip from our fist and our life will be snuffed out.'

In another famous speech before Nahal recruits in the occupied Golan Heights, two wars later, Dayan told them that no Zionist generation has the right to say that the job is concluded. Each generation had to do its job in expanding the base of Zionist settlement, and had to pass the job on to the next one.

I believe there is a profound reason for all these seemingly logical or semi-logical arguments and beliefs. The early Zionists were convinced, or convinced themselves, that the new Jewish national home would be founded in an empty country. When it became clear that this was not so, and in the face of growing Arab opposition, they still pretended that the Palestinians did not really exist, that the whole Palestinian issue had been invented one way or the other by the enemies of Zionism, that the Palestinian national movement was but a bunch of terrorists. Somewhere in the Israeli mind there is an unconscious feeling of guilt, a feeling that in doing justice to the Jews an injustice has been done to the Palestinians. These feelings are troubling the national soul, creating mental blocks, making even highly intelligent politicians and historians utter the most lamentable nonsense when touching upon the Palestinian issue.

I am convinced that this moral problem has to be faced squarely, and that a morally acceptable solution has to be discovered, before a political reconciliation and solution can be found. Until then it is a war not only between two peoples but also between two national traumas: the trauma of the Holocaust and the trauma of the Palestinian exodus. However rational a discussion among Israelis or among Palestinians — and even more so between Israelis and Palestinians — may seem, everybody is using rational arguments to mask the irrational impetus of his or her ideas and beliefs, hidden deep down in their unconscious mind.

Listening to Rabin's arguments during that conversation with him, I thought they epitomized this syndrome.

* * *

I knew that in the course of one conversation I was not going to change Rabin's philosophy. But I tried to change at least some of his tactics.

Even within the context of his policy, I suggested, he could change his tactical approach towards the PLO. Any gesture, even a small one, which would encourage the moderate wing of the PLO, would reap immediate results. It would allow people like Hammami to gain influence and demand a cessation of terrorist activities, a possibility Hammami had already announced publicly in his articles and speeches. It would save human lives and make the job of the Israeli Army easier. If, as I expected, the Americans eventually moved towards making a deal with the PLO, the Israeli government would already possess a direct alternative line of communication with the PLO leadership. I could unofficially create such a line. All I needed was some message from Rabin to be conveyed to Arafat, through Hammami — anything which would be interpreted by the PLO as a first glimmer of hope that change in Israeli policy was possible. Perhaps an amnesty for some Palestinian prisoners. Perhaps permission for some deported Palestinian leaders to return to the West Bank. In this context I brought up Hammami's request to visit Israel in secret.

Rabin was adamant. He did not accept any of my suggestions, not even the request to allow Hammami to visit Jaffa. He did not believe a moderate wing existed in the PLO, and was certainly not going to encourage one if it did. It was all quite logical: encouraging PLO moderates would lead, in the end, to the creation of a Palestinian state. I wanted that, he did not.

Near the end of the conversation, I brought up what had been a pet project of mine for many years. Since 1953, I had been proposing the creation of a new Ministry for Middle Eastern affairs, or Arab affairs; in effect, a Ministry of Peace, or at least a permanent staff of experts to deal with the Arab world. In an article, I had called this the 'white general staff', in contradistinction to the khaki-clad general staff of the armed forces. While the latter was always planning war, the former should wage peace.

I brought this up in the new context. I felt there was no need to be diplomatic with Rabin. He appreciated bluntness. I said: 'You know that you are not an expert on Arab affairs. You have never studied them the way you have studied American affairs.' Rather surprisingly, he admitted this without hesitation.

I suggested that he set up, within the prime minister's office, a regular staff of experts on Arab affairs to process all available information and suggestions, including my own, and to work out alternative contingency plans. He liked the idea, but proposed that such a staff be set up within the foreign ministry, where a miniscule and quite ineffective Middle Eastern desk already existed. I argued against this as strongly as I could. In Israel, as in any other modern state, foreign policy is made by the prime minister, not the foreign minister. Transferring the responsibility to the foreign ministry, I told him, meant shirking the responsibility.

Nothing came out of this either. Rabin did not need advisers, nor did he appreciate advice. This seems to be an occupational disease of prime ministers, presidents and kings. The lack of such a staff was evident when Israel was surprised by the Yom Kippur War, which some of us had predicted, and when Israel blundered into the Lebanese War of 1982.

* * *

I left his office much later than anticipated, and drove down to Jericho, to meet old Mussa al-Alami and Ted Hodgkin.

I was not in a bad mood. True, nothing had been achieved. Rabin had not budged an inch. But he had listened and argued, and perhaps some seeds had been planted in his mind. And, no less important, I had full permission to continue my contacts with the PLO without being molested by the security services or the law enforcement agencies. This in itself could be construed as a significant gesture towards the PLO.

In my briefcase I had two documents, which Hodgkin was to take back to England: the questionnaire for Said Hammami and the letter for Lord Caradon, asking him to prepare a meeting of Israelis and Palestinians.

# 17

*I am lying in the hospital. On 18 December 1975, there had been an attempt on my life. A young man, who had been waiting for me near the door of my apartment, had stabbed me several times, just missing my heart. It was nearly twenty-seven years to the day that I had been wounded in the war. I am talking with the mayor of Tel Aviv, who has come to visit me. For several days now members of the Knesset, peace camp activists and even an honest-to-goodness general of the Israeli army, who was known for his anti-Arab attitude, have come to visit my bedside. Each one is announced with great excitement by the nurses, for whom this is a parade of celebrities.*

*A pretty Yemeni nurse comes in, in her usual state of excitement: 'There's a call from London, a man called Sam. You must take the call from the chief nurse's office.'*

*I get out of bed as best I can. I pick up the phone. The familiar voice says: 'You got us worried, you bastard.'*

*We joke a little bit. He says: 'The old man wishes you a speedy recovery.'*

*After some more, I hang up. 'Who was that?' the pretty Yemeni nurse asks curiously.*

*'Oh, just a friend,' I say.*

*If I told her who the friend was, and who was the old man who just wished me well — the dreaded arch-terrorist himself — she would surely faint.*

# 18

The following weeks were filled with activity. Hammami called me two or three times a week from London. Never had the PLO come closer to a policy of peace, and never had this idea come as close to being accepted by the Israeli public. Both of us had the exhilarating feeling that things were moving at last, that we had helped to set in motion a great historical process. It was the first, but not the last, time we felt that great things could happen, only to have our hopes dashed by the forces set in motion against them.

What Hammami did and said became news in Israel. I talked privately with some Israeli editors, giving them background briefings. Their new awareness was reflected in the way they treated the news. Even the two evening papers, both of them ultra-chauvinistic, playing a fateful role in brainwashing the Israeli public, started to publicize Hammami's statements. A headline in *Yedioth Aharanot* on 12 October 1975, said: 'PLO Representative in London: I Recognize Israel — The Chiefs of the PLO Accept my Position.' A month later, on 20 November, *Yedioth* devoted a whole page to an interview given by Hammami to a Dutch paper with the understanding that it would be published simultaneously in Israel. The headline in *Yedioth* was: 'Only if the Israeli Jews and the Palestinian Arabs Come to an Agreement Will Peace Come to the Middle East.'

* * *

Near the end of November, Yassir Arafat paid a visit to Moscow. On the eve of his departure, Hammami called me in great excitement, saying that during his visit a public change of PLO policy was to be expected. Arafat would say that he was ready for some kind of mutual recognition. He asked me to prepare Israeli public opinion for this. I was to quote 'sources close to the PLO'.

I made a statement to the press to that effect, which was widely published. The government-controlled Israeli TV opened its evening news bulletin with a dramatic news item about my statement, giving the impression that something great and important was happening.

The next day, 26 November, I wrote a letter to Hammami: 'Dear Friend, as you see things are moving. Quicker than I dared to hope. The news you gave me was of great help. I made a statement to the press saying that I expect a change in the official PLO position concerning Geneva, etc. This was put as the first item on yesterday's TV news, with an interview with me — something virtually unheard of. It had a dramatic impact and was copied today by most papers ... Somehow I feel that we are closer to peace than we imagine. People like you and me have a part to play in this — perhaps small, but essential. Greetings to your wife and from mine. Shall they ever meet? *Maa salameh* and *shalom*, Uri.' Rachel and Khalida never met.

The following days, Hammami continued to convey information to me by telephone, which I again transmitted to the press, quoting 'PLO sources in Europe'. The Israeli foreign ministry showed its apprehension by starting a counteroffensive. At a meeting with the press, Rabin himself was asked what he would do if the PLO did indeed recognize Israel. He answered with an expression originating in Germany used by Israeli children: 'If my grandmother had wheels, she would be a bus.' Even the staid *Haaretz* rebuked him for this frivolity.

The final communiqué of Arafat's Moscow talks was inconclusive. It was exactly the kind of stuff which was useless for our job, words without impact, coded diplomatic formulas which only experts could understand. He did use for the first time, though, the terms 'the right of the Palestinian people to a free national state of its own on the soil of Palestine, in accordance with the resolutions of the United Nations'. This was a new departure, a step beyond previous PLO texts. But how do you explain this to ordinary people, who can grasp the significance of a great gesture, but not the subtleties of diplomatic texts or political formulas?

I tried. On 2 December, I convened a press conference, after a long telephone conversation with Hammami in which he pointed out the important changes hidden in the text, as well as the need for Arafat to move slowly to prevent internal difficulties.

I explained that the term 'free national state', instead of the previously-used term 'national authority', signified an implicit agreement to the partition of the country between the two national states, that it was the very opposite of the old slogan 'democratic secular state in all of Palestine', which meant the dismantling of Israel. The words 'in accordance with the resolutions of the United Nations' were, at least, an oblique reference to Resolution 242, which included the recognition of Israel, also without mentioning Israel by name.

All this was duly broadcast as printed, proving that what we were doing had suddenly become important. But it was not good enough. It certainly was not sufficient to effect that profound change of public opinion necessary to pressure the Israeli government into changing its basic policy.

* * *

The main point in my press conference concerned the immediate future.

The Security Council was going to have another debate about the Middle East. The Arabs hoped that the outcome would be a resolution calling for the participation of the PLO in a renewed Geneva Peace Conference on the Middle East. They were afraid, however, that the United States, under Israeli pressure, would veto such a resolution. In order to prevent this, the resolution would be as mild as possible. 'We are going to submit a resolution which will be so moderate that the Americans won't dare veto it', Hammami promised on the phone.

In Moscow, the Soviets and Arafat had already agreed about the reconvention of the Geneva Conference 'with the participation of all parties, on the basis of equality'. This meant, of course, with the participation of the PLO.

On the eve of my press conference, Hammami told me that I might announce, again quoting 'sources close to the PLO', that the PLO was ready to recognize Israel *de facto*, in return for an invitation to Geneva. The two moves had to come simultaneously. The Soviet Union was also ready, in this case, to resume diplomatic relations with Israel, which had been cut off by Moscow during the Six Day War — a sore point with the Israelis.

I understood that this was really a message from Arafat to Rabin, conveyed through Hammami and me. I called the secretary of the prime minister and asked her to write down this message and give it to Rabin at once. Through the press conference, it received wide publicity in the media.

I still believe that never was the prospect for a major breakthrough more promising. The Palestinians were ready to go to Geneva, and recognize Israel on the way. The majority in the PLO was willing to swallow such a recognition, as the price paid for a major political victory. Actually such an act of *de facto* recognition was not really necessary to my mind, because the very participation of the PLO in the Geneva Conference under such circumstances constituted recognition. The Geneva Conference was officially designated as a 'peace conference for the Middle East'. It was based on Security Council Resolutions 242 and 338, which recognized the sovereignty, independence and territorial integrity of all states in the Middle East, including, of course, Israel. If the PLO had been seated in Geneva behind a table marked 'Palestine' or 'Palestinian Liberation Organization', next to the table marked 'Israel' — what further *de facto* recognition could be wished for?

All the circumstances were auspicious. But nothing came of it. The Arabs submitted a moderate resolution, with the silent approval of the PLO, but the United States vetoed it. Israel boycotted the proceedings, because the PLO representative had been invited to take part in them as an observer.

Why? Had the Americans succumbed to the pressure of the Rabin government, or was Rabin following the lead of Henry Kissinger? Had Kissinger already decided to try to destroy the PLO in Lebanon in conjunction with Syria and Israel, a collusion which brought about the 1976 invasion of Lebanon by the Syrian army? The answer to all these questions is probably yes.

* * *

While all this was going on, I was working very hard to enlarge the Israeli Council for Israeli-Palestinian Peace (this was the final version of its name), and to turn it into an instrument that could exert effective pressure on the government.

My contacts with Hammami had become an open secret. When I was quoting 'sources close to the PLO in Europe', it was not too difficult to guess who was meant by this. Hammami's activities were becoming well known. *Haolam Hazeh* published a long biography of him, without directly quoting him. According to the principle we had agreed upon — 'no confirmation, no denial' — I responded with 'no comment' whenever asked about possible contacts with him.

To people who were already convinced that we must work for Israeli-Palestinian peace, the contacts proved that there was now a real chance for a dialogue with the PLO. Even to those who were somewhat less committed and more opportunistic, the chance to get a piece of the action looked attractive. Nothing succeeds like success, and the contacts with the PLO were proving to be successful. What at the beginning of 1975 was still a dangerous game seemed attractive and popular by the end of that year. During my conversations with Hammami in London, in October, he agreed that if an impressive Israeli body came into being, the PLO would start a serious, ongoing dialogue with it. The time was ripe for creating such a broadly-based organization.

The first person I asked to play a key role in the enlarged and reconstituted Council was General Mattitiyahu Peled, the former quarter-master-general of the army and a highly-respected member of the victorious general staff of 1967, who was to become important in the next stage of the contacts.

Matti, as everybody called him, had been a regular soldier for the greater part of his life. I knew him vaguely from youth, when he was briefly connected with the Canaanite group, which preached the idea that the new Hebrew nation in the Hebrew homeland should cut all links with Jewish history. He was also a member of the Palmach, the nucleus of the underground Haganah army. With the birth of the State of Israel he rose in the ranks of the army. After leaving the army in 1968, he started a new career, studied modern Arab literature and became a lecturer at Tel Aviv University.

During those years he regularly wrote articles in *Maariv*, often expressing ideas very close to my own. In Israel, generals and ex-generals are widely respected, and the opinions of an ex-general (or rather reserve general, as generals are never officially discharged from the Israeli Army) coming out for peace carried a lot of weight.

On the eve of the 1969 elections I wrote to Matti, then studying in California, and offered him the second place on my party list. He declined, however, preferring his studies. Had he accepted, he would have become a member of the Knesset. Even without the considerable contribution he could have made, however, we gained two seats.

In 1974, after the Yom Kippur War, I had cooperated with Matti in vain efforts to unite all peace groups into a new party, or at least to create a body for Israeli-Palestinian peace. When we failed, Matti was deeply disappointed and left politics altogether. Later on he joined a little party, which soon fell apart.

Now I pushed him again, told him about my contacts and asked him to become a major figure in the Council. He agreed.

Like Rabin, with whom he had served in the general staff, Peled is an introvert. He does not care for social functions, and has an incisive mind. Also like Rabin, he is his own adviser, and it is nearly impossible to influence him. But here the similarity ends. Matti has the unusual ability to change his own mind by a slow and systematic process of rethinking, analysing and drawing conclusions — a process I've always found extremely rare among politicians. In 1974 Matti was committed to the American cause in Vietnam, and categorically rejected any idea of dealing with the PLO. One and a half years later, through methodical thinking, he had come to the conclusion that the PLO must be recognized as the only valid representative of the Palestinians, and that Israel must become non-aligned.

Along with Matti came David Shaham, the former editor of the Labour Party's monthly organ, who had quarrelled with Golda Meir over nearly every aspect of policy and left the Labour Party. Shaham became active in mobilizing support for the Council. He brought with him two important figures, Eliahu Eliashar and Arieh Eliav. Later Shaham became disappointed with the Council and devoted his energies to *New Outlook*, an English-language periodical devoted to Middle Eastern affairs, close to the Labour alignment.

Eliashar was the ex-president of the World Sephardic Federation, a body representing all Mediterranean and Middle Eastern Jewish communities. He was an old-timer who had dealt all his life with Palestinians, an ex-official of the British Mandate regime and a widely-respected personality. By joining the Council and becoming its honorary president, he added much to its 'respectability'. In a country where support for an Israeli-Palestinian solution is automatically equated with left-wing radicalism — for reasons difficult to explain or even to comprehend — his liberal, moderately right-wing image helped to establish some balance. Up to his death he was a staunch supporter of the Council.

Arieh Eliav, called Lova by everybody, came from a different direction. He had been an assistant to Levi Eshkol for a long time, and had made a name for himself as an organizer of regional development schemes. He had become a deputy minister and the secretary general of the Labour Party, but quickly fell out with Golda Meir when she became the chief of the party and the government. He is an extremely emotional person, more sensitive to moods than to cold logic, more a teacher than a politician, and is imbued with the pathos of the original Zionist socialist movement. In a way, he is the exact opposite of Matti Peled.

Since the Six Day War, Lova had steadily moved towards the Israeli-Palestinian solution. In the Knesset he was one of the members who used to encourage and congratulate me privately when I submitted draft resolutions in favour of a Palestinian state, even though he did not vote for them or support them openly. He had written a book propounding the ethics of such a solution, trying to prove that it was not only compatible with classical Zionism but that it was really the fulfilment of basic Zionist ideas. When he failed to convince the Labour party of this, he quit in disgust in 1975. The Council was joined by Dr. Yaacov Arnon, an economist from Holland, who had been the director general of the Israeli finance ministry, after serving in Christian disguise in the Dutch quisling regime during the Nazi occupation of his homeland. Meir Pail, an ex-colonel and the only member of a small left-wing party in the Knesset, also joined, as did many others. We decided to hold a founding meeting on 10 December 1975. When I told Hammami about this, I asked him to send a cable of support to the meeting, but Beirut did not allow him to go so far.

The meeting took place as planned. Eliashar was elected honorary president and Matti became chairman of the executive committee. The next day I sent a letter to Hammami: 'Dear Friend, I'm sending you the press cuttings about yesterday's meeting, in which our council was officially constituted . . . this is quite impressive and a real victory. Today this is big news, we are on the radio and television and on the front pages of all newspapers. If we can keep up the momentum and attract new names and personalities, this may have a direct bearing on events. Any gestures by the PLO acknowledging the importance of the Council and moving towards a direct dialogue will have a tremendous impact, and every day now counts. Without the direct dialogue between us two, of which I informed our friends, yesterday's event would not have been possible. This is the main lesson. Mutual recognition is the key — and every step in this direction will be of great importance. Nothing would be more catastrophic to our effort than the notion that we can't make good our promises that a dialogue on the basis of our explicit principles is possible and imminent.'

The new executive committee of the Council addressed itself to the job of formulating a new manifesto, somewhat watering down the original document I had formulated with Yossi Amitai. The new version was published in the press, over the signatures of 100 prominent Israelis, in the last week of February 1976.

It read:

> We affirm: one, that this land is the homeland of its two peoples — the people of Israel and the Palestinian Arab people. Two, that the heart of the conflict between the Jews and the Arabs is a historical confrontation between the two peoples of this land, which is dear to both. Three, that the only path to peace is through coexistence between two sovereign states, each with its distinct national identity: the State of Israel for the Jewish people and the state for the Palestinian Arab people, which will exercise its right to self-determination in the political framework of its choosing. Four, that the establishment of a Palestinian Arab state alongside the State of Israel should be the outcome of negotiations between the government of Israel and a recognized and authoritative representative body of the Palestinian Arab people, without refusing negotiations with the Palestine Liberation Organization, on the basis of mutual recognition.

The twelve points of the manifesto also dealt with borders, refugees, etc. The difference between the two documents was obvious in the paragraph about Jerusalem, where Lova Eliav exerted his own pathetic style. While our original document had read:

> Six, that Jerusalem, being sacred to both peoples, deserves a special status: it should remain undivided as a municipal unit, accessible to members of all nations and of all faiths, while the Jewish section of Jerusalem will serve as the capital of Israel and the Arab section as the capital of Palestine:

the new document read:

> Six, that Jerusalem is the eternal capital of Israel. Being sacred to three religions and inhabited by the two peoples, it deserves a special status. It will remain united under a common municipal roof organization and will be accessible to people of all nations and faiths. Jerusalem will continue to be the capital of the State of Israel, and the Arab part could become, after the establishment of peace, the capital of the Palestinian Arab state. The holy places of all three religions will be administered autonomously by their respective institutions.

Paragraph 10 of the new manifesto read:

> That the two states will be sovereign in all respects including matters of immigration and return. The State of Israel will preserve its inalienable link to Zionism and to the Jewish people throughout the world, and the Palestinian Arab state will maintain the link of its people to the Arab world.

Some of the formulations were not quite to my liking, but the main points had been retained. The manifesto, like the Council itself, was an adequate basis for the next stage of the contacts.

* * *

Before moving on, I should perhaps include in this narrative some excerpts from my phone conversations with Hammami during this period, as examples of the style and flavour of our relationship. I recorded some of my many conversations with him — of course with his full knowledge — whenever I thought that things would be said or messages quoted which I needed to cite verbatim.

For example, a conversation on 7 December 1975, three days before the founding meeting of the Israel Council for Israeli-Palestinian Peace:

Hello, good evening, *massah-al-kheir*. Uri speaking, how are you?

How are things?

Things are progressing, I think. We are going to have this big meeting on Wednesday, and it may become very successful.

How was the first meeting?

No, there was no first meeting. The first meeting is on Wednesday.

How was the press conference?

Ah, the press conference. I sent you the press cuttings. You'll see, it got a very big coverage, on television, radio and the Israeli press. I sent you the press cuttings through Michael [Adams, who at that stage acted as a kind of postbox]. Now it depends how successful this meeting on Wednesday will be.

Yes.

And if you could make any gesture towards it, it would be very helpful.

OK, what other news?

You know the government has decided not to take part in any negotiations [with the PLO] and so on, and there's no news in this respect. But I think the things we are saying are getting a lot of attention. What we were saying about the possibility of a *de facto* recognition [of Israel by the PLO] has been very widely reported. And I think this is the time to show something [to prove] that there is a cover to all this. [This is a literal translation of a Hebrew expression meaning that we were not issuing empty promises.] I was wondering if you could possibly send a telegram or anything like that which we could show at the meeting and give the people a feeling that there is a mutual recognition or something.

Well, it might be an idea, but I can't do that.

You can't do that?

No.

Anything else which you think you could do?

No, that's the thing. We have to see how things develop. The meeting is on Wednesday?

Wednesday evening, yes.

Let's see how it's going to come out, the meeting.

OK.

Anything after those raids [raids by the Israeli Air Force on Palestinian refugee camps in Lebanon]?

No.

They were very bad, you know.

I can imagine, yes. And there's a big debate about it in Israel too.

Over a hundred people were killed.

I know. You know there's a big debate about this inside Israel too. We are publishing a statement against this tomorrow, I think.

Are you going to write about it?

Yes, certainly. [I did indeed write an article about it in the issue of *Haolam Hazeh* which appeared three days later, quoting American sources which speculated that the raids on the refugee camps, defined by the Israeli government as 'terrorist bases', were carried out in order to prevent Yassir Arafat from making further moderate announcements intended to facilitate the invitation of the PLO to a renewed Geneva Peace Conference.] Did you see the article I wrote about you?

Oh yes!

Did you like it?

(Laughter) It was OK, thank you, but the house wasn't mine. [Two weeks earlier I had published the first full biography of Hammami. Among the illustrations, I published a photo of a building which I supposed was the Hammami family home in Jaffa.]

Not your house?

No.

Really?

Yes.

They said that this was the house that belonged to this family.
No. Is it in Jebaliya?
It is in Jebaliya, yes.
No, it's not the house.
Oh God!
It's probably my uncle's house.
It is on what used to be [before 1948] King George Boulevard, near Bat Yam, which used to be Bayit we-Gan.
You haven't found the place yet, have you?
I thought it was this place. If you say it's not, I'll try again.
Well it's not. You know my father's name?
Adel.
Yes.
I asked for [the house of] Adel.
Try again, please!
I shall. It's becoming a big job. OK, yes, I'll try again, certainly.
I'm looking forward to hearing some more good news.
Good evening, au revoir.

Or, a conversation about a month later, 13 January 1976. After reading me the text of a long article published about our Council in *The Guardian*, he asked me about my health, saying that I had sounded weak the previous time we'd talked, when he called me at the hospital after the attempt on my life:

Yes, I'm OK. That was immediately after the operation, I was still very weak at the time. I am now OK, yes, they stitched me together, I'm like new. (Laughter) That's right. Tell me, Said, today the Israeli radio and television are giving a very bad picture about [Farouk] Kaddumi's speech in the United Nations. Was it very extreme? They say it was a most extreme statement.

Oh, rubbish, rubbish, no, no, no. Look, if you take what he talks about — Zionism and so on — well, anyone can say it's extreme, of course. Now look, Uri, if the US starts talking about communism, they end by talking about detente and peace. They talk about communism and they attack communism, but then they talk about detente. He talks about Zionism, that's true. He attacks Zionism, which is true, and it's legitimate. You don't have to be a Palestinian to attack Zionism. You see? Israeli communists [also] attack Zionism. He spoke about three points. Politically speaking, he was speaking about three points: about an Israeli withdrawal, which is very significant. Israel should withdraw and abide by UN resolutions. [Hammami meant to say that by demanding that Israel withdraw from the territories occupied in 1967 according to Resolution 242, Kaddumi was implicitly recognizing Israel within the pre-1967 borders. Next there are some unintelligible sentences, concerning Kaddumi's demand for a Palestinian state.] Then he actually speaks about peace through the implementation of the UN resolutions.

Really?

Now this is the political issue of his speech. But if you take what he talks about Zionism . . .

Could we get urgently a full text of his speech, please?

Well, hold-on . . . It's in Arabic, but I'll read it to you in English, OK? [Here Hammami reads sections of the speech] Well, look, you might probably be one of those people who can understand it very well. Remember your article following the Palestinian National Council meeting of 1974, when you spoke about the 10-point programme — you remember you said that this basic change in the policy of the PLO had been covered by many revolutionary and extremist slogans . . .

Yes.

It will always be like this, you see. If it wouldn't be for the propaganda, you wouldn't hear about the political issue in the speech, but it is important, of course. I mean for me, and I speak from within, of course, it is important to see the leadership speaking about national independence. [Hammami meant to say that it would have been impossible to make the statements indicating the new moderate line of the PLO without adding the extremist rhetoric condemning Zionism, thus satisfying the more radical elements within the PLO.]

Yes.

Of course you can understand the significance of this.

Yes I can. But it's difficult to explain to others.

Well, I don't think it's difficult, it's much easier than explaining the issue of the national authority. [When the Palestinian National Council accepted, in 1974, a resolution calling for the setting up of a Palestinian national authority in any part of Palestine, it accepted the principle of partition, but this was very difficult to explain to people not versed in Palestinian terminology.]

Yes, it's much better. I would very much like it if I could get within a few days the full text. It would help us very much. The other members of our Council would like to see the full text.

Yeah, and I'll send you what was written in our papers about you. There's a big fuss about you.

Oh really?

Well, anyway, if anyone, if anyone says that you are not a Zionist, you can show them that. (Laughter) Do you want to see what they are writing about you in the newspapers, in our paper?

In which one?

*Falastin al-Mukhtala*, which is the Fatah paper in Beirut. A big photograph, well, not a very big one, but on two columns. It's like this: 'The editor of the Zionist paper *Hazah al-Alam* has been subjected to an attempted assassination by a mentally disturbed person — mentally disturbed person is in quotes. Uri Avnery, a leading Zionist writer in Israel, has been attacked this morning while going to his office. He was stabbed three times. He was critically injured and taken to hospital. This was an emergency case. He underwent two operations immediately. It wasn't known who stabbed him. There have been many rumours that the authorities had sent someone to stab him because lately Avnery has become very active against the official policy of the government. He is the head of a newly-founded council, called the Israeli Council for Peace with the Palestinians, which urges the government to withdraw its forces, its occupation forces and authorities from the occupied territories and advocates the Palestinians' right to a state.' And some other things about you.

The significance of this was that by writing about the assassination attempt, the official Fatah newspaper informed the cadres of the organization about the creation of the Israeli Council, thus giving it the widest possible publicity among the Palestinians. In the next section of the conversation, we spoke about an incident which created quite a stir at the time. Ibrahim Souss, the PLO representative at UNESCO in Paris, had made a statement saying that the PLO was ready to accept a Palestinian state, and mentioning the pre-1967 lines as the borders of this state. This statement was denied by the PLO, as happened many times. But Hammami made clear that Souss had said these things, and, more significantly, had remained at his post as official PLO representative. The conversation went on:

Look if you want some, well, a piece of hot news: the resolution we would propose [in the UN Security Council debate, which was then going on] is not something that would make the Americans use their veto. You understand what I mean?

Yes, OK. Did you decide upon this already?

Yes, it will be very difficult for the Americans to use their veto.

Can you give me an idea what it will be?

Oh, come on, can't you understand what I mean?

I know what you mean, OK.

It will be very, very difficult for the Americans to use their veto.

Yes. [In Hebrew] *Bo, kaness* (come in)!

Who are those people shouting there? I hear some people shouting!

I said something to my wife. She just came in.

Oh, yeah.

OK, I'm very happy about that [the moderation of the PLO-sponsored Arab draft resolution].

All right, don't worry, we are very strong.

Good, I'll call you in about two or three days. Give my greetings to Khalida.

OK, bye.

In a conversation a month later, on 6 February, I questioned him about a misleading report which had appeared in a London paper, copied from a Jewish paper, indicating that Hammami had gone back on his moderate opinions and made an extremist statement. He dismissed this report contemptuously, but it was clear that he was under mounting pressure from the radical elements:

What's happening here [in Israel] is that we are going, in about a week or ten days, to publish our statement, with about ten very prominent signatures. [This was the manifesto of the Council, which was then ready for publication.] But we also got quite a number of refusals from people who say they are quite in agreement, but they want to see some sign from the other side that they are ready for a dialogue or something with this organization.

Have you read that item in the press, in that paper, about Mr. X?

About who?

About the Mr. X you are in touch with.

No. Where? What article?

It was just a short item. It was in, what is it, that evening paper.

Oh you mean in Israel? I've seen it, yes.

Well, we don't need these things these days, do we?

It depends. Don't you like it?

Well, it's still early.

What we must have here in Israel, if you want to make any real progress in public opinion, we must show that there is some kind of a dialogue going on. Otherwise we are not going to be believed by anyone.

Yes, I understand this. But don't push it too fast!

OK, OK. I thought this was more or less in line with your thinking. But if you don't think so . . .

No, no, no, don't push it so fast!

## 19

*In one of our conversations I mention a rumour that some Israeli left-wing activist is trying to set up a public meeting with Hammami. I say that all such initiatives should now be channelled through our new council. Otherwise the personalities who have joined it will be irritated. After all, why set up a new organization and risk public denunciation if it has no clear function?*

*'It's irritating to some of our people here', I say. 'I think you should take this into account.'*

*'It's always difficult to deal with the Jews, isn't it?' Hammami says.*

*'Yes it is, but it's also difficult to deal with the Palestinians. We've got two difficult peoples!'*

*We both laugh.*

# 20

30 March 1976 was an important date. On that day the Arab citizens of Israel — more than 700,000 living within the pre-1967 borders of the state — held a general strike, protesting against large-scale land confiscations in the Galilee. The government wanted to use the land in order to 'Judaize' this area, where the bulk of the Arab population in Israel is concentrated. The strike was led by Rakakh, the Israeli communist party, which is predominantly Arab and serves as a vehicle for Arab protest in Israel.

On the same day I left Israel to meet Hammami in London. At Ben Gurion Airport I heard the news that several Arabs had been killed by Israeli soldiers and policemen who had opened fire on demonstrators in several villages. A few days earlier our Council had publicly warned Prime Minister Rabin of such an eventuality.

In a sense this was a turning point. After 28 years of isolation, the Arab minority in Israel had rejoined the Palestinian people.

The Palestinians who had left Israeli territory during the 1948 War, voluntarily or, like the family of Said Hammami, forcibly, had for many years looked upon those who had remained behind as traitors. I remember a poignant scene in the early 1960s. I was attending one of the annual peace conferences organized by the mayor of Florence, Giorgio La Pira. During an intermission, talking with a high-ranking Egyptian diplomat in a piazza overlooking the city, enjoying the October sunshine and the magnificent view, I saw two friends approaching. One of them was Rashid Hussein, a young nationalist poet from a small village in Israel, who later left Israel and met a tragic death in New York, where he served as a translator for the PLO office. The other was Atallah Mansour, an Arab journalist, who had started his career at *Haolam Hazeh*. The two had been touring Europe and happened to pass through Florence; hearing about the conference they decided to pay us a visit.

I was glad to see them and introduced them to the Egyptian ambassador, with whom I had been chatting amicably. 'Please meet two young Arabs from Israel', I said. Without a word the Egyptian turned his back on them and walked away. He told me later; 'I'm ready to talk with an Israeli like you, but not with those traitors!'

All this changed radically on that fateful day in March 1976. Psychologically, the Arabs in Israel were received back into the fold of their people. A few bullets can make a big change.

When I met Hammami the next day, the deaths were very much on his mind. He talked about them at length. Naturally we had an argument about the role of Rakakh.

He tried to convince me that the Rakakh party could play a useful role. I answered that while this was true to some extent, the party is generally detested in Israel, even among well-meaning and peace-loving people, because of its total subservience to Moscow, a subservience extending even to the question of human rights in the Soviet Union. Once, sitting next to Meir Wilner, the party chief, in the Knesset, I exclaimed: 'I wish you would make one critical remark about the Soviet Union. Say that the weather in Moscow is sometimes bad, or that the Moscow underground doesn't always run on time. Something, anything!' But to no avail.

Our new council and the party I was leading were not inclined to cooperate with Rakakh too frequently, fearing that the hatred they evoked would be detrimental to the cause of peace, even when they took a stand close to our own. Also, I could not forget that after the Six Day War and well into 1969, they opposed me in the Knesset whenever I brought up the idea of a Palestinian state, because at that time the Soviets had not yet taken up the cause of the PLO.

Hammami looked at it from a different angle. Rakakh was now very popular in PLO circles, because of its championship of the Arab protests in Israel. Following the orthodox Moscow line, Rakakh was also now supporting the idea of a Palestinian state in the West Bank and Gaza, rejecting the idea of the 'democratic secular state' still advocated by Palestinian extremists, as an immediate goal. 'Any one of us in the PLO who wants to attack the slogan of the democratic secular state can do it now by quoting the Arab newspapers of Rakakh and the communist party in the West Bank', he said. 'Thus one can give the whole argument without committing oneself too much.' According to him, Rakakh had a moderating influence on the Palestinians in the diaspora.

While conceding this and giving full praise to Rakakh's activities on behalf of the Arab community in Israel, I tried to convince him that there was no use at all in meetings between the PLO and Rakakh. They were counter-productive. Adamantly anti-Zionist, Rakakh has no appeal at all to the vast majority of Israelis, who consider themselves devout Zionists. It was this majority which we had to convince and influence if we wanted to effect a change in Israeli policy. Meeting with Rakakh, the PLO only convinced these Israelis even more that the PLO was determined to fight Zionism, which to the Israeli man in the street meant trying to dismantle the state of Israel, even if Rakakh, like Moscow, did support Israel's right to exist.

All this was even more true of meetings between Hammami and militants of Matzpen, an extreme left-wing group, some of whose prominent members had emigrated from Israel. At the time a tiny group, which existed outside Israeli politics, it advocated dismantling the Israeli state to allow the creation of some kind of communist commonwealth in the Middle East.

To counter my arguments, Hammami brought up the point of loyalty. He was saying, in effect: 'Rakakh and Matzpen have supported us in difficult times. We can't turn our backs on them for the sake of expediency.'

It was only very much later that Sartawi confided to me that this argument had cost Hammami dearly. Because of it he was removed from the job of conducting the dialogue with us. Sartawi had insisted that all contacts with Rakakh and Matzpen be broken off, so as to demonstrate the PLO's readiness to talk with patriotic, Zionist Israelis, in order to come nearer the mainstream of Israeli public opinion in helping create a big Israeli peace force, strong enough to influence government policy against annexation and for an Israeli-Palestinian peace. When, in spite of this, Hammami met with extreme anti-Zionists, Sartawi insisted on taking the contacts out of his hands, and even blocked Hammami's candidacy for the job of PLO representative in Washington, when it seemed that a PLO office could be established in the American capital.

The last straw for Sartawi was Hammami's meeting with Uri Davis. I had known this man from his early youth. His father was an Englishman who had been gassed in the First World War and who had instilled in his son a devout pacifism. During the early 1960s Davis had been active, together with us, in organizing demonstrations against the expropriation of Arab lands in the Galilee. He was imprisoned for a short term, and after that was rather subdued. Eventually he went abroad, and there became an uncompromising opponent of the very existence of the State of Israel, denouncing even those who were merely extreme anti-Zionists. When Sartawi heard that Davis was going around claiming to be active in the repatriation of Oriental Jews from Israel to the Arab countries, he had had enough.

But this was all yet to come.

* * *

During that week in April 1976, I had two long conversations with Hammami. Both times he was accompanied by a young colleague who introduced himself as Mohammed Abdallah, a rather nondescript name. I wondered about this. Did Hammami suddenly feel he needed a witness, in case of trouble within the PLO?

He did not seem subdued. On the contrary, he assured me that Arafat had given him full backing and, in a private conversation, had even promised to announce in due course that he was the pioneer of the contacts with the Israelis. 'Arafat reads all your articles', he said, 'they are translated to him immediately upon the arrival of each issue in Beirut. He asks questions about them. You should take this into account when you are writing.' This, by the way, Arafat told me himself when we first met six full years later.

It gave me a strange feeling. Somehow the distance between us and the arch-enemy seemed to become much shorter. Many times after that, when I was sitting in my study overlooking the seashore of Tel Aviv and writing about peace, the idea would cross my mind: In a few days Yassir Arafat will sit in his room, perhaps overlooking the seashore of Beirut, one hundred and fifty miles north of here, and read this. As has been said, ideas penetrate where soldiers cannot.

On the plane to London, I had been reading a recently-published book about Arafat. It pretended to be an objective study, but was in fact a beautiful piece of professional disinformation, inspired, I suspected, by some Israeli body of political warfare. 'It's all rubbish!' Hammami exclaimed, when I asked him about it. The book claimed that Arafat's mother had been a relative of the famous Grand Mufti of Jerusalem, Hadj Amin al-Husseini. Hammami said that Arafat was really born in Khan Yunis, in the Gaza Strip, and that his mother belonged to a well-known Jerusalem family, the Abu Saouds, who had no connections with the late mufti.

Involuntarily, we were drawn into a discussion of the past, a subject we generally avoided, knowing we could not agree on many of its aspects. Perhaps we now felt more free with each other and dared to broach these subjects.

The mufti, he said, had been a narrow-minded person. He had been ashamed of the fact that he had been appointed by the British. Actually the British had supported both him and Ben-Gurion, two extreme nationalists, in order to foster strife between the two peoples. They had also undercut the Nashashibis, the family that had led the opposition to the Husseinis and which had supported King Abdallah of Jordan.

Adel Hammami, Said's father, had been a member of the al-Istiqlal (Independence) Party, which had fought against both the mufti and Abdallah, and had been ready to agree to limited Jewish immigration, to save the victims from Hitler's Europe. The Hammamis had Jewish acquaintances, and Said had some vague memories of Tel Aviv. When his family was deported from Jaffa, they had first lived in a refugee camp in Kantara, on the Suez Canal. But the Egyptians did not like Istiqlal people, and after a year they had to leave. They went to Sidon, in Lebanon.

Now Lebanon preoccupied him very much. The civil war was already raging. The Palestinians were being sucked into it, much against their will. The PLO was at its peak, but was facing grave danger. Hammami was certain that it was all an American conspiracy to destroy the Palestinian movement.

On the television set in my hotel room that evening I had seen Arafat embracing Georges Habash, the leader of the rejection front in the PLO, and I had voiced grave misgivings about the impact of this scene on public opinion in Israel. But Hammami explained that this was not just a drawing together in face of mortal danger, but also a way for Habash to inch his way back into the mainstream, which was now in favour of a political settlement.

* * *

From time to time, during our conversations, sheer curiosity would gain the upper hand. I would ask him questions concerning subjects I was going to write about in *Haolam Hazeh*. Few of the readers who read our reports on what was happening in the Arab world, which frequently proved to be astonishingly accurate, could guess that this information had come directly from the other side.

For his part, he bombarded me with questions about various aspects of Jewish life which intrigued him. For example: Why do Jews sway when they are praying? (Frankly, I did not know. I suppose that it was a gesture of bowing, of submission to God.) Another question: What was my attitude towards Zionism? I explained to him that Zionism was the mainstream belief in Israel, and was to most Israelis synonymous with Israeli patriotism. No peace movement would have any chance of success in Israel if it became identified with anti-Zionism. He understood this argument, without, of course, changing in the least his extreme opposition to Zionism, a term which in Palestinian eyes is synonymous with the causes of their tragedy, displacement and misery. Without quite realizing it, we were touching on a problem that was to haunt us all for many years to come — the quite different emotional implications of the term 'Zionism' for the two sides.

At about the same time, my friends and I in the Council sued an Israeli publication for libel for calling us anti-Zionists. The case went right up to the Supreme Court of Israel. We won it with flying colours and were paid damages which went a long way towards financing activities of the Council. My book, *Israel Without Zionists*, was brought up during the trial, and the judge decided that it was not anti-Zionist. Jokingly, I told Said: 'Who has an official certificate guaranteeing his sanity? Only someone released from a lunatic asylum. I am one of the few people in Israel who has an official certificate affirming his Zionism — this court judgment and the book published by the PLO six years ago, calling me a neo-Zionist.'

Speaking about Zionism, he commented bitterly on the fact that the Arab states had evicted hundreds of thousands of Jews and sent them to Israel, thereby strengthening the Zionist state. He did not believe in the moves made by the PLO for some time to convince the Arab states to invite these Jews back. 'They are Israelis now, they won't go back', he conceded — a conclusion which another PLO official, Issam Sartawi, was reaching at the same time.

He was intrigued by a remark I made that if Nasser had succeeded in unifying the Arab world in a pan-Arab state, the Palestinian people would probably have ceased to exist and merged with the other Arab peoples. Yet it was Israel, more than anything else, that had obstructed Nasser's moves towards Arab unity, thus, paradoxically, bringing about the rebirth of the Palestinian national movement.

For the Syrians, he had only bitter resentment, while he had a grudging admiration for the Israelis. 'We have a proverb in Arabic: Better a clever enemy than a stupid friend.' I said that I hoped he included me among the enemy in this context.

Israel, he said, would win the war again and again. But in the end it would spend all its blood. Then the Middle East would be a graveyard. What was the good of that, he asked, saying that he was repeating a remark made by Yassir Arafat himself.

* * *

What was the reaction to the setting up of the Israeli Council? Why had there been no public PLO gesture to welcome its birth? Why, indeed, had Hammami not answered the questionnaire I had sent him, as he had agreed to do during our last conversation?

Patience, Hammami urged, as usual. It is a process. It moves slowly. The PLO cannot recognize Israel without the support of Egypt and Syria. The quarrel between the Arab states, which continued to rage after the Egyptian-Israeli interim agreement, was hindering the move towards peace. Israeli intransigence was making things even more difficult. Arab extremists were quoting Israeli extremists, and vice versa. The automatic cooperation between the hawks of both sides was working beautifully, as usual. 'We have a saying in Arabic: you can rely on Israeli extremism!' Hammami said. He was amazed to hear that the same saying existed in Hebrew: 'Our secret weapon is Arab extremism.'

The creation of the Israeli Council had been noted, he said, and had evoked a widespread, positive response. The lack of official reaction was not important. The important thing was that the fact itself had been published throughout the Arab world. It was also well-known that the Council was a Zionist body, that it supported a Zionist state. Its composition was impressive.

By now Hammami and I had become so close to each other that we had nothing to argue about except tactics and timing. While waiting for the Fatah leadership to come to a definite conclusion about its contacts with the Israeli Council — a process about which I could only conjecture at the time, because Hammami never told me anything definite about the inner workings of the leadership body, which remained shrouded in mystery — we compared our views about the future, raising questions which had never yet been seriously faced. If the Palestinian State came to be, who would be in power? What would be the relationship between the local leaders, who had a strong base in the existing social structure, and the PLO leadership coming back from abroad? What would the social picture be? How far could Saudi money be relied on to finance reconstruction and the settling of the refugees?

Hammami thought it would take about five years for the situation in the new state to stabilize. Later on, maybe after twenty-five years, a three-state confederation of Israel, Palestine and Jordan would be possible.

He was optimistic. Arafat was now completely committed to the idea of a Palestinian state alongside Israel. The Americans were going to find out that they could not destroy the PLO, and then they would come to a settlement with it. The turning point would come when an American emissary arrived in Beirut to meet Arafat officially.

Things were moving. Soon, perhaps very soon, the PLO was bound to start official contacts with our Council. Hammami expected, of course, to be in charge of these.

* * *

On 21 April 1976, after returning home from London, I sent the prime minister a long letter reporting (or, rather, telling, since he objected to being reported to) about my conversations with Hammami and also with the Austrian chancellor, Bruno Kreisky, whom I had seen in Vienna on my way back. I had met Kreisky twice, first for a four-hour-long interview and again for a private conversation, on the day Anwar Sadat had met him in his office. There had been rumours in Vienna that I had met Sadat in Kreisky's office, but these were untrue.

The part of my letter dealing with the Hammami conversations read as follows:

> During two conversations, on March 31 and April 4, he gave me the following estimate of the situation: There is now in progress a concerted American-Syrian-Jordanian-Israeli attack on the PLO [in Lebanon]. This is the last attempt to destroy the PLO. It will not succeed because of the balance of power on the ground and because of inter-Arab relationships.
>
> After the failure of this last attempt, and after the elections in the United States [in November 1976] the US will open a new stage and work to try to achieve an alliance with the PLO. The PLO will agree. Yassir Arafat is ready for the creation of a state in the West Bank and the Gaza Strip, with American support. The present rapprochement between Arafat and Habash is for the purpose of defence against Syria, but it is also an attempt by Habash to give up his extreme positions and to come closer to the position of the PLO mainstream, i.e., Fatah.
>
> ... Hammami's estimate is: If a Palestinian state is set up in the West Bank and the Strip, it will need five years to achieve stability. After twenty-five years, a federation between Israel, Palestine and Jordan will come about. He says that there is no doubt at all that Arafat himself supports this solution completely.

If I had any hope that this would deter Rabin from taking an active part in the Lebanon tragedy against the Palestinians, I was soon disappointed. The next part of our contact with the PLO took place under the cloud of an escalating Israeli intervention in the Lebanese civil war, designed to destroy the very existence of the PLO.

While I was writing this, the Syrians were already moving into Lebanon. They decided upon this after being invited by the Maronite leadership, and after obtaining assurances from the United States that both Washington and Jerusalem approved. In later conversations with Rabin, he explained that he preferred a Syrian occupation of all Lebanon, not only because it would spread out Syrian forces and lessen the danger of a Syrian attack on Israel, but also because the Syrians could be relied on to prevent any Palestinian attacks on Israel. Experience in the Golan Heights had shown that wherever the Israeli and Syrian armies confronted each other directly, face to face, peace prevailed. Knowing that any local incident could escalate into full-fledged war, the Syrians controlled their Palestinian underlings with an iron hand.

Indeed, after the Syrian advance into Lebanon, Rabin advocated letting the Syrians move right up to the Israeli border. This move was blocked by Shimon Peres, the minister of defence. At the time, the fight between Rabin and Peres over the leadership of the Labour Party and the government was raging behind the scenes, and every move made by Rabin was immediately attacked by journalists and politicians friendly to Peres (nicknamed by us United Peres). So, when the Syrian army was advancing towards the Israeli-Lebanese frontier, a hue and cry went up in Israel: the move was decried as a mortal danger to the state and it was implied that Rabin was a wimp and soft on the Syrians. As if trying to prove that his adversaries were right, but for the opposite reasons, Rabin agreed to declare the Litani River as a Red Line beyond which any Syrian move would be considered a provocation to Israel. The Syrians duly stopped. The practical effect was that between the Litani River and the Israeli border a vacuum was created which the PLO forces quickly filled. This situation was to have fateful consequences in the following years. It was a costly victory for Peres, the 'Tireless Intrigant', as Rabin later called him in his memoirs.

While all this was happening, I did not meet Hammami. A new personality had appeared on the scene; the contacts were taken out of Hammami's hands. Issam Sartawi had taken over, after criticizing Hammami for his continued contacts with anti-Zionist fringe elements in Israel. A new relationship was born — but I'll take up this narrative in another chapter.

* * *

I met Hammami again nearly a year and a half later. The British section of the Parliamentary Association for Euro-Arab Cooperation had organized a meeting, modestly called a seminar, which took place in London from 30 September to 1 October 1977. It was a unique event, a real, genuine, public dialogue between representative PLO officials and a Zionist Israeli delegation, the first of its kind, and for a long time the only one. For two full days, Palestinians, other Arabs, Israelis and Europeans from many countries, as well as some Americans, read papers, argued from the floor and discussed the real problems involved in the quest for peace between Israel and the Palestinians.

Present were both Said Hammami and Issam Sartawi, together with some other PLO representatives. On the Israeli side both Matti Peled and I participated, with several others. From the West Bank came Karim Khalaf, the mayor of Ramallah and Dr. Nafez Nazzal from Bir Zeit University. Mohammed Sid Ahmed, the brilliant Egyptian left-wing writer, came from Cairo. Dozens of others came from other countries and from Britain itself.

It was a real debate, and all of us took the floor many times. Palestinians and Israelis spoke to each other openly, agreed and disagreed. Between meetings and at nights we spent many hours with Sartawi. But from the beginning, Hammami struck me as somewhat aloof. His public meetings with me in the corridors and during meals were much more constrained than they used to be.

I was puzzled. Only on the last day did he call me out of the hall, pull me into a deserted room behind the bar, and there we had a heart-to-heart talk. He seemed extremely discouraged. It was there that he told me that it had been wrong to describe our meeting to his superiors in Beirut as a meeting between friends, that we should have insisted that this was a meeting between enemies.

While we were talking, a demonstration of Arab students was taking place outside the hotel where the seminar was being held. Arab students carrying posters denounced the seminar as an act of treason to the

Palestinian cause, singling out Hammami as a traitor. Among the demonstrators was Uri Davis, the one whose contacts with Hammami had so upset Sartawi.

It was clear that Hammami was under great strain. In retrospect I assume there had been threats to his life by Palestinian radicals, and that he thought that he had gone too far in exposing himself as a pioneer in the Israeli-Palestinian dialogue.

This may explain many of the things he said from the podium at the seminar. Instead of concentrating upon the present and the next few years, he dwelt upon his vision of the distant future. It was, as Sartawi was to call this way of thinking later on, an escape into the future.

In practice this meant that instead of talking about the creation of a Palestinian state alongside Israel, an idea which had a chance of being accepted by the Israeli public, he talked about a unitary Democratic Secular State — an idea that frightens the wits out of Israelis, because it means to them the destruction of Israel and, probably, the destruction of Israelis. Hammami was well aware of this, after so many conversations. By taking a step forward, he was taking a step backwards.

But the way he described his vision was beautiful nonetheless. Let me quote some sentences from his paper:

> It is not my intention to reiterate the story of past wrongs or to dwell on their present consequences. Rather I wish to invite you to accompany me on a journey into the future — a happier and more hopeful future in which enmity and conflict have been laid aside and the two peoples, the Palestinian Arabs and the Israeli Jews, who both claim Palestine as their own, have begun the task which is their manifest destiny, sooner or later: the task of learning to live together as equal partners sharing the same land and respecting each other's rights.
>
> ... The time I have in mind is some ten or twenty years hence — perhaps even longer. During this time, I am assuming that events have proceeded through several phases. First, after many setbacks and disappointments, a peace settlement is at last reached in Geneva which includes the establishment of a Palestinian state. Then a considerable period of time passes while the two states, Israeli and Palestinian, exist, independently, side by side.
>
> Gradually the two peoples acquire confidence in one another and develop cultural and other relations. Also, on the political level, a dialogue opens, hesitant at first, but growing in confidence as time passes, between leading Palestinians and liberal, non-Zionist Israelis.
>
> ... I would probably go further than most of my fellow Palestinians at this stage in trying to accommodate within the vision of a 'state in partnership' the evident desire of the present Jewish population of Israel to retain a distinctive national identity of their own. I believe that, in time, we are bound to recognize and to try to live with the claim of those Jews whose home is now in Israel to retain a separate national identity — even while we continue, quite rightly, to reject the absurd Zionist contention that all Jews throughout the world constitute a separate nation centred on Israel, regardless of their present citizenship and nationality. As a first step towards a state in partnership I believe that both Israelis and Palestinians will, sooner or later, have to recognize each other's claim to nationhood.

> I am not sure how best to describe, in legal and constitutional terms, the kind of state in partnership which I am inviting you to visit with me in our excursion into the future. It has some of the characteristics of a federation, some of a condominium. But, in truth, it is *sui generis* — as it must be to fit the unique circumstances of the case. It goes by the name of 'The Commonwealth of Israel and Palestine'. Its people enjoy a common citizenship. But they have retained their separate national characteristics and symbols. The Israeli and Palestinian flags are both flown throughout the country. Hebrew and Arabic are both recognized as the official languages. Both are taught as compulsory studies in all schools, and public officials are required to have a command of both.
>
> There is freedom of movement and access throughout the country, but residents are subject to regulation ... This new commonwealth, which would be rather like Switzerland with its French, Italian and German areas, would play a significant role in the Middle East.
>
> . . . If Palestinians and Israelis learn to live together, it will not be a marriage of lovers, nor can it be a spontaneous historical process. It is the destiny of two nations who belong to one country and not what either of them would prefer. No fair-minded Israeli can claim more right to live in Palestine than a Palestinian; and no realistic Palestinian can deny an Israeli the right to live in a country to which he feels he belongs.
>
> ... The establishment of an independent state for the Palestinians in the West Bank and the Gaza Strip is a first essential, but ... this must be only a first step towards a common peace on a modus vivendi accepted and created by both Palestinians and Israelis.

Both Matti Peled and I attacked this paper, while paying tribute to the historic role played by Hammami as the pioneer of the Israeli-Palestinian dialogue. Nothing could be more unfortunate, we said, than providing ammunition to Israeli extremists, who argued that the creation of a Palestinian state in the West Bank and the Gaza Strip would only be a first step in a continued 'salami' process of cutting up Israel piece by piece, like a sausage. Many things could happen in the distant future, and everyone has a right to his own visions. But the practical job now was to achieve peace on the basis of a two-state solution.

'If eventually', I said, 'agreement were reached on a confederation of Israeli and Palestinian states, this could command acceptance among Israelis. But it is unacceptable to suggest that the Israelis are going to be denationalized into becoming a mere community. We are a nation and will remain a nation. If at some time in the future the Israelis take part in some regional superstructure, it will be as a nation.' During the seminar, one of the British participants, Dennis Walters, a pro-Arab member of Parliament, had asked the Palestinians to settle for some sort of 'rough justice', a very sensible way of saying that one should strive to achieve the possible at any given stage. Before the end of the proceedings, I took the floor and made a point about which I have thought many times since. In the summary of the proceedings, which quoted all the speakers in the third person, my remarks were quoted as follows:

> The late Professor Martin Buber, who was a great philosopher, a great friend

of Arab nationalism, also a great Zionist, told him years ago that for every political idea there was a certain moment, and Mr. Avnery thought the art of politics in the broadest sense was to grasp that moment. It might be a very fleeting moment in the life of a nation, when everything came together and everything was possible which might not have been possible a moment before and might again be impossible for a long time afterwards.

In the history of the Israeli nation there had been such a moment in 1947 when the Israelis were offered a small part of Palestine as a state, and the vast majority had the sense to accept, to reject Mr. Begin, to reject the Irgun, to reject all those forces which were in power today in Israel, and to accept the establishment of the state of Israel.

He hesitated to say what he was going to say because it might sound a typical example of Israeli arrogance, but he felt he would be shirking his moral duty if he did not say it. He believed the Palestinians had such a moment now. It might be a very short moment, but it was the moment for the Palestinian nation to realize not all its dreams, but the minimum for national existence, a basis on which to build a new national life. The time was now, and it depended to a great measure on the wisdom of their actions in the very near future. There was once in Palestine a British army camp in which there was a school for training drivers. In the centre of the school there was a badly smashed up car and on it there was a sign: 'But he was right'. To be right could be a misfortune because if one was convinced that one was right, and one really *was* right, and one neglected what had been called in the seminar 'rough justice', one committed a sin against one's own people. He believed that the Palestinian leadership should spell out as clearly as possible, at this moment, that what they wanted the international community to make possible was the creation of a Palestinian state on the West Bank and in Gaza, and the integration of the PLO in the peacemaking process. In return they would accept coexistence with Israel. He thought this should be spelt out in a language understandable to masses of people in America, in Europe, and in Israel.

Some of these words proved to be prophetic — much more than even I could have anticipated.

At that moment, Palestinian fortunes seemed at their height. The PLO had established its mini-state in Lebanon, and after withstanding the Syrian onslaught of the summer of 1976, it functioned reasonably well, in spite of the presence of the Syrian army in Lebanon. Its international prestige was rising. International trends were converging towards a consensus for the reconvening of the Geneva Peace Conference with the participation of the PLO. Several ideas were advanced as ways of circumventing Israeli objections, such as the formation of a unified Arab delegation, which would include PLO representatives, and/or the representation of the Palestinians by some well-known Palestinian academic figures, who were identified with the PLO without bearing an official PLO label. On the very day I was speaking, 1 October 1977, the United States secretary of state and the Soviet minister for foreign affairs published a joint statement containing two radical new departures. One recognized the legitimate rights of the Palestinian people, saying:

> The United States and the Soviet Union believe that, within the framework of a comprehensive settlement of the Middle East problem, all specific questions of the settlement should be resolved, including such key issues as withdrawal of Israeli armed forces from territories occupied in the 1967 conflict; the resolution of the Palestinian question including ensuring the legitimate rights of the Palestinian people; termination of the state of war and establishment of normal peaceful relations on the basis of mutual recognition of the principles of sovereignty, territorial integrity, and political independence.

The second point called for Palestinian participation in a new Geneva Conference:

> The United States and the Soviet Union believe that the only right and effective way for achieving a fundamental solution to all aspects of the Middle East problem in its entirety is negotiations within the framework of the Geneva Peace Conference, specially convened for these purposes, with participation in its work of the representatives of all the parties involved in the conflict including those of the Palestinian people, and legal and contractual formalization of the decisions reached at the conference.

These significant concessions by the new Carter administration created a panic in Jerusalem. Foreign Minister Moshe Dayan was sent post-haste to Washington, and with the help of the Jewish lobby twisted the arm of the president. The joint American-Soviet communiqué was in effect killed by the Americans two weeks after its birth.

Another red light lit up in Cairo. President Sadat had no desire at all to take part in a joint Arab delegation in Geneva, where Egypt's freedom of action would be overpowered by Syria and other radical Arab states. This certainly was one of the causes of his historic initiative; indeed, many observers, among them Rabin, as he told me privately, believe that this was Sadat's main consideration. Less than two months after my warning to the PLO in London, Sadat came to Jerusalem, astonishing the world and claiming centre stage for himself. The PLO was pushed aside for several years: the unique opportunity for an historical breakthrough by the PLO, which existed during 1977, had been missed.

* * *

A few days after the Sadat initiative, Hammami called my friend Amnon Zichroni from London. During the last year, Zichroni, my former parliamentary assistant and a successful lawyer, had become very friendly with Hammami, and they had met several times.

During one of their last meetings, Hammami had produced a gas pistol and offered it to Zichroni as a gift. 'But you need it much more than I do,' Zichroni had said. 'Oh, I'm quite safe,' Hammami replied, smiling back. Zichroni accepted the gift.

Now, after the Sadat visit, Hammami told him on the phone that he wanted to meet either me or him urgently. I was on my way to Cairo, Zichroni was extremely busy with an important trial. We postponed the meeting.

We never saw him again.

# 21

*It is 4 January 1978.*

*Said Hammami sits behind his desk in the basement of the Arab League's office in a fashionable district in the centre of London.*

*A visitor is announced. Hammami knows him well and asks that he be sent in.*

*The door opens. Smiling, Hammami rises from his seat and extends his hand.*

*Several shots ring out. The assailant escapes, unrecognized by anyone.*

*Said Hammami, a hero of peace, former Fedayeen commander, is dead.*

# PART III

## Sartawi

## 22

Enter the hero.

When I first heard the name of the Issam al-Sartawi, I did not know who he was, nor did any of my friends.

It was in the summer of 1976. A few weeks earlier we had published the manifesto of the reconstituted Israeli Council for Israeli-Palestinian Peace. I had sent the manifesto to Said Hammami in London. Earlier Hammami had indicated that if we succeeded in setting up a broad-based Israeli body for this purpose, the PLO would start a dialogue with it. I was waiting for this, assuming that the invitation would come from Hammami.

Instead, we received a signal from Paris. An Israeli professor active in the peace movement, Daniel Amit, informed our council that a PLO representative had arrived there and had asked for a meeting through the group of Henri Curiel.

I mentioned Curiel earlier in this narrative. Of all the extraordinary characters involved in our fight for Israeli-Palestinian peace, he was one of the most remarkable. I had met him in the late 1950s, when he was active in the underground Algerian FLN, and it was he who convinced me to set up the Israeli Committee for a Free Algeria.

Curiel was an Egyptian Jew. During the Second World War he set up communist cells in Cairo, which infiltrated the British Army units stationed there. He was the guiding spirit of the Egyptian Communist party — one of several such groups at the time — which was nearly exclusively composed of Jewish intellectuals. During the 1948 War, this party demonstrated in Cairo against the Egyptian intervention in Palestine.

Like the Iraqi communists, the Egyptian followers of Moscow accepted the Soviet line, which supported the partition of Palestine into an Arab and a Jewish state. This Soviet decision, which amazed the world when it was first voiced by the young Andrei Gromyko, had made possible the partition resolution of the UN. Thirty years later, an Egyptian left-winger, who had taken part in the demonstrations against the war, told me that they had been quite popular, and that by-standers had cheered the demonstrators.

For understandable reasons, King Farouk did not like these activities, and Curiel was expelled from Egypt. Since then he had been living in France as a stateless refugee. There he was soon joined by other members of his group, who were exiled from Egypt by the new revolutionary regime of Gamal Abd-al-Nasser. They had been disavowed by other Egyptian communists, who had decided to adopt a patriotic Egyptian line and supported the war against Israel.

In Paris this group became a unique phenomenon. Its members had become rich businessmen, but they continued to adore Curiel, their undisputed leader. Curiel became a one-man centre for international liberation movements. He extended his assistance to a wide variety of left-wing liberation organizations throughout the Third World — South African, Latin American, East Asian. The CIA suspected him of being a KGB agent, and leaked information to this effect to several journalists. In fact, Curiel was very far from Soviet orthodoxy and the official Communist church and its KGB priesthood. He acted alone, aided only by a few admirers and supporters, tolerated by the French secret service in spite of the fact that his residence in France was conditional on his abstention from political activity.

I never met anyone quite like him. He was the professional revolutionary par excellence, with a razor-sharp mind, looking more like an ascetic Jesuit than the dedicated Marxist he was. Whenever I passed through Paris I used to meet him in some little cafe or another, where I'd listen to his brilliant analyses of current affairs and developments and argue about Biafra or Vietnam. Whenever I needed help for some political action, he was there.

But his first love remained Israeli-Arab peace. He never wavered from his conviction that Israel had to be recognized and had to make peace with the Arabs, and in particular with the Palestinians. He was in close contact with PLO circles, as he had been with the FLN. His was, therefore, the natural address for any Palestinian seeking discreet contact with Israelis. He was not only dedicated to the cause of dialogue, but also had the means to enable both sides to meet in the utmost secrecy.

* * *

It was Curiel who informed Professor Amit that a high-ranking PLO official was staying in Paris in order to meet with a delegation of our council, of which Amit was a member. It was great news. After spending several months formulating our manifesto and obtaining the first hundred signatures of supporters, here, at last, was the signal for action.

The Council decided to send a delegation of four to Paris: Matti Peled, Lova Eliav, Yaacov Arnon and Yossi Amitai. I always regretted that I was not part of this first group, and am now therefore unable to give an eyewitness report. After I had been in contact with Hammami for nearly two years, my friends felt that as many as possible of the other members should become involved in the contacts.

During our deliberations on the eve of their departure, one question kept recurring: Who was this Sartawi, whose name had been given us by Curiel? What was his past? Whom did he represent? What was his rank in the PLO hierarchy? No one knew.

During the night before their departure a vague memory stirred in my mind. I leafed through the books about the Palestinian movement in my library, and there, sure enough, was one in which the name Issam Sartawi was mentioned in passing. It said that in 1970, a Dr. Issam al-Sartawi, an American-trained heart surgeon, was the leader of a small Fedayeen organization called The Action Organization for the Liberation of

Palestine, which was believed to be close to Iraq and Egypt. In this capacity he had been elected to the Executive Committee of the PLO, the governing body of the organization.

At 2 a.m. I called Matti Peled at his home near Jerusalem, waking him from his sleep with the news that I had identified our mystery man. He certainly was an important person.

When the delegation returned, a few days later, its report was positive. Sartawi was serious. He had identified himself as a senior member of the Fatah organization, acting on instructions from Yassir Arafat. They had had a number of important meetings. They had also gone, with Sartawi, to meet the French ex-premier, Pierre Mendès-France, at his country home. Like everything else, this meeting had been organized by Curiel. The foundation had been laid for an ongoing dialogue. Both sides had agreed to maintain absolute silence until circumstances made revelation of the contacts possible. This would be done by joint agreement.

All four were deeply impressed by the personality of their interlocutor. My curiosity was aroused even more. I was eager to meet this man. The opportunity came soon enough. A few weeks after the first meeting, Sartawi, again through Curiel, called for a second series of meetings. This time we decided that our delegation would consist of Matti Peled, Yaacov Arnon, Meir Pail and myself.

* * *

In order to avoid undue attention, each of us took a different flight to Paris. I was to arrive at Charles de Gaulle airport at a certain time, somebody from the Paris group would wait for me there, indicating by a sign that he was expecting a Mr. Levy.

As usual, when things were organized by Curiel and his friends, everything worked out exactly according to plan. I met the man waving a placard bearing the name of Mr. Levy, and he took me in his little car through Paris south, to the village of Rambouillet, a beautiful hamlet of country estates, villas and woods. At the edge of the village was an isolated villa. There the meeting was to take place.

The first man I saw was an old acquaintance of mine, Sabri Jiryes. Sabri was a young lawyer from the Arab village of Fassouta in the Galilee, who had studied at the Hebrew University in Jerusalem and had become famous as a nationalist activist. During the 1960s, a group of nationalist-minded Arab citizens of Israel had tried to set up an Arab party called al-Ard ('The Land'). He was one of the younger members. I had tried to help the founding and had met him there. The group was suppressed by the authorities. Sabri wrote a book in Hebrew about the legal discrimination against Arabs in Israel and the expropriation of their lands for Jewish settlement. Soon after, he had to leave the country, after learning that otherwise he would be arrested. Before that I met him several times. I remember a heated debate on the steps of my home, after a meeting in some intellectual club in Tel Aviv. We were debating Palestinian nationalism. In the heat of the debate Sabri had exclaimed: 'The Germans have killed six million Jews, but you made an agreement with them and now you have friendly relations with Germany. We Palestinians did not kill millions — why can't you make peace with us?'

In the street we continued to argue for several hours. We were three — Sabri, me, and the poet Rashid Hussein, another nationalist and al-Ard supporter, who had helped my election campaign in 1965. I remember that I was exasperated by Sabri's extremist views. We Palestinians must revolutionize the Arab world, he had said, in order to win the upper hand against Israel.

'Are you ready to sacrifice your own people for that?' I countered. 'If there's a war between Israel and the Arab world, the Palestinians in Israel will be the first victims!'

'I don't mind if they are killed to the last man', he said, 'if we achieve our purpose.'

When I next heard from Sabri, he was a PLO official in Beirut. He had written an article in an Arab newspaper expressing views very similar to those of Said Hammami, views favouring peace between Israel and the Palestinian people.

It was therefore with great joy that I recognized his face in Rambouillet. Here was a man I knew, with whom I could speak in Hebrew, who had had the courage to come out openly for peace, not in some European newspaper but in an Arab one appearing in Lebanon.

We embraced like long-lost friends. I introduced him to Meir Pail, who had arrived before me. Matti and Sartawi were not there yet. They were meeting somewhere in Paris, on their way to the villa, and for some reason had delayed their arrival.

Pail, who was at the time a member of the Knesset for the small left-wing Zionist party Moked, is known for his peculiar brand of sabra humour, generally identified with the Palmach underground of which he had been a proud member.

'Perhaps you bloody terrorists have kidnapped Matti Peled!' he joked. It was the wrong thing to say to a Palestinian at a first encounter. Sabri was deeply offended, and never forgot this. It cropped up later every time Meir Pail was mentioned, and he soon became *persona non grata* for several reasons.

Soon Sartawi and Peled arrived. I saw a man with a young face and grey hair, with an authoritative manner, who spoke very good English and was well-dressed. It was quite clear that he was a man used to giving orders, and that he was in charge of the Palestinian delegation which included, besides him and Sabri Jiryes, a third person, who appeared to be his aide. But Sartawi was upset; there was a good reason for it. Both he and Sabri had come straight from Beirut. Because of the civil war raging there, they could not leave from Beirut airport. They had decided to go by ship to Cyprus, and fly on from there. At the last moment they had changed their minds and flown from Damascus, a dangerous course because Sartawi was disliked by the Syrians. Upon arriving in Paris, they had learned that the ship they were supposed to have taken had been intercepted on the high seas by the Israeli navy and turned over to a Phalangist ship, which had taken it to Junia harbour, a Phalangist stronghold. There all the Palestinian passengers had been massacred.

We promised to investigate. Upon our return to Israel, Matti Peled asked Prime Minister Itzhak Rabin, with whom he had served in the general staff, to find out what had happened. Rabin denied the story, and after some time invited Peled to study the file himself. There was a report by the commander of an Israeli navy unit saying that he had indeed intercepted and searched a ship on its way from Beirut to Cyprus. While the search was going on, a Phalangist naval unit had appeared on the scene, and the Israeli ship had left. Obviously, Sartawi's story was true. We protested against this illegal procedure, but such incidents continued during the following years. Many such ships were intercepted and often taken to Haifa harbour.

* * *

The villa was very comfortable. It served as a country place for its owner, a member of the Curiel group. We were shown to our bedrooms, settled in and reassembled in the salon. Curiel and his friends chatted with us for some time, to create a cordial atmosphere; then they all left the room. We were alone — three Palestinians and four Israelis, enemies who had come from Beirut and Tel Aviv, facing each other across a small table laden with cups of coffee and sweets. Sartawi was playing with a *masbahah*, a string of beads.

The conversation lasted for two days, almost without interruption, in closed sessions, during meals with our hosts, during strolls in the woods. It was a mixture of many things: a political debate which sometimes became quite stormy, an exchange of jokes, a trade-off of analyses. We told each other stories about our pasts, trying to take each other's measure. At one point Sartawi recited some poems he had written, and Matti Peled, a lecturer in modern Arab literature at Tel Aviv University, volunteered to teach them in his courses. 'That may be a little bit too early', Sartawi remarked. At times the atmosphere became so friendly that we had to apologize to each other for forgetting that we were enemies. But we also quarrelled, and then Sartawi could be abrasive indeed. The main reason for the quarrels was a difference of approach, which was to appear again and again at many meetings, as it had already during my conversations with Hammami. It concerned the time factor. We Israelis were impatient. We needed public gestures, a confirmation that the PLO was indeed conducting a dialogue with Zionist Israelis, as an indication of its willingness to deal with and recognize the state of Israel. The Palestinians thought this a harmful course and suspected a trap. Publication could kill their effort in the first stage. 'Don't favour tactics over strategy!' Sartawi exclaimed at one point. 'A small profit today may destroy our long-range endeavour. We are progressing. Our meeting here is a sign of this. We have a strategic objective: peace. Let's judge every tactical step in the light of strategy!'

We Israelis had at the time only a very vague idea about what was happening in the PLO, what forces were at work inside the organization, who was who. In the late evening, after saying goodnight to the Palestinians, we sat in one of the rooms, compared notes and impressions, and decided to press for the publication of a joint communiqué at the end of the meeting. When Matti Peled proposed this in the morning, Sartawi was upset. We did not understand the reasons for this. We were still operating in a fog, rather like the fog surrounding the villa on that autumn day, 18 October 1976.

After listening to the exchange I said: 'The situation is like this: We are one army, fighting for one aim, peace. But we are fighting on two different fronts. Each front has its own problems, its own requirements. What we need in Israel may be different from what you need on the Palestinian side. Our job here is to reconcile our different requirements. We need to gain credibility in order to influence Israeli public opinion. We must show that we are accepted by the PLO as a valuable interlocutor, that the PLO is ready for peace. Only you can tell us what you need.' I remember these sentences, because I was to repeat them many times.

After this the discussion became easier. We talked about many subjects. How to influence Israeli public opinion. How to help our friends in the PLO convince their compatriots that peace with Israel is possible and desirable. How to gain friends for the idea of Israeli-Palestinian peace in Europe and the US. Whether and how to create some bodies on neutral ground which could facilitate a regular exchange of information, and opportunities for a public dialogue.

I promised to try to enlist the help of Bruno Kreisky, the Austrian Chancellor, with whom I had become friendly. The names of Mendès-France and Dr. Nahum Goldmann were brought up. But at that moment the subject which was uppermost in Sartawi's mind was how to build a bridge between the PLO and the US. He was quite convinced that this was essential in order to bring about progress towards peace. As we found out later, this was one of the bones of contention between Sartawi and PLO leaders like Farouk Kaddumi, who had a greater attachment to the Soviet Union and to Syria.

It appeared that Sartawi and Sabri Jiryes had been empowered by the Fatah leadership to go to the US to establish a PLO office there and to lobby for the Palestinian cause. We found the timing unfortunate, because elections were about to take place in the States, a time notoriously inopportune for any Arab lobbying. The Jewish lobby, formidable at all times, gains additional strength before elections. For reasons I never quite understood, Sartawi did not take our advice and did go to the US, a singularly ill-advised step.

* * *

Perhaps more important than the serious discussions which went on for many hours were the personal notes. We were quickly getting to know and like each other.

There was a certain similarity between us all, in spite of the vast differences of personality. None of us was an impractical utopian thinker, a born pacifist, of the type Americans call do-gooders or bleeding hearts. We had all been fighters. Peled, Pail and I had all been in the Jewish underground and later in the Israeli Army. Peled and Pail had been professional soldiers for a long time. Arnon had been in the underground during the German occupation of Holland, and later a prominent member of the Israeli establishment. Sartawi had been a Fedayeen chief, and all three Palestinians were, of course, PLO officers.

Sartawi later repeated many times an episode of his first encounter with Peled. They had talked about peace and come to a complete agreement, but then Sartawi had said: 'After we achieve a peace treaty between Israel and the Palestinian people, we must have one last war.' When Peled asked, in surprise, why, Sartawi explained: 'We have been humiliated too much on the battlefield, we must win at least one victory to restore our self-respect.' But, Sartawi added: 'General Peled convinced me that instead of having a war we should have a football match.'

During one of the meals, I confided to Sartawi that I had been entrusted with a secret mission by Ariel Sharon, whom I had told a few days earlier that I was going to meet a leading PLO official. At the time, Sharon was trying to set up a party of his own, called Shlomzion (The Peace of Zion and also the name of an ancient Jewish queen of the Hasmoneans) after leaving the Likud which he himself had created. Sharon was trying to cultivate relations with different parts of the political spectrum, including elements of the Peace Camp. He was searching for a new formula, and had asked me if I could set up a meeting between him and Yassir Arafat.

'What does he want to talk to Arafat about?' Sartawi asked.

'I believe that he wants to offer him a deal: the Israeli Army will help to overthrow King Hussein and install Arafat as president of Jordan, which will then be called Palestine', I answered.

Sartawi burst out laughing, and that was that.

Perhaps it was remarkable, and perhaps not, that during meals and strolls we talked about subjects far beyond the present. I told him of my dream: to write someday a book about the history of our common country that would be equally acceptable to both Israelis and Palestinians.

I told him a story which shed light on the psychological ramifications of the conflict. My wife, Rachel, who is a schoolteacher, had explained to her seven-year-old pupils the 23rd chapter of the Book of Genesis in which Abraham negotiates with Ephron the Hittite the purchase of the cave of Machpelah in Hebron as a burial ground. In this beautiful story, Ephron offers to give him the cave as a gift, refusing money. Abraham refuses and finally Ephron says 'My lord, harken unto me: The land is worth four hundred shekels of silver; what is that betwixt me and thee?' Rachel had explained to the children that this was a polite way of conducting business, still used by the Bedouin in the Negev.

After class, Rachel had met the teacher of the parallel class, who had been teaching the same chapter. When asked by Rachel how she had explained it to her children, the teacher answered: 'Why, I told them the truth: That this is an example of typical Arab perfidy and hypocrisy.'

Quite often during our conversations, Sabri Jiryes and I, being old friends, lapsed into Hebrew which was alien to Sartawi. Once he exploded: 'Will you two Israelis stop talking in your secret language?'

At another time, during a meal, we talked about food. Our hosts had prepared, as a special gesture, some typical Arab food, such as *falafel*. As Egyptians, the wives knew how to prepare this. When Sartawi tried to explain to us what *falafel* is, he was amazed to hear that this was a staple Israeli food. 'What, after stealing our homes you've also stolen our cuisine?' he exclaimed.

* * *

The most emotional moment during these two days came near the end, on the afternoon of the second day.

All our meetings had been overshadowed by events in Lebanon. The Syrian Army, which had been called into Lebanon by the right-wing Maronite leadership in order to help them fight against the coalition of Muslims, Druze and the PLO, had been advancing steadily in spite of fierce resistance by the Palestinian forces. One Syrian column had been wiped out in Sidon, another had been stopped for some time on the Beirut-Damascus highway near Bhamdoun, but now they were advancing again towards the main PLO strongholds in Beirut and the south. For the PLO, it was a life and death struggle. Many times during the day we stopped our talks in order to listen to the news in French and English. Once I had to translate the news which we happened to pick up from Germany. The situation looked more and more desperate.

And then, suddenly, dramatic news came over the air: the king of Saudi Arabia had intervened and delivered what amounted to an ultimatum to the Syrians. The Syrians had succumbed, also perhaps afraid of the decisive battle which was about to be fought inside the cities of Beirut and Sidon — the kind of battle in which the PLO forces excelled and in which a regular army, like the Syrian, is at a distinct disadvantage, as the Israeli Army was to learn six years later.

The Syrians had agreed to come to a summit meeting in Riyadh. The Saudi king had sent his own private plane to Beirut's closed airport in order to bring Yassir Arafat. A compromise was to be struck. The PLO mini-state in Lebanon was saved, for the time being.

The three Palestinians exploded in relief and joy. They infected our hosts, who brought in bottles of champagne, and thus we all toasted the salvation of the PLO. For Israelis who did not share our view of the future, and of the benefits of peace for Israel, this would have seemed an improbable, if not unforgivable, scene indeed.

Soon after, our meeting broke up. We were returning home, the Palestinians were going on to the States. One of our hosts took Jiryes and me into Paris. During the ride, Sabri gave me a very detailed and illuminating analysis of the state of affairs in Lebanon, describing the diverse forces and leaders, telling me about many events which had taken place during the civil war. It was one of the best lessons I ever received in my life, and I used it when analysing events in Lebanon in my paper during the following weeks and months. Readers, who may have been surprised by the accuracy of our reports about Lebanon — which were quite at variance with official analyses but proved to be completely true — may have asked themselves where we got our information from. I could not tell them that it came straight from a senior PLO analyst, just out of Beirut.

At the Paris airport I bought a book to read on my way back. It was called *Le Fou et Les Rois* by my friend Marek Halter, a French–Jewish painter born in Poland, who had at one time been active in trying to arrange an Arab-Israeli dialogue. Telling about his many disappointments, he described one of his meetings with me, mentioning, rather bitterly, my 'formidable optimism'.

On the plane to Tel Aviv I felt very optimistic. Things were moving. What had been impossible a few years ago, was possible now. We were on our way.

## 23

*Sartawi and I are sitting in a small restaurant on the Boulevard St. Germain.*

*After the main course, he excuses himself. 'I have to go to the bathroom. Keep an eye on my briefcase.'*

*His attaché case — the kind Israelis call James Bond cases — stands under the table.*

*After a few minutes he comes back, takes his seat and bursts out laughing. 'If I told anyone of my friends that I left a briefcase full of PLO secrets in the care of a Zionist, they wouldn't believe me', he says.*

*'If I tell anyone of my friends that a PLO terrorist put an attaché case under my table and went away, and I remained there, they'd think that I was crazy', I reply.*

*We laugh and order a dessert.*

# 24

To us, Issam al-Sartawi appeared out of nowhere, fully formed, *deus ex machina*, so to speak. He sprang fullblown from the head of Zeus, or Allah.

Only slowly, over the course of many meetings, did the real picture emerge. Like Hammami, he developed step by step, slowly and gradually, passing through all the stages from early 'terrorist' to champion of peace. But being unlike Hammami in nearly all respects, his course was different.

Of course during the dialogue, which lasted for seven years, his ideas crystallized and sharpened. We saw his stature grow and his philosophy deepen. But when we met him first he was already set on the course from which he never swerved. The more he told us about his earlier stages, the more our respect for him and our trust in him grew. Perhaps we would have trusted less in his ability to influence events if he had been right from the start a peacenik. The fact that he was an authentic fighter, a leader of Fedayeen, made him much more believable. Later, when we were asked how we could sit with a person whose hands were stained with blood, we answered that if a real 'terrorist' could come to the conclusion that peace is the only solution, it proved we were on the right track.

Issam Sartawi never became a Zionist, nor a lover of Israel. He was not one of the righteous ones of Jewish legend, one of those Gentiles who come to the rescue of the Jews in times of disaster. He was a Palestinian patriot, fighting for his own people, who had come to the conclusion that only through peace could the Palestinians achieve their basic national rights.

As such we respected him, and came to like, and in the end even to love him.

* * *

The long march of Issam Sartawi started in Acre, the beautiful town on the Mediterranean, one of the oldest in Palestine. Acre (Acco in Hebrew, Acca in Arabic) was already an old Phoenician town when the Israelites first entered the country. In the first chapter of the Book of Judges, Acre is mentioned, together with Sidon and other Phoenician towns, as a place which the Israelis were unable to conquer. It has had a chequered history, being for nearly a hundred years the capital of the Crusaders after the fall of Jerusalem, and later a base for various local chieftains who established semi-independent principalities there. Napoleon tried to take the town when he invaded Palestine from Egypt, but was beaten back by the Arab governor with the help of the British Navy. It had been the scene of a famous exploit of the Jewish underground, which freed its prisoners from the ancient fortress in which they had been incarcerated, and was conquered by the Israeli Army after nearby Haifa in the spring of 1948.

All these different phases of history have left their mark on the town, with its beautiful mosques and ancient fortifications. It was there that Issam was born on 1 January 1934. For some reason, the date of 1 January played a role several times in our relations, as we shall see.

The name Sartawi means 'the man from Sarta'. Sarta is a village near Ramallah, north of Jerusalem, which was occupied by the Israeli Army in 1967, nineteen years after Acre was conquered. Before that Issam Sartawi visited it once or twice, to look for his relatives, who still reside there. But his links to the place were tenuous.

As a child, Issam grew up in Acre and neighbouring Haifa, of which he retained vague memories. I used to fill in the holes in his picture, because I had lived for nearly a year in Haifa, in 1934, when I was a boy of ten. I remember it as a mixed town, the upper part of which was creeping up the Carmel Mountain and was Jewish, while the lower part, adjoining the bustling harbour, was Arab. The noises and smells of downtown Haifa are still vivid in my memory. My family lived at the time in a house belonging to a rich Arab cigarette manufacturer, near the border between the two parts of the city. On the last day of his life, Sartawi met Tamar Golan, a red-headed Israeli journalist, who told him that she also grew up in Haifa. 'If I had come across you at that time I would have dragged you under the nearest fruit tree', Sartawi had joked, as was his wont, 'and perhaps our history would have been different.'

Sartawi's family in Acre was not an affluent one. His richest relative was an uncle who was a heart specialist in Haifa, and it was this that made his mother decide that her son Issam would also become a doctor and heart specialist. In this respect, too, the Palestinians are becoming very much like the Jews. Having nothing much else, they see education as a means of survival and advancement. It's a Palestinian mother who wants to talk about her son, the doctor.

During the Palestinian disaster of 1948, which we call our War of Independence, the Sartawi family was caught up in the general tragedy. While Hammami's family went south from Jaffa to Egypt, and eventually reached Lebanon, Sartawi's family went to Iraq. There the boy Issam grew up, got his education and married his wife Waddad, an Iraqi. A picture of 1957, taken in Baghdad, shows Issam sitting next to his father Ali and his mother, surrounded by his four brothers and six sisters. Two of his brothers were born in Jenin, in central Palestine, when his family stayed there because of his father's work during the early 1940s, while the youngest were born in Baghdad. One of his brothers was later killed in an Israeli bombardment in Jordan, and another one died in an accident. Altogether a typical Palestinian family.

After beginning studies in medicine at Baghdad University, Issam went to the United States to finish his studies there and eventually became a heart surgeon.

His career could have continued, uninterrupted, on this track towards certain success. He was an imposing person, with a natural charm that attracted people to him. His English was excellent and rich. One of the specialists, who read his doctoral thesis, said: 'There is material here which can lead to a Nobel prize.' Many years later some Americans considered proposing him for a different kind of Nobel prize, the one awarded for peace efforts.

Nothing could have prevented the brilliant heart surgeon from becoming famous, from getting rich and from living happily ever after. He was married to a wife he loved and respected, and he could enjoy the things he loved — anything from good food to pretty girls — and write poems on the side. But then came the Six Day War.

The iron fist of the war grabbed Issam Sartawi, wrenching him from his new-found life, as it did many Jews who hastened to the aid of Israel.

The remainder of Palestine was conquered by the Israeli Army. The Arab armies were destroyed within hours. The humiliation of ignominious defeat was branded on the heart of every Arab. The Fatah organization of Yassir Arafat was the only Arab force which somehow continued to fight.

Sartawi knew that he could not go on living in exile and in indifference to the fate of his people. He left everything and returned to the Middle East.

Quite naturally he first joined Fatah. In his eulogy for Said Hammami, he described how he had first met him in November 1967, five months after the war. Young Hammami, seven years his junior, was then commanding a camp of Fatah forces near Damascus.

> We talked late into the night, and he told me about his dreams for his people and his cause. He also spoke about his fears. He said that the future frightened him because he felt that the Palestinian problem was far more complex than people seemed to realize. What struck me most in that conversation was a question which he kept repeating: are we going to live up to the challenge or are we going to come out losers, thus forfeiting the struggle of a whole generation as had happened to preceding Palestinian generations? And then he paused and uttered the strange remark: 'I hope I stay alive to see where we will be in ten years.' In a literal sense, Said's wish was fulfilled. He lived ten years and ten weeks, before an assassin's bullet found him. But I know that he did not find the answer because even Said — who understood the complex tragedy of the Palestinian experience as well as anyone of his generation — underestimated its complexity.

As a Fatah fighter, Sartawi received his baptism of fire on 21 March 1968, in the small village east of the Jordan — Karameh, where Palestinian forces first stood up to the might of the Israeli Army and gained what they considered a glorious victory. Sartawi was there, as was Hammami, as was Arafat.

Sartawi talked about this experience many times, in his public speeches as well as in private conversations, as soldiers are apt to do about their first battle, in which they stood the test of fire and overcame their physical fears. To every soldier this always appears a formidable and terrible battle.

But soon after, Sartawi seceded from Fatah and set up his own organization, the Action Organization for the Liberation of Palestine. In that phase, Sartawi was less a Palestinian nationalist than a pan-Arabist. As a Palestinian who had grown up in Iraq, whose family lived there and who was married to an Iraqi, he found it easy to obtain Iraqi support. In June 1970, he was elected, as the representative of this organization, to the Executive Committee of the PLO, which consisted of twenty-seven members, as well as to its much smaller secretariat, which consisted of six members only. This was a senior rank, corresponding to that of a minister belonging to the inner circle of the Cabinet.

Ten years later he told me, with some bitterness: 'When I was a man of war, I advanced to the rank of cabinet minister. When I became a man of peace, my status diminished, and now I'm barely a member of the National Council. We people of peace are really stupid.' I answered with a crack: 'We are peace*fool*.'

Sartawi's organization attacked Israeli Army patrols along the Jordan River, and executed at least one major terrorist attack: his men attacked a busload of El Al passengers in Munich airport in January 1970. In this attack, a much-beloved Israeli actress, Hannah Maron, was wounded. Her leg had to be amputated.

During one of our conversations, I told Sartawi how I had gone to Munich, on the eve of Passover 1970, to visit Hannah Maron in the hospital and bring her Israeli wine and *matzoh*, the unleavened bread Jews eat on Passover. Hannah had been a star in German films as a child, and just before the attack, had delighted Israeli audiences with her singing and dancing as Dolly in the famous musical. After losing her leg, she had moved us by learning to play while using an artificial leg, even daring here and there some dance steps. Sartawi, who by that time had come to realize how useless violence can be, said that he hoped to meet Hannah Maron and express his regrets. He asked me to tell her that, and, when I did, she accepted this with mixed feelings. But during the Lebanon War she appeared at rallies of the Peace Now movement to speak out against war and violence. The meeting I had promised to set up someday in the future never took place.

* * *

Sartawi's special character became apparent after William Rogers, President Nixon's secretary of state, published his peace plan at the end of 1969. This plan proposed a peace settlement between Israel and the Arabs, in return for the withdrawal from all the territories occupied in 1967, with 'insubstantial' alterations of the border.

In the Knesset there was only one member who came out for accepting the Rogers Plan: me. On the Palestinian side, there was only one body which advocated the same: Sartawi's new organization. He was appraising reality.

Things came to a head when the Egyptian president, Gamal Abd-al-Nasser, on the eve of his sudden death, accepted the August 1970 Rogers Initiative, which put an end to the long War of Attrition along the Suez Canel. Golda Meir, who had violently rebuffed the Rogers Peace Plan, accepted the Rogers Initiative. I voted for her in the Knesset, and

Menachem Begin seceded from the National Unity Cabinet in protest against her decision. On the other side, Gamal Abd-al-Nasser was violently attacked by most Palestinian leaders, while Sartawi's organization supported him openly.

Against this background there erupted a bloody clash between Sartawi's organization, by now pro-Egyptian, and the Popular Front of Georges Habash, which was pro-Syrian. At our first meeting, Sartawi told me, rather gleefully, how he had managed this affair. Upon receiving information that the Habash forces were about to attack his headquarters, he decided to lure them into a trap. Leaving only a small nucleus of his fighters in the headquarters, he used the others to throw a wide ring around the building. When the Habash forces attacked the building, they were surrounded and attacked from the rear. Nearly a hundred of the Habash people were killed in the crossfire.

Soon after came Black September. Reacting to provocations from extreme Palestinian organizations, the Jordanian Army attacked all the Palestinian forces. A great number of Palestinian refugees were massacred. The lesson Sartawi drew from this disaster was the need for unity among the Palestinian forces. He merged his small force with Fatah and rejoined the leadership of that organization. From there on until his death, he was a loyal Fatah member.

Yassir Arafat recognized his special qualities and sent him on various missions, not for the PLO, but for Fatah, the dominant force in the Palestinian National Movement. In the beginning Sartawi concentrated his efforts mainly on African affairs. He was instrumental in the successful campaign to induce all Black African nations to cut off their official relations with Israel after the Yom Kippur War of 1973.

* * *

It was soon after Black September, 1970, that Sartawi started on the road that was to lead him, eventually, to an unexpected destination. It all started quite innocuously. The Palestinian movement was at a stage of repudiating the guardianship of the Arab regimes, reemphasizing its authentic Palestinian character. The independence of Palestinian 'decision-making' became ever more important, and with this arose many questions about the past. One of them was a question which had troubled the minds of Palestinians for many years: Why did the Arab governments allow their Jews to come to Israel, even pushing them on their way to the Jewish state, where they swelled the ranks of Israeli citizens and soldiers striving to enlarge the Zionist Entity at the expense of the Palestinians. Indeed, while paying lip service to the Liberation of Palestine, most Arab governments had done everything possible to send their Jews there and enriched themselves in the process with the property left behind.

These questions were coupled with the idea that if these treacherous actions could be reversed, the Jews driven out of Arab lands would return to them, which would weaken the Zionist state. At the time when most Palestinians still hoped for the disintegration of Israel, this seemed a logical course to follow. The Fatah leadership entrusted Sartawi and Mahmoud

Abbas ('Abu Maazen') with the task of exploring these possibilities.

Having grown up in Iraq, Sartawi naturally became most interested in the exodus of Iraqi Jews. Very soon he became absorbed with this mysterious chapter.

First of all, he tried to find out what actually happened during the great Baghdad pogrom, which was a turning point in the history of Iraqi Jewry. In 1941, when German fortunes were at their peak, an Iraqi nationalist, Rashid Ali-al-Kilani, had engineered a coup in Iraq, kicking out the pro-British regent and his ward, the boy king who was a cousin of King Hussein of Jordan. In a swift reaction, the British Army based in Palestine invaded Iraq and retook Baghdad, helped by Jordanian units and by some members of the Jewish underground in Palestine. While the British were approaching Baghdad, a terrible pogrom took place in the city. Jews were killed, women raped, houses burned, property destroyed in a scene more reminiscent of Czarist Russia (where the word pogrom was coined) than of the Arab world. It was generally assumed that this was a last act of revenge by the departing pro-Axis nationalists, especially as the deposed Mufti of Jerusalem, Hadj Amin — who was considered a fanatical Jew-hater — was in Baghdad as a guest of the Kilani government at the time.

However, when Sartawi studied this horrible episode, a completely different picture started to emerge. As a representative of the Fatah movement, he had free access to official Iraqi files. It soon became apparent to him that the nationalists, including the Mufti, had already left Baghdad when the massacre occurred. It was a time of anarchy, a kind of interregnum. But the glaring fact was that the British Army had been at the time free to enter Baghdad, which was empty of enemy forces, and could easily have stopped the pogrom. Yet they refrained from doing so; deliberately, as Sartawi believed.

His theory was that the British and their local allies had encouraged the pogrom in order to blunt the general feeling that the king and his men were returning to Baghdad as British stooges, riding on British tanks. The pogrom provided an outlet for hatreds and frustrations and allowed the new regime to exploit the fanaticism of the people.

The more his research progressed, the thicker became the fog. All the relevant British files were kept in deepest secrecy. Sartawi waited impatiently for the publication of official British documents, after the time limit for secrecy had elapsed. He went to study the files himself, enlisting the help of his growing number of influential British friends as well as that of Said Hammami. But to no avail. It appeared that the relevant papers had been singled out for very exceptional treatment. The British authorities applied to them a seldom-used paragraph which allows them to prolong the ban on publication beyond the year 2000, if national security interests are at stake. They remained adamant, even after Sartawi convinced one of his friends to raise questions about this in Parliament. All this looked to Sartawi like confirmation of his suspicions.

But another episode concerning the fate of Iraqi Jews was even more relevant to his objectives.

In 1950, when Sartawi was a 16-year old youngster living in Baghdad, the

Iraqi government suddenly announced that any Jew who wanted to leave Iraq was free to do so upon relinquishing his citizenship and property. The obvious objective was to allow these Jews to go to the new Jewish state in Palestine, and one could assume that some kind of agreement had been arrived at between the Hashemite regime in Iraq and the Ben-Gurion government in Israel. One could also assume that not all the Jewish property left behind would be duly expropriated by the Iraqi government, but that some of it would find its way into the pockets of the corrupt Iraqi leaders.

The decree set a time limit for the exodus of the Jews. But, curiously enough, when the final date approached, only a few families had applied for exit permits. Perhaps the Jews felt safe in Iraq, perhaps they were loath to give up their property, perhaps they did not trust the government decree.

Then something mysterious happened. Bombs started to explode in synagogues and other places frequented by Jews. A panic ensued, and the ranks of those wishing to go were swelled overnight. In the end, very few Jews remained. The great Jewish community in Mesopotamia, which had lived there for 2,500 years since the first exile, practically ceased to exist. Some Jews saved some of their property by smuggling it out in gold and foreign banknotes with the help of bribed officials. But many more arrived in Israel destitute, to be housed in tents, doing hard and sometimes useless manual work, living in abject poverty. Thus began the sorry story of the Oriental Jewish refugees, which troubles Israel today more than ever.

One of these disgruntled immigrants came to me sixteen years later and told me a startling story: that those bombs had been planted by Jews, indeed by a Jewish underground cell commanded by secret agents sent from Israel. The Iraqi authorities had claimed this all the time. After a trial, two Iraqi Jews had been convicted and hanged. But the Israeli government had denounced this as a blood libel and another example of Arab barbarism.

After the disclosure of the Lavon affair — the planting of bombs in US and British localities in Egypt by a Jewish underground cell, commanded by Israeli army intelligence, allegedly on orders of Defence Minister Pinhas Lavon — the Baghdad affair became more plausible. I published a disclosure of the Baghdad affair in my magazine on 20 April 1966, stating bluntly that the bombings were indeed the work of Israeli agents, sent by the Ben-Gurion government in the spirit of what was then called 'cruel Zionism' — namely, the idea that one had to use cruel means to dislodge Jews from the fleshpots of exile and push them towards the Promised Land.

Now, a few years later, Issam Sartawi made his own study of these events. Going through secret files of the Iraqi political police and the proceedings of the trial of the two Iraqi Jews, he came across revealing facts. Two Israeli agents had been apprehended in a Baghdad department store immediately after the bombings, after they were recognized by a Palestinian refugee from Acre who worked there. By the sheerest of accidents he had once served coffee to one of the two who had been, at the time, a military governor in Galilee. The two men were arrested, but one of them, Mordechai Ben-Porat, who later became a Cabinet minister in the Likud government — was mysteriously released a few days later while all the members of the cell were rounded up. The second Israeli agent was condemned to death, but his sentence was commuted to life imprisonment, and he was released secretly after the Iraqi Revolution. Before being spirited off to Baghdad airport, he was brought for a personal meeting with Abd-al-Kareem Kasim, the Sole Leader. The prison officer who brought him to the presidential palace, and who was then brusquely ordered to make himself scarce, told the story to Sartawi.

Why was Ben-Porat released immediately? Why was the other agent released by Kasim? Why did the Iraqi government cooperate with the Israeli authorities, while publicly propounding the most extreme anti-Israeli line and declaring themselves the standard-bearers of the struggle for Palestinian liberation? There could be only one explanation: collusion between the Iraqi and Israeli governments, the former to get rid of its Jews and get hold of their property, the latter to save the Jews, whether they wanted it or not.

Sartawi had compiled a big dossier on this affair. We talked about it many times. How to publish it? When? For Israel, this was dynamite, as it concerned a very prominent Israeli politician, one of the lieutenants of Moshe Dayan, a cabinet minister. I urged him to let me publish the material in *Haolam Hazeh*, or, even better, to let me publish a signed report by him. He hesitated, postponed a decision, waiting for the right moment. The last time I saw him, he was ready to publish it. Somebody in Israel must have heaved a very big sigh of relief when he heard that Issam Sartawi had been killed.

* * *

Looking into this affair for the first time, Sartawi became interested in the whole question of the Jewish exodus from the Arab countries after the 1948 War. At the time, Palestinian consciousness was starting its Long March. The idea that Jews and Arabs should live together in a common state in Palestine was gaining ground. On the Palestinian side, among the people who had never had a close look at Israel, curiosity was growing. Who were the Jews, the Israelis, the Zionists, who were supposed one day to become their co-citizens in the ideal state? Sartawi and Abu Maazen approached Arafat and told him that no one was going to believe that Jews and Arabs could live peacefully together in the future democratic secular state of Palestine if they could not live peacefully together anywhere else under an Arab government. Therefore, it was logical for the Fatah movement to use its growing influence to convince the Arab regimes to change their attitudes towards the Jews — grant full equality to those left behind and invite back those willing to return. At the time, many Palestinians believed their own propaganda, which said that Oriental Israelis were really only Arabs professing the Jewish faith who had been lured by Ashkenazi Zionism to leave their homelands and go to the Zionist state, there to be exploited and oppressed. Many Palestinians hoped that once these Arab Jews or Jewish Arabs became disillusioned, they would gladly return to the Arab countries if only the Arab governments would invite them back.

Arafat was convinced by these arguments. At least, he set up a special task force to deal with this matter, under the leadership of Abu Maazen and

Sartawi. They were charged with changing the attitudes of the Arab governments towards the Jews and facilitating the return of the Jews from Israel to the Arab countries.

Sartawi threw himself into the job, as he did with all jobs entrusted to him. Between 1972 and 1976, he worked tirelessly. Together with Abu Maazen he met with the chief rabbi of Damascus, who recounted to them the woes that had befallen his dwindling community. The authorities were harassing the Jews, discriminatory laws and regulations dogged their every step, there were no funds for the upkeep of synagogues and schools. At the moment, he told them, he urgently needed fifty thousand pounds sterling. Sartawi saw in this an opportunity to show that Fatah was serious. He had the sum remitted to the rabbi from Fatah funds, without publishing the fact.

In order to ameliorate the conditions of the Jews, a joint Syrian-Palestinian committee was set up. The Syrians promised to change the laws, in order to allow the Jews who had left to come back. They never did.

The most famous episode was the story of the four hundred virgins. The rabbi of Damascus had complained to Sartawi and Abu Maazen that there were about 400 Jewish girls in Syria, who had no chance at all of finding husbands in the shrunken community. Sartawi found a solution on the spur of the moment: he would find 400 young Fatah fighters, who would marry the girls.

After going to bed that night, he had second thoughts. It was all wrong. His altruistic motives would be misconstrued, people would say he was destroying the Jewish faith, that the girls were raped by the Palestinians. So, instead, he and Abu Maazen went to see Hafez al-Assad with a different request. The Syrian decided to allow any Jew who wanted to marry one of the girls to come to Syria, or, alternately, to allow any girl seeking a husband abroad to leave. In the end, all 400 left for the West. The outcome was rather disappointing: most of the girls did not find husbands and eventually returned to Syria, much to the disgust of the Israeli government, which was raising hell to alert world public opinion to the terrible plight of the Jews in Syria. While this episode was quite famous at the time, no one knew the part played in it by the Palestinians. It provided Sartawi with material for many amusing stories, which he told me later on.

But the most important job was to convince the Arab regimes to officially cancel all existing anti-Jewish laws, to guarantee full equality to the Jews, and to invite the Jewish emigrés to return. It was much more difficult than Sartawi had anticipated.

In the end, only Libya complied fully. The Iraqis said they were ready to do so, but before changing the laws officially, they wanted to give the idea a trial run. They would invite the Jews back and see what happened. And indeed, European papers started to publish official advertisements from the Iraqi government, inviting Iraqi Jews to come back and enjoy the bliss of full equality in their homeland.

The easiest part of the job was in Morocco. Sartawi and Abu Maazen went to see King Hassan, starting a friendship which was to bear fruit, as will be told in a later chapter. When they asked the king to change the laws of Morocco and extend full equality to the Jews, he smiled. There was no need for that, no discriminatory laws existed in Morocco, the Jewish community was happy and satisfied.

Sartawi was insistent. The facts were not known, some symbolic gesture was called for to dramatize the king's willingness to welcome back the Jewish emigrants. King Hassan acceded to this request and sent his prime minister to Amman, where he made a dramatic announcement saying that any Jew in Israel, who wanted to return to Morocco, would be most welcome.

There was one immediate practical result of Sartawi's efforts. He had heard in Paris that about 10,000 Moroccan Jews, who had emigrated to Israel, had drifted to Paris and were living there as stateless aliens. (This was, of course, a mistake. Every Jew entering Israel automatically receives Israeli citizenship, and the Moroccan Jews who emigrated from Israel to Paris had Israeli passports.) Sartawi asked the king to grant them passports of the Sherifian Kingdom of the Maghreb. None of these Jews, who used these passports to visit their original homeland, could have known to whom they owed this privilege.

In the course of his efforts in Morocco, Sartawi did something that provided, accidentally, written proof that his account of his efforts was true. One of the Moroccan ministers had suggested that Sartawi himself meet the leaders of the Jewish community in Morocco. He accepted the idea with enthusiasm. The meeting took place in the palatial home of one of the king's advisors, Ahmed Ben Souda, in Rabat — where I was to spend some happy hours four years later.

Sartawi realized that the Jews were fearful and nervous. They had been commanded by the king to meet a representative of the dreaded PLO, the mortal enemy of Israel. They obeyed the king's request, but there was no doubt that they did so only under duress.

Sartawi used the meeting to pour out his feelings towards the Jews. He told them about his efforts, on behalf of the PLO, to ameliorate the situation of the Jews in the Arab countries. He talked about the historical relationship between the Jews and the Arabs. A short, dark chapter should not obliterate the memory of a long and glorious common past, he said. He explained his motives, adding that this meeting, as all his other efforts, would not be used for propaganda purposes. He also told them the story about his Damascus talks and the episode of the 400 virgins. A few weeks later, on 9 June 1976, a news item appeared in the Israeli daily *Haaretz*. The headline said: 'PLO Representatives Met in Morocco with Jewish Leaders and Tried to Enlist their Services in a Propaganda Effort to Convince Jews to Leave Israel. The Representatives of the Jewish Community in Morocco Have Answered: We Do Not Believe that Many Jews will Return to the Arab Countries.'

The news item said that the leaders of the Jewish community in Morocco met with PLO representatives on 24 March in the house and under the auspices of the chief of King Hassan's personal staff. In this meeting the PLO representatives officially announced the creation of a special fund designed to encourage Jews from Arab countries, and especially from North Africa, 'to return to their real homeland'.

The story, which was attributed to 'competent Israeli sources' (meaning the intelligence services), continued:

> The chief of the king's personal staff had established close relations with several notables of the Jewish community in Morocco when he sent them to the United States to act as good-will messengers for Morocco during the recent Sahara crisis. Upon their return he asked them to meet PLO representatives for an informal talk. The Jews refused and emphasized that while they are loyal to King Hassan, they have strong emotional ties with the state of Israel and do not want to be torn between the two. They also said that the job of the Jewish community organizations in Morocco is not political, but social and religious, and that therefore there is no point in meeting PLO representatives. However, sometime later, the chief of the king's staff told them that a special emissary from PLO headquarters in Beirut had arrived and was staying at his home. He invited two of the Jewish notables to come and visit him and the emissary. The Jews could not refuse, both because of the difficulty in refusing the request of a high-ranking personality and because of the sacred custom of hospitality. The meeting therefore took place. Apart from the special emissary, a member of the permanent mission of Fatah in Morocco took part as well as the host, who acted as mediator. [The story went on to say:] The meeting, which lasted for several hours, took place in a tense atmosphere. The PLO representatives said that for them Israel was an established fact, and their aim is to live in peace with the Jews. They said that they knew that some Arab countries, and especially Iraq and Syria, have treated the Jews unjustly, and that the aim of the PLO is to make up somewhat for this injustice by creating a fund which would help those Jews who have not been absorbed in Israel to return to the Arab countries.
>
> The PLO representatives added that they mean by this not only the return of the Jews living in Israel, but also those who have emigrated to the United States and Canada. They said that they hope that these Jews, upon returning to their old homes, would create a bridge of understanding between the two peoples which are caught up in an endless war.
>
> The Jewish notables answered that they do not believe that many Jews would return to Arab countries, because they have struck deep roots in the state of Israel and consider it their homeland. Anyhow, they added, if they return to Morocco, the Jewish institutions in this country, who have a long tradition of mutual help, will assist them in settling down, and therefore no PLO assistance is necessary.
>
> The Jewish notables got the impression that the aim of the PLO emissaries is to establish a small colony of a few dozen Jewish families, living in well-to-do conditions, so that they can use them as a showcase when appealing to Western opinion. The objective is to prove that Jews and Arabs can live together side by side, and that only Zionism is the root of all evil. This step, the Jewish notables said, is another phase in the sophisticated psychological warfare conducted by the PLO designed to change their image as murderers of women and children and to present them as a tolerant, enlightened and peaceful movement.

The newspaper added that the mysterious source, which had transmitted the story, had also reported to the prime minister, the foreign minister and the chairman of the Jewish Agency, but that this report had been kept secret.

Years later, when our dialogue with Sartawi had become known, the mysterious sources surfaced again. The state-run Israeli Radio suddenly broadcast a story saying that Sartawi belonged to a special task force set up by Arafat for the conduct of psychological warfare against Israel, and that we had become unwitting dupes in a campaign whose real purpose was to convince Jews to leave Israel.

This was of course nonsense. By the time our dialogue started, Sartawi had progressed far beyond this stage. The Morocco meeting was, perhaps, a milestone in his own Long March. The Jews did indeed convince him that all the efforts to get the Oriental Jews to leave Israel were futile.

Perhaps this was only the last straw. No Jews had come back to Libya and Iraq, in spite of the invitations. Neither Colonel Gadafy nor the blood-stained Iraqi dictators were living advertisements for the paradise awaiting the Jews in their former homelands.

As Sartawi later told me himself: 'I realized how pointless any effort is to grant full rights to the Jews in countries whose own citizens enjoy no such thing.' It was a bitter remark, reflecting the full measure of contempt the Palestinian had for the repressive Arab dictatorships, which had betrayed the Palestinian cause so often.

* * *

The most interesting sentence in the newspaper report about the Moroccan meeting was the one in which Sartawi had told the Jewish notables that for the PLO, Israel was now an established fact. This was certainly a turning point in Sartawi's own views, as well as in the development of PLO ideas. It showed that by now the PLO had advanced to the point of recognizing the fact of Israel's existence. This coincided with the Hammami articles, the beginning of my own dialogue with Hammami and the PLO resolution calling for the establishment of a Palestinian National Authority in a part of Palestine, i.e., the implied willingness to live side by side with Israel.

By the way, it also proves that in the middle of 1976, Israeli intelligence, and therefore the prime minister, were well aware that a high-ranking PLO functionary called Issam Sartawi was expressing such views in secret conversations. Obviously the Jewish participants in the meeting had reported to Israeli bodies.

Sartawi was a totally logical person, a man able to face facts, analyse them coldly and draw clear conclusions — a quality rare among politicians of any people.

After realizing that Israel was there to stay, that it was foolish to expect Israelis to give up their state, not to mention expecting them to return to where they came from, he concluded that the only solution to the problem was the creation of a Palestinian state alongside Israel. It was the same conclusion arrived at by Hammami a short time earlier by a different route.

Others reached the same conclusion, each in his own way. Many years later, when I met one of the most high-ranking leaders of the PLO in the presence of Sartawi, he said, only half-jokingly: 'You think that he (Sartawi) is moderate? I remember a time when I argued with him and told him that we will have to recognize Israel, and he violently objected!' This leader enjoys, in Israel, the reputation of an incorrigible hardliner.

I came to trust Sartawi implicitly, because I was aware of the long way he had come, evolving from a pan-Arab Nasserite to an advocate of peace with Israel. It is said that the human foetus passes all the stages which life forms have gone through, from primitive organisms to the human being. Something like this had happened to Sartawi.

Once he reached this point, Sartawi was uncomprisingly logical. A Palestinian state alongside Israel could only be set up with Israeli agreement. To obtain this, Israeli public opinion had to be changed. A dialogue with Israelis was necessary — not with Israeli fringe elements, such as communists and other anti-Zionists, but with people inside the Israeli mainstream, Israeli patriots and even Zionists, who were ready for coexistence between Israel and the Palestinian state.

He knew that such a dialogue had already begun between Hammami and myself. Hammami was reporting to Arafat through Abu Maazen, who gave copies of his reports to Sartawi. As he told me later, all Hammami's reports and my letters to him were in his files.

Soon Sartawi decided to take the dialogue out of Hammami's hands and to take charge of them himself. This happened just after he himself had come to the conclusion that this dialogue was a critical part of the Palestinian struggle.

Several aspects of Hammami's work upset Sartawi. Perhaps the basic reason was a fundamental incompatibility of the characters of these two remarkable men, who had so much in common, but who were also so different. Hammami, the pioneer, was an intellectual, a dreamer, a man of intuition. Sartawi was analytical, logical. Hammami was more of an artist, a man of emotion. Sartawi was a commander, a fighter, a man used to subduing his emotions.

The test was, curiously enough, the attitude towards a quite unimportant Israeli: Uri Davis. When Sartawi heard that Hammami was continuing his contacts with Davis, after the Israeli Council for Israeli-Palestinian Peace was created, he was outraged. Davis advocated the dismantling of the State of Israel, much as did die-hard Arab rejectionists. He was notorious in Israel as an anti-Zionist. Any contact with him could only destroy the very basis of the dialogue with us. We were valuable because we were accepted as Israeli patriots even by our detractors. The Council was officially defined as a Zionist body. It was an important instrument for convincing Israeli mainstream public opinion, which is of course Zionist, that peace with the Palestinians is possible and desirable for the future of Israel. Contacts with people like Davis were bound to destroy the credibility of our contacts and their very purpose.

I had made the same point with Hammami a few weeks earlier. He did not see it this way. He felt that he was bound by decency and loyalty not to forsake those with whom he had previous contacts, who had expressed their sympathy and solidarity with the Palestinian cause.

For Sartawi this was sentimental rubbish. He had a stormy session with Hammami, and when the London representative remained unconvinced, Sartawi took the whole matter out of his hands. He personally took charge of the contacts with us.

For more than a year, while our contacts with Sartawi were in full swing, Hammami was on the sidelines. Sartawi had some regrets about this. During the London seminar in October 1977, he went out of his way to laud Hammami as a great pioneer of the Israeli-Palestinian dialogue. Two weeks before Hammami's assassination, Sartawi met with him in London and settled his differences with him. They decided to meet again in the middle of January 1978, to talk things over and to establish a framework for working together. But on 4 January Hammami was killed.

On 13 February, a commemorative meeting in honour of Said Hammami was held in London. Sartawi and I were supposed to be the main speakers. I received a cordial invitation from two British members of Parliament, Andrew Faulds and Dennis Walters, on behalf of the British section of the Parliamentary Association for Euro-Arab Cooperation. A few days later, I received an excited phone call from London. Would I please send a cable that I was sick and could not attend? As I found out later, the Arab ambassadors in London, upon hearing that an Israeli was invited, had threatened to boycott the meeting, and the organizers thought that their presence was essential. I complied and cabled that I was too sick to attend, and received a grateful cable in return. Thus the very ideas for which Hammami had given his life were betrayed on the morrow.

In his eulogy of Said Hammami, a remarkable document, Issam Sartawi remembered his colleague in words that were later to apply to him:

> Said Hammami finally had to pay for his vision, courage and boundless love for his people, with his life. Said Hammami loved all Palestinians, including those who may have killed him. But above all, he had the greatest compassion and dedication to the Palestinians in the occupied territories. To our people under occupation who feel the loss of Said most, I wish to address a message from this podium: Said died for Palestine but, above all, he died for you and we shall continue to care about you as he did. And one day, our future generations will honour Said as a man who loved his country and his people with a passionate sincerity that had no use for rhetoric.

## 25

*'They were attacking me during one of the meetings back home,' Issam says. 'Some of them accused me of being friendly with the Jews. I told them: "Can you imagine our culture without the Jews? Can you imagine our heritage without Samual?"'*

*Samual is a legendary figure in Arab history. He was a Jew and the leader of a Bedouin tribe in Arabia, before the advent of Islam. One day another Bedouin chief, fleeing his enemies, had entrusted to him a valuable suit of armour. Soon after, his enemy arrived in pursuit. He grabbed the son of Samual, who was tending the herds in the field, and threatened to kill him if Samual did not give him the suit of armour.*

*'Better you kill my son than I break my word!' Samual said, and the enemy killed the son.*

*Since then, 'more loyal than Samual' is the highest accolade one Arab can give another.*

*'That shut up the bastards!' Issam gloats.*

# 26

After our October 1976 meeting in Rambouillet, Sartawi and Jiryes set out for America. Our advice to postpone the trip proved only too well-founded. The timing could not have been worse. At the best of times, PLO efforts to make friends and influence people in the United States border on the impossible. There are six million Jews in America, and their political and economic influence is disproportionate to their numbers, especially in the field of mass communications. They have a single-minded devotion to Israel — to whatever Israel does and whoever governs Israel. There are only very few Americans of Arab descent, and their influence is hardly felt.

These are well-known facts of life, even if a blunt statement of them is often construed as anti-Semitic propaganda. But very few people realize how far the ramifications of these realities extend. Even Sartawi, who had spent years in America as a student and an up-and-coming surgeon, was quite innocent when he went back to America this time. It was a quick course in on-the-job training.

The United States was in the grip of election fever. The Gerry Ford administration was wobbling, 'Jimmy Who?' Carter was knocking at the gates of Washington. The real boss for the time being was Dr. Henry Kissinger.

Kissinger has always been a paradox for me. I was profoundly impressed by his book about European politics in the first half of the last century. One of his main theses was that peace agreements are valueless if a major party to the conflict is left out and sees in the agreement a threat to its basic interests. If ever this rule were true — as it surely is — this is the case with the Palestinians in the Middle East conflict. It is also true for the Soviet Union. Yet once he became the political genius of the Nixon and Ford administrations. Kissinger behaved as if he had never read his own book — the classic example of power blinding the intellectual. He tried to make peace of some kind without the Palestinians, treating the rulers of the various Arab countries as so many Metternichs and Castlereaghs, trying to push the Soviets out of the Middle East altogether. I strongly suspected him of obstructing any real move towards peace, favouring the salami approach of little pieces of peace, so as to keep everybody screaming for American support and dependent on American protection. This was the famous step-by-step approach.

For Sartawi, in the beginning, everything looked quite simple. He was pro-American, and everybody knew that. He came to offer the Americans an historic deal: the PLO would turn away from the Soviets towards the

West; America would help them establish a Palestinian state; that state, led by the moderate PLO and allied with Saudi Arabia and Egypt, would guarantee stability in the Middle East. The PLO would, of course, recognize Israel on a mutual basis as a part of this deal.

It was all so sensible and logical that Sartawi could not imagine any right-thinking American rejecting such a proposition. The alternative should have been too terrible for Americans to consider: destabilization of the Middle East, revolution and war.

But soon enough Sartawi realized that he was up against a brick wall. Second-rate officials listened to his message, stony-faced. The media boycotted him, making it impossible for him to address the American public. Jewish leaders drew back in horror when he tried to approach them. The Jewish lobby screamed at the idea of allowing the PLO to establish an office in Washington — the main purpose of the visit.

Suddenly, it appeared that something was wrong with the passports of both Sartawi and Jiryes. Some minor details were false. The places of birth were inaccurate.

Sartawi was travelling, as always, on a Tunisian diplomatic passport. The authorities in every country he visited knew who he was — a high official of the PLO, a personal representative of Yassir Arafat, who had been provided with a diplomatic passport by a friendly Tunisian government to facilitate his work. The US authorities were well aware of this before he came to the States.

But once these facts were leaked to the press by interested parties, a veritable witches' sabbath started. The State Department, which had at least tacitly welcomed his visit and sent its officers to talk with him, asked him discreetly to leave. He was becoming an embarrassment. Sartawi bluntly refused. The situation became more than embarrassing, because the United States government had no way of deporting an official carrying the diplomatic passport of a friendly nation. Kissinger had to intervene personally.

What ensued was a diplomatic tug-of-war behind the scenes, a story so incredible that I did not believe it at first. I would hesitate to tell it if I were not certain of the facts.

American authorities approached the Tunisian government, asking it for friendship's sake to withdraw Sartawi. The Tunisians tried to comply, requesting Sartawi to be so kind as to remove himself from the United States. Sartawi, by now angry and upset, told the Tunisians that this would cause a major crisis between Tunis and the Palestinian Liberation Organization, a formidable factor in inter-Arab relations. The Tunisians hesitated. Kissinger did not. He threatened to cut off food shipments to Tunisia.

By now highly alarmed, the Tunisians asked Sartawi if he was ready to assume responsibility for starving Tunisian children. This was an argument even Sartawi could not ignore. He left.

During the weeks of his stay, he had done everything possible to break the barrier erected between him and the Jewish community. When everything else failed, he took the Yellow Pages and chose a Jewish synagogue at random. He called the office, introduced himself as a PLO representative and asked to be allowed to visit the synagogue and address the congregation. There was a stunned silence, and then, after some prevarication, he was invited to come and have a private talk with some congregation leaders.

It was the first time he saw a Jewish synagogue, and he was deeply impressed. He talked about it many times, even in public speeches. Expecting a simple house of prayer, in the style of a Muslim mosque, he was astonished to find a centre of many activities, social, sports, educational programmes. The meeting itself started in a correct but frosty atmosphere, but his charm melted the ice quickly. A lively discussion ensued, and Sartawi was well satisfied. His arguments were heard and he had the feeling that he had succeeded in changing the stereotyped image held by the Jews of the PLO as a bunch of murderers and terrorists. But this was a freak event, and his efforts were cut short by his departure.

The whole episode left a bitter taste in his mouth, a bitterness which was to grow over the following years.

The mission was a total failure. In the following weeks the PLO still considered setting up a PLO office in Washington. Hammami, who had been so successful in London, was considered for the post, but this was blocked by Sartawi, who now considered Hammami too 'erratic'.

In the end the question became academic, as no PLO office could be set up in the federal capital. Instead, a PLO mission was established in New York, when the PLO succeeded in obtaining observer status in the UN.

One can only wonder what would have happened had Sartawi been successful in the US. His own stature within the PLO would have grown considerably, the moderate elements in the PLO would have been strengthened, and the whole course of events during the following years might have been different. One must assume that Dr. Kissinger was aware of this and was determined to prevent such a development.

Why? We shall take up this question in the course of this narrative. The short-term objective may have been to prevent a clash with the Jewish lobby on the eve of elections in the States. The Rabin government, then in power in Israel, saw in the evolving moderation of the PLO a danger to its policy of preventing the establishment of a Palestinian state in the West Bank and the Gaza Strip, as Rabin had told me before, and would repeat when our council had a special meeting with him. Kissinger had officially promised the Israeli government a year earlier, during the negotiations for the interim agreement between Israel and Egypt, that the United States would not deal with the PLO in any way unless two conditions were first met: acceptance by the PLO of Resolutions 242 and 338 (which ignored the Palestinians altogether) and recognition by the PLO of Israel's right to exist. Kissinger knew, of course, as well as the Israeli government, that the PLO was unable to meet these conditions, in this form, when nothing at all was promised them in return except a dialogue between the PLO and some minor US officials.

I believe that Kissinger's long-term objective was to prevent a comprehensive peace between Israel and the Arab world, which would have made both sides far less dependent on the US.

* * *

While all this was going on, another blow fell on Sartawi.

One of the main conditions of our meetings with the PLO representatives was total secrecy. We agreed with Sartawi, as I had agreed with Hammami before, that we were allowed to report to whoever in Israel we saw fit for furthering the aims of the dialogue, including the prime minister. This indeed was one of the aims of the contact — to try to influence Israeli policy. But Israel has a free press, such as does not exist in any Arab country (except, perhaps, Lebanon at that time). The Palestinian side had not quite understood how difficult it is to keep anything secret in Israel, where even secret cabinet meetings are published *in extenso* within hours.

In September 1976, after the first meeting with Sartawi, in which I had not taken part, a story about it appeared in the evening paper *Yedioth Aharonot*. Many of the details given were false. For example, it was said that the Palestinian side was represented by Said Hammami, who was not involved at all. Therefore, this spate of stories, starting on 22 September with a report by Shlomo Nakdimon, a right-wing journalist who later became Prime Minister Begin's adviser for press affairs, did not irritate Sartawi too much. As I have told already, during the second meeting, in October, in which Meir Pail and I participated together with Matti Peled and Yaacov Arnon, the question of publication had come up and led to a heated debate. Upon the insistence of Sartawi, we promised again, and this time in the most resolute way, to prevent any publication. We were well aware by now that publishing the meetings would not only undermine the progress of our dialogue and the personal trust between the two sides, but endanger Sartawi personally. The PLO leadership was not yet ready for a public dialogue, and radicals might react violently.

It was, therefore, with consternation that we read in *Yedioth Aharonot* on 20 October, another report by Nakdimon saying that ten days before, another meeting had taken place. This time full details were given, all four Israeli participants were mentioned by name, and even some of the subjects, such as the seizure of the Lebanese boat by the Israeli Navy, were reported. Only the names of the Palestinian participants were withheld.

This was a disaster. We realized that it would be considered by Sartawi and the PLO leaders involved as a breach of confidence of the first magnitude, a stab in the back. It could spell the end of our efforts, for which we had worked so patiently.

Who had leaked the story? Several conjectures were put forth. Some supposed it was a deliberate leak by Shimon Peres, the defence minister, in order to put the blame, quite erroneously, on Itzhak Rabin, the prime minister, who knew of the contacts, though he did not approve of them. Others thought the leak came from the Mossad, in order to prevent continued contacts. The Mossad does not belong to the Ministry of Defence, but rather to the Prime Minister's Office, as does the Shin Bet, but one could assume that some Mossad chiefs were friendly with Peres.

I did not believe these speculations for a moment. I did believe, and this was confirmed by Nakdimon in a private conversation with me, that the leak came from inside our own organization. The practical conclusion we drew was to limit our future reports to general information, and not to disclose secret facts even to our colleagues. This measure proved successful, and over the years no leak ever occurred again. The drawback was that all really secret meetings were restricted to a very small group of Israeli participants, consisting in practice of Matti Peled, Yaacov Arnon, and myself.

In the meantime we had to mend fences and repair the damage done. At the end of December I was sent to Paris to talk, in the absence of Sartawi, with his closest assistant, a man we knew as Abu Faisal, who had taken part in all the meetings and whose judgment we came to trust and appreciate.

The meeting took place at the home of one of the rich members of the Curiel group. I opened it by saying: 'I come to you with a black conscience. The leaks are inexcusable. I will not even try to explain them away.'

This broke the ice. The atmosphere became cordial, as it had been in former meetings, and we sat down to consider how to minimize the damage. The leak had damaged Sartawi's prestige within the PLO leadership, and indirectly our own standing. We had to reestablish confidence.

The Palestinian was quite certain that the culprit was Meir Pail, who had boasted of the contacts. I had brought with me all press cuttings from the Israeli press about the disclosures, and Abu Faisal saw in them indications that Pail was indeed the man. He also told me that Pail's ill-conceived joke at the last meeting still rankled, and demanded that Pail be excluded from further meetings and information. When I told him that this would be difficult, he answered curtly: 'That's your baby.'

We met again the next day. During the night Abu Faisal must have communicated his confidence in our good faith to Sartawi, because at the meeting I received a telephone call from Sartawi in which he reassured me of the continuation of the dialogue. But he asked that security be tightened. 'Trust is everything', he said. 'If trust is destroyed, everything is destroyed.'

Abu Faisal told me that Sartawi had received special permission for each of the two series of meetings, and that he was now working for their regular continuation. He was optimistic. Our main discussion was about new initiatives. The dialogue could be elevated to a new level if well-known international personalities could be persuaded to take a bold initiative, call for a public dialogue and become its patrons. Four names sprang to our minds: President Senghor of Senegal, with whom Sartawi was friendly; ex-Premier Pierre Mendès-France, who was already involved in some way; the Rumanian leader Nicolae Ceausescu, who had good relations with both Israel and the Arabs; and the Austrian chancellor, Bruno Kreisky. I volunteered to go to Kreisky immediately.

* * *

This is a place to review my relations with this remarkable man, which have some bearing on our narrative.

I first met Bruno Kreisky when I visited Vienna in the late 1950s. A friend, the former Austrian Consul-General in Tel Aviv, asked me to see the deputy foreign minister, an up-and-coming Social Democrat and a Jew. When I went to see this man, whose name was still unknown outside Austria, he received me in his room in the Foreign Ministry. The first thing which impressed me was a small crocodile playing in a small basin in the middle of the room. He had received it as a gift during a visit to an African state.

But the man was anything but extravagant or flamboyant. On the contrary, he impressed me with his matter-of-fact way of speaking and his dry humour. One sentence which stuck in my mind: 'We Austrians have reconciled ourselves to the fact that we are a small country, so we don't have to produce airplanes or cars. You Israelis, being a big nation, of course have to produce such things.'

No wonder that Kreisky became vastly unpopular in Israel. The fact that he was a Jew but not a Zionist, that he considered himself an Austrian and that he criticized Israel openly and acidly, turned him quickly into a *bête noire*, one of the favourite hate objects in Israel.

Years after, I renewed this acquaintance. I had become friendly with a Viennese girl who was interested in Israel. After he became chancellor (and, as some Austrians said, a new Hapsburg kaiser, Bruno the First), he felt the need for someone in Israel to observe the scene for him. Barbara Taufar, my friend and by now a confidante of Kreisky, was sent to Israel as a member of the Austrian Embassy staff. She was immensely successful and became a social fixture in Tel Aviv, aided by her quick intelligence and good looks.

It was Barbara who suggested, in early 1976, that I go to Vienna and interview the chancellor at length, so as to dispel the growing fog of defamations and misunderstandings surrounding his name in Israel. I did this, and some kind of friendship began. We met many times and exchanged letters in between. Whenever something happened in Israel which I thought would interest him, I sent him a letter through the diplomatic post — the Austrian, of course. I came to respect his judgments and his profound political good sense, a kind of wisdom which I rather chauvinistically consider typically Jewish, and which is conspicuous by its absence in Israel. He would let himself go in my presence and often let fly biting remarks about various personalities, knowing that I would not betray these confidences — something which quite often happened to him with others.

I always suspected him of having a kind of spurned love affair with Israel. While pretending to think about Israel dispassionately, as he did any other state, a fact much resented in Israel, he was in reality deeply committed to the fate of the Jewish state, angry with its stupidities and upset about the brutal attacks on him in the Israeli press. Perhaps it was a relief for him that at least one Israeli agreed with many of his views.

Throughout 1976 he became more and more disillusioned with Prime Minister Rabin. As a dedicated Social Democrat, Austrian-style, he felt some solidarity with the Israeli Labour Party, and accused Rabin of being a bad party man, of neglecting party politics and of being a bad internationalist

— all serious crimes in his eyes. 'Der Mann hat's nicht in sich!' (more or less: this man just hasn't got it), he once told me, adding that Shimon Peres had made a favourable impression on him. As I never liked or respected Peres, and still entertained the hope that Rabin could be induced to change his mind about the Palestinian problem, I tried to mediate between Kreisky and Rabin, urging Rabin in private letters to treat Kreisky differently. To no avail.

On 26 September, I wrote one of my usual letters to Kreisky, telling him confidently about the first meeting with Sartawi and about the good impression he made on my friends. I also reacted to something Kreisky had written in a letter to me. Remarking on the situation in Lebanon and the Syrian onslaught on the PLO forces there, he had written that perhaps the PLO could not be saved any more, quoting from a famous poem by Friedrich Schiller, 'zuruck, du rettest den Freund nicht mehr . . .' (go back, you can't save the friend any more). It was one of the snap judgments to which Kreisky was sometimes prone, and in his next letter, four days later, he promised to strengthen the relations of the Austrian government with the PLO.

This was the background of the conversation I had with him on 1 December 1976, two days after my last conversation with Abu Faisal in Paris. I proposed to him the idea of an international initiative under his auspices and those of international personalities, which he promised to look into.

During the conversation I described Sartawi in glowing terms, throwing him the bait. I knew how eager Kreisky always was to meet interesting personalities. And indeed he said: 'Look, Uri, why don't you send this person to me? I'd like to talk to a real honest-to-goodness PLO man and get a personal impression. Make the arrangements with Margit.'

Margit Schmidt, his trusted and devoted personal secretary, was another member of the chain connecting Kreisky with me, making sure that my messages to the chancellor always came through within minutes. In several situations, which I shall recount later, her help was invaluable.

During the following days I made the arrangements by telephone Sartawi was to meet Kreisky in a place called Lech, a small vacation spot where the chancellor was spending some days, and there the meeting took place. I always regretted that I was not present, because it must have been a remarkable encounter. The two totally different personalities — the old Austrian Jew and the Palestinian fighter — liked each other on sight and became devoted friends. It was a friendship that was to bear important fruit for the PLO in the following years.

* * *

The leaks in the Israeli press about the contacts, unfortunate as they were, did, nevertheless, have two positive results, one for each side.

On the Israeli side, members of the right-wing Likud opposition saw in the publications another opportunity to lambast the government. Several members raised the matter in Parliament, in the form of motions to the agenda, attacking the government for not putting an end to these acts of treason by bringing us to trial. It was a stormy session. At the time I was not a member of the Knesset, but all of us culprits ostentatiously attended, taking seats in the middle of the first row of the visitors' gallery overlooking the Knesset hall.

Replying for the government, the minister of justice, Chaim Tsadock, mentioned that the official government programme included the sentence: 'The government of Israel will not conduct negotiations with the terrorist organization whose aim is the destruction of the State of Israel.' He also quoted a Knesset resolution, adopted exactly one year earlier, saying 'The Knesset affirms that the organization called PLO is a framework for the murder organizations whose declared aim is the destruction of the state of Israel. Israel will not negotiate with the terrorist organizations in any form, and will not take part in the Geneva Conference if representatives of these organizations are invited to the conference.' He vigorously denied that there was any erosion of this attitude, as alleged by the Likud. He added: 'The contacts with PLO representatives conducted by members of the body known as The Council for Israeli-Palestinian Peace were conducted by them on their own decision and on their own responsibility. According to its own stand, the government views with disapproval these contacts by Israeli citizens, organizations and persons, with representatives of terrorist organizations.'

However, he made clear that these contacts were not illegal under existing law. He analysed the relevant paragraph in order to prove that for such contacts to be illegal, there must be an absence of reasonable grounds and the existence of an intent to harm the security of the state. According to the competent authorities (i.e., the security services), these two conditions did not exist.

By majority vote, the motions were struck from the agenda. Thus we obtained an official Knesset resolution confirming the legality of our contacts.

On the other side, the results were as positive, if less official. The leaks were widely reported in the Arab press. The existence of the contacts was now public property in the Arab world and among the Palestinians, and widely commented upon. Yet nothing terrible happened. The sky did not cave in. Allah did not send his lightning to strike down the traitors. PLO radicals were content to criticize.

Greatly encouraged, Sartawi and, in the shadows, Arafat and his colleagues, saw that they could take further steps in this direction. It all reminded me of Samson's riddle (Judges 14:14): 'Out of the strong came forth sweetness.'

# 27

*It is New Year's Eve. I am at home with Rachel. We have decided to usher in the new year, 1977, alone.*

*Midnight arrives. I open a bottle of champagne, which I brought back from France.*

*The telephone rings.*

*I take the receiver. A voice I cannot quite place says: 'Happy New Year.' In the background there is music and laughter.*

*'Happy New Year to you – and who is it?' I ask.*

*'Come on. It's your friend from Paris!' says Issam Sartawi.*

# 28

1 January 1977 was an historic day — or could have been.

That day, Matti Peled met Issam Sartawi in Paris. It was Sartawi's forty-third birthday, and he was in high spirits.

The meeting between the two had begun the day before. As usual, Peled was urging Sartawi to come forward with something dramatic, something that would increase our credibility in Israel. The Rabin government was falling apart, one of the reasons being a series of economic scandals disclosed by my magazine. Rabin's candidate for the job of governor of the Bank of Israel had been arrested for corruption, his minister of housing had committed suicide. Elections were in the air, and any kind of breakthrough in our relations with the PLO was bound to increase considerably the chances for setting up an effective peace list for the Knesset. I was very much caught up in all this and could not leave the country,and therefore did not go to see Sartawi, nor did I accept the very tempting invitation from Bruno Kreisky to come and spend a winter vacation with him in Lech.

That day, 1 January, I received an excited telephone call from Paris. Matti Peled, a man who very rarely shows any emotion, was jubilant. The great breakthrough had been achieved. He and Sartawi had agreed to publish a joint communiqué, making public our contacts and endorsing the efforts of the Israeli Council. This was the breakthrough we had been hoping for.

I went into action immediately. I called my friends at the television station, told them, confidentially, about the sensation about to break, and offered them the opportunity to publish it first. I also set up a news conference for the national and international press for the next day.

Matti was scheduled to arrive at Ben Gurion Airport only a short time before the television news broadcast. I met him at the airport, told him not to wait for his luggage, and drove him to the television station, exceeding the speed limit even more than usual. Arriving there, he was ushered immediately into the studio.

On the way, I heard the details, and my enthusiasm was a bit dampened. There was indeed a joint communiqué, but Sartawi was not identified in it by name, nor did he sign it. The result was a highly unusual document, a joint communiqué by two people, only one of whom was identified, and which was not signed. The headline was: 'A Statement to be Delivered in Israel Relating to the Meeting Held Between a Member of the PLO Leadership and Dr M. Peled in Paris on December 31, 1976 and January 1, 1977.'

This was as far as Sartawi could go. As usual, he took a step forward without being authorized to do so by the leadership, hoping to create a *fait accompli* that would be accepted post factum by the movement. Usually he was correct in his judgments, and did create political facts. It is worthwhile to quote this statement in full:

> Another meeting was held between a member of the PLO leadership and Dr. Peled in Paris. The meeting lasted two days 31.12.76 – 1.1.77. The PLO leader, a veteran freedom fighter who is believed to be the man in charge of coordinating the PLO peace efforts on behalf of the PLO leadership, had been maintaining for some time regular communications with the Israeli Council for Israeli-Palestinian Peace.
>
> He has affirmed to his interlocutor that the PLO is dedicated to the policy of striving for a peaceful solution of the Israeli-Palestinian conflict on the basis of mutual acceptance of the principle of freedom, sovereignty and security for both peoples.
>
> The PLO considers the principles implied in the Manifesto of the ICIPP as an adequate basis for solving the Israeli-Palestinian conflict.
>
> He had reiterated that the PLO is not opposed to attending the Geneva Peace Conference when it is invited to participate in it. Until this becomes possible, the PLO will do its utmost to enhance the arrival of peace on the basis of mutual agreement. As one of its steps to achieve this goal, the PLO is maintaining close relations with the ICIPP and other peace forces whose activities are greatly appreciated.
>
> The PLO leader has been active lately in the USA where he endeavoured, together with his comrades, to acquaint the public with the PLO's policy as defined by its leadership. He is glad to point out that the PLO's peaceful intentions have been recognized by large sections of the American public, as well as by groups of American Jews. He finds it regrettable that the Jewish Presidents' Conference had taken a negative stand towards developing better understanding between the PLO and the American Jewish Community. He hopes that PLO representatives, in cooperation with the ICIPP and Jews inside the USA will succeed to persuade American Jews, as well as all other Jewish communities, of the urgent need for peace between Israel and the Palestinian people. Such understanding, on the part of those who wish peace for the Middle East to be achieved, is vital in order to bring an end to the state of war in the area and prevent further outbreaks of hostilities.
>
> Dr. Peled, Chairman of the Executive Committee of the ICIPP, surveyed extensively the development of Israel's public opinion relating to the Palestinian people and the PLO. Dr. Peled has stressed the significance of the Knesset debate on the Council's contacts with the PLO and recent polls showing increased willingness in Israel to deal directly with the PLO. He also pointed out that Member of Knesset A. Eliav had reported about these meetings in great detail to President Katzir on a recent occasion.
>
> Both the PLO leader and Dr. Peled are of the opinion that the relations which have developed between the PLO and the ICIPP constitute a hopeful milestone in the relations of their peoples. They expect that their cooperation in striving for peace will contribute towards the establishment of cordial and mutually respectful relations between the PLO and the people of Israel.
>
> Regular meetings between the PLO leader and members of the ICIPP have been scheduled for the future.

* * *

The disclosure of the breakthrough on the television news broadcast was a bombshell. No one paid any attention to the peculiarities of this document. It was accepted as a simple political act: here was a joint statement by Zionist, patriotic Israelis and the PLO, calling for peace. The mysterious dialogue, whose existence had been leaked to the press, was now official. Everyone understood that a new chapter had opened.

When I opened the press conference the next day, I looked into a battery of television cameras such as I had never encountered before or have after. Everybody was there, all Israeli media, all the international press agencies, the major television networks, newspapers from all over the world. We were about to publish a message the world was waiting for, drama was in the air.

When I introduced General Mattitiyahu Peled, he was the hero of the hour. The cameras clicked away, questions in several languages were thrown at him. I spoke about a 'historical breakthrough', as Matti took pains to explain the fine print of the document, pointing out its limitations as well as the achievement it represented.

The journalists did not really listen. They saw a big news story, and hastened to dispatch it in the simplest and most dramatic terms possible.

Two hours after the conference, the Reuters correspondent in Beirut went to see Farouk Kaddumi, chief of the political department of the PLO, in effect the foreign minister of the Palestinian governing body, and showed him the communiqué just broadcast by Reuters all over the world. It said that a high-ranking PLO official had signed a statement together with a Zionist leader, recognizing the Zionist State of Israel on behalf of the PLO.

Kaddumi hit back, quickly and effectively. Within minutes, the Palestinian news agency, WAFA, published a denial saying that 'the claim that a PLO representative signed a statement with Peled on the Palestinian problem is completely untrue and without foundation'. Similar statements blossomed all over the world, published by the PLO offices, all of which were controlled by Kaddumi's political department. In Paris, the PLO office stated that the PLO had signed no statement with an Israeli group, and that the PLO would never make peace with the Zionist Entity. The man responsible for this statement, Azz-al-Din Kalak, was later murdered by Palestinian extremists, who accused him of being too moderate. The PLO representative in Khartoum went even further, saying that Palestinians would continue their armed struggle to wipe out Israel. This statement was published in the international press along with Kaddumi's.

The denial was a work of art. Every word was true. No PLO representative had signed any statement, because the statement was unsigned. The statement did not endorse the Zionist ideology of the Israeli Council, but only said that the principles of the Council's Manifesto were an adequate basis for solving the conflict.

But such niceties were, of course, ignored. What came through loud and clear was that the PLO, in the most official manner, had denied the very existence of the contacts, as well as the joint statement. After the excitement generated by our statement, this was more than a mere diplomatic ploy.

It was a slap in the face, a total disavowal, making us appear ridiculous dupes at best, or liars at worst.

The next few days were field days for all the opponents of Israeli-Palestinian peace. Whoever could hold a pen, wrote articles heaping ridicule on our efforts, or denouncing us as traitors serving the enemy propaganda machine. Itzhak Rabin denounced our activities in a press conference, and the Labour party officially reaffirmed its political programme, one that precluded all negotiations with Palestinians. In the general orgy no one paid any attention to a news item, published in seven lines in *Haaretz*, saying that a Fatah spokesman, Abu Maazen, had declared that Fatah did not object to the principle of contacts between Palestinians and Israelis.

What were the Kaddumi's motives? There could be no doubt that his statement was designed to destroy Sartawi's efforts and our own standing in Israel, as effectively as if he had put bombs under our chairs. The contacts at that time were a fragile plant. The idea that Israelis could dare to meet representatives of the 'terrorist organization' was still so revolutionary that much less than such an insulting denial was needed to destroy the contacts. If he wanted only to rectify the false facts which had crept into the news agency reports, he could have done it in a different form, in a different language. Instead, he stabbed us in the back.

His motives were probably mixed. As a PLO politician, Kaddumi believed that the time was inopportune for any step towards peace, which was disapproved of by Syria and the Soviet Union. He was and remained an opponent of unilateral steps, which looked like giving something away for no concrete returns. He was also upset by Sartawi, a man working outside the PLO bureaucracy and political structure, conducting diplomacy as a personal emissary of Yassir Arafat on behalf of Fatah — an organization of which Kaddumi himself was one of the founders. No foreign minister could be expected be very enthusiastic about the political activities of a roving ambassador circumventing the authority of his ministry and reporting directly to the chief of state.

All this was understandable, but the results were a calamity for us, as well as for the Palestinian people, I believe. We were at the onset of an historic election campaign. There was a good chance, for the first time, of creating an effective political force with a platform that would include, among other things, a demand for Israeli negotiations with the PLO, for the purpose of creating a Palestinian state alongside Israel, based on mutual recognition.

As our press conference had shown, the time was ripe for it in Israel. When it seemed that we had achieved an historic breakthrough on the way to Israeli-Palestinian negotiations, we became heroes overnight. The mass media gave us headlines, the whole peace camp was electrified, the morale of many people who had despaired of peace soared. If things had developed further along those lines, there was a possibility, even a probability, of entering the next Knesset as an effective parliamentary group, perhaps changing the composition of the next government and certainly having a direct influence on Israeli policy.

All this was destroyed by one torpedo, bearing the signature of Farouk Kaddumi.

Of course, many more things happened during those fateful months before the May 1977 elections.

On 23 January, I received a call from Sartawi. He seemed extremely excited and requested that I come to Paris immediately. Something serious had developed between him and Lova Eliav, and he wanted to thrash it out. I called Matti, who advised me not to go, saying that he himself was about to go to Paris anyhow. When Sartawi called again and I told him this, he was even more angry.

Several months later, when our personal relationship had become much more relaxed, he told me what had happened. Eliav had come to Paris for a new round of talks. An argument had erupted between them, concerning a meeting with Mendès-France. For some reason, Sartawi insisted that the meeting be cancelled. Eliav decided to go alone, a decision which upset Sartawi very much. He probably felt that after having suffered such a wounding attack from Kaddumi, and being exposed to assaults from all Palestinian and Arab radicals, he deserved more consideration from his new Israeli friends.

The fact was that there was no chemistry between Sartawi and Eliav from the beginning. Eliav is an idealist, very much in the thrall of his own ideas and personality, and therefore lacks a trait necessary for these contacts — the ability and the patience to listen closely to the other side, to understand its sensibilities, to hear the things not said out loud.

During March, two things happened. All the various peace groups represented in the Israeli Council for Israeli-Palestinian Peace united in a common list for the coming elections. The resulting coalition, which later became a party, was called Sheli, the Hebrew acronym for 'Peace for Israel' as well as 'Equality in Israel'. The list of candidates was headed by Lova Eliav, Meir Pail and myself, in that order, representing the main groups who had come together. I had no illusions. While we attracted quite a number of enthusiastic youngsters, intellectuals and artists, our new group was but a shadow of the great Peace Camp which could have come into being, had Kaddumi's stunning blow not damaged our credibility and prestige.

This damage was increased by the resolution of the thirteenth Palestinian National Council, which convened in Cairo between 21 and 25 March, when the Israeli election campaign was nearing its climax. It was this Council which adopted the important Resolution 11 which called for the establishment of an independent national state in a part of Palestine. This was positive enough and, in the context of the Palestinians' Long March, a big step forward.

But in order to make this possible, this resolution was well nigh hidden beneath the old rhetoric, and it was this which met the eye of the ordinary Israeli. The Israeli press described the resolutions as a great victory for the Palestinian extremists, and the few experts who knew better kept quiet. Worst of all, the Council adopted a resolution allowing for contacts only with anti-Zionist Israelis, thus again disavowing our contacts — at least in theory.

We did our best, but on Election Day Sheli won only two seats, gaining less than two per cent of the vote. Even this meagre showing was nearly ignored, because something terrible had happened which overshadowed everything else — for the first time in the history of Israel, the chauvinist right-wing had won an election. Menachem Begin, the apostle of Greater Israel, the deadly enemy of all Palestinian aspirations, had become prime minister.

* * *

In June I visited Vienna. This came about in a rather humorous way.

Once a year an important person is invited to Vienna to give a lecture to the Karl Renner Institute. This is a very prestigious affair. The Institute belongs to the Socialist Party, but with the Socialists in power it had become practically a state affair, under the direct auspices of the chancellor, with the foreign ambassadors and the cream of Viennese society attending. The speaker scheduled for this year was Shlomo Avineri, a professor of philosophy at the Hebrew University in Jerusalem, who had acted as director-general of the Israeli Foreign Office in the now-defunct Labour government. At the very last moment, Avineri had committed an unpardonable sin: he had told the hosts he was unable to attend.

Kreisky was extremely angry and had a brilliant idea: instead of Avineri, an establishment person, he would invite Avnery, the very opposite.

Most people attending did not even notice the difference, until it was pointed out to them that there was a slight change in the lecturer's name. The event, which took place in the Hofburg, the old seat of the Kaiser, was very impressive. Kreisky introduced me to the audience in the most glowing terms, which rather embarrassed me, and then I gave an unprepared lecture, analysing the historic roots of the tragic clash between the two peoples claiming the holy country for their own, concluding with a plea for Israeli-Palestinian reconciliation and coexistence.

On the eve of this event, Kreisky had invited me to dinner at his modest home. Sartawi had come from Paris, and the three of us, together with Karl Kahane, a well-known Jewish financier and personal friend of the chancellor, had a simple meal served by his wife. I was impressed by the simplicity of the surroundings. It was a typical middle-class Austrian home, guarded by a lone policeman. Very few chiefs of government could afford to live with so little protection, or enjoyed such an absence of pomp.

The atmosphere was sombre. The main topic of conversation was, of course, Menachem Begin. As an ex-member of the Irgun underground, I had always enjoyed good personal relations with Begin, with whom I had also served eight years in Parliament. There was no personal tension between us, and he generally treated me with much cordiality. But I had no illusions about his convictions.

A few days after the elections, on 23 May, I had sent a letter to Kreisky, saying: 'I write you in a very depressed mood. For the second time in my life I experience the end of the Weimar Republic . . .' Kreisky had already voiced, in a newspaper interview, a hope that upon attaining power, Begin would become a moderate, pragmatic politician. Responding to this, I said in my letter:

> Of course it is true in principle that sometimes right-wing radical hawks are able to make concessions, which moderate politicians are unable to make. But one should not be tempted by this theory to ignore realities. I've known Mr. Begin for thirty years . . . One should not underrate the man. He is a 100 percent fanatic, with a personal line to God. He is not a de Gaulle, who was, despite everything, capable of cool calculation. He certainly is no Nixon. He comes closer to Robespierre, a basically irrational person who believes he represents sheer reason. He is totally uncompromising. The incorporation of the occupied territories (into the State of Israel) is for him a mission beyond debate.

Over dinner we had a lively argument about this. Kreisky was convinced that Begin would now become a rational statesman, while I maintained he would make no concessions at all about Palestinian territory. In the following years, we were both proven right: Begin did make concessions in order to achieve peace with Egypt, but scuttled all attempts at a compromise over the West Bank and Gaza.

At one point, upon hearing that the Begin government was dependent on the votes of the four extreme Orthodox Agudat Israel members of the Knesset, Kahane exclaimed, only half-jokingly: 'How much can it cost to buy four rabbis? If the very future of Israel is at stake, it would be a negligible price to pay!'

Seriously, we discussed the steps we could take to further the cause of peace under the new circumstances. It was agreed that the best thing to do was to call for a big conference, under the auspices of some international leaders, in which Israelis, Palestinians and other Arabs would talk about Israeli-Palestinian peace. I urged that a preparatory meeting be convened in the near future, in order to create a new momentum. Kreisky promised to examine the possibilities.

* * *

Three days after our dinner with Kreisky I met Sartawi again in Paris. There we received a call from Matti. According to reports in the Israeli press, the PLO representative in Bonn, Abdallah Franjieh, had announced that in the wake of the Begin victory in Israel, all PLO contacts with Israelis were suspended.

Sartawi was incredulous. He did not know anything about such a decision. He made some phone calls and reported: The news is true. There had indeed been such a decision.

This told me something about how the PLO apparatus worked. No one had told Sartawi about the suspension, which concerned him more than anyone else. Obviously, Arafat had had to agree to the resolution, but did not see himself obliged to enforce it. This was a procedure which was to repeat itself several times in the future.

Issam was, of course, quite bitter. During long hours of conversation, the veil of mystery shrouding the inner workings of the PLO gradually began to lift before me.

'Kaddumi had brought about the election of Begin!' Issam said. Yet he did not believe that Kaddumi was in fact against contact with Israel or against the two-state solution. He considered Kaddumi an opportunist, who wanted to be popular within the Palestinian ranks, remain a *persona grata* with the Soviets and the Syrians and prevent the ascent of a new foreign policy star and possible competitor, such as Sartawi.

During the thirteenth session of the Palestinian National Council, which had taken place in Cairo in March 1977, hardliners had attacked Sartawi, calling him a traitor to the Palestinian cause. But Arafat himself had come to his aid. In a rousing speech before the conference, Arafat had called Sartawi 'a great Palestinian patriot' and described in glowing terms his activities for the Palestinian cause, and especially his contacts with the progressive forces in Israel. The more than two hundred delegates had responded and given Sartawi a warm ovation, nearly rising to their feet.

But the Begin victory had again changed the delicate balance of Palestinian opinion on this issue — the most controversial issue for the Palestinian movement at that time and for many years after. 'Some fat Palestinians are sitting on their asses in the Gulf States, playing heroes from afar', was the way Sartawi put it. 'The people in the occupied territories want a solution. It's they who suffer. But their voice is not being heard.'

As usual, Issam had a practical proposal. Why not take the bull by the horns and address Arafat personally? I had already written open letters to Arafat and published them in *Haolam Hazeh*, and Issam knew that Arafat had read them — a fact which Arafat himself confirmed later in conversations with me. As Issam himself could not write open letters to his chief, it was up to me to do it.

There ensued a rather bizarre consultation between us. A leading PLO official was practically dictating a letter to his own chief to an Israeli journalist who would publish it in an Israeli magazine, over the signature of the Israeli. It is a document worth quoting in full, because it shows how Sartawi judged the situation inside the PLO at the time and thought to influence it.

I wrote the letter on the plane on the way back to Israel. It was published in *Haolam Hazeh* on 29 June 1977. Here is the full text, which was widely reproduced in journals around the world close to the cause of Israeli-Palestinian peace.

Mr. Chairman,

This open letter is written to you for two reasons:

This is the fastest, most direct way. Rapidity seems to me important, as my words relate to decisions which have to be adopted by yourself and by your friends in the near future.

These decisions concern every Palestinian, every Israeli and perhaps every human being throughout the world. It is therefore better to talk about this openly.

The developments now underway, which may lead to a new war, sweeping all of this area, depend now on a small number of people — among whom are to be found the Israeli Prime Minister, the President of the United States and the heads of the Arab States.

You are one of these men.

Mr. Chairman,

This letter is wholly concerned with telling you one thing:

It is in your power, now, to bring the extraordinary possibility of peace to our region.

A year ago you made a valiant decision: one which might have turned a page in the long and painful history of our two peoples.

You decided to initiate official contacts with the Israeli Council for Israeli-Palestinian Peace, a patriotic body which did not hide its Zionist identity. You asked a special team, headed by Dr. Issam Sartawi, to keep these contacts.

It is possible that your decision was influenced by the unofficial contacts I held for two years before that with the representative of your body, who acted on your instructions, and during which we discussed the issues involved in discussions between the forces working for peace.

During these conversations it became very clear to me how daring you had to be to take such a decision.

Spiritual courage was needed to put an end to the four-decades-old tradition of the Palestinian people, a tradition expressed in so many official documents, speeches and articles. Political courage was needed in order to do this, in spite of bitter opposition by the Palestinian Refusal Front and by weighty elements inside the Arab world. Personal courage was needed — both by yourself and by all those involved — at their head Dr. Issam Sartawi — who put themselves in jeopardy, baring themselves to assassination attempts by incorrigible fanatics. Those dangers were far greater than the dangers we took upon ourselves when we came to the meeting.

But it was worth it.

All these contacts evoked enormous hopes inside the Arab world and in Israel. They raised strong echoes in world public opinion.

Everybody understood that a revolutionary thing was being done — revolutionary in the positive sense of the word — something which might change the face of the area and of the world and open a new page in the history of both peoples.

The meetings proved some things to be basic truths — not as far as learned articles are concerned but in the language of everyday, real happenings which can be seen and discussed.

They proved that a possibility exists of finding peace between the two peoples, peace which will grant these peoples justice, security and honour.

They proved that on both sides forces exist which work towards peace and are ready to endanger themselves for the sake of peace, but remain, each on their side, true to their people, their land and their national aspirations.

We evoked great expectations — hopes that it is possible to save the lives of many human beings, to prevent a terrible war which may destroy the whole area.

We thus lit a small candle which shone from afar. Now our duty is to keep this candle from being snuffed out by the draught suddenly sweeping the area.

There is little doubt that these meetings opened the way to a historical opportunity. This opportunity was lost, and this may cause people to weep over the loss for ages.

There is little point in accusing anybody. It is enough to say that guilt does not lie uniquely on one side. Huge forces worked on both sides to prevent success, and each of the sides worked under various pressures and under cruel obligations.

We, the Israelis, were unable to bring about any kind of change in the totally negative stand of Rabin's government, as far as the Palestinian question was concerned. In heart-to-heart and mind-to-mind talks, we were unable to convince the central personalities of that government that they should accept even the '(General Aharon) Yariv Formula', the formula which says that Israel should agree to negotiate with the Palestinian leadership that would recognize Israel, stop hostile action and declare its wish for an Israel-Palestine peace.

The government also rejected the proposal that the PLO be invited to the Geneva Conference in return for de facto recognition of Israel by the PLO.

Rabin's government was punished for its historical lack of initiative—and along with the government were punished the parties which cooperated with it, as well as the people of Israel.

I have not the slightest doubt that the caving-in of the Israeli regime, on 17 May 1977, would have been staved off had that government taken even one small step along the way we opened for it.

The Likud's victory in these last elections would not have been possible had not the Rabin government convinced the Israeli people that there is no chance for peace, that the Arabs, and particularly the Palestinians, will never accept the existence of our state.

Had the Geneva Conference opened in April 1977 with the participation of the accredited representatives of the Palestinian people, then Menachem Begin would not be head of the Israeli government today.

I am sorry that honesty forces me to say that the Palestinian side bears a considerable part of the responsibility for what happened.

As we told your representatives several times, and as was proven in such a clear way on election day, Israel is decisively influenced by the public, free opinion of its citizens. This decides to a considerable extent the government's policies, and even its very membership.

Had our contacts reached an open target, had they ranged all over the scope covered, had they brought about, for instance, an impressive and public meeting of peace forces from both sides, and had they reached clear and openly-stated policy statements — then the Israeli public would have moved towards a completely different attitude, and would have evolved towards views very different from those it proved to entertain on 17 May 1977.

I am convinced that the PLO could have changed the situation radically, had it shown, in time, the public and political courage that the situation warranted.

I am sorry to say that we did not reach this point.

The Israeli public was confused by the contradictory voices heard in the Palestinian camp. Time and time again the official spokesmen of the PLO denied the very existence of such conversations. Prudent and general formulas, worked out during our contacts, were rejected and denied by other PLO spokesmen. How should the Israeli public have interpreted Farouk Kaddumi's words, when he said that the creation of a sovereign Palestinian state on the West Bank and in the Gaza Strip will not end the conflict, but will be, instead, 'a transitory state'? Should not the Israeli and the world's public have seen in this proof that such a state will act towards the destruction of our own sovereign state?

I have not had the opportunity to meet Mr. Kaddumi, I suppose he tries to serve the interests of the Palestinian people as best as he thinks he can.

But I have no doubt whatever that the statements and deeds of Mr. Kaddumi and his friends contributed decisively to Mr. Begin's ascent to power in Israel.

The Begin government came to power with a tiny majority. This coalition could have been denied its two or three decisive Knesset votes had not the PLO committed the faults it did during the electoral campaign. I do not mean only the PLO's denials and its double-edged statements, but also the instructions given to Israel's Arabs to vote for Rakakh — instructions which became further proof that the PLO will never recognize the Zionist State of Israel. Rakakh itself was not helped by this.

You and your friends must decide how to react to the change which happened inside Israel.

I know this is a hard decision to make. This week it was reported that Abdallah Franjieh, the Palestinian representative in Germany, stated that the PLO will cut all its contacts with Israeli elements — beginning with the Israeli left's contacts with the PLO and ending with conversations with the representatives of the Israeli Council.

I believe this to be a first spontaneous reaction to the victory of annexationist and settlers' forces in Israel. An understandable reaction — but a very dangerous one. This decision turns the clock back, inside your own camp, too.

I ask you to reconsider this decision — if indeed such a decision was taken — and to take now the opposite decision.

I know that among the Palestinian people, and in the Arab countries, as inside Israel, there are forces which do not want peace.

I know that these forces have decided to sabotage every possibility of peace. The Israeli and the Arab refusal fronts have fed and helped each other for a long while now.

I also know that the ability of any politician to withstand pressure is limited. It is clear to me that at this very moment huge pressures are being brought to bear upon you by Palestinian and Arab forces against continuing peace initiatives.

But I must say there is a historical duty to stand against these pressures and to be patient; a great deal hangs in the balance.

This is especially so now, after the forces of Greater Israel have come to power in Israel. It is now that an intelligent and pragmatic approach is needed from the Palestinian leadership, a positive approach which will further peace; and also strengthen the forces which strive towards peace.

Israeli public opinion has not said its last word yet.

Israel's internal struggle has not yet been finally decided. The process which started on 17 May 1977 can be changed. The trend can be changed.

In order to do so, the Israeli public must be faced with a credible and real alternative, which leads to peace, and promises to ensure Israel's existence and security, together with national independence and justice for the Palestinian people.

Many, inside Israel, were astonished when the decision was made in this country. Many of those who voted Likud and Mafdal, for internal reasons, were sorry the very next morning, when they saw that the new reality leads towards war.

A wise and balanced reaction from the Arab world, and particularly from the PLO, may arouse in the hearts of many of those people the conviction that one must change direction and stop the Likud's plans.

And then comes Franjieh, and his words weaken the hands of those people.

This is the greatest gift that the PLO may have given Mr. Begin. This is a direct continuation of the errors committed by the PLO during the Israeli elections.

While I am convinced of the essential need for an Israeli-Palestinian peace, I must ask: On whose side is the PLO? On that of the expansionist Israelis who want to annex territories or on the side of the Israeli peace forces?

All logical men must do everything possible to stop the coming war.

This will be a terrible war. It will strike hard at all the peoples of the area. It will spill Israel's blood. But I am convinced that, most of all, it will be the Palestinian people who will suffer from this war.

Of all tragedies which have descended on the Palestinian people in the last two generations, this may be the most terrible.

Mr. Arafat,

I write this letter feeling deeply that this very minute a heavy decision must be taken by all — Israelis and Palestinians, Jews and Arabs — who are able to see where things are leading us.

Maybe I contribute something by doing so, by making a small contribution, perhaps very small, to keep the catastrophe from happening. But a lot now depends upon you.

With peace greetings,

Uri Avnery.

# 29

*Issam and I enter a restaurant near the Rue de la Seine. Automatically, I take a seat facing the door.*

*It's a habit. I feel physically uncomfortable with my back to the door. It may be an old soldier's habit, or a result of the attempts on my life, or a manifestation of journalistic curiosity.*

*'Will you mind letting me sit there?' Issam asks.*

*I do mind, but I give up the seat. The tables are so arranged in French restaurants, that I do then have to sit with my back to the door.*

*'It's a question of Arab honour,' Issam explains. 'I don't want to be shot in the back. I want to see my assassin and return fire.'*

*After a minute he adds: 'Of course it's quite silly. If they come in and shoot me, I'll have no chance.'*

*I know he carries a small pistol in his pocket. If anything happens, he'll really have no chance at all.*

# 30

'The road to peace is paved with Palestinian graves,' Issam Sartawi said.

Said Hammami had been killed on 4 January 1978. Henri Curiel had been killed on 4 May 1978. The official PLO representative in Paris, Azz-al-Din Kalak had been killed on 1 August 1978. The last was a completely senseless murder. Kalak had been a mere functionary, taking orders, unlike Hammami, who, while an official, was also a Palestinian thinker and leader in his own right. Kalak had not been involved in any way in our contacts. Actually, Sartawi studiously avoided the official PLO delegation in Paris, which was of course controlled by Kaddumi. Kalak had refuted him publicly. The Abu Nidal gang had killed him for no reason at all, except, perhaps, the fact that he was in Paris, the city where the contacts had taken place.

I was deeply affected by Hammami's murder. I tried to express my feelings in a eulogy which I published in *Haolam Hazeh* on the morrow of his death, under the title 'Said, My Enemy, My Friend'. At that time, calling a PLO official a friend was still considered scandalous in Israel, even by many of those who approved of contacts with the enemy as a way of preparing the way for peace. Very few people indeed could imagine the kind of relationship which had sprung up between people like Hammami and Sartawi and us, a bond strengthened by shared dangers, aspirations and experiences.

As I have already said, I was prevented from taking part in the memorial meeting for Hammami, at which Sartawi made his moving and remarkable eulogy. Of course I could also not be present at Hammami's funeral, which took place in Amman.

After the murder of Curiel I rushed to Paris, to take part in the funeral of this truly remarkable human being. It took place in the Père Lachaise cemetery, and it was a singular occasion. After a silent funeral procession came a silent burial. Only one man said a few words 'on behalf of the comrades'.

Who were the 'comrades'? There were his old friends from the Egyptian Communist party, mainly Jews, who had not only been exiled from Egypt but also expelled from the party, for the sole reason that they were Jewish. This un-Marxist behaviour was explained by their former comrades as necessary in order to gain influence in Egyptian society.

There were the comrades from the Algerian underground, for whom Curiel had risked his freedom during the Algerian struggle for independence. There were strange faces, belonging to underground fighters from various countries and races, a panorama of freedom struggles, all of whom had found in Curiel a selfless friend who extended a helping hand.

Yet Curiel was only a stateless refugee himself, suspected by both the Americans and the Russians, a man who did not fit in any slot, a freedom fighter who detested terror ('Indiscriminate terror is a kind of fascism', he once told me). He was one of the few people who were really irreplaceable, because he was unique.

Among the many faces, one was missing: Sartawi's. The French police, who were responsible for his safety, had objected to his attending. Sartawi pleaded, got angry, but in the end had to comply with the wishes of his guardians. He sent a large wreath on behalf of the PLO, which was put on the grave next to the wreath of the Israeli Council – a silent demonstration of mourning for the man who had been the host of the first contact between Sartawi and us.

After the funeral I went to see Sartawi in his office. It was Israeli Independence Day.

* * *

Much had happened in the preceding months. My letter to Arafat had had no dramatic results. At the end of September and the beginning of October the London Seminar had taken place and had become the occasion for a public fraternization between Israelis and Palestinians – Sartawi, Hammami, Matti and me. But soon after, at another conference held in Paris under communist auspices, the Arab delegations had practically cut dead and silenced Lova Eliav and Meir Pail, who had come from Israel. Lova was profoundly insulted, and reacted by publishing some very blunt remarks about the PLO's cowardice and failure to respond to the Israeli peace movement.

Anwar Sadat's historic visit to Jerusalem had changed the map. After some hesitation, the PLO came out in force against this event.

Sartawi and others told me later how this came about. When Sadat made his famous speech in the Egyptian parliament, announcing his intention to go to Jerusalem and address the Knesset, Arafat was present as a guest of honour. During the previous days he had been active as a mediator between Libya and Egypt, which were, as usual, at each other's throats, and Sadat had invited him to the parliamentary session to express his gratitude. There the Egyptian president had heaped praise on the head of the PLO leader, and Arafat was happy. He was still happily applauding when Sadat sprang his great surprise. Before Arafat realized what was happening, he found himself in a position where foreign observers were bound to suspect that he was privy to the plan. He felt tricked.

Yet he did not immediately come out against the initiative, waiting, as is his custom, to see how things developed. But when he went back to Beirut he was faced with something close to revolt. The Palestinians were outraged, they felt betrayed by Egypt, a country most of them loved. Arafat had to give in to this consensus, and since then had become the implacable enemy of the Egyptian initiative.

I always felt that Sadat was much to blame for this. Not only had he failed to consult with the Palestinians beforehand, and put Arafat in an impossible position, but he also failed to mention the PLO in his historic speech in the

Knesset, a fateful omission. When I listened to the speech in the Knesset hall, to which I was invited as a former member for this historic occasion, I was waiting for a reference to the Palestinian organization, knowing how crucially important such a mention was for the Palestinians.

Sartawi said that before the speech, Begin had sent Dayan to the King David Hotel, where Sadat was staying, and told him that he was free to say whatever he wanted, but that on one point there was a specific request from the Israeli prime minister: that he does not mention the PLO. Sadat complied. I believe this was an historic mistake which turned his unique act into a partial failure. Unlike my Palestinian friends, I do believe that Sadat was sincere in his endeavour to achieve something for the Palestinians. Like his friend Kreisky, however, he did not understand the mentality of Begin.

My party and I supported the Sadat initiative. As Israeli peace activists, we could not but welcome with all our hearts an initiative which brought about a formal peace between Israel and the most important Arab state, partial and flawed as it may be.

I went to Egypt immediately, without a visa and against Israeli law. shall never forget the feeling of complete happiness I had during those first few days in Egypt, when I moved around freely in an Arab capital, being fêted everywhere like a man from Mars. It proved everything I had been saying for years: that there is no real enmity between Arab and Israeli, that once the ice is broken they will fraternize easily and wholeheartedly.

The most unforgettable moment was the first one. I arrived on a Greek flight from Athens, went up to the passport control counter, and handed my Israeli passport to a young, uniformed Egyptian policeman. He took the passport nonchalantly, and started to leaf through it. I followed his every movement, feeling a cold excitement such as I have only experienced on the battlefield. Suddenly he froze, looked up at me, and after a moment an immense smile spread across his face. '*Marhaba*', he said. Welcome.

I went to Egypt several times, and read in an Egyptian newspaper that Dr. Issam Sartawi, the high-ranking PLO official, had come out in favour of the Egyptian initiative. It was a daring act — unique — but natural for Sartawi, who had also welcomed Abd-al-Nasser's acceptance of the armistice with Israel after the War of Attrition, seven years earlier.

After the Camp David agreement, I hoped that the PLO would respond with a qualified 'yes, but' or at least 'no, but'. This was the way the Zionists had usually responded to initiatives before the creation of Israel, using every opportunity to gain an advance. But the emotional storm created among the Palestinians by Sadat's omissions made such a tactic impossible. I wonder even now what would have happened had the PLO reacted otherwise, if a Palestinian representative had shown up at the Mena House Conference the day after the Sadat initiative, on Sadat's invitation.

There was a bizarre little incident on the first day of that conference. After the Israeli delegation had entered, the Egyptians hoisted in front of the building the flags of Egypt, Israel, and all the Arab countries, including that of the PLO, which had been officially invited by Egypt but who had turned down the invitation.

On the steps of the beautiful hotel, an Israeli security officer suddenly gripped my arm in great excitement and said: 'Uri, you must save me. You are the only person who knows. What does the PLO flag look like?'

I told him that there was no PLO flag, but only the Palestinian national flag, which I drew for him on a piece of paper. 'That's it! These______ have hoisted the PLO flag!' he cried and ran off to tell the Israeli delegation. It protested, and the Egyptians reacted typically. Explaining that the flags were hoisted only for the opening moments of the conference, they took down all the flags.

Three months later, again in Cairo, I tried to pick up the news broadcast from Israel on my little transistor radio. I was standing on the balcony of the Sheraton Hotel, happily viewing the beautiful Nile, not yet inured to the dreamlike experience of being there at all, when I heard garbled Hebrew sentences coming from Jerusalem. I learned that a terrible massacre had taken place near Tel Aviv. PLO terrorists had landed on the coast, killed a photographer they had come across (a nice girl who had sold me several photographs in the past) and captured a bus full of people headed for Tel Aviv. They had been intercepted on the way and in the ensuing shootout many people, including the Fedayeen themselves, had been killed. It was one of those outrages which became imprinted on the Israeli mind. It also provided the reason - or pretext - for the first Israeli invasion of South Lebanon. When I spoke about this with Sartawi later, it again became apparent that our attitudes towards such incidents were different. Like myself, Sartawi thought that such attacks were harmful and counter-productive. But he did not condemn them on moral grounds. 'What do you want?' he asked, 'here you have some guys, probably not well-trained, entering an enemy country. You cannot compare the acts of some frightened kids like these to the coolly-planned air or ground attacks on our women and children in the Lebanese refugee camps, ordered and executed by General Staff officers.'

This was one of the psychological obstacles to an Israeli-Palestinian dialogue. To the Israelis, the Fedayeen were cold-blooded murderers, terrorists attacking schoolchildren and harmless families just to spill Jewish blood. To the Palestinians, they were heroes and martyrs, entering the land of a vastly superior enemy, facing nearly certain death, much as French underground fighters had when they faced the Nazi occupation forces in their country.

After each such outrage, a great emotional wave swept over Israel, destroying our efforts to de-demonize the PLO, as waves from the sea destroy the sandcastles built by children on the shore. It was a vicious circle, which could at times discourage even the most stalwart heart.

* * *

At times, Issam was also discouraged.

I remember a meeting where he was in a particularly depressed mood. We were having dinner in a Chinese restaurant on the Boulevard Montparnasse — both he and I liked good restaurants and good food, and all our contacts were punctuated with good dinners, accompanied by good wine and spiced with joking conversations with pretty waitresses – and Sartawi complained about our setbacks. I had to comfort him, saying that all these setbacks were temporary, that in the end the basic realities would force all parties towards peace. The most basic reality was the very existence of the Palestinian people, without whom no solution was possible. Whatever mistakes were made, an eventual solution was inevitable. This, together with the food, the wine, and also the waitress, changed his mood.

At the time, Issam was particularly upset by Lova Eliav's disparaging remarks, which had been widely distributed in PLO circles 'They tell me in Beirut: If these are the good Israelis you speak so highly of, how bad can the bad Israelis be? You must realize that I have praised you people to the skies, in order to gain support for the contacts. Because of this, if one of you says something obnoxious, the effect is much worse than if I hadn't.' Later he added: 'I can bury you in Beirut, and you can bury me in Tel Aviv. Everything we say is immediately reported on the other side. Think about this every time you say something. If I declare that we should kill Israelis, you'll be sunk. If Lova Eliav says that we Palestinians are cowards, and other humiliating and insulting things, he weakens me, after I have made you look like angels. People are shocked. I tried to explain that Lova was piqued, because Matti and you had enjoyed such a beautiful reception in London while he was rebuffed in Paris. But the prestige of the Israeli peace camp in Beirut at the moment is very low.'

In order to divert him, I asked his opinion about heart transplants. The first operation in Israel had just been performed successfully. As a heart specialist, Sartawi condemned these operations. A success rate of two percent did not justify, in his opinion, such operations. Instead, he thought, much more research should be done.

The Israeli invasion of South Lebanon had awakened Israeli interest in that country. I spent a lot of time getting from Issam a detailed picture of realities in that country, using it later for my articles about the Lebanese situation. I often wonder nowadays how many Israeli mistakes in Lebanon could have been avoided if our government had read these articles more closely. They were certainly based on information quite different, or at least seen from a quite different angle, from the evaluations gathered through Israeli intelligence channels. One of my valued possessions is a little map, drawn by Issam with my pen in my notebook, explaining the battles of the civil war of 1976. At one point Issam exclaimed: 'We have no interest in Lebanon! We hate Lebanon! We only want to survive there until we can go to the West Bank and create our own state!' It reminded me of Theodor Herzl, the founder of modern Zionism, who had once proposed to create a Jewish settlement in North Sinai, then under British control, until settlement in Palestine itself, then dominated by the Turks, was possible.

I brought up the question of the Israeli prisoner. At the end of the 'Litani Operation', as the invasion of South Lebanon in March 1978 was called in Israel, four Israeli reserve soldiers had inadvertently crossed the lines. Three were killed on the spot, the fourth had been taken prisoner. Great efforts were made to obtain his release.

Before going to Paris this time, Ezer Weizmann, the minister of defence, had sent a messenger to ask me if I was ready to try to use my contacts for this purpose. My friend Amnon Zichroni, the lawyer, and I tried several avenues. I also talked about it with Sartawi. Wouldn't it be a beautiful idea if the PLO handed the prisoner over to us, as a gesture of good will? It would certainly increase the respect for the Israeli peace movement in Israel. (Six years later this was done by the Syrian president, Hafez al-Assad, when he turned a captured American pilot over to Jesse Jackson. During the Vietnam War, American peace activists visiting Hanoi, the enemy capital, had obtained the freedom of American prisoners, and this had greatly enhanced their public standing.)

Sartawi and we still had a long way to go towards convincing the PLO leadership that the Israeli peace movement could fulfil the same function as the American movement had done during the Vietnam War. One of my stock phrases, whenever I met a Palestinian leader for the first time, was: 'The Algerian war of independence was won because of French public opinion. The Vietnam War was won because of American public opinion. The Palestinian struggle for independence will be won because of Israeli public opinion.' Once, after saying these words in a speech at an international conference, a Palestinian remarked to me that this was a typical example of Israeli arrogance. After all, the main struggle was conducted by Palestinians, as it had been by the Algerians and the Vietnamese. After that I was careful to add that of course the Palestinian struggle was the main factor.

At our next meeting, Issam told me that he had talked with Arafat about the prisoner. The main message was: There is no hurry. The prisoner is treated excellently. When his Palestinian guards get one apple, he gets two. When they get one steak, he gets one and a half. He is an object of great interest and curiosity and is being treated like a hero. The corpses of his three slain comrades are being kept in a refrigerator.

Later this was proven true. The prisoner had indeed been treated extremely well, as were, later, the prisoners of the 1982 War. It was, of course, to the advantage of the Palestinians to treat their prisoners well, and thereby gain the respect due a regular army. But I believe there was more to it. Palestinians consider themselves superior to Syrians and Egyptians, who had often mistreated Israeli prisoners. Their emotional ambivalence towards Israel also made them extremely curious about every Israeli specimen that fell into their hands.

Eventually the prisoner was returned in exchange for the release of about eighty convicted 'terrorists' held in Israeli prisons. Kreisky and Sartawi had played a role in secret negotiations, which was one of the reasons why I saw Issam frequently in Vienna. We played no part in this — another missed opportunity.

At a diplomatic party before the prisoner exchange, I met Menachem Begin. When he saw me, he came up, shook my hand warmly and said in a low voice: 'I hear you have been active for the release of our prisoner. God bless you!' The people around us were curious about what the great man had whispered in my ear.

Coming from the man who considered all members of 'the so-called PLO' despicable murderers, and who strenuously objected to our contacts, it was an odd blessing. But, somehow, one peculiar to Israel.

* * *

These years, 1978 to 1980, were indecisive. Within the Palestinian movement the struggle between the forces advocating a clear-cut peace line (nicknamed the 'Sartawi Line') and the hardliners, supported by Syria and Libya, was continuing. It was a seesaw. Camp David had been roundly condemned by the PLO. They saw in it a betrayal of the Palestinian people, and, as interpreted by Begin, it certainly was. King Hussein and the Saudis, who had not been consulted, would have no part of it. Sadat had in effect isolated himself completely from the Arab world. Instead of extricating itself from the ghetto Israel had been in for thirty years, the Israeli government succeeded in pulling Egypt in as well.

But after the condemnation came an event which was largely ignored by the West. As usual the Western press, especially the American, followed the Israeli line of ignoring Arab events and developments which did not suit the Israeli government.

On the morrow of the Camp David agreements, the Arab heads of state were called to a summit conference, which took place in Baghdad at the beginning of November 1978. To the great astonishment of many experts, the Baghdad summit unanimously adopted an amazingly moderate resolution, saying: 'The conference asserts the commitment of the Arab nation to a just peace based on the comprehensive Israeli withdrawal from the Arab territories occupied in 1967, including Arab Jerusalem, the guaranteeing of the inalienable national rights of the Palestinian people, including the right to establish their independent state on their national soil.' In Arab parlance, this meant in effect recognition of Israel with its pre-1967 borders, and the creation of a Palestinian state in the West Bank and Gaza, with its capital in East Jerusalem – a plan very similar to the programme of the Israeli Council.

This was the first time that the whole Arab world was officially united on a platform of peace. It was a great victory for Yassir Arafat, who had pushed this line behind the scenes. The prime mover was Saudi Arabia, which had assumed the mantle of Arab leadership after Egypt dropped out. The Saudis, by now afraid of Palestinian radicalization that would destabilize its regime if no solution was found soon, and also fearful of both Israeli and Iranian threats to its oil fields, were pushing actively for a peace formula. Syria and Iraq, the two rivals and arch-enemies, were united for a moment by their joint opposition to Egypt.

It was an auspicious moment for a great peace design. But it was completely ignored by West and East. Begin declared in the Knesset that the Baghdad summit had decided upon the annihilation of Israel. When I challenged him in the Knesset a few months later to prove this, he sent one of his stooges to answer from the Knesset rostrum by quoting some evasive texts.

Israeli propaganda could not have won this victory if it had not, as usual, been actively supported by Arab radicals. What actually happened was this: the final resolutions were agreed upon by the Arab heads of state at the last moment. The Arab text had to be translated carefully into European languages. This took time, but the mass communications media cannot wait. The gap was exploited by some small radical groups, who issued garbled communiqués, stressing the resolutions roundly condemning Egypt for making a separate peace and deserting the Arab front. Again as usual, the operative paragraph, with its message of peace, was submerged under a great mass of bellicose rhetoric, and uninformed journalists seized upon these sensational titbits. But for the Palestinian leadership, the results of Baghdad were important. For the first time they had a unanimous Arab endorsement for the moderate PLO line. When I saw Sartawi in the middle of December in Vienna, he said: 'I was elated. I don't have to fear being shot in the back any more.' He thought that the rejectionists within the PLO, such as Georges Habash (whom he likened to 'your Geula Cohen') had been decisively weakened. Arafat had exploited the situation and given a very moderate statement to American Congressman Finley. As usual, this was followed by a clarification from Beirut, which was no denial of what had been reported by Finley, but could be construed as such for Israeli purposes.

Sartawi also brought me a message from Arafat. He had written it down on paper. But on his way back he suddenly heard that the plane was touching down in Damascus, and had rushed to the toilet and destroyed the papers. He had to give me the message from memory.

The Chairman had read my letter to him, as he had all my previous ones. Indeed, he wished to thank me belatedly for the open letter I'd addressed to him in 1970, in which I had warned him of Jordanian designs against the PLO, which were soon after realized in Black September. He remembered this letter vividly (I myself had completely forgotten it). He was also impressed by the fact that while there had been leaks of our contacts in the Israeli press, when they were still quite secret, none of these had appeared in *Haolam Hazeh*. Sartawi also had talked with Arafat about a plan which we had been discussing: to publish, in Hebrew, a collection of the speeches and statements of Arafat, which had been largely ignored or misreported. Arafat had assented to this.

But all of this was not enough. The real great gesture, the great push which we needed, was not yet forthcoming.

* * *

During these months I met Issam many times, mostly in Vienna, which was safer than Paris. On direct orders from the chancellor, the Austrian police took great pains to protect him.

Usually we would both stay in the Hilton. Arriving there I would ask for Dr. Othman, the name which appeared in the Tunisian diplomatic passport on which he travelled. The Austrian desk clerk would shuffle through his papers and say: 'Ja, der Dr. Aussmann ist noch nicht da.' The ancient Arab name had been effectively Germanized. During such meetings, we would talk practically around the clock, meeting for breakfast, going to our separate meetings, meeting again during the day, and having dinner together well into the night, talking sometimes about other subjects, but mostly racking our brains about what to do, explaining to each other the realities on our respective sides.

I vividly remember one special dinner in one of the many wine halls dotting the Vienna Grinzig quarter. It was one of those places where an incredible variety of sausages is displayed. You walk up to the counter, choose whatever food strikes your fancy, pay and sit down at a table. There you order beer or, preferably, *heuriger*, the fresh Austrian wine of the same year.

We went to the counter and could not make up our minds which of the delicious-looking sausages – none of which was kosher for a Jew or permitted a Muslim – to choose. In the end we heaped sausage upon sausage, and the blue eyes of the Austrian countergirl became bigger and bigger in unabashed amazement, much to the delight of Issam. 'Are you gentlemen going to eat all this?' the girl asked, and Issam, in his very lame German, promised to. Before the evening was out, nothing remained on the plates.

Issam had made it a life habit to eat only one meal a day, in the evening. Until then he touched no food at all, claiming, with the authority of a heart specialist, that this was a healthy way to live. At breakfast he was content with a cup of coffee while I was consuming ham and eggs.

During that dinner, over many glasses of *heuriger*, we debated the chances of the creation of the Palestinian state. By now neither of us had many illusions left, we knew about the immense forces at work against this or any other solution. But I was more optimistic than he was. After the first few glasses, we made a bet. The dividing line was seven years. I said less, he said more. So on that evening, in January 1979, we made a bet that the Palestinian state would come into being by January 1986. Otherwise I stood to lose a bottle of whisky.

On that day I also informed him that I was about to return to the Knesset, after an absence of five years. I was replacing Lova Eliav after two years, under a rotation agreement.

One of my plans was to display a Palestinian flag, together with an Israeli one, on the Knesset rostrum at the appropriate moment. I therefore asked Issam to bring me a small Palestinian flag from Beirut. He was going to attend the Palestinian National Congress in Damascus and did indeed bring me the flag after that. As Lova had always rubbed him up the wrong way, he was glad to see me back in the Knesset, where I could propagate our line with maximum effect. Prospects for the national conference were uninspiring. The combined forces of Syria and Iraq were creating difficulties for the realists. 'They don't really want a Palestinian state', Issam said.

I volunteered: 'In the end you will find out that your only real ally is Israel.'

'And you people are going to find out that we are your only real allies in the Arab world', Issam replied.

I had also asked him to sound out Arafat about the idea of a future Israeli-Palestinian federation. This was an idea which has been close to my heart for many years. As the borders between Israel and the future Palestinian state were bound to be open for people and goods, and as reality dictated some kind of economic union, why not speak openly about some form of federation between the two states?

It was a delicate subject. The federal idea might create fear in Israel, where it could be suspected as a ploy for giving up Israeli sovereignty and the specific Jewish character of the Israeli people. It could create equal fears among the Palestinians, who might see in it a disguised form of Israeli domination. I was eager to hear Arafat's opinion about this. The answer: he was in favour of the idea, but did not think the time was opportune to raise the question.

Of course we did not speak all the time about politics. We discovered we had many other shared interests. For example we had both become absorbed by ethology, the study of animal behaviour as a means of understanding human attitudes. The books of Robert Ardrey, the man who had popularized this field, were on both of our bookshelves and we spent many hours talking about the implications of his work.

For instance, one of the examples cited by Ardrey provided, in my opinion, a possible explanation for the character of Israel. It appeared that French beavers did not build dams, as other beavers did. Through the ages, the French beaver population had been much reduced. When the French authorities imposed strict laws for the protection of the beavers, they quickly multiplied and suddenly started building dams without ever having seen a beaver do this. The probable explanation was that the dam-building instinct had lain dormant in the French beaver population until a certain population density had been restored, and that then the old instinct re-emerged.

To my mind, something like this had happened to the Jews. For many generations, while living in the diaspora, their political and military 'instincts' had lain dormant. But when they became concentrated in one country, they automatically started to behave, for better or for worse, like any other nation-building people.

As we both seemed to be admirers of Arnold Toynbee, we also argued about his view of the Jews. Sartawi objected, as I did, to Toynbee's idea that the Jews are a fossil of a dead civilization. In my opinion, the Jews were a remnant of an ancient civilization which had joined the modern civilization through the means of Zionism. Zionism as a movement was, in a way, an instrument of the collective assimilation of the Jews into twentieth-century society.

Issam agreed with most of this. His attitude towards Israel and Zionism was ambivalent. As an enemy he was interested in Israel, but the interest generated an attachment that was not merely hostile. The same had happened to us the other way around. It was a kind of symbiosis. I told him about an article I had written in 1949, entitled *Pax Semitica*, in which I had proposed a multi-national, but not anti-national, confederation of the Middle East, which I called 'the Semitic region'. His comment: 'A good idea.' Some day, we decided, we would publish a joint Semitic manifesto, calling for the pooling of resources – the oil, the manpower, the dynamism of our peoples.

When we parted, after this series of meetings, he said: 'Au revoir, if I'm not killed.'

I replied, with optimism generated more by alcohol than by reality: 'I have a feeling that neither of us will be killed.'

* * *

During this time I was in close contact with Bruno Kreisky, exchanging frequent letters, commenting on the situation. The main subject was the ups and downs of the Israeli-Egyptian relationship. Kreisky had played a big role, largely unappreciated, in creating the background for the Sadat initiative. It was he who had opened the doors of Europe for Sadat. With his typical Austrian wisdom, he now proposed to do the same for Arafat: to make him '*Salonfähig*', acceptable in polite European society. As he was unafraid of the Jewish lobby, he was the man to create the precedent, which other European governments could follow, and which, he hoped, the American administration would eventually be able to emulate.

In the summer of 1979, Kreisky had won a resounding election victory. On election night there had been exuberant victory celebrations. My friend Barbara Taufar and her friend, Kreisky's secretary Margit Schmidt, had celebrated with Issam and got marvellously drunk.

One of the first acts of the reconfirmed *Bundeskanzler* was to invite Arafat to Vienna, not yet as the Austrian chief of government, but as the leader of the Austrian Socialist party. When I read the news that Arafat had arrived in Vienna I called Kreisky at his home, in order to urge him to convince Arafat to make some gesture towards the Israeli peace movement. Kreisky answered the phone himself, and when I started to speak he asked: 'Why don't you talk with Arafat himself? He's sitting here right next to me. I'll ask him.'

A few minutes passed, and I could hear voices. I had an odd feeling. I had never come so physically close to Arafat.

Then somebody picked up the receiver and I heard the familiar voice of Issam. 'The Chairman does not think it opportune to talk with you now, but he's sitting here and asks me to convey to you and to your friends his most cordial greetings.'

* * *

In September 1979, an international conference, with the participation of Palestinians and Israelis, was convened in Rome. Matti Peled had to go to the United States, and Sartawi urged me to attend. He was not invited, because this was an enterprise organized with Kaddumi, his opponent. But he was very eager to get more and more Palestinian leaders involved in direct meetings with Israelis, and therefore thought that it was imperative for me to be present, especially as the Palestinian delegation was to include two very important personalities: Ahmed Zidki Dajani, a respected PLO diplomat, and, more importantly, Magid Abu-Sharar, the secretary of the revolutionary council, the highest governing body of Fatah. Abu-Sharar was the leader of the pro-Soviet section in Fatah.

When he sensed my hesitation – I was also very busy at the time – Sartawi told me that Arafat had given the delegation personal instructions to treat the Israelis with the utmost cordiality.

At the conference, Dajani did indeed treat the Israeli delegation very cordially. Besides me, the delegation included Dr Yaacov Arnon, as well as two communists and two university professors. As the leader of the delegation, I made the first Israeli speech, addressing the Palestinians directly. The PLO delegation was present and listened attentively. Afterwards Dajani gave a press conference, to which Israeli journalists were invited and allowed to ask questions. Dajani was very forthcoming, declaring in unequivocal terms that the PLO wanted a Palestinian state in the West Bank and Gaza, and was ready for peace with Israel. Abu-Sharar was much more discreet, and avoided any real controversies. As we shall see, this was significant. It was an expression of the highly ambivalent attitude of the Soviet Union towards our peace efforts. While advocating a clear peace programme based on the coexistence of Israel and the future Palestinian state, the Soviet Union obviously looked with great disfavour upon any direct Palestinian-Israeli contacts outside the communist camp. It wanted all peace efforts to be channelled through its own agents, and did not hesitate to torpedo any other efforts. In practice they behaved very much like the Americans.

The Rome conference was widely reported in the Israeli press, and left behind a positive impression, which was, however, quickly dispelled by an event following classical lines. French journalists had seen me talking with Dajani and assumed that Dajani's remarks were the outcome of secret discussions between us. This was published in an exaggerated form, which must have frightened the Palestinian. Dajani published a denial in Beirut. Again.

* * *

This was a forerunner of much more serious events.

At the beginning of 1979, during one of our conversations, Kreisky had asked me what I thought about an idea he had. Somebody had donated a sum of money for the purpose of celebrating his anniversary. Rather than accept the money, Kreisky had asked that a prize fund be set up. The 'Bruno Kreisky Prize' was to be awarded every three years to a person or persons who had done outstanding work for the cause of peace and humanitarian endeavour. Kreisky wanted to use the prize to promote Israeli-Palestinian peace. He proposed to award the 1979 prize to Sartawi and an Israeli, and asked me what I thought about awarding the prize to Lova Eliav. He preferred Eliav to others, because he was the former secretary of the Israeli Labour Party, and Kreisky hoped quite openly to convince Eliav to leave our party, Sheli, and rejoin the Labour Party. I did not like this at all, but I favoured the idea of giving the award to an Israeli and a Palestinian, and therefore wholeheartedly endorsed the candidature of Eliav. When I went back to Israel and told Lova about it, he was at first incensed that such a decision had been made without consulting him, but then he relented and accepted.

On the other side, the situation was much more complicated. The PLO was not ready for another demonstration of Palestinian-Israeli fraternization, and therefore instructed Sartawi not to take part in the prize-awarding ceremony.

This was a direct affront to Kreisky, especially after the chancellor had gone out of his way to invite Arafat to Vienna. Issam was angry with his colleagues, and he therefore behaved in his typical way: disregarding his instructions, he went to the ceremony, which took place after a long delay in October 1979, but, at his request, with little fanfare. No one was invited from Israel, and therefore I was absent. Later I regretted this very much, because I might have prevented things from happening the way they did.

During the ceremony, the two recipients were asked to address the meeting. Sartawi of course praised the PLO and took pains to make a speech as unprovocative as possible. He hoped Lova would do the same.

But Eliav is not the person to pay too much attention to other people's sensitivities. He took the opportunity to make a speech, praising Zionist ideology and action.

For Palestinians, Zionism is still the number one hate object. They could at best tolerate the idea that they had to accept Zionist partners in the dialogue, but any gratuitous mention of Zionism still riled them. In theory, the Palestinian National Council resolution of March 1977, calling for a dialogue with democratic and progressive forces 'inside and outside the occupied homeland, which are struggling against the ideology and practice of Zionism', still stood.

Sartawi was greatly upset. He smelled trouble. As he told me later: 'Okay, Lova could have mentioned Zionism once, in order to dispense with the formality. But knowing in what a delicate situation I was in by even appearing at this ceremony, why did he have to rub it in?"

Soon news items in Arab papers all over the Middle East prophesied that Issam Sartawi would be put on trial for appearing at the ceremony with a Zionist leader. Some called for his execution. It was a golden opportunity for all the opponents of Sartawi and his line to unite and destroy him.

On 5 December, I called Sartawi, in Paris. I was worried about the news reports, which had been given great prominence in the Israeli media, about his imminent trial. 'They have asked for my neck, and they are still out for my neck', he said. 'I am under enormous attack all over. I'm going back to Beirut.'

'What are you going to do?' I asked.

'I'm going back, you know, to face the music.'

'When will you be back?'

'*If* I come back . . .' Then he said: 'Why don't you raise the question a little bit? It wouldn't do any harm to call the common friend, you know which one I mean, and tell him what you've heard, without mentioning me of course, you know.' I promised to call Bruno Kreisky the next day.

'It won't do any harm. It will give it an international dimension.'

A year earlier, at the end of the dinner Issam and I had had with Bruno Kreisky at his home, Kreisky had volunteered a promise: 'If either of you are persecuted, we shall mobilize international public opinion.' This was the time to take him up on his offer. The next day I called Vienna, and not finding Kreisky there, I called Margit Schmidt about the developments. A few hours later, I spoke with the chancellor himself.

For a month Issam disappeared completely. Kreisky did his utmost, making it clear that if any harm befell Sartawi, it would do incalculable damage and practically destroy all Kreisky's efforts to make the PLO acceptable in the Western world, as well as everything we had built in Israel.

On 5 January, Issam Sartawi miraculously reappeared, flamboyant as ever. He called me, and not finding me at home, left a message on my answering machine. When I called him the next day, in Paris, he sounded confident and reported that the other side was continuing its struggle against him, but that 'the mainstream is solidly behind, you know, our activities. Well, it had to come to the open and this is what we are doing, you know . . . It was a little bit risky.'

At the end of the conversation, he added: 'Give my regards to all our friends. Ask them to have more courage. We have to face the music. After all, we are the only hope for the whole area. So we have to win.'

'We shall!'

'Okay, Uri.'

'Rachel says we shall overcome.'

'We shall.'

Rachel had been standing in the doorway listening, and when she heard me saying 'We shall', she automatically added the word associated with this phrase. We had sung the Martin Luther King song, 'We Shall Overcome', in English and Hebrew, during many a demonstration.

When we went over this episode at our next meeting, it appeared that the Kreisky prize was not the only pretext for the onslaught against Sartawi. There was a second, and perhaps even more damaging one.

While in Vienna, Sartawi had been asked by Kreisky whether he would like to meet with the Egyptian prime minister, Mustafa Khalil, who was staying in Austria. The meeting was arranged in utmost secrecy in Salzburg. No one knew about it, except Khalil and Sartawi, and of course Kreisky. Yet a few days later a story about it appeared in an Egyptian paper. Understandably, it incensed the PLO radicals, who saw in it an act of treason.

Sartawi was certain that this was a deliberate provocation by the Egyptians, who were out to create havoc among the Palestinians, irrespective of the danger to him. During my next visits to Egypt, I raised the question in no uncertain terms. The Egyptian officials apologized profusely: it was all a misunderstanding, sheer stupidity. But it could have killed Sartawi.

The brightest point of the story was that Arafat had defended Sartawi throughout. He had made it clear that Sartawi was his man, and nobody dared touch him.

If anyone had hoped that Issam would be cowed by this experience and lower his profile, he was mistaken. it was quite the opposite.

# 31

*'I've told your joke to everyone in Beirut. It's now called the Avnery joke', Issam says.*

*I have told him this joke several times. Originally, I heard it from Ezer Weizmann, the minister of defence, who must have heard it, judging from his language, when he was a fighter pilot in the Royal Air Force. Weizmann used it to describe the attitude of the Begin government towards the Sadat initiative. I used it to describe PLO tactics.*

*In an expurgated version, it goes like this:*

*A stately British lady arrives at a railway station, only to find she's ten minutes early for her train. Spying a penny-operated scale, she decides to check her weight while she waits. She puts in her penny, and the machine spits out a ticket saying: Your weight is 140 pounds and in five minutes you will receive a kiss.*

*This is preposterous! She thinks, and stalks off to find the station master to lodge a complaint. On the way, she runs into an old friend she hasn't seen for many years, and he takes her into a dark corner of the station building and kisses her passionately.*

*Odd, thinks the lady. How could the machine have known? She still has time before the train comes, so she puts another penny in the scales. The ticket comes out, and this time says: Your weight is 140 pounds and in five minutes you will get a kick.*

*A kick! She is outraged. This time she heads in earnest for the station master. Not finding him in his office, she speaks instead with a porter. There is nothing he can do about the machine, he informs her insolently, and as he turns on his heel to leave her, he accidentally kicks her in the shin. She is speechless and rushes back to the scales, overcome with curiosity.*

*How could the machine know?*

*This time her ticket reads: Your weight is still 140 pounds, but between a kiss and a kick, you've missed your train.*

# 32

We were back in Rambouillet. Issam had called us and invited us three – Matti Peled, Yaacov Arnon, and me – to come urgently for consultations. Henri Curiel's comrades, who were insisting on continuing his work, put the villa at our disposal and conveyed us there. It was the end of September 1980.

The four of us were now thoroughly comfortable with each other. A personal pattern had been established. We had by now complete trust in each other, after Eliav, Pail and one or two others had abused Sartawi's confidence, or so he thought. Between us four, the most secret matters could be discussed openly without fear or reservation.

Each of us had a different kind of relationship with Issam. He respected Matti Peled, who as a person was his very opposite. Matti does not care very much for the simple delights of life, such as good meals, and certainly would not be a party to a discussion of the merits of girls. The fact that he was a general impressed Issam, knowing that it would also impress other Palestinian leaders. In speeches he sometimes said: 'I talked with General Peled, as a Palestinian general to an Israeli general . . .' alluding to the fact that he was a former chief of a Fedayeen organization.

His relationship with Yaacov Arnon was quite different. Arnon is ten years older than both Matti and me (there is only a few week's gap between us) and he was a kind of father figure. Issam liked to trade jokes with him, and respected his common sense. Arnon, who had survived the German occupation of his native Holland, was a veteran of the Labour Party and the Israeli government administration, and had that particular brand of earthy wisdom which one needs to run a big corporation.

The relationship between Issam and me was different again. In many respects we were very similar to each other. We shared many likes and dislikes, a sense of adventure, a certain devil-may-care attitude, an enjoyment of the good things, a general curiosity about things. An American woman journalist, who became friendly with both of us, once told me: 'When I'm with Issam I think about you, and when I'm with you I think about Issam. To me you are two different versions of the same person.' I took it as a great compliment.

* * *

Sartawi had called us because he wanted to launch a great plan, a grand design, and felt that he should consult us before submitting it to his leaders.

The situation in the PLO was developing positively, and he thought that great things were now possible.

This was not so readily perceived in Israel. To us the picture looked much more confused.

Several things had happened in 1980. In May, the Fatah leadership had convened in Damascus and immediately afterwards the world press blossomed with news stories that Fatah had decided to destroy Israel. This was gleefully taken up by the Israeli media as another proof of our naïveté.

According to Sartawi, the story was quite different. The radical elements in the movement had prepared an introduction, saying that their aim was 'to liquidate the Zionist entity politically, economically, militarily, culturally, and ideologically'.

This introduction was never discussed, much less adopted. But the Syrians, who of course controlled the media in Damascus, leaked it to foreign journalists, who assumed that these were the resolutions of the secret caucus. It was the old, old story all over again.

When no denial was forthcoming, Sartawi got more and more angry. The news had had a catastrophic impact on European public opinion, which he was courting so arduously. He threatened to resign from Fatah, and in the end succeeded in convincing Arafat that something must be done. He chose an American journalist, Joseph Fitchett of the *International Herald Tribune* in Paris, and took him to Beirut, where Arafat gave him an exclusive interview, which was published on 6 August. It said, inter alia:

> In an effort to defend the Palestine Liberation Organization's political gains and credibility in Europe, Yasser Arafat denied today diplomatic and press reports dating back to May that his guerrilla group recently called for the destruction of Israel and had abandoned any interest in negotiating for a Palestinian mini-state to co-exist alongside Israel.
>
> In response to a question in an interview, he said that he had let the report stand unchallenged for weeks because he had been too preoccupied by other issues, although there were disavowals of the strong anti-Israel statement by other PLO officials.
>
> In the interview, Mr Arafat accused Israel of carrying out an international operation to misrepresent the PLO, based on misleading documents widely publicized in Western newspapers and circulated at the United Nations purporting to prove that the PLO had reverted to its old hardline goal of never compromising with Israel.
>
> "It is the latest part in a long series of attempts by Begin to falsify and denigrate the Palestinian political position", he said, in accusing by name Israeli Prime Minister Menachem Begin.

This was a victory for Sartawi. By denying that the PLO aimed to destroy Israel or that it had given up the idea of establishing a Palestinian state in the West Bank and Gaza, Arafat had come closer than ever before to confirming the Sartawi line.

There could be no doubt that an Israeli department for political warfare was at work, using titbits provided by Arab radicals and sometimes resorting to outright falsification and disinformation.

The most blatant example was an interview widely distributed by Israeli officials throughout the world. It purported to be an exclusive interview given by Yassir Arafat to a South American magazine, *El Mondo*, which very few people had ever heard of before. In this interview, Arafat expressed the most extreme views, calling for the total destruction of Israel.

Upon Sartawi's urging, a thorough investigation was set underway. It appeared that *El Mondo* was an insignificant girlie magazine, and that Arafat had never granted it an interview. When called to account, the editors explained that their correspondent had been present, together with sixty other journalists, at a press conference given by Arafat. But none of the others had heard the remarks quoted by the magazine in its 'exclusive' interview. It was a textbook example of planted misinformation. But the PLO was powerless to counteract the manufacture of such stories, which were distributed by the brilliant Israeli propaganda machine, which is much maligned at home but which, I believe, has no peer.

Developments now in the Arab world were positive. At the Baghdad summit of November 1978, Iraq had shown surprising signs of moderation. Now the Iraqi dictator had started a war against Iran, and was becoming more and more dependent upon Saudi assistance and supplies passing through Jordan. He had joined the moderate Arab bloc, which was isolating Syria and Libya, whose influence was diminished. Damascus could not pressure the PLO leadership as it had done before. The PLO leadership was freer now to conduct an independent policy.

A few days before the Rambouillet meeting, Arafat had made a revolutionary gesture. An Israeli communist delegation had taken part in one of the many communist gatherings, this time in Sofia. By prearrangement, Arafat was there and 'happened' to run into them in the corridor. The members of the delegation – two Knesset members and a Jewish woman lawyer – were introduced to him. He embraced them and kissed the woman. This created quite a sensation in Israel, but was shrugged off by most. What's the big deal? An Arab embraces an Arab, a Moscow ally embraces a Moscow stooge, a Palestinian terrorist kisses a female traitor.

Having no time to consult anyone, I wrote a cover story explaining that this was a big step forward. Such a meeting could hardly have been a coincidence. By embracing a member of the Israeli Knesset, and a Jewish one, the PLO leader had gone one step further towards recognizing the State of Israel. By doing this in Sofia, and by choosing communists for this first gesture, he had avoided the criticism of the PLO hardliners and the Syrians, who were allied with the communist bloc. Thus a precedent had been set, which would enable Arafat to meet, in due course, other members of the Knesset and other peace activists. Meeting Sartawi a few days later, I asked him to explain the episode. I was quite pleased when he explained it to me in nearly exactly the same words as I had put in my article. It proved to me that I was starting to understand the inner workings of the PLO. After six years of studying, I was becoming a professor of Palestinian realities.

The practical upshot was that things were progressing, that Sartawi's position was strengthened, and that he was ready now to move on to bigger and better things.

* * *

The grand design which Sartawi put before us, in the quiet, comfortable living room of the Rambouillet villa, was ambitious indeed. The time had passed, he said, to work *ad hoc*. From now on, we must work according to a plan. The crucial date was Israeli election day in 1981. The objective was to send fifteen people committed to our programme to the next Knesset.

We had to smile at this figure. For a small or new party to gain fifteen members of parliament was an immense undertaking. It had been done only once, in 1977, when the new Dash party, under General Yigal Yadin, had gained exactly that number. But soon after, the party had fallen apart, and nothing remained but a sad memory.

We were quite ready to settle for a much smaller objective – say, a parliamentary faction of five or six members. Experience showed that even such a small faction, in the 120-member Knesset, could play a crucial role if the government was dependent upon its votes. As a matter of fact, the existing Begin government depended for its very life upon the four votes of the ultra-orthodox Agudat Israel faction, which could practically dictate its wishes to the government and often did. But Issam would not hear of this. The objective had to be big, in order to impress the PLO leadership.

Unfolding his ideas, Sartawi drew a picture which made the impossible seem possible. Assuming the new elections would be held in the fall of 1981, there was a year left for action. During this year a series of dramatic events would take place, on an ever-grander scale, such as Israeli-Palestinian conferences, meetings between Israeli peace activists and high-ranking PLO leaders, and so forth. This would help us become heroes in Israel, and create a great coalition of peace forces, the nucleus of which would be the Israeli Council. At the same time we would organize supportive movements all over the Western world, with the active help of Sartawi himself, and this would enable us to raise money on a scale we had never dreamt of. We would become a force in Israeli politics, the next Labour Party government (everyone assumed at that time that Labour would come back to power) would be dependent on our votes. We would use this power to turn Israeli policy towards peace. Our achievements would vastly strengthen the realistic elements within the PLO. Sartawi himself would become much more important, Arafat would be able to make the unequivocal statements about the PLO's readiness for mutual recognition and peace which we needed.

A long time had passed since I first tried to impress this line of thought on Said Hammami in London. Here it was as a practical plan, proposed by a PLO official.

We discussed practical steps. A joint committee should be set up to direct the whole enterprise. A detailed plan should be worked out and confirmed at a meeting with the leadership of both sides. An all-Arab peace initiative, led by Saudi Arabia, should coincide with our effort. International personalities should be called upon to play their part. We examined various possibilities of approaching heads of states. What could be done about King Hassan of Morocco or President Bourguiba of Tunisia, with both of whom

Sartawi had good relations? How to approach President Valéry Giscard d'Estaing of France? How best to use the good offices of Bruno Kreisky? (Issam called him 'the most dedicated Jew in the whole world', adding, 'he is deeply committed to Israel. He believes that peace is the sole guarantee for the future existence of Israel.') What could be done about the German leaders, such as Willy Brandt and Helmut Schmidt? Sartawi himself could not enter German territory, because the Bavarian government had issued a warrant for his arrest in February 1969, after the attack by his former organization on the Israeli passengers at Munich airport. The Bavarian right-wing leader, Franz-Josef Strauss, was an ardent supporter of the Israeli government, and all efforts to rescind the warrant against the ex-Fedayeen, who was now a peace hero, had proved futile. Sartawi could also not go to the States, where the State Department refused to grant him entry, using as a pretext the passport irregularity which had created such an extreme diplomatic incident in 1976. Even the personal intervention of Nahum Goldmann, who spoke about this several times with Cyrus Vance, was to no avail. At the same time, well-known leaders of the rejection front were allowed to enter the United States freely, move about, make speeches and collect money for organizations devoted to the destruction of Israel. No one cared about that.

We brought up many problems. Could we bring the PLO to stop acts of violence? How and when? Could we perhaps achieve a temporary, limited moratorium on such attacks, and present it to the Israeli public as another achievement of the peace movement? Could we establish immediately an Israeli-Palestinian peace centre, for the exchange of information? Could we publish a joint newsletter in Europe, which would publish all information about peace initiatives and actions on both sides?

What could we do to put an end, once and for all, to the foul practice of PLO denial after every advance? How could we make sure that declarations by either side would be coordinated with the other side before being made public?

It was by far the most practical discussion we had ever had. We were moving into another stage.

Over a dinner prepared by our hosts, who discreetly hovered about us without being present at any of the discussions, we relaxed and traded memories. Again we compared notes about the Baghdad bomb of 1950. And I told Issam about the so-called 'security mishap' of 1954 in Cairo, which had given rise to the famous Lavon Affair.*

We were in an excellent mood.

On the way home, in the airplane, we exchanged impressions. In the light of our long experience, we were a bit sceptical. We were convinced of Issam's total sincerity, but was he able to pull it off? Wasn't he over optimistic in his assessment of the balance of forces within the PLO? As usual, Arnon was the most sceptical, and warned of premature enthusiasm. Matti was much more optimistic and I was somewhere in the middle.

* See the relevant chapter in my book, *Israel Without Zionists*.

* * *

But this time things did move. At the end of December 1980, we received the expected message: Come immediately.

Anna Best, Henri Curiel's devoted assistant for many years and an expert on Kurdish affairs, an Ashkenazi Jewish girl from Egypt, received us at Charles de Gaulle airport. We crammed into her little car, along with our luggage, and on the way into the city she told us the news: We were all going to Morocco, to meet the king.

'I don't believe it,' Arnon said.

At the private apartment of one of the Curiel group members, we prepared for the journey. Issam appeared, radiating confidence. Everything was prepared. We were to receive false papers in order to enter Morocco. All three of us would receive Arab names, and fly to Rabat on a Royal Air Maroc airliner. Everything was arranged by the Moroccan Embassy in Paris, on direct orders of His Majesty.

A few minutes later we were on our way to Orly airport. A young Moroccan gentleman accompanied us. He gave each of us a typed document, with our photograph affixed to it. (I always carried passport photographs with me, but Matti and Arnon had to find a photo booth in Paris.) I was now Dr Omar Kharaki, a Moroccan citizen with improbable blue eyes. I was born in Casablanca on 16 June 1927, thus becoming younger by four years. Arnon was Dr Ahmed Sabar, born in Meknes in 1917, also gaining a few years. Matti was Dr Abd-al-Salaam Murabet.

Rather fearfully, we approached the French passport control officer. With a cursory glance at our papers, without batting an eyelash, he waved through the three improbable Moroccans. In the exit lounge, waiting to receive our boarding passes, we found ourselves in a long line of Moroccans. The Moroccan gentleman had disappeared. Among ourselves we spoke as little as possible, in English, with subdued voices. The wait was interminable, but eventually we found ourselves installed in the first class of the airliner, surrounded by beautiful Moroccan hostesses who offered us champagne for starters.

It was all much too smooth. Something was bound to happen to spoil the miracle. And sure enough, it did. But something quite different.

Still on the ground, there was a little commotion. An elderly Moroccan couple, exuding an air of privilege and importance, entered the first class. There was no place for them left. Peremptorily, the purser pointed at Dr Murabet and Dr Othman - Matti and Issam - and with a perfunctory apology told them to seat themselves in the economy class. Our position being as delicate as it was, they could not put up a fight. They followed the purser quietly to the very rear of the plane, near the lavatories.

Issam never forgot this experience. He recounted it many times. He could forget dangers, assassination attempts, failures and rebuffs, but he could not forget the indignity of being forced to sit in the cramped economy class, eating inedible (for him) food, on his way to see the King of Morocco.

As he told it, the crowning indignity was my appearance in the doorway of the first class, carrying a bottle of exquisite champagne and sweets, solicitously inquiring after them. 'You really rubbed it in. You were practically gloating!'

And indeed this flight was one to remember. I never fly first class. But this was not even a usual first class, such as exists in American airliners, not to mention El Al. It was a flying paradise. Champagne flowed like tap water. Meal followed meal, sweets followed cigars, excellent cognac was served with Arab coffee. All this on top of the singular experience of being in an Arab airplane at all, surrounded by Arab ladies and gentlemen, served by Arab cabin attendants in grand style, on the way to an experience which we couldn't have dreamt of 24 hours earlier.

At Rabat airport, a gentleman in a flowing black robe received us and asked us to sit in a comfortable lounge while the other passengers were processed. After a short conversation with Sartawi, we were whisked out to a big limousine and brought to a beautiful villa on the outskirts of the town where our host, Ahmed Ben-Souda, the king's *chef de cabinet*, was awaiting us.

Our mood, already very good, became euphoric. Ben-Souda is a charming gentleman. Within minutes we were launched into a discussion of Arabic poetry, in which Matti Peled excelled. They were reciting to each other classical Arab poems. The sight of an Israeli general who could recite, at length, pre-Mohammedan Arab poems must have impressed our host, who was joined by another adviser of the King. Ben-Souda recited some poems he had written himself as a youngster, and Issam, another lover of Arab poetry, who occasionally wrote poems himself, did not lag behind.

After the poems came the jokes. The caliph Haroun al-Rashid is visiting the palace of one of his viziers, which was more beautiful than his own. He asks the son of the vizier, whose palace is more magnificent? The child has to choose between lying, which is a sin, and telling the truth, which would insult the caliph. He answers, 'our palace is more beautiful, now that the caliph is staying in it'.

The door opened and two other gentlemen were ushered in. One was Abu Marwan, the PLO ambassador in Rabat. The other was one of the most important persons in the PLO, Khaled al-Hassan, Yassir Arafat's political adviser, a member of the first rank of Fatah and the PLO, one of the half a dozen top men around Arafat.

After six years of meeting, Hammami, Sartawi, Jiryes, Abu Faisal, and two or three others, we had reached the top. As Sartawi told us later, he had told Arafat: 'They have been seeing Sartawi, Sartawi, Sartawi. They are sick and tired of seeing my face. New people must enter the dialogue!' From the first moment, the most cordial friendship sprang up between Khaled al-Hassan and us. He is a rich merchant based in Kuwait, an importer of Japanese electronic equipment. He is of imposing stature, with a wonderful sense of humour, a man of great wisdom and political sense. After a few minutes we called him Khaled, and he called us by our first names.

The serious discussion started. Matti opened it with a well-reasoned, concise exposition of the Israeli peace movement, its potential and problems. Ben-Souda and his colleague, Ahmed al-Khadera, listened attentively. Their job, as they explained, was to brief His Majesty before our meeting;

to discuss the problems with us in advance so as to put concrete proposals before His Majesty which could be discussed with him. No one took notes, but, as it appeared in the end, they were experts at listening, digesting and analysing material. They did not miss a point.

After an hour or so, during which we all talked and traded ideas, we were told, to my consternation, that dinner was ready. On the airplane I had eaten immense quantities of the food and sweets, unable to refuse such excellent fare. Now we were conducted into the dining corner, where we sat on cushions on the floor. In front of us immense heaps of food were waiting. Not partaking would be an insult to our host, so I ate a second dinner, even bigger than the first. Fortunately, the food was so interesting that my appetite was whetted again. The host would dip into the food with his hand, choose the choicest bits for us and serve it from hand to hand.

Conversation turned again to the humorous. There was this young alcoholic gentleman in Damascus who was informed that his uncle, a most devout Muslim hadj, was passing through his city on the way back from Mecca and expected him to serve him. In panic, the gentleman hides the numerous bottles of alcohol in his house. The sheikh arrives and eats a very leisurely meal. The craving of his host for a drink becomes unbearable. Uncle, he says, I must tell you something. I am very sick and the doctor has ordered me to drink a glass of whisky with water with every meal. Allah forbid! cries the sheikh. The host suffers for another few minutes, and then says: Ya sheikh, my life is at stake, I must have a glass of whisky with water immediately. Allah forbid! says the sheikh, never mix whisky with water!

Between the jokes, the food and the Moroccan red wine, the political discussion continued, interspersed with personal notes. Our host told us that his family came originally from Granada. One of his forefathers had been the pupil of a famous Jewish doctor, and all members of his family had been lawyers or physicians. 'All of them, except me, are poets', he added modestly. The King himself, it was noted, belonged to a family which had a centuries-old tradition of Muslim-Jewish cooperation. I told them what I had learned in school about the 'Golden Epoch' of Muslim-Jewish culture in Muslim Spain, when some of the greatest Jewish poets had written their works in Arabic and Hebrew, and when many Jews had become famous as viziers, advisers and physicians of Moroccan princes.

Listening to the conversation, observing the perfect blend of authentic Arab Moroccan and French European cultures, I could not help thinking about a topic which was to occupy me constantly during the following two days: Why were the Moroccan Jews in Israel looked down upon and discriminated against by the Ashkenazis? What has happened to their cultural heritage?

I told my host that during the 1948 War, when I was promoted to section leader, I had chosen my men from among the new immigrants coming from many different countries. I had chosen a group of Moroccans and led them into battle. I had never regretted this decision, because it was four of my Moroccan soldiers who saved my life when I was wounded, carrying me back from an exposed position under fire.

I discovered that no one in the Moroccan elite was angry with the Moroccan Jews who had left their homeland and gone to Israel. They still considered them Moroccans.

At the end of the evening, the King's advisers asked us to try and condense our requests to His Majesty into a few concrete items. Matti drew up a list, Arnon and I added to it and Khaled al-Hassan amended it, moderating several items. In the end it was condensed into four concrete proposals:

1) That the King, as chairman of the Islamic Conference due to be convened in a few days, see to it that peace with Israel be mentioned in its resolutions. This was Arnon's proposal.

2) If this was impossible, that the King interpret the resolutions in his own speech and add that the comprehensive peace in the Middle East includes peace with Israel. This was my proposal. Matti proposed that the King address the Israeli government in his speech and draw its attention to the fact that it was missing a great opportunity to achieve peace, now that the Arab world was ready for peace with it.

3) That the King address the Moroccan Jews (who were forming, in Israel, the electoral base of the Likud) and ask them to work for peace. This was my suggestion. Matti and Khaled formulated it as follows: That His Majesty address all the Jews who had come to Israel from Arab countries, remind them of the long history of brotherhood between Jews and Arabs, and ask them to use their influence in the cause of peace.

4) That after this visit, which was secret, His Majesty invite to Morocco, officially and publicly, a delegation of the Israeli peace camp.

* * *

When I woke up in the morning, the sun was shining brightly and I had a glorious view of the sea.

I was rather surprised, because I had had no idea that Rabat was actually on the coast. The whole trip had been so hurried that I had had no time for any preparation, such as looking at a map.

We had arrived in Rabat after dark and spent the evening in the palatial villa of Ben-Souda, who had brought us personally to the Rabat Hilton just before midnight. He told the manager that we were personal guests of His Majesty, and from then on we received royal treatment.

After getting up, I inspected the hotel with great curiosity. It was here that the famous Rabat Summit resolution of 1974, which had recognized the PLO as the sole legitimate representative of the Palestinian people, had been adopted.

All four of us – Dr Haraki, Dr Sabar, Dr Murabet and Dr Othman – had our breakfast together at the al-Foroussia Coffee Shop, eating Moroccan dishes I didn't know existed: khareira soup and eggs with honey. Soon after we went up to Issam's room, expecting to be called any moment to the King. We knew that Ben-Souda and al-Khadera were to be received by the King at ten thirty, and naively thought that after half an hour of briefing he would summon us. So we sat around the room, discussing this and that and waiting for the telephone to ring. The subjects, as usual: the power struggle within the PLO, the relations between the PLO and Jordan, the PLO vis-à-vis

Saudi Arabia and the Gulf States. After an hour or so Khaled al-Hassan joined us. He spread his bulk on the bed, for lack of any more chairs.

Twenty-four hours before, Khaled al-Hassan had been just another name for us, a remote figure in the PLO leadership. Now we were intimate. In between serious discussions, a lot of jokes were exchanged. I remember one of Khaled's: Two butchers are having a fight in the market. One butcher cuts off the nose and some fingers of the other, who bursts out laughing, exclaiming: But I cut off something else, and he's getting married tonight!

The time stretched out, but we were far from bored. Whenever Israelis and Palestinians meet for the first time, they have a lot to tell each other, a lot to explain and to argue about. In a few hours we had to condense for Khaled all we had told Issam in four years. Fortunately he has a very quick intelligence. We were also interested to hear Khaled's point of view, to hear about PLO realities from someone other than Sartawi so we could compare the two versions.

'By God, I'm glad you're here. These people must have started to suspect that I'm quite alone, that my pose of representing the PLO is just make believe', Issam said, only half jokingly. He was not far off the mark.

After talking for four hours, crammed in the little room, we were getting a little bit impatient. 'You must get used to dealing with kings', Khaled, who had a lot of experience of this kind, said. 'Kings are like beautiful girls. They can afford to let you wait.'

We learned some facts about Khaled's personal background. He was born in Haifa. For generations his family had been the keeper of Elijah's cave, a famous site near the city, venerated by the Jews as well as by the Arabs. On Jewish holidays, his father's house had been full of rabbis. He asked me to bring him some photos of the site as it looked now – a promise I kept. For a fleeting moment the sad memory of Said Hammami, and his house in Jaffa that I never found, sprang to my mind.

Khaled told us something about the way the historic resolution to establish a Palestinian national state was adopted at the 1977 National Council session. The former resolution, adopted in 1974, spoke about the 'independent combatant national authority'. Somebody wanted to speak about the 'combatant national state', somebody else wanted it to read 'liberating national state'. In exasperation, Khaled had proposed to call it a 'jet national state', because in order to fight you had to have modern instruments. In the general laughter, the simple formula was adopted.

I was surprised to hear that he had great respect for Georges Habash, the hardliner. He said that Habash wanted peace as much as anyone, but did not believe that Israel and the imperialists would ever agree. He did not want the PLO to entertain illusions.

The so-called Jordanian option, according to Khaled, was a ridiculous proposition. King Hussein would never accept the West Bank without Jerusalem. Khaled believed that eventually some kind of federation of the Palestinian state and Jordan would come into being, and this could also include Israel and Lebanon. He was surprised to hear that some Israelis, including Eri Jabotinsky, the son of the famous nationalist leader, had at one time proposed much the same thing.

The Gulf States couldn't exist without the Palestinians. It would take five years to replace them in their jobs. While other foreigners could be repatriated from the Gulf States and Saudi Arabia, there was nowhere the Palestinians could go from there. Even more, the Saudis were afraid of quarrelling with the Palestinians, because this could lead to their radicalization.

As for Syria, she fed on the war. She was not really interested in getting back the Golan Heights, if this meant peace. As a confrontation state and defender of the Arab world, Syria received five billion dollars a year from the Arab world. It was a question of money and honour. Peace would be a catastrophe for Syria.

At around five o'clock we received the awaited phone call. The audience with the King would take place the next day, at eleven o'clock. We were irritated. But the next day we found out that the time had not been spent in vain: the King had been very thoroughly briefed, and many points had been checked. As one of his advisers told us: 'By now he knows the exact rank of Matti Peled and the exact collar size of Uri Avnery.'

In the meantime we were free to do as we pleased. We decided to see the town, and especially the bazaar.

On the way out, Issam took a photograph with his pocket camera. This was a very secret picture, with us standing under the sign of the Rabat Hilton. Then a doorman took a picture of all four of us. It was a measure of Issam's trust in us that he gave me a copy a few days later. Only when the time was ripe did I publish the lower part of the picture, cutting off the sign that indicated the location. It was the only picture ever taken of us four together until then. After our meetings with the King were made public by His Majesty himself, I published the full picture.

After the obligatory visit to the impressive mausoleum of King Mohammed V, Hassan's father, who had been considered a friend and protector of the Jews, we went to the souk. It was an incredible experience, adding to the dreamlike atmosphere of the whole adventure. Here we were, three Israelis and a Palestinian, moving through the throng, speaking English, and only sometimes, in subdued voices, in Hebrew. We were neither accompanied nor shadowed by the Moroccan security services. Each of us was looking for different things: Matti was eager to discover some rare editions of Arabic literature and poetry, I had set my heart on buying some cassettes of Moroccan music, Arnon was looking for souvenirs for his wife, Luce. Among the three of us, he was the one who found it most difficult to believe that we were actually there. 'It's not true, it's all a dream', he kept repeating. He said that if he did not buy some authentic presents, even his wife would not believe him.

There were shops displaying an incredible variety of dates and nuts, and some very picturesque butchers' shops featuring various internal organs of animals. Matti wanted us to pose for a photo in front of one of them. Issam joked: 'Butchers and soldiers must have something in common.'

In the end we each bought a colourful dress for our wives, spending a lot of time choosing the right one. For myself I bought a beautiful black Moroccan robe with a hood, the same I had seen on the security officer who had received us at the airport. When I dared to wear it, years later, at a costume party in Israel, I was taken for a monk.

I was continuously wondering about the difference between the Moroccans and their Jewish counterparts in Israel. They looked different.

Leaving the souk, on the way to our taxi, I crossed the path of a very beautiful young woman. Being happy, I smiled at her. For a moment she hesitated, and then she smiled back, a radiant smile which lit up her face.

* * *

In the evening we went up to the Bab es-Sama (Port of Heaven) restaurant on the eighth floor of the Hilton. It was an evening of complete happiness, one of those occasions one remembers for a long time.

Here we were in a foreign country, about to be received by the King in the presence of one of the highest PLO leaders. At long last things were moving. Our long, frustrating effort for peace was bearing fruit.

Relaxing in the Moroccan atmosphere, we tried to choose between *Couscous Tfaia* (couscous with onions and dried raisins) and *Charia Madfouna* (steamed vermicelli with sugar and cinammon), between *Bstila* (flaky pigeon pie, the Fassi way) and *Houte Fassi* (marinated whole fish in *chermoula* sauce with stuffed peppers and tomatoes). We talked about future plans. Everything seemed possible. One of the suggestions: to propose Issam Sartawi and Matti Peled jointly for the Nobel Peace Prize. As a member of parliament I had the right to do so, but perhaps – we thought –we should make this suggestion to Willy Brandt and Bruno Kreisky.

Sartawi thought that they owed him such a gesture, after what he considered a betrayal. He had appeared at the last meeting of the Socialist International, which was held in Madrid in November 1980, but only as an observer in a private capacity. Brandt, who had promised him much more, had reneged on his promise – on the urging of Shimon Peres – to recognize him as the PLO representative, and so had denied him a very important achievement. He had reacted by publishing in an English-language Beirut magazine, *Monday Morning*, a scathing indictment of the Israeli Labour Party's programme, asserting that it was a war programme, and that only Sheli and some other groups were following a sincere peace line. This was in response to the resolution of the International declaring that the Israeli Labour Party was the only peace force in Israel, which had been adopted in order to help the Labour Party's forthcoming election campaign.

The bitterness with which he told us about these events quickly dissolved under the influence of Moroccan wine, Moroccan music, Moroccan food. A girl got up from one of the tables, where she was sitting with a family, and started to move, quite alone, on the dance floor. With the subtlest of movements, she circled the floor to the suggestive Moroccan music. We followed her with our eyes as if hypnotized, and perhaps we were. It was a unique experience, spellbinding and bewitching. We could have looked at her all night, but after some twenty minutes she sat down, breaking the spell. We could not guess whether she was a professional dancer or not; in any case, Arnon, the perfect European gentleman, went up to her and thanked her.

* * *

We met the King the next morning, on the last day of 1980.

We were told to be ready early. When Ben-Souda took us from the hotel, we understood why. His Majesty was not staying in Rabat, but on a royal farm, somewhere between Rabat and Casablanca.

Our little convoy traversed the Moroccan countryside, and I looked with great curiosity at the country from which so many of my friends and acquaintances had come. After something like an hour we came to a large, enclosed estate, and were led to a large reception room. We had to wait a little while, the King was getting up.

We were sitting around little tables – the two royal advisers, the three Israeli musketeers (as we called ourselves at the time), and the three Palestinians, Khaled, Issam and the PLO ambassador to Morocco, Abu Marwan, whose real name was Wajia Hassan Ali Kassem. On the wall some very modernistic abstract art was displayed. White-clad retainers served us cold drinks, Moroccan *khareira* soup with milk, and the most excellent yogourt I've ever tasted. 'It's from His Majesty's own animals,' Ben-Souda commented. 'His Majesty is having his breakfast, and he sent us some of it.' The suppressed tension found an outlet in an endless string of jokes – some Jewish, some Israeli, some Palestinian, some Arabic, some of undefined nationality.

Unlike Matti and Arnon, I had not brought a suit with me, and was wearing a dark blazer. I felt too casually dressed, but then the King entered, wearing a blue blazer with gold buttons and grey trousers, white shirt and black tie. He shook everyone's hand – the Moroccans bowed – and conveyed us to his private office. On the way I succumbed to a momentary weakness and stole a book of matches imprinted with the royal insignia and the French inscription: S.M. le Roi Hassan II.

The King is about my age, slightly shorter than me, and from the first moment I was struck by his modest, unassuming but quietly confident manner. It was the good breeding one associates with long established royal houses. As a direct descendant of the Prophet Mohammed, the King is both a temporal and spiritual leader.

The King started the conversation in a jocular vein. He complained that he had put on a tie only because Khaled al-Hassan always dresses formally. But here was Khaled, without a tie, rather sloppily dressed in a brown jacket. The King added that he had brought a general to the meeting, out of respect for Matti's rank. The Moroccan general, in civilian clothes, was sitting quietly on the side. He was General Dlimi, the King's chief security adviser, who later died in an accident.

We had been told in advance by the advisers that there was no need for a lengthy exposé of our proposals. Having been thoroughly briefed and having considered the matters, the King would respond to our proposals, and we were to discuss his views.

Matti Peled opened with an Arabic greeting, then the King came straight to the point. He spoke Arabic, Sartawi translated into English, and from time to time the King corrected the translation, displaying a perfect command of the language.

About our suggestion that the King, as chairman of the Islamic Conference, try to convince that body to adopt a pro-peace resolution mentioning Israel, the King was cautiously optimistic. It would be easier to convince an Islamic than a purely Arabic conference, but even so it would not be easy.

About the idea that the King publish a statement saying that Israel was committing a grave error by disregarding the Arab world's readiness for peace with it, he expressed his willingness to do so when the proper opportunity arose.

About our request that he address the Moroccan community in Israel and ask it to support the peace forces (instead of as now constituting the bulk of the Likud electorate), the King was more than willing. There were flourishing Jewish–Moroccan communities in Canada and Paris, and the King believed that those would also be amenable to such an appeal. He also hoped that the Jewish community in Morocco and its chief rabbi, whom he considered his personal friend, would issue similar appeals.

The King brought up several other points. He preferred, he said, the discreet approach of going from door to door. Would we be ready for meetings with other Arab leaders, such as President Bourguiba of Tunisia? Matti started a lengthy reply, but Issam hissed to him: 'Say yes! Yes!' Unperturbed, Matti changed his tone in the middle of the sentence and said that we were most eager for His Majesty to arrange such a meeting. (I later remarked to both of them that if there had been a table between them, Issam would have kicked his shin.)

Unfortunately, the King said, there were some Arab regimes which fed on the war. He did not mention any names, but I assumed he meant Syria and Libya.

In passing, the King mentioned that he had been the first Arab leader to call for peace with Israel. In 1958, seven years before the historic peace initiative of President Bourguiba, he, Hassan, had, in Beirut, called on the Arabs to recognize Israel and admit it as a member state to the Arab League. (By the way, I had made much the same proposal in the early 1950s.)

King Hassan also thought that much could be done in Europe. Under the leadership of Valéry Giscard d'Estaing, France could take the lead. He thought we should do the utmost to help Giscard against François Mitterrand in the coming election.

But what about the United States? Did we have connections with high administration circles? If not, General Dlimi had very good relations with Vice-President George Bush. He would arrange a meeting.

On this note, the audience ended. Both Matti and Arnon helped themselves to His Majesty's matchbooks, as souvenirs, and the King led us to the guestroom, which, like his office, was redolent of incense, and shook our hands warmly.

Outside, in the glorious winter sun, the tension gave way to exuberance.

The audience had gone well, much better than any of us could have expected. The King was more than friendly, he was an ally.

We stood around, exchanging impressions and making last-minute suggestions. 'Don't push him, please!' Khaled advised. I told him that once, during one of the Florence peace conferences, Mayor La Pira, who was deeply religious, had said: 'God is almighty. He can do anything He wants, even make peace between Israel and the Arabs overnight. But He wants to be pushed!'

We exchanged cards, telephone numbers, embraces and kisses. Ben-Souda joked: 'I know these are friendly kisses – only.'

From the royal estate we went straight to King Mohammed V airport, south of Casablanca. On the way we passed through the outskirts of that city, from which so many Moroccan Jews had come to Israel. A security officer received us at the airport and led us to the VIP lounge, where we were served scented Moroccan tea. From there we were taken straight to the plane without any formalities. Issam saw to it that we could keep our Moroccan laissez-passers as souvenirs.

This time all four of us remained in the first class section. Between the glasses of champagne, the meals and the sweets, we made plans. From time to time we dared utter a few words in Hebrew. The plane touched down in Oujda after flying over the Moroccan Atlas Mountains and the towns of Meknes and Fez. A group of impoverished Moroccan labourers came on board, obviously en route to work in France.

In Orly we had a problem. This time we had to use our Israeli passports. We also had to fill out disembarkation cards that demanded the origin of the flight. We looked at the great arrival board, noticed that a plane from Portugal had just come in, and wrote down: Place of embarkation – Lisbon. The passport control officer did not even look at us.

At the airport, Anna Best was waiting for us. She had been worried and was greatly relieved to see us. Everybody was jubilant. I told her: 'Issam reminds me of a magician who has time and again failed to produce the rabbit from the top hat. *Voilà*, this time he has produced it.'

And Arnon asked: 'Was this an adventure, or did we really make history?'

* * *

1 January 1981 seemed to promise a year of achievements. It was also Issam's birthday.

On New Year's Eve I called Rachel from his office, to wish her a Happy New Year. Apart from Amnon Zichroni, my friend and lawyer, whom I had prepared for any eventuality, Rachel was the only person who knew that I was flying off to Morocco where I would be totally at the mercy of the PLO. She was happy to hear my voice. We spoke guardedly, knowing that at least two security services were listening in, but she knew from the tone of my voice that we had had a great success. Apart from other presents, Issam had also insisted on buying, on the airplane, a bottle of expensive perfume for each of our wives.

During the conversation, Issam took the receiver to wish Rachel a Happy New Year as well.

I spent the night in his office, which had two bedrooms, and where I felt more comfortable and safe than in a hotel. I made this a habit until Issam's death, wondering many times at the complete trust he had in me, often leaving me alone in the office with its many files. He himself lived with his family nearby, and the office was generally guarded by Fatah bodyguards. Israeli propaganda would probably have called it 'a nest of terrorists'.

On 1 January, we all met to chart the course for the near future. Matti mentioned that the Israeli Council for Israeli-Palestinian Peace was about to commemorate the fifth anniversary of its founding in a meeting in Jerusalem, and asked Issam to send a message to it. Sartawi went to the next room, spent half an hour composing a handwritten message, and came back to show us the text. It read:

> On the occasion of the fifth anniversary of the foundation of the Israeli Council for Israeli-Palestinian Peace, I extend to you my heartiest congratulations and best wishes. Your valiant struggle for a just peace in the Middle East and your enormous courage in recognizing and advocating that such a peace can only be reached through the implementation of Palestinian National Rights under the leadership of the PLO has earned the respect of all the peace-loving forces all over the world. I realize that the price which you paid for your courageous position was a heavy one, but so do all pioneers and visionaries whose sacrifices are so vital for the orderly progress of history and the evolution of a more mature and responsible social order as well as more advanced models of interhuman relationships. But the suffering was not on your part alone, your Palestinian counterparts had to pay an even heavier and more painful price. Precious lives were lost in the long, arduous road toward peace. Said Hammami and other comrades gave their lives so that our two peoples might live together in peace and coexistence. Let these noble examples be an incentive for all of us to continue our difficult struggle for peace until we achieve our common goal and the flags of peace will fly proudly over our holy land.
>
> Slow as our progress may seem to be, we must admit that, by historic criteria we have come a long way. Chairman Arafat states that the ongoing peace talks with Sheli* have for their purpose the creation of new political facts in the Middle East, and the world takes this astonishing declaration in its stride, because peace through your valiant efforts and ours has come to stay.

Reading the text, I thought that something was missing. 'Somewhere the State of Israel has to be mentioned specifically', I said, 'it's what our opponents always look for first. Without such a mention, everything else will be explained away.'

Without a word, Issam took the paper back and went to the other room again. When he reappeared, he had added a sentence which became a slogan for us during the following months and years: 'Sooner than all our combined enemies think, peace shall and must reign between the Palestinian and Israeli states and their peoples.'

* In *Al-Hawadess*, 19 December 1980.

## 33

*We are at Charles de Gaulle airport. I am going back to Israel, Issam is going somewhere else.*

*We are buying duty-free alcohol – he whisky, I vodka.*

*For some reason he is in a sombre mood.*

*'We are fools', he says. 'All of us working for peace in the Middle East are fools. If we had been working for war, we would be respected, macho, adored by the masses. We, the peaceful ones, are fools.'*

*'We are peace*fools*', I crack, to cheer him up.*

# 34

The year 1981 started auspiciously enough.

On 11 January, the Israeli Council for Israeli-Palestinian Peace held its fifth anniversary meeting in Jerusalem. Issam Sartawi's congratulatory message was read out, and created excitement. On the wall, on a big poster, the crossed flags of Israel and Palestine were displayed, expressing in the simplest and most concise way what our struggle was about.

It put the State Attorney into a quandary. As I put it to him: 'This flag is forbidden because it means identification with an organization devoted to the destruction of Israel. If this flag is crossed with the Israeli flag, it obviously cannot mean that. So either it is not the PLO flag, because according to you the PLO wants to destroy Israel, and then the flag is not illegal, or it is the PLO flag, and it follows that the PLO does not want to destroy Israel, and then the flag is certainly legal'.

This argument was accepted by the Attorney General, who several years later officially informed the police that the display of our emblem as such does not constitute an offence. But in the meantime our members were arrested several times for wearing it, and both Matti Peled and I were investigated by the police.

All this explains why the first public display of the flags created so much excitement. On 13 January, the French news agency reported from Beirut that the official PLO spokesman, Mahmoud Labadi, had declared that the display of the Palestinian flag in Jerusalem was 'a very important and interesting development'. The same news item mentioned that at the meeting of our council a message by 'Mr. Issam Sartawi, a close assistant to the PLO chief, Mr. Yassir Arafat', was read. The agency concluded that 'it is reasonable to assume that Mr. Sartawi sent this message on the personal instructions of Mr. Arafat himself.' Thus the sentence speaking of peace between the states of Israel and Palestine, which Sartawi had added on the spur of the moment, upon my urging, was publicly endorsed by Arafat.

On the same day, the Jordanian minister of information, Adnan Abu Oudah, published a statement saying that the display of the Palestinian flag by Israelis in Jerusalem was an 'important phenomenon'. In a statement to the French agency, he said that, 'the Palestinian flag is a symbol of Palestine and the struggle of the Palestinian people. Its display is important, because it shows that certain Israeli groups recognize the identity of the Palestinian people and its historic rights on the soil of Palestine.'

Never before had the 'Sartawi Line' been so clearly endorsed by the top Palestinian leadership, and never before had so many signals been addressed to Israeli public opinion. The first significant signal had been given already on 13 December 1980. The official Fatah organ, *Falastin al-Thawra* (Palestine Revolution), published a long interview with Issam Sartawi, who was introduced as an official representative of the PLO and a close adviser to Chairman Yassir Arafat. The paper considered this interview of such importance, that it published it twice: once in its daily issue, and again in its weekly supplement.

In the interview, Sartawi for the first time explained his views at length in an official PLO organ. The most important paragraph read:

> Inside the Zionist movement exist, in our times, three currents: 1) The Likud bloc, which denies the rights of the Palestinian people and would like to annex all the occupied territories; 2) The Labour Alignment bloc, which is willing to give back part of these territories but refuses to recognize the right of the Palestinians to self-determination and wishes to annex a considerable part of the territories; 3) The Peace Camp, which acknowledges the rights of the Palestinians and is willing to accept the existence of a Palestinian state alongside Israel.

A few weeks later, in deepest secrecy, Sartawi showed me the original of the article. Several passages had been corrected in handwriting. 'This is Arafat's own hand', Sartawi said, and pointed out a handwritten remark in Arafat's handwriting, saying 'Muhim (important)! to be published! J.A.' Sartawi was very conscious of the importance of our work, and therefore, like myself, kept a full documentation of it for future historians. He had photocopied the manuscript of the article with Arafat's remarks. The important point: Arafat had not made any change in the passage about Zionism.

This was of immense importance, not easily understood by outsiders. The idea of Zionism still sticks in the throat of even the most realistic Palestinian, who has come to terms with the fact that Israel exists and must be recognized. The emotional impact of this word on a Palestinian can only be compared to that of words like 'fascism' or even 'Nazism' on Jews. Whatever the historical facts, every Palestinian associates Zionism with the chain of tragedies which has led to the expulsion of a major part of the Palestinian people from their homeland, and to the subjugation and oppression of the rest. For the Palestinians, Zionism is the devil incarnate, the worst form of racism, Jewish fascism.

Yet nearly all Israelis consider themselves Zionists, whatever they mean by it. Peace between the Palestinian people and Israel has to be made by the Palestinians, who identify themselves with the PLO, and a people and a state which identify themselves completely with the Zionist idea and movement. There, as Hamlet said, is the rub.

We consciously did not want to make it easier for the Palestinians to avoid the issue, and therefore we stressed the fact that the Israeli Council is a Zionist body. We saw no use at all in any recognition of non-Zionists by the PLO, because it did not bring it nearer to mutual recognition — much as we insisted in Israel that all peace forces, and eventually the state itself, must recognize the PLO.

Sartawi came to see this clearly, and adopted this line unequivocally. In this interview, he took the bull by the horns, setting forth a theory designed to make it possible for the Palestinians to come to grips with the problem. The fact that Arafat had approved this passage was therefore doubly significant.

Indeed, Arafat was sending quite a number of signals himself. He had clearly become very conscious of the importance of Israeli public opinion, and of the need to support the peace movement in Israel. Especially, he singled out the Sheli party, which had been founded by the Israeli Council, and which at that time was represented in the Knesset by me. Sheli was also officially a Zionist party.

On 19 December 1980, Yassir Arafat gave an interview to one of the most important mazagines in the Arab world, the Beirut *Al-Hawadeth*, which was read by millions of Arabs, including Palestinians. One passage reads:

> Following the decision of the Israeli government that impedes Israeli politicians from carrying out negotiations and having contacts with the PLO, what is the future of your relations with the Israeli peace party Sheli?
>
> "We continue. Our decision is that of the Palestinian National Council, taken in 1977. It deals with initiating a dialogue with the democratic and progressive forces in Israel as well as outside. We shall continue to do this. Whoever is willing to continue to hold this dialogue, let him come too.
>
> "I have the obligation to hold this dialogue, as the Chairman of the PLO Executive, since I was elected to office according to this programme."
>
> Is this dialogue causing a rift among politicians inside Israel?
>
> "The aim of this dialogue is not and was not to cause a rift among politicans. The aim is to lay new political foundations in the Middle East".

This was almost a repetition of a passage of the Sartawi interview published four days earlier in *Monday Morning* magazine in Beirut, in which he said: 'There are peace forces in Israel, including the Sheli party, the Peace Now Movement, the New Outlook group and others'. All these groups were Zionist.

My friend Eric Rouleau, the eminent expert on Arab affairs and Middle East editor for *Le Monde,* told me that he had gone to Saudi Arabia to cover the Islamic Conference which took place in Taif in January 1981 — the same conference about which we had talked with King Hassan, its chairman. Spending the night in Jeddah, and having nothing better to do, Rouleau turned on the television set in his hotel room and saw the face of Yassir Arafat, who had also arrived in Saudi Arabia, and was giving a live interview to the local TV station. Asked about the achievements of the PLO, Arafat told his Saudi listeners that one of his organization's most important achievements was its dialogue with Israeli peace forces, who supported the principle of Palestinian self-determination. To me this was of the utmost significance, because nobody could accuse Arafat of pandering on this occasion to Western public opinion. It was a strictly local broadcast aimed at a local audience.

* * *

I was nearing the completion of the second year of my membership in the ninth Knesset, and I was resolved to resign in order to turn over my seat to an Arab member, the next on our list. For two years I had talked continuously about the Palestinian problem, warning of the dangers of another war, and pointing out the signals coming from the PLO. Altogether, during my ten years in parliament, I must have made about a thousand speeches, speaking nearly every day the Knesset was sitting.

On 2 February 1981, I proposed a motion to the Knesset agenda in order to draw attention to the latest developments in the PLO. I would like to quote it *in extenso* from the Knesset record, in order to give the flavour of this kind of discussion, where I stood quite alone against the whole Knesset, except the communists whose help did more harm than good because of the universal hatred of them.

*Uri Avnery* (Sheli): Mr. Chairman, respected Knesset.

I shall refrain from addressing myself to the speech of the last speaker [Moshe Shamir, a famous writer, who was once a rabid Stalinist and who had become an equally rabid Jewish fascist]. We listened to a speech, to an orgasm of ignorance and hate, and I do not know which was stronger: the hate or the ignorance.

I will only say this: if the leaders of the Muslim world had but a modicum of gratitude, they should send a telegram thanking Knesset Member Moshe Shamir and his faction, because the silly and imbecilic Jerusalem Law [introduced by Shamir's Techiya faction reaffirming the annexation of East Jerusalem to Israel] helped them unite, for the first time, eight hundred million Muslims into a single front against Israel. Speeches such as Mr. Shamir's evoke the biblical question: "Hast thou killed and also taken possession?"

I would like to speak seriously about the subject I raised. I hope that the Foreign Minister [Itzhak Shamir] when answering this speech will deal with the real significance of this important political event [the Islamic Conference in Taif], and not be tempted to exploit it for unimportant and propaganda purposes.

The conference held at Taif was a most moderate one. But perhaps we should first of all try to define what 'moderate' and 'extremist' mean in contemporary Arab terms. One could say: A 'moderate' is one who agrees with the Israeli government, and an 'extremist' is one opposed to it. I, on the other hand, take the liberty of proposing another definition: 'Extremists' are those who deny the very right of the State of Israel to exist; 'moderates' are those willing to accommodate themselves to the existence of Israel, even if their terms for this are not acceptable to us, or to some among us.

If this definition is accepted we must say that the Taif Conference was moderate, since all its resolutions remain in the framework of decisions taken by the Arab Summit conference held in Baghdad in December 1978, at which for the first time a unanimous resolution was adopted saying that the aim of the Arab world is a just and permanent peace, based on the return of the territories occupied in 1967 and the creation of a Palestinian state in the West Bank and the Gaza Strip, i.e., alongside Israel.

*Shmuel Toledano,* MK: Would you mention the word jihad [holy war]?

*Uri Avnery:* I shall.

*Yossef Rom:* He [Avnery] wants to prove that he has a sense of humour.

*Shmuel Toledano:* [Unintelligible comment.]

*Uri Avnery:* Couldn't you have this stupid conversation in the cafeteria? That's where it belongs.

Foreign Minister Shamir gets important information from his sources, including some most important sources. [An allusion to the Mossad.] I take the liberty of saying that my friends and I also have sources of our own, and although they are different from his, they are no less good. [None of the listeners could even imagine that only a few days before I had met King Hassan on Moroccan soil.]

What was really resolved at the Taif Conference? *Le Monde*, a universally-respected newspaper, said that "the head of Saudi Arabian diplomacy [and I suppose this means King Fahd] gave two explanations for the use of the term jihad: the struggle is aimed at liberating 'the territories occupied since 1967' and thus Israel's territorial integrity is not being questioned". This means the State of Israel inside the pre-1967 borders. As to the character of the jihad, "the purpose is to explore peaceful ways, outside the framework of the Camp David accords, in order to return to the Palestinians their legitimate rights to self-determination and an independent state in Palestine".

*Amnon Linn,* MK: And for this they declare a jihad?

*Uri Avnery:* The word jihad, as it appears there, is a . . .

*Deputy Defence Minister Mordechai Zipori:* . . . friendly word.

*Uri Avnery:* . . . word that should be rejected completely, because of its religious and historical associations. But the resolution talks about a "military, political, and economic jihad". The King of Morocco, who cannot be suspected even by the members of this house of being an 'extremist' — I remind you that King Hassan II of Morocco was the first Arab ruler who, as early as 1958, addressing an Arab audience in Beirut, proposed that Israel be admitted to the Arab League — King Hassan declared that the aim is to conduct a political and economic struggle in order to abolish the annexation of East Jerusalem. He said so specifically: *East* Jerusalem.

Mr Chairman, the main phenomenon in Taif, on which I would like to enlarge, is a strengthening of the position of the leadership of the Palestinian Liberation Organization, led by Yassir Arafat, who was the third deputy of the president of the conference.

In order to understand at all what happened in Taif, one must understand what happened in the last few weeks inside the Palestinian Liberation Organization. Since the Israeli media do not usually report on these developments, which are most important for our future, I take the liberty of submitting to the Knesset — and I'm glad that the prime minister [Begin] and the foreign minister are present in the house — some facts which they should know, and which I am not convinced were brought to their attention.

During the last six weeks, a series of official statements have been made by the leadership of the PLO, statements which indicate — and I choose my words carefully — a fundamental change in the approach of the PLO towards the State of Israel, and even more importantly, to the Zionist movement.

*Deputy Defence Minister Mordechai Zipori:* [Unintelligible remarks.]

*Uri Avnery:* I suggest that the deputy minister of defence . . .

*Zipori:* No, I correct your statement . . .

*Uri Avnery:* ... I suggest that the deputy minister listen to the facts, and if he has something to add, I shall be glad to listen.

A whole series of official statements have been made by highest-ranking PLO leaders. Here are the facts [here I quoted at length the statements of Arafat and Sartawi mentioned earlier].

This is the PLO that came to the Taif Conference, this is the PLO leadership headed by Yassir Arafat which went there after making these statements; statements which were not secret, which were not made for Western audiences but Arab newspapers read by millions of Arabs, such as *Falastin al-Thawra* which is read by every Palestinian, or *Al-Hawadeth*, read by important people in all Arab countries. Arafat came thus to Taif and was elected third deputy president of the conference, and the PLO received a promise of help from this conference.

Mr. Chairman, I do not deceive myself that the government of Israel would today accept our approach and our peace programme. We have fundamental differences on this subject, and this is well known. Yet I ask: Can the government of Israel, whatever its policy, can the Knesset afford to ignore completely what is happening around us? Should we ignore what is really happening in the Arab world just for the sake of a propaganda statement that will be released tomorrow and forgotten a few days later, condemning this or that? Should we lose ourselves in a kind of onanistic emotional exercise, such as we just witnessed in Mr. Shamir's speech?

I move that the Knesset confront these new developments in a serious manner, collecting all the facts, both from official and from other sources.

Mr. Foreign Minister, other sources, other contacts, and other kinds of information do exist. Hasn't the time come for the Knesset to receive all information at hand, from all sides, in order to review the situation in the Middle East as it is now? Perhaps this would induce the government of Israel to effect some changes in its own perceptions, considerations and statements.

Answering this speech, the foreign minister of course rejected all the facts I had submitted, reiterating the extreme government line. But in the end the Knesset resolved to transmit my motion, together with the opposite motion of Moshe Shamir, to the Knesset Committee for Foreign and Military Affairs, which in a way gave it the stamp of at least minimal approval. This, and the fact that my words did not provoke the usual storm of protest and accusations, and that I was not called a PLO agent and traitor, as at other times, proved that this barrage of PLO signals was beginning to have some effect on Israeli public opinion, and indirectly on the politicians.

A week later, on 11 February, I made my last speech in the Knesset. I had already announced that I was about to resign my seat, and that this was going to be my farewell speech. As such a resignation is a rarity in the Knesset — no politician in his right mind ever keeps a promise to resign — there was no established procedure for such a speech, but Prime Minister Begin and other members of the cabinet paid me the courtesy of attending.

I put the speech in a very unusual form. At the beginning of the century, Theodor Herzl, the founder of modern Zionism, whose picture is the only one displayed in the Knesset hall, had written a futuristic novel, describing the future Jewish state in Palestine. It is a rather naive, simplistic book, whose motto is 'If Thou Willed It, It Shall Not Be A Fairytale'.

I took this up in my speech, describing how the grandson of the hero of Herzl's book comes back to Israel in the year 2001, and finds it flourishing after peace with the whole Arab world has been achieved. In this way I described, in a futuristic style, how peace could be achieved and how Israel would benefit from it.

Near the end of the speech, while my listeners were absorbed, half-amused, half-thoughtful, in this tale, I suddenly produced a cardboard sign displaying the flags of Israel and Palestine and concluded: 'Mr. Chairman, these two flags, when they appear together, do they constitute a threat? Isn't it our most cherished dream that these two peoples, who live in this country, each with its own flag and its own national consciousness, shall combine their destinies in peace and mutual respect? Let me finish my tale with the old slogan of Herzl: 'If Thou Willed It, It Shall Not Be A Fairytale'.

For a few moments, Mr. Begin and the whole Knesset looked aghast at the abomination, the terrorist PLO flag, being displayed in the Holy of Holies. But before they could react, and before the chairman could take any steps, I concluded my speech, bowed to the audience, and resumed my seat. The cameras, which had been alerted in advance, had focused on the unusual spectacle of a Knesset member on the rostrum displaying the Palestinian flag with the Israeli.

According to Knesset procedure, a cabinet minister was to answer my speech. The task was given to the minister of justice, a Likud member, who was quite unprepared for my gesture, and therefore did not react to it at all. Instead he made a rather mild speech, lauding my contributions to the Knesset and expressing regret over my resignation, speaking more in sorrow than in anger about my misguided attitude towards the problem of Palestine — or, rather, Eretz Israel.

The flags incident was reported in the media throughout the world, and *Le Monde* asked me to contribute an article to its opinion column entitled 'Why Did I Display the Palestinian Flag in the Knesset?'

But the most significant reaction was published on 12 February in *Falastin al-Thawra*. The Fatah organ published, on the first page, a news story entitled 'The Palestinian Flag For the First Time in the Knesset! Avnery Attacks Begin Government'.

* * *

When I went to see Sartawi again, on 12 March 1981, I expected to find him in a radiant mood. I was surprised to discover him depressed.

I did not notice this in the first moment. He had come to Charles de Gaulle airport to fetch me in his new big black Citroen. Coming out of the arrival hall I did not see him at first. He was half-hidden in a corner, with two American girls, whom he had told to look out — as he told me the second he saw me — for a handsome, white-haired gentleman. One of the two girls had become his assistant, the other was her girlfriend who, according to him, had fallen for me at first sight. This became a standing joke between us.

After eating a lunch prepared by Issam and the girls, whom he had instructed in Arab culinary art on this occasion, we settled down to serious business. It was grim.

It appeared that something had happened in Rabat after our departure. The King was unable to go on with his efforts to arrange meetings between us and the American vice-president, President Bourguiba of Tunisia or other Arab leaders, or to publish our meeting, or to convene another, public one.

Using his own sources, Issam had tried to find out what had happened. He had obtained a clear-cut answer: some part of the United States administration had intervened and requested that the King abstain from any action designed to facilitate a dialogue between Israelis and the PLO.

Here, for the first time, Sartawi had clear-cut proof that the US was indeed directly responsible for many of the failures of his efforts. For many hours during that afternoon, evening and the early hours of the morning, we sat and for the first time seriously discussed the United States' involvement in our conflict. Pooling our experiences, we tried to compare what had happened to us over the years. Like the stones of a mosaic, events which had happened to him and us in Israel slowly fell into place, gradually forming a picture so conclusive that its implications could not be avoided.

For many years now we had kept having an experience that repeated itself like a bad dream: following a new road we had seen our efforts rewarded by success until, suddenly, we found ourselves confronted with an iron wall, which had often seemed to us inexplicable. It now appeared that in many of these cases there had been American intervention.

It was not an easy conclusion for us to draw, but it was an inescapable one. Neither Issam nor I had any love for the Soviet Union. Both he and I had been often denounced by our opponents as American agents, if not outright operatives of the CIA. Issam was the only leading person in the PLO who openly advocated that the organization meet the American conditions for a dialogue. I am a neutralist by inclination, but I've never hidden my conviction that the US must play a leading role in the peace efforts in our region.

Moreover, neither of us doubted that if the conflict continued, sooner or later the whole region would blow up in the face of the Western world, causing a historical shift in the global balance. This was so obvious to us (and still is to me) that we were puzzled by the American attitude. What could be the motive? The famous Jewish lobby? The immense sales of American arms to both sides of the conflict? The idea that American interests would be best served in a situation where both sides were afraid of each other and in need of American protection? Sheer stupidity? None of the explanations, or even all of them together, seemed to us an adequate solution to the puzzle.

But here we were, recounting to each other for hours on end experiences, big and small, which all pointed in the same direction. For example: Brzezinski had visited Israel and come to Matti Peled's house. He had been visibly impressed by Matti's line of logic. But when he became Jimmy

Carter's security adviser, Matti found it impossible to gain even an audience with him. Exactly the same thing had happened to me earlier with Harold Saunders, with whom I had had a very long and satisfying exchange of opinions about the Palestinian problem in the executive suite of the White House in 1969, but who thereafter, upon climbing to the more rarefied atmosphere of the State Department, avoided me like the plague. This was in spite of the fact that I had been the only member in the Knesset, one out of 120, who had come out in favour of the peace plan announced by Secretary of State William Rogers at the end of 1969.

Why had Kissinger taken such pains to deport Sartawi from the United States in 1976? Why had the American-Soviet communiqué of 1 October 1977 — such a big step forward on the way towards peace — been immediately repudiated by the United States? Why had the Tunisians abandoned a plan hatched in 1978 to invite Lova Eliav on our behalf to Tunis?

After checking and comparing dozens of such examples, we felt that we could no longer avoid the conclusion that the US was actively and sometimes physically obstructing our efforts, much as the Soviet Union was doing for rather similar motives. It was a grim conclusion for us, but the practical lesson was: we must work for a direct dialogue between our peoples, we could not rely on any outside force — neither on the superpowers nor the Arab regimes.

I told Issam a fact which had come only recently to my attention. During the negotiations held at Kilometre 101 (from Cairo) after the Yom Kippur War, the chief Egyptian negotiator, General Abd-al-Ghani al-Gamazi, had approached his Israeli counterpart, General Israel Tal, and told him that Egypt was now ready to sign an Egyptian–Israeli accord. Tal had rushed to Prime Minister Golda Meir and told her so in great excitement. Golda had cooled him down. She told him that she had an agreement with Henry Kissinger that such an instrument would have to be signed under American auspices in Geneva. And, indeed, negotiations at Kilometre 101 were stopped at this point, and started all over again in Geneva. But there could be no doubt that it was in the interests of Israel to have a direct, bilateral agreement with Egypt, which could have become a precedent of the utmost significance.

This conversation with Sartawi made a deep impression on me. Later in the year I summarized it, without mentioning Sartawi, in an article which I published in *New Outlook*, an Israeli magazine, under the headline 'Does America Want Peace?' I would like to quote the opening paragraphs:

> The question mark in the title is much more than just a grammatical nuance. It is the essence of a quest of many months.
>
> Like many of my friends, I have for a long time subscribed to a political axiom best expressed by Dr Nahum Goldmann. It goes more or less like this: the US has a basic interest in achieving peace in our region. Since 1967, the successive governments of Israel have obstructed peace, in order to hold on to the occupied areas. Sooner or later the Americans will have to impose peace on an unwilling Israeli government. If they have not yet done so, it is only because of the stupidity or naivete or cowardice of some American politicians. Once this is overcome, the inevitable imposed peace will come about.

It is an easy idea to swallow. It makes life much easier. It shifts the weight of responsibility to someone else. It makes the weaknesses of the Israeli peace movement easier to live with. It is in tune with the certainty, so beloved by so many intellectuals, that something 'is bound' to happen.

It is also an idea close to the heart of people like myself, who have an inherent sympathy for the US and the American way of life. Of course, America has erred in Vietnam, but basically US policy must reflect a love for peace. Or so, at least, we would like to think.

But there is a sounder basis for this belief. Objectively, so it seems, the US really has a profound interest in peace in the region.

The Palestinians are there. Their nationalist fervour cannot be ignored by anyone who looks at the scene with open eyes. You cannot deny to a nation of four million intelligent people their nationhood, without causing an explosion. Unlike the Kurds, the dispersed Palestinians are located in vital areas of the world struggle. Sooner or later the Palestinians are going to blow the Middle East, with all its mineral riches, sky-high. When this happens, the US and the West will suffer a terrible, perhaps fatal, blow. The breakdown of Western industry, nuclear holocaust, total revolution — all these are definite possibilities.

So America MUST want peace. We just have to wait. A big power like this will wake up, in due time, and act according to its interests.

Logical? Yes, perfectly logical. But it has not happened. And when an illogical situation persists for fourteen years, something must be wrong with the logic.

That's where the question mark comes in. Since the end of last year I am in the throes of an 'agonizing reappraisal', to borrow a phrase. I am trying to rethink. I have not yet come to any definite conclusion, but I would like to set forth some of my reflections.

In the article I set forth the possible explanations for American behaviour and concluded:

There is certainly some truth in each of these theories and they may be all quite true. In politics, many factors are at work simultaneously, their paths crossing and recrossing.

But I find myself dissatisfied by all these explanations. The gap between the short-range benefits of this situation and the immense long-range risks involved is just too great. Even the fact that politicians and officials habitually prefer short-term solutions to long-term reckoning, familiar to anyone who has been in politics anywhere, does not provide a satisfactory key to this enigma.

This article had a curious footnote. Some months later I received, out of the blue, a letter from Dr Nahum Goldmann, dated 30 January 1982. More than anyone else, Goldmann had preached over the years the idea that only the United States, in conjunction with the Soviet Union, could impose a reasonable peace on Israel. My relations with him had been sometimes warm, sometimes distant, since I proposed in 1953 the creation of a special ministry for peace (or for Middle Eastern relations) with Goldmann in charge of it.

His letter read as follows:

Dear Mr Avnery,

I am writing to you in German because I am leaving on a trip within the hour and it would take me longer to dictate the letter in Hebrew. I would like to tell you that during the last two years I have been reading *Haolam Hazeh* with great interest, and that I admire and appreciate again and again your courage and your journalistic talent.

The motive for this letter is your article 'Does America Want Peace?', which I read yesterday [in the Hebrew translation published in *Haolam Hazeh*]. As you know, I've had over many years — until the Reagan administration — rather close relations in Washington, especially with Kissinger, Brzezinski, Vance, before that with Dean Rusk, not to mention a number of high officials, and that therefore, until the present era, I was rather well-informed. It is well that you are putting a question mark after your title, but it is good that you are expressing publicly your doubt as to the Americans' desire for peace. I, too, lately ask myself this question, even if one should not underestimate the lack of statesmanlike wisdom of the Americans who are in charge of foreign policy.

I could write a whole book and cite the symptoms of the American desire for peace, and I could also cite other examples which show that America does not want peace. To mention only one which is now topical — because it concerns your article about Sartawi — by the way I saw him the day before yesterday and am trying to help in various ways — I asked Vance, with whom I have a personal friendship, at the time, to give Sartawi a visa so that he could come to the *New Outlook* conference in Washington [in October 1979]. Vance, who is a very decent and honest person, and by the way much more talented and wise than Brzezinski, informed me that he had tried to induce the Justice Department to cancel the order prohibiting his entry and that it would take some time to achieve this. I don't believe that this was just a pretext.

On the other side, apart from Carter's interest in Camp David, I could mention — to cite only one of many exampales — that both Vance and Brzezinski urged me throughout all these years to meet Arafat publicly, because that would make it easier for them to do the same.

But many things support your question, and it is difficult to have a clear, definitive opinion about it. More than everything, there is in America a fear that a total peace is impossible without Rakakh, and because of their anti-Soviet obsession, especially under Begin, they prefer the continuation of the present situation to an agreement that would be possible only with American–Russian participation and joint guarantees. You will remember that Vance and Gromyko agreed in 1977 to convene a Geneva Conference with Israel and the PLO, and that it was Dayan who induced American Jews to exert pressure on Carter, in order to get him to cancel the agreement. As I know from personal contacts, the Soviets were furious about this.

I wanted to make these remarks to you personally. They are not intended to be published, even if I often declare publicly that America is more to blame than Israel for the absence of peace in the Middle East. I havc believed this for the last ten years.

To summarize, I would say at this moment, without being quite certain about it, that the reason for the American policy in the Middle East, which totally lacks understanding and results, and which will cost Israel dearly one of these days, is a combination of American diplomatic incompetence, their fear of Russian participation in the peace, and the fear in Washington of the pro-Israeli lobby, which consists not only of Jews but also of people like Senator [Henry] Jackson.

* * *

The only immediate result of King Hassan's intervention was a meeting he had arranged between me and a close aide of President Giscard d'Estaing. Issam told me about this and in due course I presented myself at the gates of the Elysée Palace, from where I was conducted to the elegant office of M. Chapot. The meeting took place on 14 March 1981, when the presidential elections in France were nearing their climax. Chapot was reasonably certain that his man would win, but the result was in doubt. He received me with the words: 'So you are the man who raised the Palestinian flag in the Knesset!'

We soon agreed that nothing could be done before the elections. Contrary to what King Hassan seemed to believe, the French Jewish community, and especially the Jews who had come from Morocco, were raving supporters of the Likud, and any support for Giscard expressed by Israelis like myself would be counterproductive.

But if Giscard were re-elected, there would still be time to do something to help us in the Israeli elections, which were going to take place in two months.

What could be done? I made several proposals: that the president receive a delegation of the Israeli peace camp, and that a prestigious meeting between us and PLO leaders be convened under his auspices in Paris. In the meantime, he promised to help Sartawi's activities in every possible way. This was important, because Sartawi needed efficient police protection more than anything else.

Issam was happy to hear this promise when I met him later that day. That evening we had one of our many memorable dinners, this time in an Indian restaurant, whose owner received him as an ambassador. For the first time I met Issam's wife, Waddad, a very impressive, self-contained woman. Usually Sartawi tried to keep his family far from his activities, in order not to endanger them. The ever-present danger was very much on his mind. Before starting his car that day, in the sinister subterranean garage of the huge luxury building in which his office was located, he asked me to stand behind a concrete column while unlocking the car and starting the engine. 'No use us both being blown up', he said.

I urged him to take many precautions. After several threatening letters were sent to me in the Knesset, the Knesset security officer had sent me a police demolition expert, who had given me a short, concise course of how to take such precautions, as well as a written checklist. I tried to follow the instructions for several days, but then I gave up. It was too cumbersome and time-consuming. Sartawi felt the same way about it, but he promised to read the checklist if I translated it into English for him. In the end I never did.

By the way, Issam never asked girls to hide behind columns, before opening the car for them. He thought it bad to frighten them.

Over dinner and during the following days, Issam brought me up to date about happenings in the Arab world and inside the PLO. Surprisingly, his many pro-peace statements, and those of Arafat, had not evoked any violent reactions in Syria. Quite the contrary, Sartawi's articles and a long interview he had given to the Arab section of Radio Monaco — the most widely-listened-to station all over the Arab world — had been widely and prominently quoted in the Syrian press, without adverse comment. The government-controlled Syrian papers had omitted only the passages relating to Israel.

Issam did not believe that the Soviet Union had any influence on Syria. He thought the opposite was more probable.

About our visit to Morocco, he revealed that it had been personally approved by Arafat, who had asked his colleagues whether they were ready to attend. They had all been in favour of the meeting, but only Khaled al-Hassan had volunteered to go on this mission.The fact that none of them, except Khaled, had been ready to go even on such a secret mission was by itself a revealing fact.

An interesting story: Asked by a foreign journalist what price he could pay for peace with Israel and the creation of a Palestinian state, Arafat had raised his pen and said: 'This is my most important weapon, because this is the only pen in the whole Arab world which can sign a document recognizing Israel. Without recognition by this pen, any other Arab recognition of Israel will be worthless'.

In 1977, Kaddumi had been asked by *La Stampa* whether he was ready to recognize Israel and had answered: 'This is our most important card. We shall not play it before coming to the negotiating table'.

I asked Issam about a nice young PLO diplomat in the States, who had come several times to our meetings and approved of our line, but who had said recently in a public debate that he is for a Democratic Secular State of Palestine — the very idea which, to Israelis, was synonymous with the destruction of Israel. 'He's an excellent person', Sartawi said. 'I only asked in Beirut why we pay his salary. He should be paid by the Israeli Embassy.'

Late at night I went back to Issam's office, where one of the bedrooms had been prepared for me. Before going to sleep I tried to call one of my correspondents in Jerusalem. A strange voice answered sleepily; it was a wrong number. I nearly started laughing at the thought: What would this anonymous Israeli think if he knew he'd been awakened from his dreams by a call coming from a 'terrorist headquarters' in Paris?

* * *

A few months earlier, in the fall of 1980, while expounding his great design to us, Issam had made us a proposal whose daring for a moment took away our breath.

At the first moment it sounded incredible. He asked us whether we were ready to go to Beirut to meet Yassir Arafat.

He made it clear that he had absolutely no idea whether Arafat or anyone else would agree to such an unprecedented move, but before airing the proposal in Beirut he wanted to be certain of our willingness. It was, he said, a very dangerous enterprise, but he was sure that with the proper planning the risk could be reduced to acceptable proportions.

The idea went like this: The three of us — Peled, Arnon and I — together with Issam, would go by plane to Beirut airport. We would probably use a private plane; for example, that of Kreisky's Austrian friend, the financier Karl Kahane. Beirut airport was officially operated by the Lebanese government, but in practice was dominated by the forces of the Muslim-PLO coalition. We would arrive under false names and be received at the airport by reliable Fatah officers, who would take us to a safe place in West Beirut. There we would confer with Arafat and other Fatah leaders. From there we would return to Israel by the land route, inspecting on the way the refugee camps so frequently bombed by the Israeli Air Force. We would present ourselves at the Israeli border post at Rosh Hanikra, and put the Israeli government on the horns of a dilemma: Put us on trial and dramatize the exploit throughout the world, or let us go? On the eve of the Israeli elections, such a sensational enterprise could electrify the Israeli peace camp, raise our stature and credibility, demonstrate the possibility of Israeli-Palestinian dialogue and peace, and enhance our chances on election day.

Of course there were many risks involved. Could the Fatah security forces prevent attempts on our lives by the more fanatical Palestinian groups in Beirut? Was the way from the airport into the city safe enough? How long could such a visit be kept secret, so that the first news of it would be made public upon our arrival at the Israeli border? What would the effects be on Israeli public opinion and on the Palestinian rejectionists?

But none of us three hesitated for a moment. If the PLO agreed to the proposal, we would take the risk.

Now, in March 1981, Sartawi brought up a different idea in his conversations with me. The Beirut visit had not, of course, materialized. The risks had been considered too great, and perhaps the situation inside the PLO, as well as the relationship between the PLO and the Lebanese and Syrian governments, had made such an exploit politically impossible. After all, it would have been a clear violation of Lebanese sovereignty, on top of everything else.

Issam's new idea was even more daring and incredible: to enter the lion's den, go to Damascus. The 15th session of the Palestinian National Council was due to convene in the Syrian capital. The Knesset elections were about to take place in June. The efforts made during the last few months, our secret visit to Morocco, the various statements by Arafat, Sartawi and others — all these seemed to have gone well. Perhaps the time was ripe to do the really big thing, something so dramatic that it would change the very texture of the Israeli elections and enable us to enter the next Knesset as a significant political force.

The idea was simply to get the PLO to invite an Israeli peace delegation to the PNC in Damascus, much as other delegations were invited from all over the world. We would be present at the sessions, make a speech expressing our best wishes for the conference and demonstrate by our very presence that a new chapter in the relations between our two peoples had started.

I immediately expressed my willingness to go and said that I was certain that Peled and Arnon would also agree to come, in spite of the dangers involved.We could, of course, be accused of committing several crimes, such as having contact with the enemy and entering enemy territory. Unlike Lebanon, Syria was universally feared and hated in Israel.

In order to make the idea more palatable to the left-wing groups in the PLO, and to the Syrians, Issam proposed that the Israeli delegation be composed of two parts: we three Israelis who defined ourselves as Zionists and three members of the Israeli Communist Party. Under the circumstances, I found this reasonable.

We agreed that I should do two things: write a personal letter to Yassir Arafat explaining this proposal and talk privately with Meir Wilner, the leader of the Israeli Communist Party, to obtain his agreement and induce him to use his ties with Moscow in order to bring their influence to bear on their friends the Syrians and the PLO.

Issam and I wrote the letter to Arafat jointly. First we talked about it at length, then I wrote a draft which Issam corrected, and then I typed it. Dated 14 March, 1981 it read as follows:

> Dear Chairman Arafat,
>
> I am writing with a great sense of urgency.
>
> I view with great apprehension the potential developments in the next months. There can be no doubt that the USA is doing everything possible to obstruct any move towards peace. Anti-Palestinian feelings are being actively fostered in Israel in a degree never before experienced. The Labour Party, which is likely to return to power, has a programme of active combat against the PLO. If these tendencies go unchecked, the war between our peoples may reach new and unprecedented stages. The Palestinian movement may be in greater peril than ever before. While I am certain that it will overcome, the price may be great and the damage to the chances of peace incalculable.
>
> I therefore urge Israelis and Palestinians alike to consider measures which are daring and dangerous, but which are demanded by the situation, because the dangers of not doing what has to be done may be even greater.
>
> The coming elections in Israel may be of crucial importance, because they may either enlarge or contain these dangers. If the Labour Party wins a decisive victory, while the forces of peace are wiped out, all signs point towards catastrophic possibilities.
>
> On the other hand, these elections may prove to be a turning point. If the forces of peace — and especially the Zionist peace movement — win a significant victory, they may create a completely new atmosphere. If they obtain enough seats to change the composition of the next government, they may change official policy. Even more important, they may change public opinion in a way that may induce Shimon Peres, an unprincipled opportunist, to take a new line.
>
> I believe that it is in our power to effect such a change by bold action. The US and other outside factors can obstruct peace as long as there is no directly concerted action of the peace forces in the PLO and Israel. Once there is direct concerted action, their power to sabotage and obstruct is greatly reduced, if not nullified.

The most practical action in this direction is using the platform of the PNC to create facts that will electrify the world. I suggest that the PNC invite a delegation of two Rakakh members and two Sheli people to attend the council and make short congratulatory speeches.

The advantages of such an unprecedented and bold move would be enormous. To mention a few:

Sadat would be upstaged. While he came to Jerusalem, here Jerusalem would come to the PLO, and to Damascus.

All tricky arguments about the PLO being opposed to the very existence of Israel — irrespective of its policies — would be disproved. After that, nobody will dare to bring up again the Charter, etc. as grounds for destroying the PLO.

American policy will be confounded, even in the US itself. The Reagan administration, faced with a *fait accompli*, will have to change its line, whatever its real intentions.

In Israel, the whole election campaign will rearrange itself around this event, the peace forces will be the centre of debate, their credibility will be vastly increased, and their chances of gaining a significant number of seats — enough to become a coalition partner — enhanced.

The mass media in the US, Europe and Israel, which have practically ignored your remarkable interview in *al-Hawadess*, Sartawi's important message and other declarations and texts, will be unable to ignore such a visible event. The logic of mass communications will take over and create a snowball effect.

April will be exactly the right timing. Israeli elections will just begin in earnest, the Reagan administration will just consider its first moves in the Middle East, French elections will be at their height, the death of the Camp David accords will be obvious. What better time to move and influence developments?

The Syrian government will gain additional advantages for such a move, taking place on Syrian soil, confounding its enemies, putting the Golan problem in a different perspective. In a way, President Assad would replace Sadat as the hero of peace, without paying the same price.

A special chapter is the influence of this and similar moves on the votes of the Palestinian citizens of Israel. More than a half of them used to vote for the Labour Party and other forces of the same kind, against their own interests and the interests of the Palestinian people as a whole. A move like the one outlined here, as well as direct appeals explaining to them the situation, would help to change their vote. After all, they are fifteen percent of the voting public, electing fifteen to eighteen members of the Knesset — a most important potential factor.

I conclude this letter with a profound sense of the dangers ahead, but also with great hope for joint measures to change the picture completely.

You have done great things, taken great risks, shown great courage in adversity. I am certain that these qualities — reflecting the spirit of the Palestinian people — will make a revolutionary step possible.

Shalom, Uri Avnery.

In order to mobilize support for the idea, I also wrote short letters to Abu Jihad (Khalil al-Wazir), whom I had never met, Ahmed Sidki Dajani, whom I had met in Rome, and Khaled al-Hassan.

Upon returning home, I called Meir Wilner and asked to talk with him in private. We met in a little cafe in Tel Aviv, where I told him about the idea and asked him what he thought of it.

I had been sitting next to Wilner in the Knesset for ten years, and our personal relations were friendly, though we had argued many times. This time he was noncommittal, and finally said: 'I'll consult my comrades and give you an answer'. I wondered who the 'comrades' were — members of the Israeli party or somebody else.

A few days later, while I was sitting in a meeting with my staff, Wilner called. The answer was negative. His comrades thought such an idea would backfire, be detrimental to the cause et cetera.

And that was that. After our Moroccan visit we had run up against the American iron wall. Now we were running up against the Soviet one.

* * *

The 15th session of the Palestinian National Council, which took place in Damascus, convened in April 1981. Instead of becoming the occasion for a dramatic breakthrough, as proposed by Sartawi, it became the very opposite. But there was drama, and its hero was Sartawi himself.

Whenever the PNC is convened, the choice of the location is in itself of the utmost significance. Choosing Damascus in 1981 meant that the radicals, who were serving Syrian interests, would have a decisive advantage. In a conference taking place in its own capital, Syria could bring the utmost influence to bear.

For any Palestinian leader in disfavour in Damascus, even attending the conference presented a grave risk. The Syrian secret services, notorious throughout the Middle East, had never had any compunction about killing Palestinians seen as obstacles to Syrian aspirations. Many members of the PNC did not attend the Damascus session for this reason. Characteristically, Sartawi did.

By now he was considered the number one enemy of Syrian designs within the PLO. He had no illusion about this step. He was putting his life in danger. But, again characteristically, he went about it in a clever way.

Issam Sartawi went to Damascus as a member of Yassir Arafat's personal entourage. He supposed, quite rightly, that the Syrians would not dare touch him while he was keeping close to Arafat, because this would have been an intolerable affront. The Syrians were not yet ready for this.

At the time, Damascus was engaged in a little war with Lebanon. A few days before the beginning of the PNC, the Phalangists had set in motion a train of events designed to drag Israel into a war with Syria. They attacked Syrian positions in the Christian town of Zahla, the famous capital of Arak and a vital strategic point for the defence of Damascus against a potential invasion from the west. The Syrians reacted violently, laying siege to the town. The Maronite leaders sent SOS messages to Israel, calling upon its government to save the Christians from genocide. It is now generally believed in Israel that the whole plan was hatched in collusion with the Israeli Chief of Staff, Rafael Eytan, nicknamed Raful, a rabid right-wing nationalist, who had conferred with the Phalangist leaders a few days earlier.

In the end, Menachem Begin drew back from the precipice of war. But he permitted the Israeli Air Force to shoot down Syrian helicopters. At the time, Begin was acting also as minister of defence. Ariel Sharon's time had not yet come.

With the Middle East teetering on the brink of war and a battle going on not far from Damascus, the atmosphere in the Syrian capital was even more warlike than usual. If war broke out, the PLO mini-state in South Lebanon would be the first to bear the brunt of an attack. Therefore, the PLO was at the moment more dependent than ever on Syrian military protection, and both the PLO and Syria were dependent on Soviet arms and other assistance.

This was the situation in which Issam Sartawi dared raise his voice.

Things started peacefully enough. Television viewers in Israel, aided by exceptional climatic conditions, could watch the opening of the Palestinian Council with Issam Sartawi clearly visible near Arafat. The Tunisian general secretary of the Arab League made a relatively moderate speech, mentioning Israel by name. Assad's congratulatory speech was routine. But when the general debate got underway, the radicals launched a concentrated attack on Sartawi, condemning any contacts with Israelis, with the possible exception of the communists.

The leader of the pro-Soviet faction in Fatah, Majid Abu-Sharar (the man I had met at the September 1979 conference, whose death later in Rome will occupy us later), made a violent attack on us, declaring that Matti Peled had recently said that he had killed Arabs since the age of 16: these were the kind of people Sartawi was meeting.

This was, of course, a double falsification. Not Matti but Lova Eliav had once made this remark, but in a very different context. In one of the emotional speeches for which he is famous, Lova had said that he had been killing Arabs from the age of 16, when he became a member of the Haganah underground, and that he does not want this to happen to his sons and grandsons. It was a powerful plea for peace with Palestinians.

Abu-Sharar's vitriolic attack was significant, because it proved beyond doubt that the Soviet Union was out to destroy any possibility of direct contacts between the PLO and Israeli forces, except the communists who are totally subservient to Moscow. But Abu-Sharar was joined by a whole chorus of extremists, Syrian and Libyan agents and others.

Sartawi was not the kind of person to take this lying down. Near the end of the debate he requested the floor, and started to reply to his detractors. He was shouted down, and the president of the Council, Khaled al-Fahoum, a person known to be a member of the Syrian faction in the PLO and a resident of Damascus, cut him off.

Sartawi responded with an act unheard of in Damascus. He not only resigned from the PNC, but also called in the foreign press and explained his resignation to them — in effect attacking the policy of the Syrian dictatorship and its agents in the Syrian capital. It was an act of unequalled courage.

His statement, as quoted by the Western news agencies, went as follows:

Since the Palestinian National Council, in its 13th session which took place in 1977, adopted the resolution calling for a dialogue with the progressive democratic forces in Israel and outside, I have taken on the responsibility for the implementation of this resolution.

While meeting the forces to whom this resolution applies, I have made certain that they would include the groups recognizing the legitimate rights of the Palestinian people, including the right to establish its independent state, and to recognize the PLO as the sole legitimate representative of the Palestinian people.

On this basis, meetings took place first with the Israeli Council for Israeli-Palestinian Peace, the Sheli Party, and the Israeli Communist Party, Rakakh.

On the Palestinian side, views about these contacts were divided, and this subject became the centre of debate in all Palestinian forums. Opinion was also divided about the definition of the forces to whom the PNC resolution applied.

Some of the [Palestinian] organizations insisted that the resolution applied only to the Israeli Communist Party. But I, and many of the high-ranking Palestinian personalities, believed that the resolution must apply also to the Sheli Party, in view of the published positions of its leaders.

In light of the controversy regarding the meaning of this resolution, and the many questions which arose as to the legitimacy of these contacts which became more and more numerous before this session of the PNC, the need arose to present the problem to the council, in order to enable it to on the one hand decide whether it wants to continue this contact, and to define on the other hand the forces to whom the resolution applies, if it does decide to continue with them.

For me personally a third problem presents itself. It is important to me, in view of my responsibility towards the Palestinian revolution, to present to the Council a report about the actions which have taken place in the course of the implementation of this resolution.

I came, therefore, to the present session of the PNC in order to give a report and present the two problems: whether to confirm the continuation of the contacts and how to define the forces concerned. There was no limit to my surprise when the president of the Council refused to give me the floor or even allow me the right of reply, thereby contravening the statutes and denying the Council the right to hear my report about the contacts. The president thereby undermined the function of the Council as the legislative body and as the supreme leadership of the Palestinian people.

In view of this situation I had no alternative but to tender my resignation from the Council, and I did so at the end of the session of 15 April 1981, a few minutes before the closure of the general debate.

I feel obliged to make the following statement:

One, following my resignation from the National Council, I do not have from now on any representative authority for the PLO. As the contacts, which have taken place until now, were based on my membership in the National Council and followed its official resolution, these contacts must now be considered as suspended, as far as I am officially concerned.

Two, this resignation does not change my views concerning the legitimacy of the contacts conducted in the past by me and other members, and which will be conducted in the future by whoever is entrusted with this task by the PLO.

Three, in spite of the bitterness accompanying it, this experience has increased my trust in the PLO as the sole legitimate representative of the Palestinian people and in the eventual victory of the legitimate aims of our people.

The resignation was a bombshell and overnight became an international sensation. The name of Sartawi, until this moment known to only a few, appeared in headlines all over the world, especially in Israel.

During the preceding months, the Israeli press had studiously ignored Sartawi's articles and messages, such as his message to the Israeli Council and his article in the Fatah newspaper, in which he had recognized the positive role of a part of the Zionist movement. If mentioned at all, Sartawi was described as a PLO terrorist entrusted with the job of deluding naive Israelis like us.

Now suddenly Sartawi appeared in the Israeli media as a peace hero, the only member of the PLO advocating peace with Israel who was, therefore, thrown out of the organization. On the evening of his resignation, Israeli television opened its news broadcast with a dramatic story about him.

Sartawi's resignation succeeded in achieving his aim. The problem of his contact with us became the central theme of the PNC, and the only event of this session which was widely reported. The problem of contacts with the Israeli peace camp, meaning the Zionist one, had to be faced squarely.

But, as had happened so often, differences were patched up. On Arafat's instruction, the president of the Council announced that Sartawi's resignation had not been accepted. (In fact, such a resignation has very little practical meaning. PNC members representing the component organizations are appointed by these organizations and can be recalled by them at any time. It was for Fatah to decide whether Sartawi was one of its representatives in the Council or not, and Arafat had no intention of letting him go.)

Arafat's leadership was soundly reconfirmed, and the new executive committee, the governing body, was relatively more moderate than the one it had displaced.

But on the issue raised by Sartawi, nothing changed. The old obnoxious formula calling for a dialogue with the democratic progressive forces inside the occupied homeland and outside, who were opposed to the theory and practice of Zionism, was left intact and in effect reaffirmed.

It was also completely ignored by Arafat. When asked about it in later interviews, he blithely disregarded the second part of the resolution and announced that the PNC had adopted a resolution that practically compelled him to conduct a dialogue with all peace forces in Israel, mentioning Sheli by name. When asked by a pro-Saudi paper appearing in Paris whether he was continuing 'his discussions with Uri Avnery', he answered: 'I've never met Avnery, but my people have met him and are continuing to do so'. When asked about Sartawi's contention that he no longer had the right to continue the dialogue with us, Arafat asked: 'What does Sartawi want? No one has instructed him to break off his contacts with the Israeli peace movement. He must continue with them'.

* * *

All these equivocations had very little effect on Israeli public opinion. The only fact which registered was that Sartawi had had contacts with the Zionist peace movement, and that Sartawi had been kicked out of the PLO. Not only had the dramatic breakthrough planned by Sartawi not happened, but, quite the contrary, the PNC had dealt us a decisive blow on the eve of our elections. The official propaganda of course saw to it that the PNC decision allowing for contacts with anti-Zionists only was widely reported in the Israeli media. Thus, by implication, we were branded as anti-Zionist, which in Israel means anti-Israeli.

In May 1981, I met Sartawi again. We had both been invited to a singular event — a conference on peace in the Middle East convened by the Ditchley Foundation in one of the stately homes of England.

For an Anglophile like me, this was an enchanted atmosphere. A butler straight out of P.G. Wodehouse catered to our needs, discussions took place in elegantly-appointed parlours, in between we could stroll on the lawns in the slight drizzle. Many international experts took part in the debates, which were all held in closed session with the understanding that they would not be published. Present were, among others, Harold Saunders and several American ex-ambassadors to the Arab states; David Owen, the former British Foreign Secretary; several assorted lords and Foreign Office experts from Britain and a dozen other European countries.

The discussions were extremely interesting and informative. Sartawi and I urged the assembled experts to use their formidable influence to facilitate the Israeli-Palestinian dialogue. We had many conversations with the participants about the real situation in Israel and the PLO, and about what must be done to avoid a new catastrophe in the region. One of the participants was a young man from the United States, John Edwin Mroz, and our conversation with him was going to bear unforeseen fruit.

But between ourselves, we were both pessimistic. I sensed that we in Israel were about to suffer a major defeat, and Sartawi was bitter about the failure of his grand design at the Damascus PNC. He realized that the disappearance of the peace forces from the Knesset and the re-election of an even more extreme Likud government could spell disaster for his people.

On 30 June, all these forebodings were proved only too justified. Our party, Sheli, suffered a disastrous defeat, gaining, incredibly, only 8,691 votes, less than the one percent needed to gain entry to the Knesset. Exactly four years earlier, in the heydey of our first known contacts with the PLO, we had gained 27,281 votes. If the PLO had been set to destroy the peace forces in Israel and make an Israeli attack on it inevitable, it could not have conducted the PNC better.

* * *

On both sides the forces of war, in their unholy alliance, were triumphant. But after a few months of bitterness, during which we hardly met at all,

Issam's usual self reasserted itself.

At the end of our series of meetings in March 1981, he said, by way of a parting remark: 'Victory and defeat are but states of mind.'

## 35

*We are sitting in Issam's Paris office, overlooking the Seine.*

*We have both agreed that the time has come for me to officially interview him for* Haolam Hazeh, *letting him speak about his past, his convictions, his views about Israel and Israelis.*

*Earlier that day, Sartawi had returned from a short visit to London. We had a small lunch together in the office, had our delicious Arab coffee and settled down. He is sitting in his comfortable armchair, in which no one else ever dares to sit. I am sitting in my usual place, on the sofa.*

*I take out my pipe and pouch of tobacco and start to light a pipe. Suddenly I remember that Issam has told me he has decided to stop smoking, after being a compulsive chain-smoker.*

*'Sorry', I say, 'I don't want to smoke in front of somebody who's just kicked the habit!'*

*'On the contrary', he answers, 'I love the smell, now that I can't smoke myself.'*

*I take out a block of writing paper and my small tape recorder, prepare everything for the interview, and turn towards him with a bright 'Now . . . '*

*Issam is asleep.*

# 36

The most important result of the disastrous 1981 elections was the elevation of Ariel Sharon to the post of minister of defence.

The first Begin government, which was established in 1977, had been equipped with some brakes. Compared to Begin, Moshe Dayan was a moderate. After the Sadat visit to Jerusalem, Ezer Weizmann, an extreme hawk, had a change of heart comparable only to that of Saint Paul on the way to Damascus. He became a dove.

In the new government, however, all brakes had been removed. The real Begin emerged, flanked by Sharon and the chief of staff, Eytan.

Soon after Ariel Sharon entered the office he had so coveted, I visited him there. The Ministry of Defence in Israel is a centre of power second only to that of the Prime Minister's Office. It receives half of the government's budget, excluding the part devoted to servicing the national debt, and controls an important part of the economy. It employs at least a quarter of the Israeli labour force.

All this power was now concentrated in the hands of man for whom power is the essence of life, a man who exudes power, who has all his life used brute force as his main instrument.

I had been friendly with Ariel Sharon at various times. During and after the Yom Kippur War he had used my magazine to reveal many hidden facts of the war, when he was waging what was then called in Israel 'the war of the generals'. After leaving the Likud, in 1976, when he was toying with the idea of creating a new party, he cultivated many Israeli doves. I had visited his home several times. On the way home I used to have heated arguments with Rachel, who insisted that the man was stupid, while I argued that he had a shrewd mind, even if a coarse and non-intellectual one.

The minute Ariel Sharon assumed the office of defence minister, it was clear to me that from now on things would move on a different course. I therefore decided to write a long essay on his personality, character and intentions. Once a year, on the eve of the Jewish New Year, *Haolam Hazeh* chooses a Man of the Year, rather like *Time* magazine, and devotes a long article to him, one sometimes running up to twenty thousand words. We chose Sharon for the year 5741, which came to an end in September 1981.

Sharon, who knows the value of publicity, agreed to cooperate. I spent many hours with him at his farm and in his office. He reminisced, told me about his childhood and his many struggles. For several hours he explained to me, with the help of maps he had prepared for his consultations with the Pentagon, his plans for the future.

I was therefore in a unique position. There was no doubt that Sharon was planning a big war in Lebanon, with the triple purpose of destroying the PLO, evicting the Syrian Army from Lebanon, and installing there a Phalangist dictatorship subservient to Israel.

It may seem curious that the minister of defence was revealing his most secret plans to an Israeli peace activist, who had open contact with the PLO. But this is Israel. Sharon did not request me to keep this information secret; on the contrary, he encouraged its publication, stipulating only that he not be directly quoted, in this context. He probably thought that the article would help him sell his war to the public and the government. Be that as it may, the full plan of the Lebanese War appeared in the issue of *Haolam Hazeh* dated 27 September 1981, more than eight months before it started. No war has ever been more publicized in advance.

It was therefore with an increasing sense of foreboding that I followed the train of events both in Israel and inside the PLO. Too many people were fiddling while Rome was about to burn.

* * *

The events of the PNC session in Damascus had put Sartawi in a highly equivocal situation. According to the letter of the resolution adopted, he had no right to have any contact with us. While we condemned certain trends in the history of Zionism, and bitterly criticized the policy of our government, it could in no way be said that we 'condemned the theory and the practice of Zionism'. Our council is a Zionist body according to its manifesto.

During the months following the adoption of this resolution, Arafat either ignored it or explained it away. Sometimes he said that for him we were not Zionists, because anyone who respects the national rights of the Palestinians could not possibly be called a Zionist. This reminded me of the mayor of Vienna at the beginning of the century, Karl Lueger, an avowed anti-Semite, who when caught rooting for a Jewish football team in a match against the hated Hungarians, made the memorable remark: 'It's I who decide who is a Jew!'.

In internal discussions, Sartawi told Arafat that this line was no good. Marking us anti-Zionists, as our enemies in Israel were trying to do, would not only be wrong but would also destroy any chances we had of success in convincing the Israeli public. Arafat therefore pretended that the second half of the resolution did not exist, but that the PNC had called only for a dialogue with democratic and progressive forces in Israel, period.

Issam was not about to be satisfied with this. He opted for another trial of strength. This time he sent a memorandum to the Executive Committee, the 15-member governing body of the PLO, demanding a clarification of the resolution. He requested that copies of this memorandum be distributed to all members of the committee. Arafat prevented this, saying that he first had to consult with the Syrians. This was in February 1982.

On 22 January 1982, Sartawi had already dropped another bombshell, moving to the attack. In an interview with our friend Eric Rouleau, he had accused the PLO of aiding and abetting the victory of Begin, by destroying the credibility of the Israeli peace movement.

The Arabs, and in particular the Palestinians, [the article read] encouraged Israel to put its expansionist policies into action; this is the theory that was outlined to us by Doctor Issam Sartawi, member of the Palestinian National Council (parliament) and one of the advisers on international policy to Mr Yassir Arafat, president of the PLO. It is obvious, he declared, that Mr Begin is trying to annihilate the Palestinian people, and take away their country completely, but this is not a reason for us to supply him with pretexts and means to attain his goals.

The annexation of the Golan, according to the Palestinian leaders, would not have been possible if the Israeli peace movement had had at their disposal at least ten members of the Knesset who, due to parliamentary distribution, could have acted as arbitrators. "We did not manage to contribute to the success of the democrats and the progressive Israelis who, contrary to appearances, have the support of a comparatively wide electorate." The peace movement according to Dr Sartawi, is not composed only of the Rakakh Party (communist) and Sheli, but also groups and personalities, Zionist or not, who accept the following principles: Israel's return to the 1967 borders, recognition of the right of the Palestinian people to self-determination and to a sovereign state, with the understanding that the PLO is their sole legitimate respresentative.

If Sheli — a group animated noticeably by General Peled and Mr Uri Avnery — did not obtain their four or five seats in the last election, stated Mr Sartawi, it is because it was not credible in the eyes of the Israelis, largely due to the fault of the Palestinians. "My secret conversations with the progressive Israelis as of autumn 1976, first at the request of the Executive of the PLO, then with the endorsement of the Palestinian National Council (March 1977), should have been publicly admitted, justified and defended in the core of the Arab world and before Israeli opinion." Such a spectacular gesture, audacious as it may seem, was indispensable for the Palestinian leaders: "We should have invited our Israeli counterparts to Beirut for a direct exchange of views with Mr Yassir Arafat: better still, they should have been invited to address the Palestinian National Council, which held its meeting in Damascus last April, two months before the elections in Israel. The PLO could then have concretely demonstrated its willingness to bring about true peace, acceptable to both parties, which could have granted a measure of credibility to the Israeli pacifists in the eys of their countrymen."

Mr Sartawi was disavowed implicitly by his superiors. Not only did the Palestinian National Council not invite him to present a report on his conversations with the progressive Israelis, but a resolution was adopted forbidding contacts with any Jew who was not an anti-Zionist "both in theory and practice". Mr Sartawi's protest resignation to the PNC was not accepted. But Mr Arafat's adviser immediately broke off talks with his Israeli partners in the dialogue. "I am a disciplined militant", he explained, "and I have never acted beyond the directives of the representatives of the Palestinian people." He thinks more or less that his superiors were mistaken in giving way to discouragement. "The intransigence of Mr Begin's coalition and the lack of sensitivity of the Labour Party should have, on the contrary, incited us to double our efforts rather than fall into the trap that the enemies of peace held out to us."

Accordingly, Mr Sartawi took various initiatives with a view to resuming the dialogue between Israelis and Palestinians "on a more solid and wider basis." He hoped to obtain first the backing of the PLO and then that of the Arab League, preferably on the occasion of a forthcoming summit meeting.

Does he feel that he is carrying on a solitary battle? No, he said, on the contrary: It is enough to mention that over a million and a half Palestinians in the occupied territories understand, like him, the vital importance of Israeli public opinion and highly appreciate the moral and material support given them by the democratic Jews, when faced with the repression of the occupying forces.

The PLO should take into account the opinion and aspirations of all the sectors of the Palestinian people, especially those of the occupied territories, otherwise the PLO would risk its representativity and its function, stated Mr Sartawi vehemently.

The reactions of both sides to this challenge were interesting.

Sartawi's enemies tried to get the Executive Committee to condemn him outright. But Arafat came to his defence. 'What do you want to condemn? Which passage exactly?' he demanded. The hardliners did not find any particular passage they could put their finger on. 'I have my own criticism of Sartawi,' Arafat said, 'who told him to break off the contacts?'

Following the interview in *Le Monde*, al-Saiqa, the organization which is in effect the arm of Syria inside the PLO, published a statement calling for Sartawi's execution, as well as that of Elias Freij and Rashad al-Shawa, the mayors of Bethlehem and Gaza, who had voiced similar views. The official organ of the Popular Front for the Liberation of Palestine, led by Georges Habash, *al-Hadaf*, published a cover showing Sartawi, Freij and al-Shawa as dice in front of an Israeli flag, calling them 'dice in the game for Palestinian capitulation'.

After the Executive Committee had rejected the proposal to condemn Sartawi, Arafat felt strong enough to instruct his spokesman to announce to *Le Monde* that Sartawi was continuing to act as his representative. He also served secret notice to everybody concerned that any attempt on the lives of Sartawi, Freij or al-Shawa would meet instant retaliation by Fatah. 'If they are killed, we also know how to kill!'

On the Israeli side reactions were no less instructive. As the acting chairman of our council, I called a press conference with Yaacov Arnon and Yossi Amitai. Then I read a statement, which was widely quoted in the Israeli press, calling for mutual recognition between Israel and the PLO, and suggesting that Sartawi receive the Nobel Peace Prize. As Sartawi had already disclosed the plan for our visit to Damascus as guests of the PNC, I was free to disclose the details of this aborted project. I did so at the press conference and in a detailed report published in *Haolam Hazeh*.

The positive reaction of parts of the Israeli public encouraged two cautious doves, Yossi Sarid of the Labour Party and Victor Shemtov of Mapam, to declare that they were ready to meet with Sartawi. They were immediately silenced by Shimon Peres, the leader of the Alignment of the two parties. In fact, both Sarid and Shemtov refused to meet Sartawi and never did, even when invited.

The most telling reaction came from the Israeli Communist Party. The party's number two man, Tawfiq Toubi, violently attacked Sartawi in a meeting of the party's central committee. This seemed rather peculiar, until this attack was published prominently in *al-Safir,* a Lebanese paper known to be run by Libyan agents. There could be no doubt that Toubi's attack had been prompted by the pro-Soviet and pro-Syrian elements in the PLO, who were after Sartawi's blood. Indeed, all the machinations of these elements were aimed at eliminating all contacts between Israelis and Palestinians, except those controlled by Moscow. The communist attitude which aborted our invitation to the PNC, the PNC resolution allowing for contact only with anti-Zionists and this attack by Toubi were all part of the same picture.

Continuing his offensive, Sartawi published a long interview in *al-Majallah,* a pro-Saudi paper appearing in Europe. There he called for the legitimation of the contacts with the Israeli peace movement. Reacting to the initiative of the (then) Saudi King Fahd, which called for a clear statement of the Arab peace plan, he said that its principles were insufficient and should be enlarged.

* * *

I met Sartawi again in Vienna, on 18 March 1982. He explained to me the latest moves inside the PLO, which I've just recounted. It was clear that he was again confident of his ability to push the PLO leadership in the right direction. He had been to Jeddah and Amman several times, and found receptive ears there. He wanted the Saudis to finance directly his growing activities, which would enable him to set up a worldwide network of Palestinian peace groups. He also wanted the Jordanians to allow him to speak on Jordanian TV, which was widely watched in Israel and the occupied territories. He was certainly on the move.

While we were talking the telephone rang and Beirut was on the line. At another time, when he talked with me on the phone, Jeddah was on the second line. Sartawi's office was becoming a factor in inter-Arab politics. But it was clear that no Arab government could support him decisively, without a clear PLO decision endorsing his line. Arafat's sporadic statements to this effect were not enough.

* * *

Sartawi was staying in Vienna in a small hotel in the inner town. It was nearly a hiding place. Vienna had become a centre of terrorist activity.

This formed the central theme of this series of meetings. During one of them the Austrian minister of the interior, Erwin Lanc, had dinner with us. Lanc was one of Kreisky's ardent supporters and later became, as foreign minister, in a way the heir of his Middle Eastern policy.

Dinner was a pleasant affair. Long before we met, Lanc had read the serialization of my book which had appeared in the German *Der Spiegel,* and therefore knew a lot about me and my views. We quickly found a common language.

But during the long hours we spent in Issam's little hotel room, we were concerned with a much more practical problem. The Abu Nidal group had killed a Viennese Jewish functionary, Heinz Nittel. Afterwards, two Abu Nidal terrorists were intercepted on their arrival at Vienna airport. The Austrian police had established, through Sartawi, close relations with the Fatah security services, a collaboration designed to prevent Syrian-inspired attempts on Kreisky's life and other acts of terrorism.

When the two terrorists were arrested, Sartawi was informally called in to assist in their interrogation and was allowed to talk with them in private. When this became known, it created quite an uproar in Austria.

Sartawi, who realized the terrible danger of the Abu Nidal group and the secret services hiding behind it, was exasperated by the cumbersome processes of the Austrian law-enforcement agencies. At one moment he exclaimed: 'Turn these two bastards over to me for one hour, and I'll tell you who sent them, where they got their weapons from, everything!'

With a helpless gesture, Lanc turned to me and said: 'Please, Herr Avnery, explain to our friend that such methods are not accepted in Austria'.

But by patient policework, exchange of information with other European police forces, comparisons of bullets etc., a picture began to emerge. There could be no doubt that under the label of Abu Nidal, a well-organized, well-equipped, well-trained and well-financed organization was operating throughout Europe, undoubtedly with the help of the security services of at least one Arab government, if not several.

And who is Abu Nidal?

For several hours Issam gave me a rundown on the man and the organization, soliciting my advice on several aspects.

Sabri al-Banna, nicknamed Abu Nidal ('Father of the Struggle'), was one of the Fatah veterans. I had heard about him for the first time from Sabri Jiryes, during my first meeting with Sartawi. As Jiryes told it, Abu Nidal had been the official PLO representative in Baghdad. There he had gone over to the Iraqis and become their agent against the Fatah leadership. At the time the Iraqis were the most radical of Arab radicals, and were conducting an active fight against the new moderate line of the Fatah leadership.

As a refugee from Palestine, al-Banna had been a menial worker in Saudi Arabia — the lowest possible status in the aristocratic kingdom, which despised foreigners in general and working men in particular. It seems that there he had become imbued with a violent hatred of Saudi Arabia and all conservative Arab regimes. This turned into a consuming hatred of Arafat and his colleagues, who were trying to manoeuvre between various Arab camps and coming close to the moderate Saudi line. Saudi Arabia was, of course, the main source of financial support for the PLO.

Openly denouncing Arafat as a traitor, Abu Nidal broke away from Fatah and set up his own organization, which was in effect an arm of Iraqi intelligence. He called it Fatah and also published a paper under the name of the legitimate Fatah organ *Falastin Al-Thawra*. His publications were, therefore, practically indistinguishable from the real Fatah ones, and only a trained eye could tell the difference, mainly because Abu Nidal used to add to the name of Fatah the designation 'Revolutionary Command'.

When Iraq became more moderate, as of 1978, mainly because its terrible war with Iran made it dependent on Saudi assistance and Jordanian roads and Aqaba harbour, Abu Nidal branched out. He established a second centre in Damascus — a most odd move, because Syria and Iraq were deadly enemies, each claiming to be the true guardian of the Baathist pan-Arab flame.

It was Abu Nidal who had killed Said Hammami and several other PLO representatives in various countries, whom he suspected of having contacts with Israelis or advocating the line of peace. Thus he murdered Ali Nasser Yassin in Kuwait in June 1978, Azz-al-Din Kalak in Paris in August 1978, and Naim Khader in Brussels in June 1981.

Worse, Abu Nidal had already committed a series of anti-Semitic outrages throughout Europe, attacking Jewish synagogues, children's homes and other institutions. All these acts provided the most effective ammunition for the Israeli propaganda machine, which was constantly trying to convince world public opinion, and especially the Israeli public itself, that the PLO was not just fighting Israel or its policies, but was a truly anti-Semitic organization in the Nazi spirit. The fact that the murderers used the name Fatah made it even easier for Israeli propaganda, which relied on the fact that only a very few insiders knew that, in fact, these atrocities were committed by an organization outside the PLO, whose main aim was to kill Arafat and destroy the PLO leadership.

Who could have an interest in this? Using simple logic, Issam was convinced that Abu Nidal's organization was serving Israeli interests, or was at least infiltrated by the Israeli services. 'This is a veritable orgy', he exclaimed, 'Abu Nidal is sleeping with everybody, the Iraqis, the Syrians, the Mossad, and perhaps also the CIA and KGB!'

Another odd fact was that the great majority of all the Abu Nidal hitmen arrested in European countries and in Morocco, where they had tried to assassinate Arafat, were from the occupied territories. The percentage of West Bank people in the Abu Nidal group seemed to be 90%, higher than in other Fedayeen organizations, in spite of the fact that Abu Nidal had no office in Amman, and therefore would have found it difficult to recruit members in the occupied West Bank. Issam claimed that several captured Abu Nidal terrorists had admitted under interrogation that they had been recruited on the West Bank by Israeli officers and been sent to a certain address in Baghdad.

In his *Le Monde* interview, Sartawi hinted at this. This passage read:

> Is he not afraid to be the next victim of a dissident group of Palestinians of Abu Nidal who threatened to kill the "Traitors"; those who preach, like him, a policy of dialogue and compromise? "Contrary to appearances", replied our speaker, "Abu Nidal is not a maximalist serving the cause of the rejection front, but a renegade who is in the service of Israel. The Austrian Security Services have established, without any doubt, that the right-hand man of Abu Nidal not only killed the municipal councillor Heinz Nittel, on 1 May 1981, and attacked the synagogue in Vienna in August, but also murdered, on 1 June, Naim Khader the representative of the PLO in Brussels. They intended to attack Yassir Arafat during his scheduled visit to Vienna the following week. Who, but Israel, could be interested in eliminating our

leaders? Who was interested in discrediting the Palestinian resistance by committing crimes of such a scandalously anti-Semitic nature?"

"We do not ask ourselves these questions anymore", continued Mr Sartawi, "since the members of the Abu Nidal group, whom we hold in Beirut, admitted to having been recruited by the Mossad [Israeli Intelligence] in the occupied territories. Curiously, Abu Nidal benefited equally from the help of certain Arab countries who utilized him for their own aims."

Mr Sartawi refused to name the Arab countries to which he referred, but it is widely known that Syria and Iraq have granted their hospitality and support to the commandos of Abu Nidal. "In spite of the advantages which they derived", concluded Mr Sartawi, "we hope that the Arab countries will put an end to their cooperation once the documents in our possession, that incriminate their protégé, are brought to their knowledge."

There was one item which to Sartawi seemed conclusive proof of the Israeli connection with Abu Nidal. Sometime earlier, the leader of the pro-Soviet faction in Fatah, Majid Abu Sharar, had been murdered in Rome. This was the same person who had taken part in the Rome conference of 1979, in which I had made my speech. After the murder, the PLO had claimed, as usual, that he had been killed by Israeli agents.

A few days later, Abu Nidal's newspaper had published the picture of Abu Sharar on its cover, claimed him as one of its own, and accused Arafat of murdering him. This, by the way, also seemed to prove that there was a close connection between the pro-Soviet Fatah faction and Abu Nidal, and indirectly, involvement of the Soviet Union and Syria with Abu Nidal outrages. Abu Sharar was succeeded as the head of the pro-Soviet faction in Fatah by Abu Saleh, who later became the chief of the so-called Fatah dissidents, the group which broke away from Fatah and took up arms against it under Syrian auspices in 1983.

What excited Sartawi was another fact. As the PLO had claimed that Abu Sharar was murdered by the Mossad, it would have been logical for this organization to seize upon the Abu Nidal publication accusing Arafat of this crime, because it would have proved how untrue was the incrimination of the Mossad. Yet, curiously enough, neither the Mossad nor any other Israeli agency took this up. It was not mentioned in any of the Israeli media, until I published it. What clearer proof could there be — according to Sartawi — of the Mossad's interest in aiding and abetting Abu Nidal?

* * *

Issam was staying this time in a small hotel, because Vienna was full of delegations from the Arab world. An important meeting of OPEC, the Organization of Petroleum Exporting Countries, was taking place in the Hotel Imperial, and Sartawi wanted to be discreet.

For some unfathomable reason, my travel agent had put me exactly there — in the Hotel Imperial — not having found any other accommodation.

Arriving there, I found the place surrounded by police and army units. After having passed through a variety of security devices, and having been thoroughly searched, I presented myself at the registration desk.

'What delegation, please'? the reception clerk asked.

'I'm from Israel', I answered.

'I didn't know there was an Israeli delegation', he said, leafing through his lists to find out which rooms had been assigned the Israeli delegation.

Having established that I was merely a private guest, he assigned me a room which had been ordered by the Kuwaiti delegation, but which had not been claimed by them. When I left the elevator, ten pairs of dark eyes scrutinized me, and followed me to my room. For three days I was one of the most protected persons in the world. At least ten bodyguards, Arab and Austrian, safeguarded my security, at any rate during my stay in the room.

When I asked Margit, Kreisky's secretary, whether I could see him, she had a nice invitation for me. The chancellor was going on an election tour through the Burgenland, near the Hungarian border, and would be pleased if I would accompany him.

The chancellor's limousine picked me up in the morning from the fortress hotel, and for the whole day we travelled between election meetings, wine-drinking sessions with local notables, engaging in conversation in between. I told the chancellor about Sharon's ideas and plans, including his scheme to invade Lebanon in order to destroy the PLO, kick out the Syrians and install a Phalangist quisling regime.

'Dear me'! Kreisky exclaimed at one point, 'how awful! This is exactly the kind of person who will impress the Pentagon!'

As it transpired, this was an exact prediction.

While we were spending this nice spring day among the rural Social Democratic stalwarts, to whom Kreisky insisted on introducing me as a valiant Israeli comrade and peace activist, preparations for the war were underway.

* * *

Yassir Arafat knew, of course, that Sharon was preparing for war. He did not have to read *Haolam Hazeh* — as he did, in translation, prepared for him by his assistant Imad Shakour, who later became my friend — to know what Sharon intended. He also knew that the one way to prevent this plan from being executed was to change his relationship with the United States, without whose consent Israel could not go to war.

He was caught in a dilemma.

Very few people realized this. A year earlier, in March 1981, Issam and Anna Best had arranged for me to see Pierre Mendès-France at his elegant home in Paris. I had talked with the frail old man for an hour or two, giving him a run-down on the situation in Israel, which confirmed his pessimistic views — like many people, he had completely despaired of Shimon Peres — and told him about our ongoing contacts with the PLO. I was surprised by the vehemence of his criticism of Arafat. 'A real leader should make decisions, and not wait for a consensus to be reached', he insisted, 'unity is important. But if unity means that you cannot do anything, then unity must be sacrificed. Action is more important.'

I asked him what Arafat should do.

'He should announce that he is going to Jerusalem to negotiate with the Israeli government! And then he should go to the bridge and try to cross!'

Anna Best, who was listening with increasing exasperation, exclaimed 'But the Israelis would arrest him! They would shoot him!'

The wizened old man turned to her and said mildly: 'That would be very good. Arafat in prison, or martyred, would be of greater value to his cause than alive and unable to act.'

It was easy to be impatient with Arafat, but the situation was vastly more complicated than outsiders believed.

In the spring of 1982, every knowledgeable person knew that war was imminent. To prevent it, the PLO had to convince the US government to start an urgent dialogue with it in order to prepare a peace solution including the Palestinians. But America was committed by a written understanding given to Israel by Henry Kissinger in 1975 stipulating that it would not deal with the PLO unless the organization recognized Israel's right to exist and accepted Security Council Resolutions 242 and 338. Even if the mainstream leadership of the PLO was ready for this, psychologically and politically, it would be impossible to do without provoking a dangerous confrontation with Syria at a time when Syria practically occupied Lebanon — including the PLO mini-state — and commanded the support of several organizations within the PLO.

Also, facing the imminent threat of an Israeli invasion, the PLO was more dependent than ever on its military alliance with Syria, the only Arab 'confrontation state' left on the potential battlefield after the defection of Egypt.

Faced with this dilemma, Arafat manoeuvred. Without confronting the Syrians directly, he tried to find out in discreet ways whether the Americans were serious about starting a dialogue with the PLO if their two conditions were met — and what that meant in practice.

At the Ditchley Conference in May 1981, Issam and I had talked to a young American, John Edwin Mroz, who was in charge of one of the many semi-private institutions dealing with political affairs in the States. Since then Mroz had taken the initiative of implementing our ideas, trying to act as a go-between between the State Department and the PLO. He later recounted that he had spent more than 400 hours with Yassir Arafat in frequent visits to Beirut, carrying messages and trying to find a formula acceptable to the Americans and the PLO.

Issam Sartawi was doing the same. At the time I could only guess what he was doing, but visiting his office one could feel that his standing in the organization had risen considerably, and that his relationship with Arafat was closer than ever. In private conversations he expressed his growing impatience with the leadership which, in his view, was not taking the audacious course demanded by the terrible dangers facing the organization. He thought that the PLO should meet the American demands squarely, express its willingness to recognize Israel and accept the Security Council resolutions, and challenge the Americans to either fulfil their obligations or renege on them publicly.

'My God', he exclaimed more than once, 'we have already recognized

Israel *de facto* by accepting the Brezhnev Peace Plan and similar documents. Why beat around the bush! Let's say so clearly and unequivocally! It's the only way to get Israel into a corner!'

But it was not that easy. A much more circuitous route had to be found. Acting on Arafat's orders, Sartawi was hard at work following it.

As he could not go to the US because of the political ban camouflaged as a visa irregularity, he had to find an intermediary. He consulted with Kreisky, the British Foreign Office and the Elysée Palace, and finally decided that the best go-between would be a Tunisian. Using his excellent relations with the wife of Habib Bourguiba and other top figures in the Tunisian government, he went to see President Bourguiba and asked for his help. Bourguiba, who had called for Arab recognition of Israel 17 years earlier, was enthusiastic. He instructed the prime minister, Mohammed Mzali, to go to the States and negotiate for a dialogue.

The problem was finding a formula which would be acceptable to the majority of the PLO and which would meet the American conditions. Arafat had to be certain in advance that the Americans would indeed accept this formula and honour their obligation to start a dialogue accordingly. A final text had to be agreed upon by the two sides ahead of time, the form of the American response had to be worked out, the timing had to be fixed — all this without the two parties meeting each other face to face and keeping the indirect contacts in total secrecy, while working under the cloud of imminent war.

As a diplomatic exercise, nothing could be more complicated. In actual life, it was an exercise in frivolous cynicism. The lives of many human beings were involved. The governments of both Israel and Syria were adamantly opposed to any such settlement, which could — perish the thought — lead to peace. The good intentions and even the intelligence of the American officials were in doubt, while Arafat and his colleagues in Beirut were walking on very thin ice indeed.

How difficult all this was was already shown in 1981, when the Saudis had worked out a formula calling for peace in the Middle East, the setting up of a Palestinian state, and an implied recognition of Israel within the pre-1967 borders. This formula was in reality a PLO proposal, drafted by Khaled al-Hassan and edited by Arafat himself. But after its publication it came under intense fire from the Syrians. Arafat's intention of having the Saudi plan officially endorsed by the PLO was torpedoed by the pro-Syrian elements in the organization. When the Fez Summit convened in December 1981, it was impossible to reach a consensus, and the host, King Hassan of Morocco, postponed the meeting in disgust. The same plan was eventually adopted when the summit was reconvened in Fez in September 1982 — but in the meantime there had been a war which had changed the map.

Oscillating between fits of optimism and gloom, Sartawi continued. He met with the Tunisian prime minister several times. Mzali had come back from America, giving the impression that things were progressing satisfactorily. Sartawi proposed a formula enumerating the many decisions taken by the Palestinian National Council and other PLO bodies which implied the recognition of Israel, such as the decisions to set up a

Palestinian national state in a part of Palestine, the welcoming of the joint American-Soviet declaration of 1 October 1977, the welcoming of the Brezhnev Peace Plan which confirmed Israel's right to exist, et cetera. The crux of the formula was a positive statement saying that by these resolutions, the PLO had in fact recognized Israel. As all these resolutions had been adopted unanimously, they superseded the Palestinian Charter, which stated that the PNC was empowered to amend it by a two-thirds majority.

By this formula, Issam hoped to overcome all internal opposition, basing himself on existing resolutions, making it unnecessary to adopt new ones.

Sartawi proposed making the announcement himself, speaking on behalf of Yassir Arafat and the PLO, in as prestigious a forum as he could find. He decided upon the French Institute of International Relations in Paris, which he was invited to address on Monday 14 June 1982. As he told me later, among other considerations he also took into account the dateline of *Haolam Hazeh* — Monday night — in order to give us the scoop and make sure that it would make the biggest possible splash in Israel.

I don't know if Issam was aware of the parallel efforts of Mroz, which were progressing simultaneously on the same lines. Mroz also had the impression that he was nearing the finishing line, and that Arafat was ready to make the expected announcement in late June. It is quite possible that some more secret initiatives, which have not yet been disclosed, were also in progress at the same time.

Everything was moving towards a crucial point, the historical breakthrough which would mark the beginning of the end of the Israeli-Palestinian conflict. The month of June would be the dawn of a new era.

# 37

*'I told them', Issam storms, 'you have to choose between General Peled and General Sharon. Either General Peled and his friends come here on a peace mission, or General Sharon will come here with his tanks. They did not understand what I was saying. Now they do.'*

*We are sitting in his office, looking down at the peaceful Seine River. The date is 15 June 1982.*

# 38

On Thursday 3 June 1982, the Israeli Ambassador in London, Shlomo Argov, was shot and critically wounded in front of the Grosvenor Hotel in central London.

The next morning, the Israeli cabinet convened an emergency session and accepted a proposal by the prime minister, Menachem Begin, to bomb Beirut, thus putting an end to the unofficial armistice which had been achieved by the American emissary, Philip Habib. That peculiar agreement between two sides which did not recognize each other's existence, Israel and the PLO, had safeguarded Israel's northern border for eleven months, during which not one single Israeli was hurt, a remarkable demonstration of Yassir Arafat's ability to control even the extremists in his organization.

During the cabinet meeting, the Israeli intelligence chief said that he had brought along an expert on Palestinian organizations, who was ready to give the cabinet a short lecture on the Abu Nidal organization, which had been identified as the perpetrator of the shooting.

Begin brushed him aside. 'That's not necessary', he said, 'they are all PLO.'

On Friday, 4 June, the Israeli Air Force subjected West Beirut to the most intensive air attack until then. The PLO retaliated on Saturday, 5 June, by shelling Israel's northern frontier. During the bombardment of Beirut, about 500 people were believed to have perished. During the PLO shelling, one Israeli was killed.

That evening, the Israeli cabinet decided to invade Lebanon. The war was on.

* * *

On the fourth day of the war, Wednesday 9 June, I decided to visit the battlefront. No permission was granted at the time to Israeli journalists to cross the border. I took a photographer and a correspondent, both girls, in my private car and tried to cross the border at the main crossing point, but was prevented from doing so. For a few hours I drove along the military fence, which marks the border, trying to find a way to cross. At every point I was intercepted by army patrols.

I was ready to give up when, near Metulla, I found an open gate guarded by a soldier who was reading *Haolam Hazeh.* His face lit up when he saw me. I am ashamed to say that I lied to this faithful reader, telling him that I was expected on the other side by Major Saad Haddad, the commander of the Israeli-commanded quisling militia in South Lebanon. The soldier waved me on in a comradely fashion.

During the next few hours we travelled peacefully through the countryside sometimes alone, sometimes in army convoys, being warmly received everywhere. After crossing the Litani River and skirting Nabatiyeh, we came to the outskirts of Sidon, which was not yet occupied. Fighting was going on in the city and in the neighbouring Ein Hilwa refugee camp. Some convoys of Israeli tanks and armoured cars broke through the main road to Beirut, but the officer in charge refused to let my private car join them.

At the end of the day, I returned by the short route, south to the official crossing point at Rosh Hanikra, when we were arrested, interrogated and duly charged with illegally crossing the border of Israel into enemy territory. This charge was eventually dropped, when much weightier charges were introduced.

Thus I was full of vivid impressions when I met Issam next, less than a week later. He was raging. He felt that the rejectionists in the PLO and vacillating leaders were to blame for not following his line, the only one which could have prevented war. He cursed the 'bloody fools', was frustrated about sitting in Paris, while his friends and co-fighters were fighting in Beirut, which was now besieged and completely surrounded by the Israeli Army.

Issam's office in Paris was now a vital life-line for the PLO. By a curious coincidence, the telephone switching station of Beirut was located in West Beirut, unlike most other services. The Israeli Army could cut off water and electricity for the besieged city, and at times did, but it could not cut off telephone and telex communications. Issam became the main connecting link between Arafat and the outside world. Every few minutes the two telephones in his office were ringing with calls from Beirut and from all over the world. For me it was an eerie feeling, seeing Sartawi speak with some PLO leader in the besieged city, while my friends and relatives were among the besiegers, shooting and shelling. One of these was Rann Cohen, a member of the Sheli central committee, who was commanding an artillery unit in Beirut. I had met him on the outskirts of Sidon, where he was boarding a landing craft for an amphibious landing north of the city. His role in the war became a major factor in the later split of Sheli.

Between the calls, we pieced together the story of the conspiracy that led to the war. For the first time, Issam told me the full story of his endeavours to bring about an American-PLO rapprochement over the last few months. He was quite certain that the American Secretary of State, Alexander Haig, had double-crossed him. Knowing that Sartawi was about to make a historic statement on behalf of the PLO meeting the American demands, as agreed with the Tunisians, he had told Sharon to attack a few days earlier. Issam was going to make the statement at the French Institute a few days later, but of course its impact would be drowned by the impact of the war. Holed up in Beirut and fighting for his life, Arafat would not be able to endorse a statement, as foreseen.

Most of our efforts were devoted to trying to unravel the events which had led to the war. Issam's extensive investigation of Abu Nidal and his gang stood him now in good stead. Together we were able to piece together a plausible theory. When I told Arafat about it a year and a half later, he concurred with it completely, adding some more items confirming it.

There could be no doubt at all that whoever gave the order for the shooting in London intended to bring about the outbreak of the war. The question was: Who was it, and why?

One thing was absolutely certain: the shooting was done by Abu Nidal's people. London police were able to round up the perpetrators and their collaborators within a few hours, and had ascertained that they were all members of the Abu Nidal organization. One of them was the nephew of Abu Nidal, Marwan al-Banna.

The first fact which stood out was that this operation was carried out in an amateurish fashion not characteristic of Abu Nidal. Usually, hitmen are brought in from abroad, using diplomatic passports, execute their mission and are quickly spirited away. Everything, including the escape route, is meticulously prepared in advance.

Nothing like this had happened in London. The hitmen were caught, their assistants were easily apprehended. It was stupid to use a close relative of the leader, even more so considering the fact that the newphew was not a trained terrorist, but a bumbling student, who had been sent by his uncle to complete his studies in England, using the organization's funds. Far from being a terrorist disguised as a student, he was really a student disguised as a terrorist.

It was obvious that unacceptable risks had been taken in order to carry out the shooting in great haste. This indicated a deadline to be met. Why?

In the middle of May, Sharon had visited Washington and met Alexander Haig. As later disclosed by Haig himself, Sharon had told him about his plan to invade Lebanon within a few days. As he recounted in his memoirs, Haig had strenuously objected to the operation, unless it was launched in reaction to an internationally recognized provocation. This meant that he had told Sharon to prepare such a provocation before attacking. The shooting of an Israeli ambassador clearly constituted such a provocation.

Sartawi always suspected Abu Nidal of being in the pay of the Mossad, Israeli's central intelligence agency. For him it was obvious that Sharon had simply ordered Abu Nidal to kill the Israeli ambassador on 3 June, in line with his other preparations.

I could not accept this theory. It was and still is inconceivable for me to believe that even a man like Sharon could give such an order, or that the Mossad would act on such an order. But if not the Israelis, who?

Our first theory pointed to the Iraqis. It was they who had set up Abu Nidal in the first place. At the moment the Iraqis were in dire straits: their invasion of Iran had failed, and the Iranians were massing for an attack on Baghdad. It was conceivable that in their desperation the Iraqis would facilitate the outbreak of a war in Lebanon, which would provide the pretext for an emotional appeal to the Iranian fellow Muslims and the Arab world at large to put an end to the Iraqi–Iranian war.

But the fact was that in June 1982, Abu Nidal was staying in Damascus and operating from there. It was inconceivable that he would order an action inimical to the Syrians. Indeed, the conditions in Syria were such that Abu Nidal would not do anything like this without express orders from the Syrian dictator.

But was this reasonable? Why would Hafez al-Assad order an action which led to an Israeli onslaught on the Syrian Army in Lebanon?

The answer was quite simple, but it took us some time to see it. The Syrians did not expect Sharon to attack them. They were certain that the full might of the Israeli Army would be directed against the PLO forces, and that Yassir Arafat and his organization would collapse within a day or two. The PLO mini-state would be destroyed, Arafat would be killed or captured by the Israelis, and the Syrians would achieve their major aim: the obliteration of the PLO as an independent Palestinian force. In preparation for a possible Israeli attack, the PLO had already set up, in Damascus, duplicates of all its offices. These were of course manned by people acceptable to the Syrians, and were ready to go into action on a moment's notice if the offices in Beirut were unable to function. Thus another PLO, totally subservient to the Syrians, but entirely legitimate, would take over. It was a beautiful plan, and if it had succeeded nothing of what happened later — the so-called rebellion in Fatah, the Syrian attack on the PLO in Tripoli, etc — would have been necessary.

Certainly the Syrians were surprised by the Israeli attack on their forces. They did not believe that one of Sharon's war aims was to oust them from Lebanon. Why should he? After all, the Syrian Army had entered Lebanon six years earlier with the full consent of the Israeli government, then led by Itzhak Rabin. Assad could not imagine that any Israeli would be foolish enough to believe that Lebanon could exist for any length of time outside the parameters of Syrian hegemony.

For several days the Israeli Army did not attack the Syrian forces, and these did not fire upon the Israelis who crossed the border to fight the PLO. Syrian prisoners later testified that they had received express orders not to open fire and not even to return fire unless directly shot at. When the government allowed the Israeli Army to attack the Syrians, it achieved full tactical surprise.

A few months later, at the Fez Summit Conference, the Iraqi dictator, Saddam Hussein, berated Assad in public for not fighting the Israelis as he should have. 'You have more advanced MIGs than I have, yet you did not fight as we fight the Iranians!' he stormed.

In exasperation, Assad exclaimed, in the presence of some 150 Arab foreign ministers and their assistants: 'But they told me they would not advance more than 45 kilometres!' It was an inadvertent admission.

According to PLO intelligence, the brother of the Syrian dictator, Rifaat al-Assad, chief of Syrian intelligence, had met Ariel Sharon in the US on 5 May 1982, just a month before the Israeli invasion.

Only on the fourth day of the war did the Israeli Army open its attack on the Syrian positions in Lebanon. The Syrian missiles were destroyed in a brilliant air attack, but the missiles in Syria proper, which were much more important, were not attacked. Under the Soviet–Syrian agreement, the Soviet Union was bound to come to the aid of the Syrians if attacked in their own country, though not in Lebanon.

On the ground, the Syrian Army acquitted itself well. The Israeli forces ran into an ambush near Sultan Yaaqub, sustained a stinging defeat and were unable to obtain their objective — the Beirut-Damascus highway — before the ceasefire came into effect on Friday, the sixth day of the war.

This ceasefire agreement was in itself an act of treason in Arab eyes. When it came into effect, Ariel Sharon announced that it did not cover the 'terrorists', meaning the PLO forces. Thus the mighty Syrian Army deserted its comrades on the field of battle, leaving the Palestinians alone to face the full might of the Israeli Army. There could be no clearer answer to the question about Syrian intentions.

To everybody's surprise, the Palestinian forces were acquitting themselves well. They had been unable to confront the Israeli Army in the open field, being too ill-trained and ill-equipped for such a task. They had no air force at all, and such heavy weapons as they posessed were largely left in their crates and stowed away, because they were unable to use them. But in the towns and refugee camps, they fought tenaciously and well, gaining accolades from some Israeli officers and commentators.

The decisive point was Sidon. Only one road passes from the Israeli frontier to Beirut, and this goes through the middle of Sidon. Sidon had already been the scene of an important battle for the Palestinians. It was there that a Syrian armoured column was destroyed in 1976 by Palestinan forces, using the advantages which irregular and semi-regular forces have against enemy armour in street-fighting. At the time the victorious Palestinian force was commanded, curiously enough, by Abu Mussa — the very same officer who in 1983 joined the Syrian conspiracy against his people.

The Israeli forces could not mount a major attack on Beirut without conquering Sidon. But there the Palestinians put up an obstinate struggle, which went on for days in the city and the Ein Hilwa refugee camp (which is not a camp at all, but an adjacent town built by refugees, as are all the so-called refugee camps in Lebanon). Until this resistance was overcome, the bulk of the Israeli Army and supplies could not come up to the outskirts of Beirut, and even the amphibious landings at Damour, between Sidon and Beirut, could not gain sufficient force. The war, which should have lasted between 24 and 48 hours, turned into something quite different. It dragged on, allowing Israeli grassroot opposition to it to develop and turn into a major political force.

North of Sidon, at the entrance to West Beirut, another major battle developed at Khalde, a vital road junction near the international airport. For days, the Palestinian resistance held up the Israeli Army there. As Arafat told me later, he, Abu Jihad and Abu Walid, the political and military commanders of the Fatah forces, visited the front line there every day, realizing the crucial importance of this battle. One hundred and sixty Palestinian fighters were killed there, but the time gained enabled West Beirut to prepare its defence, which held out for more than seventy days. 'Before the war started, not a single mine was in place, we were quite unprepared', Arafat told me.

The resistance at Khalde was strong enough to compel the Israeli Army to find another way to go around West Beirut. The forces who did this did not come from the south, but from the east, where they crossed territory supposed to be defended by the Syrians. These forces conquered Baabda, to the east of Beirut, and linked up with the Phalangist forces controlling East Beirut and the north, thus achieving one objective of the war a week later than planned.

Now Beirut was surrounded, and the long siege began. The Israeli Army and leadership had neither foreseen or planned such a lengthy operation, which completely changed the very texture of the war and turned Yassir Arafat into a national hero.

* * *

'Thus were they eating and drinking while the Jews of Europe were slaughtered!'

The thought crossed my mind while I was sitting with Sartawi in an expensive Chinese restaurant, not far from the Eiffel Tower, on the fifteenth of June. I was thinking about the ruined buildings of Tyre I had seen a few days before, the corpses near the roadside. Every day French television was showing terrible pictures from inside battered West Beirut: destroyed houses, mutilated children, crying women, crowded hospitals without medicines. And here we were sitting among a crowd of French bourgeois, who were meticulously choosing the right kind of wine for their food.

A few hours earlier, while I was sitting in Issam's office, there had been a call from Abu Faisal, who had been Sartawi's assistant for several years. His message was short: 'I am going out to fight. If anything happens to me, please look after my parents.' Abu Faisal, with his big moustache, his short rotund body, his sense of humour — it was difficult to imagine him fighting in the streest of Beirut against our tanks.

What could we do? Sartawi was working round the clock. While we were talking, we listened to an interview with him broadcast by the BBC. Issam recalled the steps taken by the PLO to recognize Israel and called upon the Israeli peace forces to oppose the war. He had rushed to Vienna to see Kreisky and had asked him to invite Arafat for an official visit to Austria. In this face-saving way, Issam thought, it would be possible to save Arafat from perishing in Beirut. He didn't know that Arafat would never dream of leaving the city, where he stayed to the very end. In Vienna he had also met Mitterand, who was visiting there, and had pleaded with him in vain to do something. Afterwards, Kreisky had said of Mitterand: 'He's half a fascist'.

Arafat himself called early the next morning. According to Issam his mood was euphoric. He made it quite clear that he would not leave Beirut. 'I shall die with my men', he said.

Matti, who was staying in Paris during these months to do academic work on modern Arab literature, went with me to see the functionaries of the French Socialist Party. What were they doing, we asked. The Israeli Labour Party had voted for the war. Why did the French sister party abstain from condemning this? The functionaries smiled politely, expressed their great concern, even invited us to a press conference where they spoke about

French politics, and included two or three wishy-washy sentences about Lebanon.

The French Socialist government, like the Americans, like the Russians, was biding its time for the outcome, cynically calculating the profits to be derived from the catastrophe. I was thinking constantly about the Holocaust. This silence, this cynicism, these polite expressions of regret — it was a repetition, on a smaller scale, of the world's attitude during those terrible years. It was a subject often talked about in Israel — Why was the world silent? Why did nobody do anything at all while the Jews were 'going up the chimneys' except the few Righteous Gentiles?

We felt that it was our duty, as Jews, to behave like the Righteous Ones, the way we would have wanted others to have behaved in our time of need.

The next day our French friends arranged a press conference for us three — Issam, Matti and me. We sat together on a platform, facing about 100 deeply-concerned people, conscience-stricken Jews, desperate Palestinians, worried Frenchmen and other Europeans.

Opening my remarks, I made a statement:

> We consider ourselves Israeli patriots. We are deeply concerned about the future of our state and its moral base. The killing and destruction of this war have made our job of putting an end to the conflict even more urgent and important. Mr Sharon says that this war is intended to destroy the PLO once and for all. We say: After this war the Palestinian problem must be solved, once and for all. We want Israel to offer the Palestinian people immediate negotiations on the basis of mutual recognition of the right to self-determination.

When the conference was finished, a woman who had been quietly sitting near the wall came up to me, shook my hand, and introduced herself. She was Claude Hamshari, the widow of the PLO representative in Paris who had been killed some years earlier by the Mossad, which had connected an extremely sophisticated electronic device to his telephone.

That night I slept in one of the bedrooms of the apartment which served as Issam's office. In the next bedroom slept two Palestinians, a doctor from Gaza and a Fatah bodyguard. Before leaving for home, Issam had given me his pistol. During the night the phone rang several times, calls from Beirut. Before dropping off to sleep, I was conscious of the singularity of my situation. Here I was, sleeping in what would certainly be called by Ariel Sharon a 'nest of terrorists', while the army of my country was trying to destroy the 'terrorist base' in Beirut. My relatives and the relatives of the two young people in the next room were trying to kill each other. Our effort to put an end to the slaughter and destruction would look like treason to many Israelis.

* * *

We were not alone.

Before the first week of the war was out, signals came from the fighting army that many Israeli soldiers had grave misgivings about the war. The first of these came from the Syrian front, where some of the units had been ambushed. But the feeling spread quickly along the whole front. The military promenade had turned into a large-scale war, there had been hard fighting, and the fighting was still going on. Before the ceasefire with the Syrians was one day old, Sharon was breaking it, trying to advance along the Beirut-Damascus highway, which the army had failed to capture in the eastern sector.

Already during the first week, hundreds of Israelis had signed a petition headed 'Enough!' At the end of the third week, on Saturday 25 June, the newly-formed Committee Against the War in Lebanon had called for a demonstration in Tel Aviv's central Kings of Israel Square. An hour before the appointed time, I was asked by foreign journalists how many people I expected to come. I answered, quite sincerely, that if one thousand people turned up I would consider it a great achievement. Never before had there been an anti-war demonstration in Israel while a war was going on.

An hour later, twenty thousand people were there. Many among the demonstrators were young people, who had already seen fighting in the war as reserve soldiers and been discharged.

This success emboldened the Peace Now Movement, which had been very quiet during the first few weeks, to call a demonstration of its own for the following Saturday, 3 July. An hour before the starting time, the Israeli radio broadcast a PLO communiqué just published in Beirut, saying that Uri Avnery had met with Yassir Arafat in West Beirut.

Ten days later I met Issam again in Paris. Friends in the United States had asked me to come over immediately to report on my meeting with Arafat. While the meeting had been a sensation in European papers — *The Times* of London had called it an historical encounter — it had not been mentioned at all in the American media. My friends felt that by coming to the States I could break what was obviously a conspiracy of silence. And indeed, during a 48-hour visit to New York and Washington, I spoke on five television networks, and interviews with me were printed in the major newspapers. But what struck me most during this visit was the determination shown by both officials and journalists to ignore everything indicating a readiness by the PLO leadership to achieve a settlement. Anything which tended to undermine the existing stereotype of the PLO and the Palestinians in general as a bunch of terrorists — an eastern version of the Red Indians in old Hollywood movies — was simply ignored.

On the way there I made a stopover in Paris and spent the day in discussion with Sartawi. Then the three of us — Matti had joined us — travelled together to London for a press conference. It was there that Issam voiced his suspicion that Abu Nidal was working for the Mossad, and that the attempt on Ambassador Argov's life had been engineered by Sharon. The journalists turned towards me and asked me to comment on this. I replied: 'I do not believe it, and I do not want to believe it.' Matti, when asked the same question, was less explicit, saying that he would reserve judgment until he'd seen all the evidence. This noncommittal answer led to many complications. A right-wing Israeli lawyer demanded that Matti be put on trial for collaborating with the enemy in wartime, and this case went all the way to the Supreme Court, which finally decided that the Attorney General was the sole authority to decide whether General Peled should be prosecuted or not. The Attorney General decided there were no grounds for prosecution, and that even ordering an investigation would besmirch the reputation of an Israeli Army general.

Both Issam and I believed that an all-out attack on West Beirut was probable, and that the aim of Begin and Sharon was to kill Arafat and all the other PLO leaders in the city. During my visit to West Beirut I had gained the impression that this was what Arafat and his soldiers expected, too. We asked ourselves: If it did happen, what next?

All our energies were devoted at the moment to preventing the final assault on West Beirut. For me, I believed that such an assault would be a disaster all round. I had heard competent estimates predicting that 700 Israeli soldiers would be killed in the ensuing street-fighting, where the vast technical superiority of the Israeli Army would be reduced by the terrain. The terrible price to be paid by the civilian population was unimaginable. The political and psychological effect of storming and destroying an Arab capital would cast a shadow for generations. Palestinian moderation, for which we had worked so hard, would be wiped out. A new generation of Palestinians would be totally devoted to vengeance.

Issam's labours had borne one important fruit: On the day I saw Arafat, the press reported that three outstanding Jews had called on Israel and the PLO to negotiate on the basis of self-determination. The three were Nahum Goldmann, the American Jewish leader Philip Klutznick, and Pierre Mendès-France.This was the first time in his life that Mendès-France publicly identified himself as a Jew, a sign of how deeply his emotions were stirred.

The text of a statement had been prepared by Sartawi, and was published together with a response by Sartawi, welcoming the statement on behalf of the PLO. Just before meeting me, Arafat published a statement of his own congratulating the three. It was a clear expression of the PLO's willingness to negotiate with Israel for the two states solution, followed immediately by his interview with me and, a few days later, by a meeting with Congressman Paul McCloskey, in which Arafat signed an improvised statement on a piece of paper, saying that the PLO accepts all United Nations resolutions concerning the Palestinian question. All UN resolutions are, of course, based on the recognition of Israel, a UN member-state created according to a specific resolution of the UN. A few days later, Arafat received in Beirut an Israeli journalist, Amnon Kapeliouk, who went there as a representative of the French newspaper *Le Monde*

For Sartawi, my meeting with Arafat was more than a victory, it was a complete vindication of all his work. Forgotten were the days when Kaddumi had denied the very existence of our contacts, forgotten were the PNC resolutions forbidding contacts with Zionist Israelis. The meeting symbolized the victory of 'the Sartawi Line', after all Sartawi's warnings had proved to be only too right.

A curious thought: Only a year and a half earlier, Sartawi had been threatened with a trial for treason for accepting a prize along with a Zionist Israeli. Now I was threatened with a treason trial for meeting the chairman of the PLO.

Issam had made a statement at IFRI, the French Institute for International Relations, saying *inter alia*: 'We are intelligent people. When we talk about peace, it is clear that we are talking about peace with the enemy. Peace creates new relations. Peace serves the interests of our people and of the Arab nation.

> In 1981, the PLO accepted the plan of Chairman Brezhnev calling for an international conference of all the parties concerned, including the PLO and Israel, the implementation of the national rights of the Palestinians, and the right of all the states in the region, including Israel, to live in peace and security.
>
> We have postponed the meeting in which I was about to make this statement, because we did not want it to look an act of capitulation. Now we are doing this because we have proved we are unvanquished, fighting for forty days against the third biggest army in the world.
>
> The supreme institution of the Palestinian people has recognized Israel's right to be accepted on a mutual basis. Only this same institution, the Palestinian National Council, can nullify this resolution.

But our main concern was, of course: If the worst comes to the worst, and the present leadersiip of the PLO is destroyed, what will happen?

In deepest confidence, Issam told me his views, as they were evolving in the face of the dramatic events. By that time he was convinced that Syria had had a hand in the events leading up to the war. Indeed, the PLO representative in Peking had already published a statement denouncing Syria and Israel for conspiring together against the Palestinian people.

If as a result of the war the remnants of the PLO became Syrian puppets in Damascus, it would be a catastrophe for the Palestinian people. Their supreme interest — the creation of a Palestinian state in the West Bank and Gaza — would be sacrificed on the altar of Syrian interest. Damascus was clearly interested in the endless prolongation of the conflict, which enhanced its standing in the Arab world and its claim on huge Arab financial assistance. It had no interest at all in seeing a truly independent Palestinian state set up in what it still considered a part of Greater Syria.

Therefore, a new idea sprang up in Issam's mind, first hesitatingly, then quickly assuming clearer and bolder outlines. If the legitimate leadership was destroyed, the independent forces within the Palestinian people, those which rejected foreign domination and strove for a peace settlement which would bring about national independence, should resurrect the PLO in some other country. This would mean a split between a Damascus-based PLO, radical and rejectionist, and a moderate, realistic PLO somewhere else.

After initial hesitation, Sartawi became increasingly resolved to take the initiative in such a development, if the need arose. It was an agonizing decision, which we talked about over and over again, attacking it from different angles. I was all for it and encouraged him to be ready for such an eventuality. I even proposed that he ask Arafat for authorization over the phone and record the conversation, and volunteered to cross the lines into

Beirut again, if necessary, to obtain written confirmation for him.

In the end, the critical moment for making this decision did not arrive. On the edge of the precipice, even Begin and Sharon recoiled from ordering the final onslaught, compensating themselves by ordering murderous air attacks on the beleaguered city of half a million, while Itzhak Rabin advised Sharon to cut off water and electricity.

Many factors combined to prevent the attack: the tenacious Palestinian resistance, the growing peace movement in Israel, world public opinion, in which we had played some part. But above all, it was the opposition of the Israeli Army itself, which abhorred the idea of fighting a battle inside a densely-populated city.

After fighting for 79 days, the Palestinian forces evacuated West Beirut, after an agreement had been reached under American auspices. I stood on the roof of a building in the Beirut harbour area while the first truckloads of Palestinian soldiers passed by on their way to the ship, waving their flags and their arms and portraits of Yassir Arafat. A battle had come to its end, but the war was far from finished. The illusion that the national movement of a people could be destroyed by conquering a piece of territory, an illusion entertained by Sharon and Begin — who at least should have known better — had been proved ridiculous. When the smoke of battle cleared over Beirut, the Palestinian problem was still there.

Everything had changed, and everything remained the same.

# 39

*'Is there a shop nearby where I can buy some earrings?' I ask Issam.*

*'What do you need earrings for? Who's the lucky lady?'*

*'It's my wife, Rachel. Her hairdresser cut her hair too short, and she's terribly upset. I promised her I'd bring back a pair of green earrings to make up for it.'*

*Later in the afternoon, Issam takes me to a nearby luxury hotel, where there are several expensive-looking shops for rich tourists.*

*Upon entering one of the shops, we are approached by a salesman who shouts to me in Hebrew: 'Uri Avnery! What are you doing here?' It appears he is a Moroccan Jew, who had lived in Israel and emigrated to France.*

*'Do you know this gentleman?' Issam asks him.*

*'Everybody knows him!' the Moroccan says.*

*'He's the king of the Jews,' Issam declares.*

*There are no earrings in the shop. While I am looking through a rack of ties, Issam disappears. When he does not come back after ten minutes, I start to worry. We could have been followed.*

*After another ten minutes he reappears. In his hand he has a small parcel. Attached to it is a tiny card: 'To Rachel from Issam.'*

*When Rachel opens the package back home, she finds a beautiful pair of green earrings.*

# 40

It was a terrible, terrible evening.

It had started off well enough. A peace group in Amsterdam had invited me to take part in a public discussion with a representative of the PLO. I had expected Issam, but instead Imad Shakour had turned up. Issam also came, but Yassir Arafat had decided to enlarge the number of PLO officials appearing on public platforms with Zionist Israelis. In order to emphasize his determination to move forward towards a peace initiative, after the battle of Beirut, he had sent Imad, a member of his personal staff and adviser on Israeli affairs. Shakour was an Israeli citizen, who had left Israel after being arrested several times. He was the man who translated excerpts from the Israeli press, and all my articles in *Haolam Hazeh,* for Arafat. I had met him in Beirut during the siege.

I was sitting with Imad on the platform, after we had seen a performance of a Palestinian dance troupe, and the discussion was underway, when a piece of paper was handed to us. It said that news had just been received about a massacre in the Palestinian refugee camps in Beirut.

It was 18 September 1982, the evening of the first day of Rosh Hashana, the Jewish New Year.

We continued our debate as if nothing had happened, talking about peace, coexistence between Israel and a Palestinian state, negotiations between the Israeli government and the PLO. And while we were talking, new slips of paper were handed to us. Hundreds had been massacred in the refugee camps of Sabra and Shatilla, two shanty towns I had visited only two months earlier after my interview with Yassir Arafat

After the meeting, Imad and I walked together to the small hotel, where both of us were staying.We were speaking in Hebrew, which Imad spoke perfectly, having studied at the Hebrew University in Jerusalem. 'They want to destroy every possibility of Palestinians and Israelis ever talking to each other', he said, adding, 'but we shall not let them!'

At the hotel Issam was waiting for us, surrounded by a group of Palestinians who had come to Amsterdam for the meeting, Palestinian activists and functionaries from Holland and nearby countries. We went together to a pub, a rather questionable one. There we sat around a table, talking about the outrage committed by Lebanese Christians, in an area controlled by Israelis, on Palestinians. Out of curiosity I asked Issam whether the people around the table were all Muslims. He didn't know, and asked them. Some were Muslims, some were Christians, all were Palestinians. It gave me an idea about one interesting aspect of the Palestinian situation: religious differences, which played such a terrible role in Lebanon, had been nearly obliterated among the Palestinians by their common tragedy. Nationalism had taken their place.

The next day I flew back to Israel. Rarely in my life had I been so full of rage. I expressed it in an article I wrote on the plane. For the following months I thought, talked and wrote continuously about the massacre. I became an expert on every minute detail of the events, interviewing generals (mostly in secret) and soldiers. When the Kahan Report came out, I was one of its most outspoken critics.

The appointment of the commission of inquiry headed by Judge Itzhak Kahan was the result of a moral outcry, such as Israel had never seen before. When the government refused to investigate, a huge protest rally took place in the Kings of Israel Square, the same place where the first big rally against the war had taken place. But this time 400,000 people showed up, an emotional experience of rare dimensions. Per capita, this would be equivalent to a demonstration of 20 million Americans or of five million Britons assembled in one place.

The government had to give way, and a judicial board of inquiry was set up. The whole world followed its proceedings. Nearly everyone in Israel and throughout the world expected its report to be followed by the fall of the government. But this did not happen. The commission established the facts, and decided that several Israeli leaders and officers bore 'indirect' responsibility for the massacre. Chief among those implicated was Ariel Sharon. After a drawn-out battle, Sharon was relieved of the job of minister of defence, but stayed on in the cabinet as a minister without portfolio.

I had no quarrel with the factual findings of the report, but did not agree that the responsibility of Sharon and the others was 'indirect' — a definition which does not exist in Israeli law. They were clearly accessories to the crime and should have been indicted for murder. And so I said.

But while the outcome was not yet clear, the imminent downfall of the government still seeming probable, I was transported to another world.

* * *

Nearly two years had passed since our visit to Rabat. King Hassan had promised us then to invite us again, and this time publicly. American intervention, as Issam believed, had prevented this. Now, suddenly, we received an urgent message from Issam: Come immediately, the King wants to see you.

The background, as we learned later, was the developing peace offensive of the Fatah leadership after Beirut, which I shall discuss in the next chapters. Arafat and Abu Maazen had asked the king to receive us, publicly, so as to prepare the ground for a direct and public meeting between them and us. After the whole world had heard about my meeting with Arafat during the siege of Beirut, King Hassan found it possible to accede to this request. He was going to the United States to talk with President Reagan and address the United Nations General Assembly, and on this occasion would be pleased to grant us an audience. The date, as Issam understood it, was to be 21 October 1982, and we went post-haste to Paris, to be briefed by Issam, who could not go to the States himself, because of the continuing

American refusal to grant him a visa. We stayed the day in Paris, and flew on to New York. There, we were told, an emissary of the King would receive us at the airport, and from then on we would be guests of His Majesty.

We passed passport control at Kennedy Airport, waited for our luggage to arrive and then stood in a long line for customs control, an anachronistic procedure peculiar to the US and rather infuriating. All the time our eyes roved around the hall, trying to identify a Moroccan-looking gentleman. By the time we passed customs we were becoming a little nervous, but then a young gentleman materialized and greeted us. He was an official of the Moroccan Consulate.

He whisked us away to a big, luxurious limousine. In our brisk Israeli way, we showered him with questions: Would the King see us today or tomorrow, would we have time to change clothes, would we go first to an hotel or straight to His Majesty? The young gentleman smiled politely. All in good time, all in good time. His job was to take us to the Waldorf Towers. Then we would hear all.

The Moroccan, it appeared, was a Berber, and during the drive into Manhattan Matti Peled conversed with him in Arabic about Berber culture and about Moroccan Jews. To our surprise, the Moroccan official told us that about 5,000 Israelis of Moroccan descent visited Morocco every year, a fact not well-known in Israel.

At the Waldorf Towers we were received with the most profound respect. An elegant suite had been prepared for us, and two other rooms. We decided that Matti would occupy the suite, and that it would become our temporary headquarters.

What followed was a chapter of hilarious frustration. The gentleman took his leave after depositing us safely at the hotel, having done his duty. Before leaving, he told us that as guests of His Majesty we were absolutely free to do as we pleased, to order anything we wished in the hotel, to enjoy ourselves at any nightclub or any other form of amusement. The luxurious limousine would be at our disposal around the clock.

And there we were in the most luxurious suite any one of us had ever stayed in, with paradise at our feet, furious. Our time was extremely limited. I had to be back at home within three days, having left all my work up in the air. Matti had to give an important lecture at the university. Only Yaacov Arnon was free, but he wanted to visit his son in California. We had not the slightest inkling about the timetable, having been told only that someone in the King's entourage would contact us in due time and give us all the details. His Majesty, so the gentleman told us, was due to arrive within a few hours in Washington D.C to see the president. Perhaps we would be called to Washington, perhaps we would be asked to stay in New York until the King arrived there, within a few days. His Majesty's visit to the States would last only a week, and during one of those days His Majesty would receive us.

Hours passed, and nothing happened. Expecting a call, we did not dare leave our island of luxury. The most sumptuous meals, fit for kings and their guests, were brought to us. As we were determined to keep our visit a secret until we got permission from the King to announce it, we could not even contact our friends in the city. We were voluntarily incarcerated in a gilded prison.

In the evening we called Issam in Paris, giving vent to our frustration. He laughed. 'It's the usual mess', he said, 'because of this you Israelis have been able to screw us for thirty years!' But he promised to call the King's advisers to speed things up.

The day passed, and then another, and yet another. We made small sorties in the limousine to buy electronic games for Arnon's grandchildren and Arabic books for Matti. The idea that this wonderful limousine was just standing there, without our being able to use it for a long journey, drove us crazy. But even so, the short trips could be eventful. Once when all three of us were in the limousine talking Hebrew, the chauffeur turned around and asked: 'You're speaking Hebrew?' It appeared he was a Russian Jew. Fortunately, he did not find it peculiar to be conducting Israelis around in a limousine ordered by the Moroccan Consulate.

I broke the rules of secrecy to call my friend Lally Weymouth, a freelance journalist, and to visit her in my limousine. When she called back to the hotel, asking for me and giving my room number, the telephone operator said ingenuously: 'Oh, the gentlemen from the Moroccan delegation!'

Our only comfort was our daily meetings with Khaled al-Hassan, who was staying incognito in the same hotel. We had several meals together.

I had met Khaled in New York three months earlier, when I was in the States to report about my meeting with Arafat. After I had been publicly received by the Chairman, Khaled saw no reason to keep our meeting a secret, and allowed me to report on it. That was, of course, still during the siege of Beirut. He gave me an important statement saying that the PLO was ready to cease all hostilities, including all guerrilla attacks, once agreement about mutual recognition between Israel and the PLO was reached. At that time Khaled had been also staying at the Waldorf Towers. He had received me in his room, his huge frame encased in a flowing white robe. We had talked, of course, about the war, enabling me to publish in *Haolam Hazeh* an account of the war which was very different from anything appearing in the Israeli press. It prepared my readers for the ongoing war which at that time no one foresaw.

Khaled, like his brother, Hani, is one of the political brains of the PLO, a diplomat by nature, a founder of Fatah. He is also a big conservative businessman. I was amused the next day when I saw a banner headline on the front page of the *New York Post* screaming 'Terror Chief in New York!'

Now we were sitting around a table that had been wheeled in laden with exquisite food and were talking about the situation. It was a serious debate about the future of the PLO and peace, but it was quite impossible to talk with Khaled without a continuing flow of jokes, most of them risqué.

There was this Palestinian whose wife had been killed in Beirut and who had fled with his ten children to Damascus. Needing a mother for his children, but not wanting to have more children, he looks for a woman who cannot bear children. He is introduced to a widow who had been married three times and had no children at all. But, after the wedding night, she becomes immediately pregnant.

'How's this possible?' the poor man cries upon hearing the news. 'You had no children with your first three husbands! How is that?'

'Well, it was like this. The first husband was a Lebanese Maronite, who was educated in France. No children. The second husband was a Turk. No children. The third husband was a Syrian. He was a Baath party member. Every night he came home after a party meeting and started to shout: Long live the Baath! Long live the Baath! When he finished shouting he was so tired he went straight to sleep. No children.'

Khaled told us about a secret message sent by President Reagan to Syria, Jordan, Saudi Arabia and Egypt, explaining the real meaning of the so-called Reagan Plan which had been published on 1 September 1982, a few days after the evacuation of the PLO forces from Beirut. In this message, Reagan had said that 98 percent of the occupied territories would be returned to the Arabs, that Jerusalem would remain united, and that the fate of these territories would be decided in free elections. He also made it clear that he was 'against' a sovereign Palestinian state, but that he would not refuse to accept such a solution.

Khaled also told us about Arafat's proposal to King Hussein, which had been more or less accepted by the king. According to this, a confederation between Jordan and a Palestinian state in the West Bank and Gaza would be set up. The Palestinian state would have its own passport, flag and 'symbolic' army. The foreign service would be divided between Palestine and Jordan, so that if the ambassador in Paris was a Palestinian, the ambassador in Bonn would be a Jordanian. Both states would have their own parliaments, and a super-parliament would be shared. (As it turned out, the Syrian agents within the PLO torpedoed this agreement in 1982, as they did the Fahd Plan a year earlier.)

Al-Hassan, who had accompanied Arafat on his visit to Rome and to the Pope, told us that the Chairman had toasted the Israeli peace movement before a cheering crowd of 1,500, who applauded him for three solid minutes. He also told us that Sharon had recently stayed in America in the same hotel as Rifaat al-Assad, the brother of the Syrian president and chief of the Syrian security services. He believed the two had met. I told him that under the old British law, it was enough to prove that a woman and her presumed lover had stayed a night under the same roof in order to obtain a divorce.

Our main topic was, of course, the Sabra and Shatilla massacre, which was at the moment being investigated by the Kahan Commission. Two days before the massacre, the Israeli Army had moved into West Beirut, in direct contravention of the agreement achieved by Philip Habib, President Reagan's representative, on the eve of the PLO evacuation. At the time, the Israeli government had contended that the PLO had left behind 2,000 fighters, thus making this action imperative. No proof of this was ever found, even by the Kahan Commission. Khaled shrugged off the very idea. 'Under the agreement, we had to evacuate 6,000 fighters. We took away 15,000. Actually, we evacuated everyone who had no valid Lebanese papers, because we were afraid of Lebanese retaliation.' He also explained the big arms caches found all over South Lebanon. 'We are a guerrilla army, and therefore we have stashed away arms in many places. Actually, we had many more arms that we could use. Several Arab states sent us arms in abundance, whether we needed them or not.' (Israel later conducted a thriving arms trade with these weapons, mostly of Soviet origin, which were ideal for sending to guerrilla forces when the identity of the supplier had to be kept secret.)

Again and again we brought up the time element. Khaled agreed with us that now, after Beirut, when the prestige of Arafat among the Palestinians was at its height, the climate for peace was the most propitious, and that this opportunity should not be allowed to pass by, as so many others had in the past. He mentioned that such an opportunity for Israel had been immediately after the Six-Day War. 'If Israel had voluntarily returned the occupied territories immediately after that war, it would have been king of the world. No one would have been able to touch it with a rose, not to mention bullets. At the time there was a meeting of the Fatah leadership, and somebody said "Let's start operations immediately, because if Israel returns the territories we are finished!" ' I told him that on the fifth day of the Six Day War I had proposed to Prime Minsiter Levi Eshkol that he make a dramatic offer to the Palestinian people offering Israeli assistance in the setting up of a Palestinian state.

All this was extremely stimulating and enjoyable, but Matti and I had by now become very impatient. On the third day of our stay in paradise, Matti called the Moroccan Consul and told him that we had to leave the next day. A few minutes later the foreign minister of Morocco called from Washington. He expressed his regret over the delay. His Majesty would be pleased to receive us on Tuesday, 26 October, in New York, immediately after his speech before the General Assembly. He hoped that everything was done to make our stay as enjoyable as possible.

The next day both of us returned to Israel, leaving the suite to Arnon. We were probably the first people in the history of the Waldorf Towers who gave up free rooms. Our Moroccan hosts could understand even less our insistence that we had to go back to Israel for two days before taking the long flight back again to New York. And indeed, we started to feel like air stewards, spending interminable hours going back and forth, each flight taking 18 hours with stopovers and other delays. But on the 26th we rushed from Kennedy Airport to the Waldorf Towers ('home sweet home'), and hardly had time to change into dark three-piece suits, before a very impatient young gentleman — the same — urged us to please hurry. His Majesty was waiting.

* * *

His Sherifian Majesty, Hassan II, was residing in a beautiful villa at 4 Durham Street, Bronxville, N.Y. For his visit a big Oriental tent, lit up in different colours, had been erected. Several trailers equipped with telephones had also been set up for the security people. We were ushered into one of these. His Majesty had not yet arrived from the United Nations, where he had made his great speech, speaking in Arabic, without notes.

The premises were swarming with journalists, not one of whom took the slightest notice of the three gentlemen, nor of the crossed flags of Israel and Palestine they were wearing on their lapels. In the trailer, Khaled joined us to brief us on the situation, but to our surprise he told us that he was not joining us for the audience with the King. He was keeping his meetings with us secret — excluding those with me. As I had already met Arafat, he felt free to meet me publicly.

Eventually we were ushered into the villa. The King, in a grey suit, was awaiting us on the steps. We shook hands, bowing slightly, and the King cordially seated us around him, in front of a table laden with a huge heap of Arab sweets. After our long flight and hasty departure for the audience, both Matti and I were ravenous, but as His Majesty did not take any sweets himself, we did not eat either.

At the beginning a great horde of journalists rushed into the hall, but all except the Moroccans were evicted immediately by the guards. The Moroccans took pictures and filmed us, and were then also requested to leave.

The King, with his keen perception, sensed our disappointment. So this meeting was not to be a public one, as we had hoped. 'We have to devise a strategy in our fight against Mr Begin', he explained. 'We have to save our ammunition. This meeting shall be made public, but please allow me to decide exactly when.'

Khaled had already explained to us the delicacy of the situation. The King had arrived in the States at the head of an Arab League delegation including the foreign minister of Syria and Farouk Kaddumi of the PLO, both of whom would have strenuously objected to any meeting with Israelis. He felt that having a public meeting with us while serving in this capacity could be construed as an insult to them.

In an extremely amiable atmosphere, we had a serious discussion. It was not a debate, because we had no differences of opinion about any subject brought up. The King thought that the most important thing was to bring about the downfall of the Begin government, which he considered disastrous, but he had no illusions at all about Shimon Peres.

'I know him', he said 'he's more polite than Begin, but there's little else to separate them. The important thing is to give more power to people like you, who have a clear concept of the Palestinian problem.'

It was clear to him that this was the main purpose of our meeting: To lend us credibility and importance in our fight for Israeli public opinion, especially in view of the coming elections in Israel. The King also expected the Israeli government to fall after the publication of the Kahan Report. He apologized for doing so little. 'I'm six thousand kilometres away from the conflict', he explained, 'I'm not a part of the conflict. I can only help. The decisions have to be taken on the scene, preferably by the PLO together with King Hussein. The burden is too heavy for either of them alone. It would be easier for both of them together. I shall help them come together.'

Speaking about the Kahan Commission hearings, he impressed me with the shrewdness of his observations. 'It was stupid of Sharon to attack the army. It's very dangerous for him.' The King, with long experience with his own security people, some of whom had conspired against him, obviously knew what he was talking about.

He also showed us that he was well informed about domestic politics in Israel. He was keenly interested in the affair of Aharon Abu-Hatzeira, a cabinet minister under investigation for corruption. Abu-Hatzeira is the descendant of a distinguished Moroccan family of rabbis, and he was about to form a new party led by Moroccan Jews. 'I know him', the King remarked. Some of the King's advisers, icluding Mohammed Boussita, the foreign minister, and Khadera, who had been present at the Arafat meeting, were present but did not speak, unless asked specific questions by the King. Another adviser, Ben Souda, who had been our host in Rabat, entered in the middle of the discussion, after sending in a valet with a request to join us. Upon entering he bowed and kissed the King's hands. Out of cosideration for us, the King spoke in English, which he speaks very well, but he was obviously much more at home in French.

The King agreed with us that now was the time to take decisive action to bring about a settlement. In the wake of the war, all conditions were propitious — Israeli public opinion was fed up with the war and with the government, the Kahan Report might bring Begin down, Arafat could act without Syrian obstruction, America seemed ready for bold new iniatives. At his meeting with Reagan, the King had explored the possibilities.

'We must do everything to make you stronger in Israel', the King repeated when he accompanied us courteously to the steps of the villa, where we took leave with handshakes and bows. He had promised to make the meeting public soon — which he did three months later, after our meeting with Yassir Arafat.

Conducting us to our limousine, the Moroccan consul, who confided to us that he had been in Israel, but secretly, remarked that the situation was complex. 'But so is everything in our region', he added. He was only too right.

The next day Matti and Arnon went home, after another long conversation with al-Hassan. I was left alone for another 48 hours in the beautiful suite, with the beautiful limousine.

'Have you any idea where Khaled al-Hassan is?' Lally Weymouth asked me. 'The whole world is looking for him. No one has met him, and no one has met the King. Everyone wants to interview them.' I couldn't tell her yet that three Israelis had seen both.

## 41

*Lova Eliav, who had been a soldier in the British Army during the Second World War, used to tell a story about our job.*

*In the British Army, he says, they found a way to overcome the enemy barbed wire during infantry attacks on its positions. One soldier would run ahead and throw himself full length on the barbed wire, and the others would then run over him and storm the position.*

*'It's an unpleasant job, but someone has to do it!'*

# 42

When he came out of Beirut, proud and unvanquished, Yassir Arafat was determined to move ahead and conduct an independent Palestinian policy, in order to achieve a political solution.

Paradoxically, in the beleaguered city Arafat was, perhaps for the first time in the history of the PLO, really independent. He was rid of the Syrians, who had deserted him on the battlefield by concluding a ceasefire agreement with the Israelis on the sixth day of the war, leaving the Palestinians to fight it out alone. The remnants of the Syrian Army inside Beirut were demoralized and an object of ridicule. The Soviet Union, which had not lifted a finger to help the Palestinians in their darkest hour, was not in a position to veto any move. Arafat himself had gained immense prestige among his people and in the Arab world at large by remaining with his besieged forces, sharing their lot and risking his life every minute, knowing that hundreds of Phalangist and Israeli agents inside the city were looking for him.

The most precious of all Palestinian possessions, the one called by them 'the independence of decision', seemed secure. It was this which enabled him to receive me publicly, to give an interview afterwards to an Israeli correspondent representing *Le Monde*, to give Congressman Paul McCloskey a handwritten statement saying that the PLO was ready to accept all United Nations resolutions concerning Palestine, and to welcome the statement of the three Jewish leaders calling for mutual recognition between Israel and the PLO.

Coming out of Beirut, Arafat continued this course. Going to Tunis, instead of Damascus, was a declaration of independence. He went to Rome and toasted the Israeli peace movement, which had made such a deep impression upon the Palestinians with its mass demonstrations against the war ('the only demonstrations in the Middle East against the Israeli invasion', as many Palestinians put it). In Rome, he told Italian politicians that the PLO was ready to meet with leaders of the Israeli Labour Party in a public conference — but this was publicly rebuffed by Shimon Peres and his colleagues, who announced that any member of the Labour Party who met with PLO members would be evicted from the party. Our meeting with King Hassan, which had been held on Arafat's request, was a part of this campaign.

During his interview with Amnon Kapeliouk, the Israeli journalist sent by *Le Monde*, in an underground parking lot in Beirut, Arafat had suggested that after the war, Israeli and Palestinian 'thinkers' meet to talk about all aspects of the conflict, including ways of amending the Palestinian Charter.

This now seemed the most promising avenue. To a delegation of the Curiel group from Paris, Arafat said in Tunis that such a meeting could now take place anywhere, perhaps in Paris, perhaps in Cyprus.

With this in view, I went to Paris on 11 January, 1983, to see how the conference could be organized. I knew that the Palestinian National Council was about to be convened within a few weeks, and I thought that a great event before that would have an impact on that session, where, I hoped, decisive new resolutions would be adopted.

When I met Issam, he scoffed at the idea of a conference. Much more important things could and should be done, he believed. He was reviving his pet idea of 1981: that an Israeli peace delegation be invited to the Palestinian National Council, dramatizing the dialogue between the PLO and Zionist peace forces in Israel. His immediate object was no less than revolutionary: to organize a meeting between Arafat and us.

In the evening I went with Issam to eat at a famous restaurant, the *Pied de Cochon,* in the old Les Halles district. It was bitterly cold and we walked briskly along the streets lined with sex shops and other tourist attractions. Issam tok me to a bar he liked, where he joked with the pretty bar girls, and then over a substantial meal, accompanied by good wine, we discussed the situation inside the organization.

One of the subjects was the creation of a Palestinian provisional government in exile. This had been an idea close to my heart for a long time. It would help us shatter the demonic image of the PLO as a terrorist organization, so prevalent in the world. Sadat had proposed it several times. Why wasn't it done?

Eric Rouleau, the *Le Monde* expert on the Middle East, with whom I had talked that day, thought that the creation of such a government might now be possible. Instead of the top leadership of the PLO, it could consist of secondary figures identified with the PLO, such as the mayors of Hebron and Halhul, Fahd Kawasmeh and Mohammed Milhem, who had been deported from Israel. 'Ezer Weizmann or Arik Sharon could decide the leadership of the Palestinian people by deporting certain leaders and turning them into national heroes', Eric had joked. Weizmann was the defence minister who had ordered the deportations. 'If Sharon deports Bassam Shaqa [the deposed mayor of Nablus] he certainly would be a likely candidate for prime minister.' Shaqa had indeed been threatened with deportation by Weizmann, but the order was revoked after the Supreme Court intervened. Immediately afterwards Shaqa lost both his legs in a Jewish terrorist assassination attempt. In a simultaneous attack, his colleague in Ramallah, Karim Khalaf, had lost one leg.

Riding on a wave of optimism, but frustrated by the slowness of the process, Issam was hatching great plans, which he confided to me during the evening. One of the biggest problems was organizing the population in the occupied West Bank into a big peace movement, in order to make their pressure felt within the PLO. Issam was thinking about creating some kind of pressure group, consisting of some of the more courageous leaders in the West Bank and Palestinian personalities throughout the diaspora, especially in the United States and Europe, who could influence proceedings in the PNC and perhaps provide the decisive push towards a clear and unequivocal peace programme. He asked me to see several West Bank personalities immediately, in order to give them this message and see what help they needed.

The next day Issam had to go to London for several meetings arranged by June Ward, a very attractive and efficient young British woman, on whom he relied more and more. I spent the day with Abu Faisal.

The evening before, while I was having dinner with Issam, Abu Faisal had arrived. Entering the apartment which served as Issam's office, he saw a suitcase standing in the hall. He recognized this as mine, and left the main guestroom for me. When I came in late in the evening, he was already asleep in the other guestroom.

In the morning he told me his exciting stories. When the PLO had evacuated Beirut, he had stayed behind. He was not a combatant, and had valid Lebanese papers. One morning he had heard a strange noise, and realized that the Israeli Army was invading West Beirut. He dressed in a hurry and went into the street, just in time to meet a group of Israeli officers who asked him for the apartment of Abu Faisal. He sent them to his apartment and rushed to the French Embassy, where he found asylum. The Israeli officers could be forgiven for not suspecting him, because nobody could look less like a terrorist than Abu Faisal, a short, rotund, mustachioed, humorous fellow. He was now in Paris, torn with anxiety for his old parents, whom he had left behind all alone in Beirut and whom he was trying to get out of the city, which was rapidly becoming an inferno for Palestinians, being at the mercy of the Israeli Army, the Phalangists, the Lebanese Army, and especially the notorious Lebanese security services. Shafiq al-Hut, the official PLO ambassador to Lebanon, was staying on, practically underground, after his office was invaded by the security services, and my friend Sabri Jiryes was holding out as the only visible symbol of the Palestinian presence, in the empty premises of the Palestinian Research Centre, whose contents had been impounded by the Israeli Army and shipped to Israel. (They were later returned as part of a prisoner exchange agreement. The Palestinians took great pride in this, saying that their books were as important to them as their prisoners.) Later, a bomb exploded near the Centre, and Jiryes's wife was killed.

I heard all these stories about friends and acquaintances while walking through the streets of St Germain. Abu Faisal was on a shopping spree, not for himself but for Abu Amar, as whose personal aide he was serving temporarily. We bought an exercise bicycle as well as a plastic substance for exercising the hands. It seemed that Arafat needed this because he got cramps after signing so many documents. During the siege of Beirut he had suffered from an attack of gallstones and been inactive for several days, giving rise to a spate of rumours that he had been killed by an Israeli bomb. In all this activity, between perpetual trips to world capitals, he tried to keep as fit as possible.

Indeed, it was not easy to organize a meeting with Arafat, because communications were difficult. As a security measure, he never announces his movements in advance, appearing suddenly here or there, making it difficult for his enemies — Syrian, Israelis, and many others — to plan an assassination attempt. Even while arranging a meeting with Kreisky, he had driven the meticulous Austrians crazy by not informing them in advance when and how he would arrive. Kreisky had to go to the airport quite suddenly, when informed that Arafat would arrive within the hour from Sofia on the private plane of the Bulgarian leader — and then had to wait for an hour, because the plane was late.

It appeared that now Arafat was somewhere between Yemen and Iraq, and his office in Tunis found it hard to contact him. Throughout the day Abu Faisal tried to establish contact, but to no avail.

In the evening we gave up and went to a Chinese restaurant, where we had dinner with Maxim Ghilan, an Israeli emigré living in Paris, who publishes a unique publication called *Israel and Palestine*, providing the two sides with interesting information about happenings on both sides. As usual, Maxim, who had once worked on my staff in Tel Aviv, had many interesting tit-bits, and we had a highly informative conversation over the Chinese food.

It was quite late when Abu Faisal and I went 'home', to sleep in our guest-rooms in Issam's office. The telephone was ringing like mad. It was Tunis. 'We've been looking for you all evening', the man on the other end of the line said, 'where the hell have you been?' It was Ramsey Khouri, the chief of Arafat's personal bureau. He had received a message from Arafat, who was in Baghdad. The Chairman would see us in Tunis on the following Tuesday.

In a flash, the place was filled with tension. The effects of two bottles of wine, which we had consumed, evaporated. Abu Faisal called Issam, who was at his home nearby, while I took the other phone and called Matti Peled at his home near Jerusalem, where the time was well after midnight. Trying to control my excitement, I told him that he and Arnon must immediately come to Paris, for an important meeting, *the* important meeting. I knew that at least two secret services were listening and recording, and tried to phrase my message as cautiously as possible.

Matti was unmoved. He was busy. He had lectures to give at the university and couldn't come.

'But this is the moment we have been waiting for all these years!' I exclaimed. Matti was not convinced.

In desperation, I said: 'I'll come back tomorrow. Let's meet tomorrow night and talk it over!' When I told this to an unbelieving Abu Faisal, an expert on air travel, he began leafing through booklets of airline timetables, trying to figure out how I could fly to Tel Aviv the next day and return two days later to Paris. A reservation had to be made — Paris-Tel Aviv for one, Tel Aviv-Paris for three, Paris-Tunis for four.

When we called Issam to tell him about this project, he used some expressions quite unsuitable for the ears of an Israeli general.

* * *

The next evening I was sitting with Arnon and Matti in Matti's villa in Motsa Illit near Jerusalem, trying to convince the sceptical gentlemen to leave everything and rush to Paris. I wished for the tongue of Demosthenes so as to infect them with my enthusiasm.

'Are you quite sure that Arafat will be there?' Arnon asked.

'Absolutely!' I lied. Of course no one could ever be sure of Arafat arriving at a certain time in a certain place. Other things might crop up suddenly, security considerations might interfere, a prior meeting might drag on beyond the allotted time, the political situation might change overnight. 'At least, I'm 95 percent sure', I allowed.

Later, after the historic event, Arnon accused me of 'manipulating' them. By then he knew that I had been only, perhaps, 60 per cent certain. Thus are the ways of the peace-maker.

There were some grounds for Matti's scepticism and hesitation. He had already been to Tunis a few weeks earlier, but Arafat had not shown up, and after idling away a few days he had to leave, after seeing only two leading members of Fatah. At the university, his frequent absences had been noticed, providing ammunition for his opponents, who disliked his well-known political views.

In the end, both agreed to fly to Paris on Monday. But Matti made one firm condition: Whatever happens, he must be back in Tel Aviv for his five o'clock lecture at the university on Wednesday. He might as well have asked for the moon.

* * *

The next day I fulfilled a promise to Issam: I went to see Mayor Elias Freij at his home in Bethlehem. He was the only important elected Palestinian mayor in the West Bank still in office.

The mayors had been elected in 1976, by mistake. As Itzhak Rabin, at the time the prime minister, told me gleefully immediately after the event, his enemy, Shimon Peres, the minister of defence, had been convinced that free elections would give a renewed mandate to the old notables, who were Jordanian stooges. The elections had been really free, and the results were revolutionary. In nearly all the important towns of the West Bank there had been a pro-PLO landslide victory. A new group of young pro-PLO nationalists had assumed office, proving, by the way, that the Palestinian people stood solidly behind the PLO. Paradoxically, these were the only free elections anywhere in the world in which Palestinians could really express their preference. Of course, this exercise was never repeated by the Israeli authorities, and most of the mayors were deposed or deported in the following years.

Freij is a controversial figure. The Christian mayor of a mainly Christian town, he was suspect to the more religious-minded Muslim conservatives. He tried to 'walk between the raindrops', as the Hebrew expression goes, not giving the Israeli authorities any pretext to depose him, keeping his good relations with the Jordanian regime and being loyal to the PLO. He also kept good relations with all the elements of the Israeli peace movement, appearing at our public meetings and symposiums. All this needed great courage, which was somehow incongruous with his rather Chaplinesque appearance, emphasized by his small moustache.

He received me on the big verandah of his home, which commanded a wide view of the surrounding countryside. Sadly, he pointed out the Jewish villages and towns springing up everywhere. 'Every day I look and see new buildings going up.'

Freij wished for an accommodation between Arafat and Hussein and bemoaned the prevarications of the Palestinian organization, which prevented this from happening quickly. 'They don't realize what is happening here, that time is running out, that we are losing our homeland while they are talking', he said bitterly, 'they' meaning the extremists within the PLO, and the demagogues and opportunists who pretended to be extremists.

He was in complete agreement with Sartawi, and believed that a peace pressure group should be organized in the West Bank. He told me what was needed for this and asked me to convey his ideas to Issam.

When I hinted to him that I might see Abu Amar soon, he exclaimed: 'Tell him! Tell him that we in the West Bank want decisive action to achieve a political solution that will remove the Israeli occupation! We are being asphyxiated!' And waving his hand at the countryside, he added: 'Tell him what you are seeing! We are losing our homeland! Time is running out!'

It was an emotional moment. Here I was, an Israeli, supposed to carry this cry of despair to the leader of the Palestinian people. It underlined the pathos of Palestinian dispersion. It also underlined a particular aspect of the Palestinian situation which had already given me much food for thought.

Most, if not all, liberation organizations are based on the population of the occupied country. But the PLO had been created by Palestinian refugees, who had been dispersed all over the Middle East by the 1948 War. The main movement, Fatah, had been founded in Kuwait by people from several countries, mainly from Egypt. The development of the PLO in the diaspora had been predominantly influenced by the half of the Palestinian people which was living outside Palestine, by the hopes of the abject refugees in the camps who dreamed of eventual return, by parties and organizations recruited from among the exiled. The Jordanian dictatorship in the West Bank, and later the Israeli occupation regime, had done everything possible to prevent the population in the West Bank from playing an active role in PLO politics. West Bankers had been prevented from attending the PNC, and the slightest expression of sympathy with the PLO could lead to long prison terms, deportation and other punishments.

As the municipal elections had shown, the Palestinians in the West Bank and the Gaza Strip were completely loyal to the PLO and considered it their sole and legitimate political representative. Israeli attempts in the early 1980s to create a quisling leadership and militia had failed miserably. The so-called Village Leagues, which included some unimportant frustrated local notables, criminal elements and other riffraff, had become a sorry joke. Incredibly, the PLO loyalists did not resort to terror to impose their convictions, and only very few outright collaborators and informers were killed. This self-restraint was the result of an historical trauma. During the Palestinian revolt of 1936-39, the Grand Mufti of Jerusalem, Hadj Amin al-Husseini, the nationalist leader, had conducted a wholesale murder campaign against his opponents, crippling the Palestinian leadership for many years. No one wanted to repeat this experience. The controversies between PLO loyalists and the remaining pro-Jordanians, as well as between the adherents of the various factions within the PLO, did not lead to bloodshed.

After the battle of Beirut, admiration for Arafat in the West Bank was nearly unanimous. He was more than a political leader. He had become a national hero. Loyalty to him and to the PLO was unswerving. All efforts by Americans and others to induce the leaders in the West Bank to assume an independent role were sharply rebuffed. But, at the same time, many West Bankers were becoming impatient with the PLO politicians, suspecting that they were not aware of the urgency of the situation.

There was some ground for these misgivings. The PLO was a force in inter-Arab politics. It had been forced to play a role in the domestic politics first of Jordan and then of Lebanon. Much against its will, it had been dragged into the Lebanese civil war. Much of its energies had been absorbed by military and political struggles which had very little direct connection with Palestinian national objectives.

One of the results was that the West Bank population was never organized for the struggle against the Israeli occupation as it could have been, much to the relief of Israeli governments. There was no effective leadership for the organization of civil disobedience along the lines of Mahatma Gandhi, such as a general strike. A hundred thousand workers from the occupied areas were crossing into Israel daily, playing a major role in many Israeli industries. Even the Jewish settlements in the occupied areas, which directly threatened the national existence of the Palestinian people, were built by Palestinian labourers. Jewish construction workers, once the pride of the Zionist movement, had practically disappeared.

It was the dream of Issam Sartawi to reaffirm the role of the West Bank and the Gaza Strip Palestinians in the structure of the PLO, to enable them to play a major role in formulating Palestinian policy. He quite correctly assumed that these Palestinians, having the most intense personal interest in a solution that would remove the Israeli occupation from their back and save their lands, could constitute the backbone of Arafat's peace policy, reducing the influence of the rejectionists, who played a role in the PLO quite incommensurate with their real strength.

Freij was in total agreement with this line of thought. But how could this be implemented, when the slightest move of every West Bank personality was supervised by the Israeli authorities? What could the Israeli peace movement do to change this situation? How bring the situation home to the PLO leadership?

While we were discussing this, Freij's wife was preparing a parcel for me to take to Paris: homemade bread baked on an open oven ('tabunah') and goat cheese from Nablus. This was my standard gift to Issam.

When I was about to take my leave, ambulance sirens began to shriek on the road to Hebron, which passed in front of the house. Ambulances were racing south, in the direction of Dheishe refugee camp, which was in a perpetual state of revolt and siege. Freij rushed to the telephone to find out if anything had happened.

* * *

Matti was adamant. He woldn't go to Tunis.

It was Tuesday, 18 January, 1983 — a date which was to have great significance in our lives.

We had arrived in Paris the day before. Anna Best — selfless, indefatigable, ever-ready Anna, the ministering angel of all our efforts in Paris — picked us up at the airport and saw to our accommodation for the night. At eight thirty in the morning we all met in Issam's office. the plane to Tunis was to leave at eleven o'clock, so we had to leave at about 'nine for Orly.

But Matti's mind was set. He had to be back in Tel Aviv the next day at five o'clock. He would not go to Tunis unless two terms were met: he must be assured that Arafat would be there ready to receive us, and also must be assured of his return flight.

The only way to make it in time to Tel Aviv was to leave Tunis that very same Tuesday and take the flight the next day from Paris to Tel Aviv. But how could we be certain that Arafat would receive us immediately upon our arrival in Tunis, so that Matti could fly back a few hours later? How could we be sure that Araft was in Tunis at all? The minutes passed. Issam tried frantically to contact Arafat's office in Tunis, to ask whether the Chairman had come back from his travels. Nine o'clock was long past, and so was nine-thirty. In vain we tried to move Matti from his decision. Like a true general he can be very, very stubborn.

At ten-twenty the telephone rang. It was Abu Faisal, who had gone to Tunis the day before as our advance party. The Chairman had arrived and was waiting for us.

Reluctantly, Matti rose. Anna whispered to him, 'You can go to the airport, you won't make it anyhow. There's no way to be there on time for the flight.'

Within seconds, the room was filled with incredible activity. Arnon and I had heavy suitcases, Matti, travelling lightly, took only an overnight bag. Somehow all this luggage was heaved into the lift and we all rushed down and into the street like a stampeding herd of buffaloes. Issam and Matti were rushed into a waiting police car; Arnon and I, with Anna, took Issam's own car. Anwar Abu Eicha took the wheel.

Anwar, who was destined to be at Issam's side when he was shot to death, had been the chairman of the Palestinian students in France. He had studied law and become Issam's assistant, after Abu Faisal had gone back to Beirut before the war. He had written a moving book about his youth in Hebron under Israeli occupation. His father was a bus driver, and Anwar had been driving cars since he was a child. But his real driving test was now.

The police car in front, blue light flashing, sirens wailing at full blast, dived into the Paris morning traffic, our car right behind. For miles and miles we went through the traffic like a knife through butter. We weaved back and forth, ran red lights, miraculously escaped hundreds of near accidents, driving at more than 100 kilometres an hour. The dense city traffic, and the no less dense traffic on the autoroute parted before us like the Red Sea before the children of Israel.

I saw the hairs on Arnon's head stand up one by one. As for me, I was exhilarated. I am used to my own driving.

We arrived at Orly at five minutes to eleven. the check-in counter was closed. 'Leave the suitcases here. Anna will take them back home!' Issam commanded. With a police officer in front, we rushed to passport control. The officer flashed his police card, we waved our Israeli passports, and were let through. Running, we navigated the endless corridors.

The aircraft was waiting. The police had radioed an order for it to wait. The bewildered passengers were waiting in the lounge. Then there was a snag. By some mistake our flight had been booked economy class. Issam insisted on first class. A discussion ensued, tickets had to be reissued. Suddenly we had a lot of time, because the flight had to be fitted into the airport departure pattern, and this caused more than an hour's delay.

Issam was anxious, because there had been a rumour that Ibrahim Souss, the official PLO representative in Paris, would be on the flight. Souss was not supposed to know anything about our meeting. A gifted musician and certainly a moderate, Souss, who had taken the job after his predecessor had been murdered by the Abu Nidal gang, tried to remain detached from all contact with us. At the height of the battle of Beirut, when Matti had gone on French television to denounce the bombardment conducted by his own army, Souss had refused to appear with him on the same programme.

On the flight we spoke English, drank champagne. Issam charmed the stewardesses, and we prepared ourselves for the events to follow.

At Tunis airport there were no problems. Abu Faisal was waiting for us along with a high-ranking Tunisian security officer. We left our Israeli passports with Abu Faisal, and a young Palestinian took us to Sidi Bou Said, a small holiday resort on the sea, north of Carthage and east of Tunis. We were installed there in a beautiful hotel, which was quite empty at that time of year.

There Matti's troubles started again. It appeared that we were to meet the Chairman in the evening, much too late for Matti to return to Paris. But now we had Abu Faisal with us, the wizard of air timetables. He discovered that Matti could go early the next day from Tunis straight to Rome, and from there, through Athens to Tel Aviv — just in time for his lecture. It took some phone calls to Anna in Paris to arrange all this.

* * *

In the afternoon, Abu Maazen arrived at the hotel for a preliminary meeting. It was the first time I had met this man, who had hovered over all our contacts since I first met Said Hammami. At the time, Said had confided to me that the two ranking Fatah leaders in charge of the contacts, besides Arafat himself, were Abu Jihad and Abu Maazen. Abu Jihad, the Fatah defence minister, was relatively well-known in Israel. Abu Maazen was quite unknown, and has remained a kind of mystery man who does not visit Western countries. He is mainly concerned with the organization and finances of his movement.

Looking rather like a schoolmaster, soft-spoken and informal, Abu Maazen — whose real name is Mahmoud Abbas — quickly settled down to business. But first we exchanged the usual small talk between Israelis and Palestinians: who is from where. Abu Maazen, it appeared, was a refugee from Safed. My wife, Rachel, who was born in Berlin and came to the country at the age of one, also grew up in Safed. Her father had been a pediatrician on Mount Canaan, which overlooks Safed, and it was conceivable that the young Mahmoud had been treated by him. He did not remember, but he did remember some of the eccentric people who lived at the time on Mount Canaan, who were familiar to me from the tales of my wife. By now, very little of the wild beauty of the mountain remains. It is a densely populated place. But I did not tell him this.

I also did not tell him about a lecture given by Yigal Allon, who commanded the Palmach brigades at the beginning of the 1948 War. Describing the 'liberation' of Safed, Allon had said: 'The Arab population fled. We did everything to encourage them to flee.'

Abu Maazen, who was considered a pro-Western PLO leader and who was very popular with the Saudis, the chief financial backers of the PLO, had been cleverly invited by the Soviets to do his doctorate there. He was, in fact, a doctor of Zionism – this being the subject he had chosen. In particular, he was interested in the Kastner Affair, a famous trial which had taken place in Israel during the 1950s, dealing mainly with the efforts of the Zionist leadership in Hungary during the Holocaust to deal with the Nazis. The main figure, Rudolph Kastner, was a hero to some, a traitor to others. He had been assassinated by Jewish extremists.

The conversation was devoted mainly to a preliminary discussion of the subjects which we wanted to raise with the Chairman. We spoke English, which Abu Maazen understood perfectly, but he preferred to speak in Arabic, lapsing into English from time to time. He took copious notes, obviously in order to go over them with Arafat before our meeting. I wrote down the subjects we wanted to put on the agenda: the general situation after Beirut, our endeavours to create a united peace front in Israel, future relations between the PLO and such a peace front — and our Council, the idea of a conference of Palestinian and Israeli thinkers, the relations between the Israeli peace movement and the population in the occupied territories, the forthcoming Palestinian National Council and the possibility of an Israeli peace delegation attending that meeting. And, of course, the publicizing of this meeting in Tunis.

We asked Abu Maazen about our meeting with King Hassan, which had been arranged by him. Why had the King not yet published it? He told us that he had already asked the king about it, telling him: 'Our friends are impatient.' His Majesty had proposed that we meet again, and that on that occasion all our prior meetings would also be made public. We discussed a possible date, and Abu Maazen took it upon himself to arrange it. Eventually, a few days after our meeting with Arafat, the King himself announced our meetings.

The conversation, of course, returned several times to Lebanon. I told Abu Maazen, 'Sharon did you a great service by taking you out of the Lebanese mess and by putting us into it.'

* * *

It was already dark when our motorcade drove north to the palatial villa which serves as the official embassy of the PLO in Tunis. The ambassador, Abu Marwan — a different Abu Marwan from the PLO ambassador in Rabat who had taken part in our first meeting with the King — received us. His real name is Hakim al-Bal'awi, and he is a writer who has published many short stories highlighting the Palestinian condition. He ushered us into a big salon, which was a little piece of Palestine in exile: a tapestry with the map of Palestine, another tapestry showing a Palestinian girl, a golden bas relief of the world highlighting the country which they call Palestine, and we call Eretz Israel. It crossed my mind that these two names actually form the crux of the conflict which accounted for our presence here.

A little girl came into the room and served us some sweets, the ambassador's wife came in and was presented to us. Matti spoke with the ambassador about Arab literature, and then a familiar face appeared in the door. It was Fathi, Arafat's chief bodyguard, who had taken such great care to keep me safe in besieged Beirut. In Beirut he had at first looked formidable, with his big moustache and army uniform — he had the rank of major in the Fatah forces — but during the day I spent in his company I had come to see him as a friendly person. Now he was wearing civilian clothes, because Fatah personnel were not allowed to wear uniforms in Tunisia. I embraced him warmly.

And then there was Arafat himself. He entered the room quietly, embraced and kissed me on the cheeks, as is his custom. I introduced him to Matti and Arnon, and then we were seated: Arafat in the middle of the sofa, flanked by Matti on his left and me on his right. At my side were Arnon and Abu Maazen, and next to Matti Sartawi, Shakour and Abu Marwan.

The first few moments were awkward. Neither Arafat nor Matti are good at small talk, so I took the initiative. 'Do you feel better now than last time in Beirut?' I asked.

'I felt fine in Beirut', Arafat answered in English.

Coming in, he had worn a fur hat with the insignia of the commander-in-chief of the PLO forces. Upon sitting down he took it off. He was wearing a well-pressed khaki uniform, with the inevitable little pistol in his belt. I was struck again by the difference between his television image and the real person. His beard was well-kept, partly black, partly grey, his quick brown eyes much softer than his pictures. In Beirut he had been tense, rather euphoric, facing death in a battle to the end. Now he was relaxed, smiling. I suspected that this is the perpetual smile of a rather shy person.

To open the serious conversation, I told him about my meeting with Elias Freij and the view from his verandah, about the ambulances going to Dheishe. Freij had asked me, I said, to convey to him a great sense or urgency.

Arafat listened attentively. 'I appreciate the steadfastness of Brother Freij', he said (Palestinians always say brother, where we would say comrade). 'What practical steps does he propose?'

I explained that in Freij's opinion, the PLO should recognize Israel even unilaterally, in order to achieve at least a dialogue with the Americans.

'But a day after we do that, Begin will announce that he will not recognize the PLO', Arafat said. 'Such a step would not bring about any change in Israeli policy'.

'But it will prompt the Americans to move', I said.

Matti put in: 'You might state that you will recognize Israel if Israel recognizes you. Or, even better, you could state that you would recognize Israel if the Israeli government adopts the programme of our council.'

'That's the French-Egyptian proposal', Arafat quickly pointed out. The French and Egyptians had indeed submitted such a proposal for mutual conditional recognition to the UN Security Council, but had withdrawn it when it became clear that the Americans would veto it.

I added: 'Freij also said that several leaders in the West Bank are still afraid to cooperate with the Israeli peace forces, as long as there is no clear PLO statement approving this.'

'We have said this already', Arafat interjected, 'but we shall do it again. I shall call upon them by name and ask them to do so', he added, looking at Abu Maazen, who was taking notes. So were Sartawi and Shakour. Arafat himself took a small notebrook from his breastpocket from time to time, jotting down notes or looking up points. I was interested to notice that he had the rare quality of listening while he wrote. This was clear when he interrupted a speaker with questions, while still busy writing.

At his request, Issam gave a concise resumé of the points that had been discussed during our conversation with Abu Maazen in the afternoon. This was Issam's great day, the great personal victory he had been looking for for years, after Kaddumi had denied his contacts and after he had been contemptuously dismissed by Israeli journalists and politicians as an outsider, a marginal figure, an adventurer acting alone, representing nobody and nothing. Among others, Yossi Sarid had said so publicly during the battle of Beirut, when Sartawi had openly invited him and others to meet him in Paris.

When Arafat lauded him and his work, Issam did not refrain from remarking: 'I paid for all of you. I have been ostracized because of this work.' Arafat answered with an eloquent gesture of his hand, as if to say 'it was worth it'.

'The most important point is the credibility of the Israeli peace forces', Issam stated. 'If our friends can go home and announce that we have met here, this is very important.'

Without a moment's hesitation, Arafat replied: 'OK, there's no problem. You publish whatever you want, and we shall confirm it.'

We were amazed, because we had expected that this would be the main sticking point. I suggested that we formulate a joint communiqué after the meeting. Arafat readily agreed.

Whenever I met Arafat, I was struck by this ability of his to make quick decisions, unlike some of his colleagues. It brought to mind the figure of David Ben-Gurion. Ben-Gurion and Arafat are, of course, quite different. But there are some points of similarity: the same height, the same ability to make quick decisions, the same self-confidence, the same air of authority without formality. In his time, Ben-Gurion in a way personified the Zionist movement and the Jewish condition. Much in the same way, Arafat is not just the leader of a movement but, in some strange way, the personification of the Palestinian tragedy, pathos, tenacity and endurance.

'We also need photographs', I insisted, and again Arafat acquiesced without hesitation.

His official photographer was called in. we arranged ourselves in one line on the sofa and chairs, with Abu Maazen moving next to Issam, and Abu Marwan staying out of the picture. We had already agreed not to identify the country of our meeting, so as not to embarrass the Tunisian government.

Arafat put on his fur hat again, and several photos were taken. Then Arafat was suddenly struck with the thought that it might be bad for us if the picture showed him wearing military headgear. So he got up, put on a *keffiyeh*, carefully draped around his head, and then the same pictures were taken again. (In the end, I took both sets of pictures. They were both published in Israel, causing an Israeli magazine to put two pictures together to ask its readers: 'Find the difference between these two pictures'.)

Looking at the pictures today, I am fascinated by the different kinds of smiles displayed, from the well-known broad smile of Arafat, to the victorious smile of Issam, the restrained smile of Matti, and Abu Maazen's ghost of a smile

The conversation ranged over many subjects. The political situation in Israel was, of course, of great interest to our hosts, who never before had had such an opportunity to have insiders' views of Israel. Why was the Labour Party behaving the way it was, what were the differences between Begin and Peres, what was Peace Now up to? When I explained that the Labour Party was competing with the Likud for the votes of the middle-of-the-roaders, Arafat interrupted me and finished my sentence 'and is therefore veering to the right'. As a political practitioner of the first rank, he easily understood political realities in our state. We, of course, were interested in the array of forces inside the PLO. Arafat and Abu Maazen were confident of their ability to command an impressive majority in the forthcoming, sixteenth, session of the Palestinian National Council due to convene within three weeks' time. Fatah had a commanding lead, the Democratic Front of Hawatmeh was joining their position, it was now possible to adopt far-reaching resolutions for a peace solution.

In a short lecture, Matti expounded the views of the Israeli Council. We had a chance to influence public opinion in Israel, things in Israel were in a state of flux. But in order to gain prestige and power, we had to prove to the Israeli public that there was a definite change in PLO policy, that the Palestinian leadership was indeed ready to make peace, that the creation of a Palestinian state would put an end to the conflict, and not just be a stage in an attempt to destroy the State of Israel, as our opponents at home contended. We needed unequivocal PLO positions, which could not be twisted by the enemies of peace. We hoped that the Palestinian National Council would adopt such resolutions. this would give new courage to the Israeli peace forces, which had already done important things during the Lebanon War, but which had not yet reached the clearcut positions our council propounded. It would also enable us to take the lead in forming a united peace camp, which could become a powerful force in Israeli politics.

Arnon interjected that Begin feared nothing more than a PLO peace initiative which would have an impact on the Israeli public. 'That is Begin's greatest nightmare!' Matti added.

I voiced my view that diplomatic texts and political statements would be much less effective than large dramatic gestures, which ordinary people could see and hear on television, which would exert both an unconscious and conscious influence on them. After a war going on already for three generations, nothing less would change deep-seated prejudices and fears. 'Our meeting today is such a dramatic event. We must continue along this road, moving towards bigger and bigger things. 'Of course', I apologized, I'm speaking as a professional mass communication person.'

'So am I', said Arafat.

* * *

In the middle of the conversation dinner was announced. We moved to the other side of the big room, where the dining table had been arranged, laden with exquisite oriental food prepared by Abu Marwan's wife.

Before we sat down, Arafat took command. With diplomatic finesse he seated each of us, preventing anyone from feeling slighted. He put me in the middle of the broad side of the table, opposite himself, while seating Matti at the head of the table on one side, and Arnon at the other. Abu Maazen was on Arafat's right, Issam on his left. I was sitting between Abu Marwan and Shakour, with whom I could converse in Hebrew. Over the meal I raised the point uppermost in my mind: the one big dramatic event which would create a historical breakthrough. It was Sartawi's old idea of having us invited to the PNC. We had been told already by Abu Maazen that this was not feasible. But in view of the optimistic forecast of what would happen at the PNC session, I felt justified in bringing up the matter again. Enlarging on the idea that dramatic events could bring profound changes, I mentioned the Sadat visit to Jerusalem.

'Whatever the opinion about the political content of the Sadat initiative', I dared to say, knowing the PLO's vehement objection to it, 'everyone has to concede that Sadat's technique was masterful. He changed Israeli public opinion about giving back the Sinai practically overnight. I once told Sadat what happened during the moments when Israeli television was broadcasting live his arrival at Ben-Gurion airport. I live on one of the main streets of Tel Aviv. During the broadcast I looked out of the window and there was not a single thing moving on the street except one lonely cat, which was probably looking for a television set.'

I hastened to add:'Of course, you cannot come to the Knesset, but we can come to your Knesset. Imagine the impact it would have in Israel, and indeed throughout the world, if a delegation of patriotic Israelis attends the Palestinian National Council. It would completely shatter the demonic image of the PLO in Israel, it would put the Palestinian issue on the agenda as the central theme in our elections. We shall have the initiative, instead of being marginal elements.'

I believe that this made an impression on Arafat. Like all great politicians, he is also a showman. He realized the dramatic potential of such a move. 'It's difficult', he said. 'Some elements will make trouble. You know which ones.'

'Are you afraid of violence?' I asked, 'is it a question of security?'

'No, no violence. It wouldn't go as far as that. But there would be heckling, an uproar.'

'So what?' I asked, 'we are used to that in the Knesset. When President Carter addressed the Knesset, Geula Cohen heckled him. We can take it. It will only show that you have a democratic parliament. It will be a world-wide sensation, headlines in all the newspapers, drama on television.'

I saw him wavering.

'We shall think about it again', he promised. Somebody raised the question whether Israelis could go to Algiers, where the PNC was to be held, without being arrested upon their return to Israel for entering enemy territory. 'Algeria is not an enemy country under Israeli law,' Arafat remarked. 'Like Tunisia and Morocco, it was not an independent country in 1948, and therefore did not declare war on Israel.' This rather suprised me, but when I checked it later with my legal advisers, I found it to be true. Even our visit to Tunis was perfectly legal from this point of view.

In order to emphasize the possibilities of change in Israel, I told him about an encounter I had had with Begin during one of the Knesset sessions, two years earlier. After I had made a speech about the necessity of solving the Palestinian question by negotiations with the PLO, the prime minister got up to reply and said, more in sorrow than in anger: 'Knesset Member Avnery, you know that 110 (out of 120) members in this house are against every word you said in your speech!'

'I know that', I responded, 'and I would be suitably impressed if I didn't remember that one week before Sadat's visit to this house 110 members of the Knesset were against giving back the Sinai to Egypt!'

* * *

After the leisurely meal, during which we exchanged views about many people and organizations on both sides, we got up. Issam, Imad and I sat down together in a corner of the room to draft the communiqué. On his way to the bathroom, Arafat tossed two Arabic words to Issam meaning: 'Stick to generalities.' He obviously thought that the very fact of our meeting and publishing a joint communiqué was dramatic enough, and that this moment, on the eve of the Palestinian National Council session, was not the right time to come forward with explicit new formulas.

In the end we produced the following statement in English, which we simultaneously translated into Arabic and Hebrew:

> Chairman Arafat met with a delegation of the Israeli Council for Israeli-Palestinian Peace, consisting of General (Res.) Mattitiyahu Peled, Uri Avnery and Dr Yaacov Arnon. On the Palestinian side Dr Abu Maazen, Dr Issam Sartawi and Imad Shakour took part in the meeting. In the meeting, the situation in the Middle East was reviewed in depth, as well as the ways of joint action for permanent and just peace in the Middle East. Chairman Arafat expressed his appreciation for the role of the Israeli peace forces and their struggle for a just and lasting peace.

This deceptively simple formula was arrived at after several drafts and alterations, in which Arafat himself took part. Surprisingly, it appeared that he was very sensitive to the nuances of the English language. 'He doesn't write English, but he's great at editing other people's texts', Imad Shakour said jokingly. It was Arafat who inserted the words 'joint action' in the text.

After my meeting with Arafat in Beirut, Mahmoud Labadi had published a communiqué about our meeting before I even had time to reach home. I was thus unable to make any preparation for the proper reception of the report in Israel. In order to avoid this eventuality, we agreed that the joint communiqué would be published simultaneously in Tunis and Tel Aviv on Thursday evening, at eight o'clock Israeli time, allowing us to return and prepare the Israeli mass media, print and distribute pictures, et cetera.

While washing his hands in the bathroom after the meal, Arafat confided to Matti Peled a detail which shed light on the circumstances of our meeting. A few days earlier the leaders of the rejection front had met in Tripoli, Libya, and adopted a hard-line programme which they wanted to impose on the National Council. After concluding their meeting and publishing a communiqué, they contacted Arafat in Baghdad and requested him to repair immediately to Damascus, in order to receive their proposed draft resolution. Arafat hotly replied that he was unfortunately unable to be with them, as on the proposed date he was meeting with the leaders of the Israeli peace forces. This explained why the initiative for this meeting had come from Arafat while he was in Baghdad, and why all the arrangements had to be made by telephone between Baghdad-Tunis-Paris-Jerusalem.

* * *

It was nearly midnight when our motorcade returned to the hotel. There was no question of going to sleep. We were much too excited. Issam was jubilant and so, of course, were we. We all congregated in his room, where he opened a bottle of whisky which he had bought on the plane.

For Issam this was a day of victory, a total rehabilitation after all the attacks he had endured throughout the years not only from the rejectionists and the Syrians, but also from Farouk Kaddumi and others. All his untiring efforts were retroactively confirmed by the stamp of approval from Yassir Arafat.

For us it was an unqualified achievement. Not only had we met with the supreme leader of the PLO, but this meeting had been dignified by a joint communiqué and raised to the status of a meeting between delegations. While deliberately vague, the communiqué mentioned joint action with an Israeli body which was avowedly Zionist, and which had an explicit programme of mutual recognition, peace and coexistence.

Perhaps the most important achievement was the picture. Millions of Israelis and Palestinians were about to see a photo of Yassir Arafat sitting between a general in the Israeli Army, a former member of the Knesset and a former director-general of an Israeli ministry. The visual impact of this was bound to change, consciously or unconsciously, the perception of people on both sides.

For Matti there was an additional consolation: his flight to Rome early the next morning was assured, so he would be able to make his lecture on time.

And indeed, when Arnon and I got up the next morning, Matti had already gone. Issam told us that he had safely delivered him to the airport. There was a story to go with that, which Matti told us later. When Issam had presented him to the Tunisian security chief at the airport, they found that there were no empty seats left on the plane. Issam impressed upon the officer the utmost importance of getting Matti on the plane nevertheless. The officer took up the phone and called one of his subordinates. 'Wasn't there somebody on the plane whose papers were not in order?' he asked. The man on the other end of the line said yes, there was such a person, but he had been allowed to board the plane. 'Take him off and check his papers again', the officer commanded and, smiling radiantly, turned to Matti and said: 'It's OK, you've got your seat'. Years later, Matti's conscience was still troubled by this incident.

For Arnon and me, it was a peaceful morning. We bought presents for our wives in the hotel shop and had a few leisurely drinks with Imad Shakour and Abu Eisha. Imad was worried about his two brothers, who were still living in Sakhnin, in Israel, and who had once again been arrested for displaying a Palestinian flag. I was happy to tell him that they had been acquitted and released — until the next time.

Imad was also angry with *Maariv* for publishing a story about him which was incorrect. I proposed that he write a letter to the editor in Hebrew. I assured him that even *Maariv*, a very right-wing anti-Arab evening paper, would not be able to resist the temptation to publish a letter addressed to it in Hebrew by a close assistant to Arafat. But in this I was wrong. Imad wrote a letter, in good Hebrew, correcting the facts, and gave it to me. Upon my return I sent it to *Maariv*, explaining the circumstances. Eventually they sent the letter back to me with regrets — they were unfortunately unable to publish it.

Before noon Issam took us to the airport. We were ushered to the VIP lounge, where the Tunisian officials returned our Israeli passports to us. Arafat's photographer gave us the pictures. To our pleasant surprise, Abu Maazen and Abu Marwan also appeared to see us off. They gave each of us a beautiful big package of delicious Tunisian sweets, which we took home to our wives. Matti was a loser.

Not only in this sense. When we arrived in Paris and sat down with Issam in his office, to deliberate upon steps to exploit our achievement, the telehone rang. It was Matti from the Rome airport. A strike had broken out in Athens, causing the cancellation of all flights there. There was no way he could get to Israel from Rome, so he was coming back to Paris.

We saw him again late in the evening. We had just finished a very good French meal in the company of our Parisian friends from the Curiel group, who had helped us so much, when Matti appeared, tired and furious. He could not even eat good French food, because he had already eaten on the plane.

So he returned the next day together with us.

# 43

*We are in The Hague. Issam had come late for the conference which we were both attending. Only after the meeting could I give him the parcel I had brought for him: home-baked tabunah bread and Nablus cheese. Rachel had packed the cheese as well as she could, but somehow everything in my suitcase was permeated with its pungent odour.*

*The minute I give him the parcel in my hotel room, he rips it open and begins to eat, gulping big chunks of bread and cheese.*

*'I don't know why it is so wonderful', he says. 'To me, this is the taste of home.'*

# 44

Everything proceeded according to plan. The pictures of our meeting with Arafat appeared on the front pages of all the papers and television screens in Israel. We gave interviews, my detailed report appeared in *Haolam Hazeh* and was widely read. Foreign Minister Itzhak Shamir appeared on television to denounce the meeting as 'the very depths of human degradation', and everyone who wanted to be mentioned in the media demanded our prosecution for all imaginable crimes.

For three weeks we were busy talking and writing about the dramatic change in the PLO, when lightning struck. The news agencies reported that Issam Sartawi had made a row during the meeting of the Palestinian National Council in Algiers. After confronting Arafat on the floor, he had stormed out, resigned, made a violent attack on the leadership in a press conference and flown back to Paris.

* * *

The 16th session of the Palestinian National Council took place only three weeks after our meeting with Arafat. They were fateful weeks for the Palestinian movement. Only during the following weeks and months could I piece the story together.

First, the revolutionary council of Fatah, the highest body of that organization, held a secret meeting. There, Arafat and Issam were violently attacked by some members for meeting with Zionists like us. These meetings, it was held, directly contravened existing PNC resolutions, which allowed for contacts only with Israelis who opposed Zionism in theory and practice. Arafat found himself in the minority. The majority in the governing body of his own organization objected to any further meetings, and expressly forbade them unless approved by the organization in advance.

This meeting foreshadowed the events to follow later that year, when a group of Fatah functionaries and officers 'revolted' against Arafat — a Syrian-inspired move.

The situation was even worse in the Palestinian National Council. It was clear that any move to adopt far-reaching resolutions as envisaged by Arafat, would cause a split in the organization. This Arafat wanted to avoid at all costs.

When the session was convened, speakers for the rejectionists stood up one after another to make long denunciations of Israel, Zionism, the United States, imperialism, rejecting any idea of peace and dialogue. Some of these speakers represented tiny splinter organizations of no importance whatsoever, while the majority kept quiet. Journalists from abroad, unversed in the intricacies of Palestinian politics, received the impression that the PLO rejected peace with Israel altogether.

Sartawi was furious. He demanded to be heard, to voice the views of what he believed to be the vast majority of the Palestinian people and of the PLO, and especially the views of the population in the occupied territories, whose representatives had again been prevented by the Israeli authorities from attending the PNC session. But Arafat was afraid that such a speech by Sartawi would so inflame the rejectionists that it would lead to the break-up of the organization. His attitude was: 'Let them talk to their heart's content, afterwards we shall do what we have to do.' But Sartawi believed this to be a cardinal mistake. Media reports of a rejectionist PLO would destroy our chances in Israel at the next elections, as well as any chance of getting US public opinion to accept the PLO. Moreover, if the policy of peace and dialogue was not explained to the Palestinian masses from the rostrum of their parliament, it would not receive the poular support needed to move forward along this course. In all this he was right.

Arafat, on the other side, felt responsible for the preservation of the PLO as a unified body. I could understand this. I remembered that for Zionists, before the State of Israel was created, the existence of our 'national institutions' was of paramount importance. The efforts of Zeev Jabotinsky to create a competing 'New Zionist Organization' had come to naught, and even the Irgun had been ostracized for contravening the 'national discipline'. For a people without a state, and especially for a dispersed people, the very existence of a recognized national leadership is an invaluable asset.

Possibly Arafat was aware that a split with the Palestinian elements supported by Syria was inevitable, but tried to postpone it. At the time, his peace line had achieved nothing. Israeli and American attitudes towards the PLO remained totally hostile. There was no sign whatsoever that a different PLO, adopting an unequivocal peace policy, would achieve anything at all. In such a situation it was impossible to convince the Palestinian masses that the radical change needed would be anything but surrender.

As a consummate tactician, Arafat wanted to put the onus of creating the rupture — if it was inevitable — on his opponents, thus causing the vast majority of the Palestinians to rally around him. In this he was also right.

At the session, the Fatah leadership arrived at a typical compromise. They decided that only one person, Abu Iyad, would speak for Fatah. No one else would be allowed to speak. Issam thus was effectively silenced.

One of the bizarre peculiarities of the session was that an Israeli was present throughout. Amnon Kapeliouk, an Israeli sabra of Russian descent, speaks perfect Arabic, carries a French passport and is accredited to *Le Monde*; this enabled him to come to Algiers, where he took a seat in the press gallery. He was well-known to many Palestinians, and they pointed him out to others. Between meetings they crowded around him, speaking mostly in Hebrew to show off their proficiency in the language of the enemy.

He reported daily to *Yedioth Aharanot*, an extremely right-wing evening paper in Israel, which published his stories *in extenso* on the front page for the sake of the journalistic scoop. When Kapeliouk sent his first report from Algiers to Paris in Hebrew, using Latin letters, the Algerian security authorities were certain it was a code used by a dangerous spy. They called in the PLO security people, who read the text and burst out laughing. 'It's in Hebrew', they explained to their flabbergasted Algerian colleagues, 'please send it.'

During one of the intermissions, Kapeliouk was tired and asked his Palestinian friends if there was a place where he could rest. They took him to a nearby rest house and rang the doorbell. The man who appeared in the door, wearing pyjamas, was Abu Iyad. 'This is too much', he joked upon hearing the request. 'First you take my home, then you take my country, and now you want my bed, too!'

Abu Iyad was known as a hardline Fatah leader, but this reputation was quite undeserved. Once when he met some foreigners in the presence of Sartawi, he exclaimed: 'You think Sartawi is moderate? I remember that I used to argue with him for years, when he was an extremist and I tried to explain to him that we need a political solution.' His moving book *My Home, My Land*, with a foreword by Eric Rouleau, made it clear that he was for the two-state solution.

Giving his speech on behalf of Fatah, Abu Iyad did indeed propound the peace line, but in diplomatic and equivocal terms. He highlighted the contacts with Israelis, and this was duly noticed by the press. As very few journalists understood Arabic and had to rely on translations, they did not notice that Abu Iyad defined us as anti-Zionists, and therefore justified the contacts with us as being in accord with previous PNC resolutions. Fortunately, this was not reported. When Issam realized that he would not be allowed to speak and make his report on the contacts with us, he exploded. A shouting match between Arafat and him took place on the floor. Peremptorily, he dashed off a letter of resignation from the PNC and sent his aide to deliver it to the chairman of the meeting. Arafat noticed this and sent his own aide to intercept the messenger. 'Abu Amar wants to see the letter for a moment', Arafat's aide said and grabbed the letter, which, thus, was never officially submitted.

But Sartawi had already stomped out. He called a press conference, condemning the leadership and making the point which he had wished to make in his speech on the floor: the need to recognize Israel and to change the Palestinian Charter. He also exposed Abu Nidal, and the Arab states supporting him, for his anti-Semitic outrages and the murder of loyal Palestinians working for peace.

Sartawi's dramatic departure created a world sensation and underlined the negative character of this session. In fact, it ended with a draw. Arafat was unanimously re-elected, thus enhancing his personal position, but he was unable to get the PNC to elect a new executive committee more in line with his ideas. The old committee was re-elected. The Council was even unable to elect a fifteenth member, to replace one who had resigned, leaving the committee with only fourteen members, who were evenly divided between supporters of the Arafat line and others. The same happened to the other resolutions. They were vague and did not change the general line, at best allowing Arafat to operate in a grey zone of equivocal resolutions.

Most importantly for us, the old resolution about contacts with only anti-Zionist Israelis remained unchanged.

For us it was a total disaster.

* * *

A few days later after the PNC session, Issam and I were to appear together in a public meeting in London. This event had been planned in advance by a group of Jews and Israelis living in London, who were devoted to the cause of Israeli-Palestinian peace.

When I arrived in London, the young lady who received me on behalf of the organizers told me that Issam had called from Paris and wanted me to call him immediately. I telephoned from the airport and was asked by Issam, in a tense voice, to take the first plane to Paris. He wanted us to consult. Matti also happened to be in Paris. So I collected my suitcase and boarded the plane to Paris. I took a taxi at Charles de Gaulle airport and went straight to Issam's office, where I found him already in session with Matti.

The situation, I learned, was much more serious than I thought. In deepest secrecy, he told us about the meeting of the Fatah revolutionary council, whose decisions were much more important than the public resolutions of the PNC. Every contact with us, even our sitting together at that moment, was a direct contravention of these decisions. Issam no longer had any mandate at all to meet us.

What to do? What about the London meeting? What about the future of our effort?

Even in this situation, Issam was unchanged. When the time came he decided that we had to have a proper dinner. He wanted us to try something new, an Argentinian restaurant which he had discovered. So the three of us took his car from the underground garage and went out together — openly and illegally — to eat thick Argentinian steaks. Over the meal, Sartawi told us more about what had actually happened in Algiers, and the more he told us, the graver the situation looked.

We decided that Matti and I should write a personal letter to Arafat. We had no time to have it typed out, so we wrote it by hand on pages from my notebook, which we both signed. Issam undertook to have it delivered.

We hesitated about what exactly to say. As usual, Matti was more extreme, while I proposed to say the grave things we had to say in as moderate a tone as possible under the circumstances. Matti wanted to 'condemn' the PNC resolutions: I was content with expressing our 'regrets'. Matti wanted to say that the PNC resolutions were incompatible with what was achieved at our meeting in Tunis. I proposed to phrase it as a question: How to reconcile the two? Upon Issam's urging, Matti relented a bit.

The letter asked the Chairman how, in light of the PNC resolutions, our effort could continue. We reminded him that we had decided upon a monthly meeting of representatives of the PLO and our council, on the convention of a broad-based Israeli-Palestinian conference, and on a public call by him to the West Bank leaders to cooperate with us.

But the most urgent question was what to do about the London meeting. Issam could not possibly appear with me there without publicly flouting the explicit decision of his own organization and provoking all his enemies to the utmost. On the other hand, failing to appear would discourage and insult a valuable group of well-meaning people. In the end, Issam decided to fly with me to London, and there to explain to our would-be hosts why he could not possibly appear on the platform.

I slept at his office, and in the morning he collected me. He was accompanied by an officer of the French police, who took us to the airport in his car and whisked us through the formalities. It was clear that he belonged to some political branch of the French police: remarks he let drop on the way revealed a sound knowledge of our situation.

In London we were received by June Ward, Issam's newly-found assistant there, a charming young lady who took us to her Hampstead home. Soon we were joined there by our hosts, some of them well-known British Jewish personalities, and an agonizing discussion ensued.

All preparations for the meeting that night had already been made. The event was scheduled to take place in the ornate hall of the Greater London Council, and ample security arrangements had been made by the police. It was the starting point for a public campaign of our hosts.

Issam tried to explain, without giving the details, that his participation was impossible. It was obvious that our hosts felt slighted by what they thought were inadequate reasons. Issam proposed that he plead sickness, and that I speak for him, too. I said that his participation was much more important, and that therefore it was I who should plead sickness. Our hosts pleaded with us both to appear.

At one crucial point Sartawi suddenly sat up and made his decision. He had been leaning back, slumped on the sofa, looking tired and indecisive. Now he sat up, with a resolute expression, and said: 'OK, I'll come!'

I have often thought back to this moment, which, perhaps, decided his fate. Why did he do it? Had I pressed him too hard, making him act against his better judgment? Had the presence of a beautiful young woman, who obviously admired him, something to do with it?

There was a logical reason for his decision. As I knew already, Sartawi had decided to create a Palestinian peace party, and he attached great importance to the creation of a network of independent peace groups, like this one in London, which would provide a worldwide support system for our movements.

But remembering the expression on his face at that moment, I feel certain that the deciding factor was personal. It was the pride of Issam Sartawi the fighter which tipped the scales. It was not his nature to knuckle under to threats, to take the path of caution, to shirk a challenge. Basically he was a fighting man, and he was ready for battle.

At that moment I was perhaps closer to him than at any other time.

* * *

When the time came, it looked like a battle.

We drove to the Greater London Council palace in a convoy. The place was surrounded by police. We were ushered in through a side entrance, where several policemen in mufti took charge of us and conducted us through long corridors to a little room behind the stage. An Israeli journalist was waiting for us there, wishing, not incongruously, to interview Issam about the Abu Nidal gang. He was writing a book about the subject. After the Argov shooting, a year before, interest in England in this group was running high.

Issam was tense as a spring, showing all the signs of a soldier going into battle, and even I felt some tension. The chairman, Steven Rose, a highly-respected academic, looked at his watch and said, 'It's time'. We trooped through the thick curtains on to the stage.

What we saw was a round hall, very elegant, filled to the brim. One could feel the excitement in the air. We knew from the first moment that this was not going to be an ordinary meeting.

While the chairman made his opening remarks, we had time to look around, trying to analyse the audience. Some of the people were obviously British, concerned intellectuals and just well-meaning ordinary people. But there were groups of Jewish militants, as well as pockets of Palestinians.

Issam and I sat next to each other and compared notes. Looking at the Arabs, Sartawi said: 'We must get them photographed. They are Abu Nidal people.' The young Jewish militants were members of Beitar, an extreme right-wing Zionist organization with a name for violence.

I was the first of us to speak, and was heckled throughout by the Jewish fanatics. I enjoy heckling, being used to it from Knesset debates, but when things got too rough, the uniformed British police went into action and forcibly evicted some of the hecklers. When Issam stood up to speak, the spectacle was repeated, but this time it was the Palestinian militants who got into a shouting match with him.

Things got even hotter after the first round, when the audience was allowed to question us. Most of the questions were aggressive and provocative, the Jews grilling me and the Palestinians grilling Issam. Never in my life had I seen so graphic a demonstration of a statement I had repeatedly made in my articles; that the fanatics of both sides collaborate with each other and really belong to one party — the party devoted to the endless prolongation of the war.

Fortunately, I recorded the meeting on my small tape recorder. Following is a transcription of the beginning of Issam's concluding remarks:

> I would like to tell you, ladies and genetlemen, that for the last 72 hours I was debating with myself whether I should attend this meeting or send an apology. Finally I decided to come in the face of heavy schedules. After listening to what I listened to, I'm very glad I came. I needed this experience, I needed to see what I thought, and I would like to depart from my unwritten text to say what I wasn't going to say and to serve notice. And I hope the world will take me very seriously. If anybody thinks that sissies make peace, they are mistaken. Peacemakers are very tough and so help us God if challenged we are going to demonstrate how tough we are. We cannot be shouted down.

Nor can we be scared into abandoning our chosen path, because this path for which we bled precious blood is the moral path, the patriotic path. I feel guilty, ladies and gentlemen, I feel guilty because I bear a responsibility for the tragedy of Lebanon. This man [pointing to me] offered his life to save Lebanon, he and General Peled. He offered to come to us on a pilgrimage to Beirut. He offered to come at the head of an Israeli peace delegation, and furthermore, offered to come to our national council in Damascus. The delegation which wanted to come wanted to split into two groups, one group traversing the borders through the Golan and the other through the south of Lebanon. And somebody mentioned my resignation — yes, I went to Damascus to fight, to fight for Peled and Avnery to be heard, to be invited. We couldn't invite them. Lebanon was raped and for those Palestinians who are acting tough and mighty in the halls of London, I tell them that their honour was violated in the refugee camps of Lebanon — not because of me, because of you! You cowards! No, shut up! You cowards, you despicable cowards! Now, those who are acting as tough heroes, those, who through their lack of vision, through their fanaticism, through their inability to look into the realities of Palestinian interests, to the fate of their people who are being massacred in the absence of anybody being able to do something... I think I needed this experience, I needed to be strengthened in my determination to fight for peace because I saw the two sides meeting together, I saw so-called Arab Hitlers joining hand to hand the extreme right-wing of Zionism. Congratulations for both sides, *mabruk aleikum* [in Arabic: blessings on you], congratulations for both of you! Congratulations, yes! [Prolonged shouting in Arabic] *Na'am* [yes,] *Na'am.* Shut up! Shut up! Shut up! You have no rights! *Na'am!* Now I want to tell you this. [Shouting from the audience in English and Arabic: 'Traitor, your end will be like Sadat, it's because of you and Avnery that Beirut was invaded'.]

The chairman tried to calm down the shouting: 'Can we ... can we ... can we allow ... can we allow ... Dr Sartawi ... to ...'

Sartawi: 'No, no, no, I can shut them up, but I want to listen to them, I want to see who they are. Now, all right, all right, you've said enough. Now I want to say that I am glad I came because I really needed this experience to strengthen my determination to continue fighting for peace. Because this is the only way I will serve my people. Thank you.'

He sat down, amid thunderous applause from the great majority of the audience, which demonstrated by its prolonged ovation its rejection of the extremists of both camps. But while the chairman was making his concluding remarks, Issam wrote me on a slip of paper: 'How can we get these people photographed? They are the Abu Nidal murderers! They must be identified!' But we had no photographer at our disposal.

Our police bodyguards again spirited us away through the long corridors of the County Hall building, and we rushed to our car.

We met half an hour later and had a quiet dinner at an Indian restaurant not far from Marble Arch. June Ward was there, as well as Edward Mortimer from *The Times*, the man who had helped me set up the first meeting with Said Hammami, more than eight years before. After the excitement, Issam was exuberant and so was I. The adrenalin in our blood needed time to abate.

The exuberance was misplaced. Perhaps at that very moment, while we were eating curry and drinking good red wine, talking about his plans to create a Palestinian peace party, somebody was deciding upon his death.

A few days later, Issam sent me a cutting from an Arabic paper appearing in London. It was a statement by the Abu Nidal organization announcing that it was condemning Issam Sartawi, Yassir Arafat and me to death. Issam was charged with being a CIA agent, who had sold Palestinian secrets (about Abu Nidal) to a British paper. Arafat was condemned as a traitor and a CIA agent. I was condemned as the Mossad operative charged with infiltrating and subverting the PLO.

The date of the London meeting was 27 February 1983. Issam Sartawi had 42 more days to live.

* * *

During these weeks we talked often. I felt closer to him than ever, because now he confided to me his innermost thoughts. He was hatching great plans, ceaselessly turning them over in his head, using me as a sounding board, asking for reactions and advice. There were very few people in whom he could confide such dangerous ideas.

He was planning a revolutionary step: no less than the creation of a new force in Palestinian politics — a Palestinian peace party.

I had seen these ideas begin to evolve during the siege of Beirut. When all of us believed that Ariel Sharon was preparing the final assault on the city and the annihilation of Yassir Arafat and his associates there, Sartawi was thinking aloud in my presence about the next step, in case that happened. While doing everything possible to help Arafat and save the PLO in the beleaguered city, he was thinking about creating a new PLO that would compete with the Syrian-dominated PLO being readied in Damascus. Like de Gaulle after the fall of France, he considered himself the right man to issue the dramatic call for a new patriotic realignment, a PLO conducting an independent Palestinian policy leading towards the setting-up of a Palestinian state.

This eventually did not arise. The PLO forces, with Arafat at their head, had been safely and proudly evacuated from Beirut, the PLO was functioning. But something was missing.

The Algiers experience had left its mark on Sartawi. He was bitter. He felt that he had been left exposed to the enemies of peace. The activities he had conducted on behalf of the Fatah leadership had been again left outside the scope of Palestinian legitimacy.

During the first days after Algiers he thought of abandoning his efforts altogether. But Issam was not the man to relinquish a task because its enemies had won a tactical victory. I saw him rally, determined to fight back. With his analytical mind, he tried to pinpoint the causes of the defeat and to find a way to change the situation.

In Paris, on the way to London, in London and later in Holland, we talked about the problem constantly. The trouble was, he believed, that inside the PLO there existed a strong minority, led and financed by Syria and Libya, that wanted to obstruct any independent Palestinian move towards peace. There was no organized force to counteract these pressures. There was no pressure group for peace, no organized party that could spread the gospel of a peaceful solution, explain it to the masses of the Palestinian diaspora. This was a weakness perceived by many Palestinian intellectuals, such as the noted scholar Edward Said, who once told me that Arafat was unable to carry out his policies because neither he nor Sartawi had ever really tried to explain them to the Palestinian masses.

How could such a pressure group be set up? On whom should it be based? What kind of body should it be? What should its relationship be with the PLO, Fatah and Arafat?

These were the questions we talked about for many, many hours, sitting together in airplanes, sipping drinks in hotel rooms, walking the streets.

My own fondest dream was — and has been since I wrote my first booklet about the conflict in 1946 — a joint party of Israelis and Palestinians, a party joining the patriots of both sides and integrating the patriotism of both sides into a common policy for peace and the reorganization of the Semitic world. I voiced this idea again, but Issam thought, probably quite rightly, that this was premature. the Palestinian peace forces had to be organized first. But how?

His ideas oscillated between two different approaches. One was to draft a manifesto, clearly setting out the objective of a two-state solution, the need to redraft the Palestinian Charter and to recognize Israel, and the paramount importance of close cooperation with the Israeli peace movement in order to change the face of Israel. The next step would be to get an impressive number of Palestinian intellectuals in the West, leaders of the Palestinian population in the occupied territories and other like-minded Palestinian personalities to sign and publish this manifesto. Such a move would certainly be supported by several Arab regimes, such as Morocco, Tunisia, Saudi Arabia, Egypt and Jordan. With the help of generous financial support, a worldwide organization could be set up, cooperating with a network of peace groups in Western Europe and other parts of the world. A parallel Israeli peace organization would cooperate with it closely.

Another, more ambitious scheme was to create a real party. There already existed a Palestinian communist party, propounding communist ideology and loyalty to Moscow. Why shouldn't there come into being an independent peace party, organizing branches wherever there are Palestinians? Such a party could appear at the next session of the Palestinian National Council as an independent force, standing up to the mindless radicals, who had nearly monopolized the debate in Algiers. Sartawi clearly saw himself as the leader of such a party.

Many questions presented themselves. Would such a party be inside Fatah or outside all existing organizations? Would it accept the overall leadership of Yassir Arafat or not? What would its exact status be vis-à-vis the PLO?

At times, in his exasperation, Issam entertained heretical thoughts, but he always quickly snapped back to reality. I strongly discouraged him from planning anything that could be construed as an attempt to undermine the foundation of the PLO and the leadership of Arafat. To my mind this was both dangeous and unrealistic. Recalling our own experience before the creation of the State of Israel, I knew the paramount importance of a unified national institution. I also emphasized to him the unswerving loyalty of the Palestinian masses in the West Bank and Gaza to Arafat, and the immense value of this personal leadership as a unifying force. After moments of bitterness, Issam himself acknowledged these facts, and based his plans upon them.

During these weeks Sartawi burst into activity, explaining his views and ideas in a great number of interviews and articles, trying for the first time to systematize his thoughts and bring them home to the Palestinian masses. The drama of the Algiers conference had made him newsworthy, and he exploited this to the hilt in order to draw attention to his line. I saw him spending endless hours on the telephone and in direct conversation with journalists of all kinds and countries.

It was as if he sensed that his time was short. Radio Monte Carlo, perhaps the most important medium of electronic communication in the Arab world, broadcast an hour-long interview with him. Friendly Arab papers devoted pages to his views, he himself rushed around giving speeches to every group, however small, which invited him to voice his opinions.

Perhaps the most important interview with him was published in the Egyptian weekly *Al Musawar* on 25 March 1983. The interview was given to a young Egyptian journalist in London. Never before had he set out his views so clearly. As this interview was given only days before his death, it merits quotation at length.

On the PLO:

> It is not true that Issam Sartawi is a thing apart from the PLO. The PLO is for us the symbol of Palestinian national identity, and we cannot depart from it ... when I criticize the PLO, or take up an opposite position in its institutions, I do this in order to strengthen and support it, and not for any other reason.

On the Reagan Peace Plan:

> We should have defined the Reagan proposal as the starting point of the American position, and matched it with a starting point of our own. The art of negotiation is, after all, the art of taking two diametrically opposed starting points and reconciling them through arduous joint sessions and tough confrontations.

The Algiers session of the PNC:

> I did not call it a session of the silent majority but in conversations I did express my appraisal — this is only an appraisal, and I have no way to prove the assertion — that my views represent the opinion of the silent Palestinian majority. I base myself on several criteria. For example, when Brother Abu Amar recently met with General Matti Peled and a delegation of the Israeli

Council for Israeli-Palestinian Peace, several voices expressing strong criticism and even insults were heard. But from the refugee camps in Lebanon there came messages of support for this meeting, and statements of support were published. These were the camps in which the massacre occurred, and these are the Palestinians who understand the danger of posing as patriots in order to gain prestige, who know how harmful and destructive such an attitude is. These Palestinians in the refugee camps, where the massacre occurred, learned in the face of death what political wisdom is and what the meaning of sane, realistic attitudes are which deal with the world as it really is and not with a world which has no bearing on reality. Those who stayed alive understood that if Palestinian wisdom had prevailed before the invasion, they would not have been massacred in their camps. They understand what the extremists call treason is not treason, but that extremism itself is the height of national treason.

On the Palestinian majority:

Therefore I say: Yes, there is a Palestinian silent majority that has started to speak up, and I believe that what I propose and what I do expresses the opinions of this majority ... Of all those who devote themselves to the service of our people, I am the only one who speaks out frankly. As a result of this I have suffered all forms of hardship and defamation. The list is long and I do not want to go into it here. I want my people to attain their rights to the furthest possible extent. I shall struggle with all my power so that my people shall have a state, an entity, an identity and a passport.

On three different approaches:

How shall we achieve our goal? On this our opinions differ. There are those who argue that we not act in a hurry, and this opinion is voiced often. Those who think so believe that we are unable to achieve anything in the present situation, that every political movement can only harm us, because it will compel us to give up very important political cards. Israel will never be a legitimate entity as long as we do not recognize it. Therefore let's wait 100 years until circumstances change, and then we shall throw Israel into the sea. This view is being put forth to us. Our comrades in the organization of popular liberation struggle, or al-Saiqa, propose this view.

There is another approach which says that we should freeze all political activity and strive instead for revolutions in the Arab world. Let's leave Israel alone and make revolutions in the various Arab states. Instead of the existing regimes; let's set up revolutionary regimes which shall mobilize all their forces for the attack on Israel and its destruction. Those who hold this view are also entitled to their opinions. But it's my right to say that it means that we shall freeze all our activity for the Palestinian cause and forget our people for an indeterminate number of years, and only Allah knows how long it will take.

We must take into account that in this case we would be in the position of one who buys a fish that is still in the water. Nobody can guarantee us that the revolutionary, pioneering forces, who propose these slogans, are able to carry out the revolutions which they want.

All the views which propose to escape from reality are groundless, both theoretically and practically. It is our duty to face reality as it is. How can we attain for our people everything that can be attained in the existing circumstances of the balance of power and possibilities for political action?

On Israeli expansionism:

I am convinced that Israel plans to get to the Persian Gulf, by expanding to the east, in order to secure the Arab oil. The aim is to put its hand on the source of basic power, which will make it independent of the United States and liberate it from total dependence upon it and give it the economic power base it lacks today. This would also give it a greater military capability, because in this way Israel will break the Arab nation from Egypt to the Gulf into little religious states, each one of which will be dependent on Israel for its daily needs. Israel will also exploit the Arab wealth for the development of its technology and industry, in order to produce all the arms it needs. It would export the surplus in order to create an economic-industrial empire, which will allow it to maintain its independence and hegemony even after the oil is depleted.

On the Arabs:

Our duty is to face this reality, to see Israel as it is, powerful and superior. We must admit to ourselves that it is Israel who has the military option against us, and not we who have the military option against Israel. It is Israel who shall stand, and we have to recognize that the balance of power was not in our favour when Lebanon was invaded and the tragedy occurred.

We have witnessed the legendary heroism of the Lebanese people and the Palestinian fighters, which allowed this pitiful force to hold out against the Israeli Army for three months, during which all the foreign factors had time to act. What did we find out?

The great powers — what did they do? The Arab brothers — what did they accomplish?

If the Arab brothers and we ourselves were frank with ourselves, and if we had said to ourselves: This is Israel and these are our borders with her, we would not have found ourselves in the humiliating situation where two Arab peoples, the Lebanese and the Palestinian, were massacred, and the Arab world stands by and watches. In the whole of the Middle East — oh shame! — there were only three demonstrations [against the refugee camps massacre], a real big demonstration in Israel, or rather many demonstrations, a very small demonstration in Cairo and a third one in Kuwait.

On Arab aims:

I believe that the Palestinian State, for which we strive, is not only a local aim, but also a pan-Arab aim, because this state will be the line of defence against Israeli expansion towards the Arab Gulf.

On Palestinian aims:

This is the challenge facing us, the historic and intellectual challenge. It faces first of all me, as a Palestinian, and only after that all other Arabs, because every other Arab people is protected in its country, may Allah be blessed for that. They have a passport, they have institutions for providing food, they have hospitals. Nobody doubts that Egypt is Egyptian or Jordan Jordanian.

But I am a Palestinian, my identity has been stolen and lost, I cannot give my people the minimum it needs for its existence. Therefore my Palestinian task is stupendous, beyond every description.

On heroism:

First of all, I have to decide if I want to serve my people or myself.

If I want to serve myself, the media of communication and propaganda will turn me into a great hero if I escape 100 years into the future. I shall be a great hero, my picture will be in all the papers, I shall be described in glowing terms, I shall have at my disposal luxury cars, elegant apartments, I shall be an honoured guest in all the Arab capitals and send my children to the school of the Arab organization. All this on condition that I escape from the tragedy of my people today into a vague solution which will be realized after 100 years.

Or I shall decide to serve my people in spite of everything others are saying, armed with unending love for my people, with an unbreakable bond with my people, for the confrontation is bitter and lonely, very lonely.

A person not armed with love for his people, not bound to them with ties that prevent him from escaping from his conscience, will find it easy to sit in a big armchair of heroism and public acclamation.

On radicalism:

The strategy which we have devised is unprecedented: To start a dialogue with parts of the Israeli society, in the middle of a bitter war. When we broke into Israeli society, offering our hand to the democratic and progressive forces, we rejected capitulation. It is we who are the radicals, and not those who reject and escape.

On Fatah:

We must remember that Fatah fired the first military bullet, which started the revolution in 1965, and that Fatah ten years later fired the political bullet which started the political revolution. Why Fatah? Because it is the pioneer. Fatah is the Palestinian body that represents the national interests as they really are — the simple Palestinian, the will of the Palestinian human being and his well-being. The basis is the love of Palestine and the bond with it, and not the loyalty to some other party.

... ten years after Fatah fired the first bullet, the movement understood that there exists a world in which we have to act, and that the defeat of Israel is not a little pleasure trip and that we must realign our ideas ... This breakthrough and the new precise thinking was a common venture of several personalities in the Fatah leadership, and not my own personal line. Those who took part in working out this line were Abu Amar, Abu Jihad, Abu Maazen, Abu Said (Khaled al-Hassan) and others. The mainstream of the PLO leadership turned to face this historical challenge and respond to it. This is how the new line evolved, and this is how we entered the bitter struggle, which had numerous reverberations in the Arab world and in Fatah, and during which many comrades who are irreplaceable like the late Said Hammami, the late Naim Khader, the late Ali Nasser Yassin, the late Azz-al-Din Kalak fell. These are the martyrs who cannot be replaced.

. . . Now we have some differences of opinion about the details, but there are no differences of opinion about the principle. Who are the forces with whom we have to talk? . . . We have addressed ourselves to the Israeli society, in order to establish bonds of dialogue and friendship with forces inside this society with whom and through whom we can change the balance in favour of peace in our region, and only this peace can enable our people to realize their rights.

On dialogue with Israelis:

If the circumstances facing us are bad, we have to create new circumstances in which we can act. This means first of all the need to face reality courageously, without escaping from it, because the escape from reality means escape from the solution, capitulation and surrender. And when we face reality we have to rethink. Nations cannot give up their aims and their existence even when the attack on them is heavy and circumstances too hard to bear.

Our experience [in the dialogue with Israeli peace forces] has no precedent in the history of nations or liberation movements. And indeed when we started we had no one else's experience to draw on.

Therefore, we had to devise our own rules of behaviour as we went along, in the light of positive and negative reactions from here and from there. Because the dialogue is a beginning of strategic, not tactical, dimensions; for us it is a strategy and not, as many believe, a tactic. We want the development of a process within Israel which will bring about the recognition of the national rights of the Palestinian people, the acceptance of the PLO as the sole legitimate representative of this people and the agreement to the full withdrawal of Israel from all the occupied Arab lands.

The appearance of such a tendency in Israel is a basic change. We hope that in time this tendency will spread and attain such power as to enable it to influence the political decisions of Israel.

On Israeli public opinion:

We must distinguish completely between two experiences, the Egyptian and the Palestinian. First, the Palestinian experience antedated the Egyptian one by many years. Second, the Palestinian experience was not aimed at the official Israeli establishment, but at public opinion. The Israeli peace forces do not possess today the power to influence Israeli policy, but they have the ability to develop in such a way as to gain a hearing for their arguments and to convince the Israeli public of the necessity of the solution we are propounding.

In contact between states, the decision is in the hands of the government which has the majority in parliament and controls the instruments of power, while we want to bring about in the opinion of Israeli society a change from enmity to a recognition of the rights of the Palestinian people. This means that our point of departure is that we have to convince the public before we negotiate with the government.

* * *

On 25 March, I was to appear together with Issam at a conference of European parliamentarians in the parliament building in The Hague. This was a preparatory conference for the United Nations International Conference on the Question of Palestine which was to take place in August.

Arriving in The Hague, I met Abu Faisal and Zouhedi Terzi, the official PLO observer at the UN. I was disappointed to hear that Sartawi was unable to attend. He had been called to Tunis to meet Yassir Arafat. In spite of the disappointment, these were tidings of joy. It meant that Arafat had taken the initiative to mend the rift between him and Issam which had been created in Algiers. The Chairman was much too wise to dispense with the services of Sartawi, and much too fond of him personally to let the wound fester.

Abu Faisal, Terzi and I spent the evening in the home of a rich local Palestinian, discussing the situation in a cordial atmoshere, and then Terzi drove me to my hotel. The Dutch police obviously feared terrorist attacks on me, and four policemen in mufti, their hands on concealed pistols, conducted me in the morning to their car and drove me the few hundred yards to the parliament building. There I found Issam.

It appeared that he had been waiting for Abu Amar in Tunis and become impatient. As often happened, Abu Amar was detained for a few days, so Issam got up and left. He arrived just in time for the start of the conference.

Many of the parliamentarians did not believe their eyes when they saw the senior PLO representative and the guest from Israel sitting next to each other throughout the conference, conferring with each other during dull speeches and sticking together even during intermissions. A part of the meeting was devoted to the dialogue between us, and some of the audience was again astonished when our speeches complimented and complemented each other when we defended each other from aggressive questions, when either of us explained the importance of the activities of the other. If we had been members of the same party from the same country, we couldn't have been more united. While I pleaded for the recognition of the PLO by Western Europe, as the most important means of strengthening the forces of moderation inside the PLO, Issam made a strong case for the invitation of the Israeli peace forces to the forthcoming UN conference.

This time there was no heckling and no excitement as there had been in London. In the quiet conference room of the parliament building, in a most civilized atmosphere — smoking was allowed on the right hand side of the hall, but not on the left— both of us spoke quietly. Yet, reading the text of Issam's speech which I had recorded on my small machine, I am struck by the force of his plea.

* * *

At the end of the conference that day, the security people bundled us into the same car and sped us to the nearby hotel. It was already quite late, and there was to be an official banquet with speeches and toasts. But before that Issam came to my room to take the ubiquitous parcel of bread and cheese I had brought with me. He devoured some of it on the spot. His appetite must have been blunted by the time we got down to the hall, where the wholesome

Dutch food was waiting for us.

Afterwards, after the parliamentarians had gone to sleep, we went to look for the bar. There we spent an hour in the company of our numerous bodyguards. I would have liked to discuss several issues with him, but that was quite impossible, because of one of the bodyguards.

She was the most unusual bodyguard we had ever encountered: a tall, blonde, blue-eyed beauty, quick and intelligent. If anyone had tried to find a girl who was the epitome of everything Issam Sartawi was looking for in a woman, there she was in front of us, in flesh and blood, an armed Venus risen from the waves.

After an hour or so I was extremely tired. I had to get up early the next morning to catch my plane back home, and so I excused myself. I took the lift to my room. To simplify security, Issam had been given the room next door, and the corridor had been equipped with electronic machinery that enabled the security personnel to scan the approaches to our rooms from another room. Threading my way through the tangle of wires, I went to my room and fell promptly asleep. Very early the next morning I got up and left. I did not wake Issam in his room, which was guarded by several alert guards.

I did not see him again. The last glimpse I had of him he was in the bar of the hotel, joking with the blonde beauty.

He had still sixteen days to live.

## 45

*Matti is sitting in Issam's office. They talk about developments. Suddenly the phone rings.*

*Issam picks it up. He listens gravely and exchanges a few sentences with the caller. Matti realizes that he is talking with Abu Amar.*

*'It was the Chairman', Issam says to Matti after putting down the receiver. 'He is warning me. Our intelligence has found out that a group of Abu Nidal people have left Damascus. Their mission is to kill me. Abu Amar is sending some bodyguards to protect me.'*

*They resume the discussion.*

# 46

Several people had warned Issam not to attend the meeting of the Socialist International, scheduled for April 1983 in Albufeira, Portugal. The meeting was publicized in advance, and so was his intention to attend. It was inviting trouble.

I had once told him the first rule in avoiding assassination. I had learned it from my neighbour in the Knesset, Isar Harel, who had been for many years the chief of the Israeli security service, and later of the Mossad. He had told me that in order to carry out an assassination, one had to know the location and the time well in advance, so as to draw up a plan, bring in the hitmen and the weapons and prepare the escape route. The first rule of protection was, therefore, never to be in a place where people expect you. Yassir Arafat adhered to this rule scrupulously, and thus he was staying alive.

Issam did not adhere to this rule. I suspect it was against his nature, his natural pride to do so. To him it means yielding to the will of the enemy. He did not want to be dictated to. If so, it was misguided pride.

But Issam insisted that the Socialist International was an important area in the PLO's battle for international recognition. He believed that the International, professing socialist internationalism, owed it to the Palestinian people to take up their cause. Moreover, in the International he had influential friends and allies. Bruno Kreisky was an important figure there, the head of a socialist government. Willy Brandt, the former German chancellor, was the president of the International. Several other important socialist leaders were his friends and admirers.

But his battle for recognition had been frustrated time and again by Shimon Peres. As leader of the Israeli socialist party, he demanded that no recognition be extended to the PLO. This was in line with the four noes which had been proclaimed by the Labour Party as the Israeli national consensus: no withdrawal to the pre-1967 borders, no Palestinian state, no change in the status of East Jerusalem which had been annexed to Israel, no dealings with the PLO. Behind the scenes, Peres was pleading with Brandt, Kreisky and the others that any resolution in favour of the PLO would be considered a personal defeat for him and deal a blow to the Labour Party in its efforts to regain power in Israel. It is one of the main functions of the International to help any socialist party gain or retain power in its country.

In previous sessions, some personal status had been given to Sartawi. He had been working behind the scenes. But to no avail. In the 1980 session, the International had declared that the Israeli Labour Party was the only peace force in Israel. Furious, Issam had published in the English-language

Beirut weekly, *Monday Morning*, an indictment of the Israeli Labour Party, analysing its programme and proving that it called for the destruction of the Palestinian community in Lebanon, under the guise of an anti-terrorist crusade. 'Under a Labour government, the Israeli armed forces would launch a concentrated attack on the PLO bases in Syria and Lebanon', he said, adding that the so-called PLO bases were the organs of civil administration, health care, schools and social welfare in South Lebanon. It was a good prediction of what was to happen later — not under a Labour government, but in a war conducted by the Likud government with the full support of Labour. While Labour was a war party, Sartawi stressed, 'there are in Israel peace forces, including the Sheli Party, the Peace Now Movement, the *New Outlook* group and others'.

He wanted to go to Albufeira to continue the fight, hoping to be seated this time as an official PLO representative. Gaining such a position, he thought, would strengthen the moderate forces in the PLO, enhance his own personal status and further his plans for the creation of a Palestinian peace party.

* * *

The last journey of Issam Sartawi was a sad one.

He arrived in Lisbon Airport quite alone. On the plane he had met some Israeli journalists, who were going to cover the conference. He had started a conversation with Tamar Golan, a correspondent for the BBC and the Israeli paper *Maariv*, and discovered that she was born in Haifa, not far from his own birthplace in Acre, at about the same time. He flirted with her in his usual way.

At Lisbon airport no one was waiting for Issam — no Palestinian, no Portuguese security official.

This was strange. During our last joint appearances in London and The Hague, I had been impressed by the elaborate security arrangements made by the local police forces. In Paris and in Vienna, Issam was under constant police protection. In Portugal he was not only left without any protection whatsoever, but, on his travels, he also could not take arms with him. He was defenceless.

What struck Tamar Golan was the great fanfare that greeted Shimon Peres at the airport. Portuguese officials surrounded him, and a large security squad was provided for his stay in Portugal. Who could have any designs on Shimon Peres?

Seeing that Issam was stranded, Tamar suggested that they all take — the PLO activist and the Israeli journalists — a taxi for the 200 kilometre drive to Albufeira, located on the southern coast of Portugal. Issam accepted.

Something must be said about Tamar Golan, as unusual an Israeli type as can be found. I met her first thirty years ago, during a visit to a kibbutz in the Negev. She was a member of the kibbutz, which had good relations with the neighbouring Bedouin tribes, and we went several times to visit them. Tamar, a very intense sabra, an idealistic member of Hashomer Hatzeir, the left-wing kibbutz movement, was a great believer in Jewish-Arab brotherhood. Like her husband, Avihu, she was from Haifa, where she had joined the youth movement in early youth and gone to found the kibbutz not far from Beersheva. Later she left the kibbutz and went to Ethiopia where her husband had found a job with an Israeli company. There, while attending a folk festival in the wilderness, he had been run over by an Ethiopian Army car, the only one in the neighbourhood. Tamar had taken him on the long way to hospital, cradling his head while he slowly died.

After that she had become attached to the African continent. She went to Kinshasa during the civil war, fell in love with a Nigerial Muslim diplomat, whose wife's family had her thrown out of Zaire. She was also not allowed into Nigeria, so she set up her headquarters in the nearby Ivory Coast. There she had become an expert on African affairs for the British and Israeli media, and kept close relations with several African personalities after she moved to Paris. She always wears white ('I'm staying in mourning for Avihu, but black is too depressing. So I chose white.') and always uses green ink, which suits her red hair.

All in all, she reminds one of the eccentric British ladies who used to roam the dark continent in the last century.

So Issam travelled in the company of this extraordinary Israeli, who must have intrigued him very much, to Albufeira. There he was not quartered in the hotel where the conference took place, as most delegates were, but in a far-away hotel. At least twice a day he had to travel alone on deserted roads, an ideal target for an ambush.

At the conference, all his moves were blocked by Peres. Brandt and Kreisky tried to have him seated as an observer for the PLO and let him be allowed to read his prepared speech, but on the insistence of Peres this was denied him. In the end, some *modus vivendi* was found to allow him to attend the conference as a private observer.

This did not deter Shimon Peres later from eulogizing Issam Sartawi from the rostrum as a great human being and peace hero. That's the kind of person Peres is. He also did not object to Issam's speech being read from the rostrum by Willy Brandt. Posthumously.

On 10 April, Issam was standing in the lobby of the hotel where the conference was taking place, chatting with some delegates. Next to him stood Anwar Abu Eisha, his assistant. A hitman of the Abu Nidal group approached him from behind, drew a revolver equipped with a silencer, and shot him in the head. Abu Eisha was wounded in the legs.

Issam died instantly. Contrary to the wish he had so often voiced, he did not see his assassin.

A few hours later, the Abu Nidal group published a communiqué from Damascus:

> The Fatah — Revolutionary Committee — is happy to announce to the Arab masses, to the Palestinian people inside and outside Palestine, to the militants and to the free people around the world that it has succeeded in executing the death sentence passed on the criminal traitor Sartawi, who was an agent of the Mossad, the CIA, and British intelligence.

The Portuguese police started a hunt and captured the Abu Nidal hitman. The murderer, identified as Mohammed Hussein Rashid, smiled throughout the trial, which lasted for eight hours. He readily admitted that he was a member of the Abu Nidal group, that he had entered Portugal with a false passport and that he had been a member of the hit group sent to kill Sartawi. But he denied having shot him himself. After a strange trial the judge passed a strange judgment. The man was acquitted of murder, and condemned only on charges of entering Portugal with a false passport. For this crime he was sentenced to three years in prison and forbidden to enter Portugal for five years. Hearing the verdict, the accused laughed.

# 47

*It is 10 April, just before ten o'clock in the morning. A friend of mine who works for the French news agency is on the line.*

*'We have just received news that there has been an attempt on the life of Issam Sartawi in Portugal. It's still very unclear. He's either wounded or dead.'*

*I don't feel anything. It's like receiving a bit of news you have been expecting for a long time.*

*'Do you want to comment on it for publication?' the journalist asks in his French-accented Hebrew.*

*'Let's wait until the news is definite. Please call me when you have a definite confirmation.'*

*I try to get back to work and find it difficult to concentrate. I call Matti in Jerusalem to tell him what I've heard.*

*Neither of us says anything more.*

*Ten minutes later my friend calls again. It's quite definite. Issam Sartawi has been shot dead. I give him a short statement.*

*At eleven o'clock the Israeli radio broadcasts the news.*

*Matti Peled calls Waddad, Issam's wife, at his home in Paris. When he starts to express our profound sense of shock, he realizes that she does not know anything. No one has told her yet.*

# PART IV

# Arafat

# 48

On 22 April 1983, Issam Sartawi and I were scheduled to appear together in a meeting at Cambridge University in England. The organizers were members of a small group of concerned Jews, much like the one which had organized the meeting in London. After the murder they called me in desperation, asking my advice. I told them to hold the meeting and turn it into a memorial event.

This time a police escort waited for me at the airport, and another one met me in Cambridge. I felt like an actor in one of the many British police serials, which are so frequently shown on Israeli television. These were either very serious, very accurate in their portrayal of the British police or else the British policemen were consciously modelling their style on the programmes.

With the policemen lurking discreetly behind the scenes, I made my speech about Issam. It was one of the most moving meetings I've ever attended. I concluded my speech with the words of Hamlet describing his dead father: 'He was a man, take him for all in all, I shall not look upon his like again'.

* * *

Issam Sartawi was buried in Amman. The loyal Abu Faisal had been sent by the PLO to Albufeira to bring him back. The Portuguese authorities refused to put a light chartered plane at his disposal for this purpose. In the end, it was the King of Morocco who sent a plane.

Surprisingly, thousands followed his coffin through the streets of Amman. He was buried near the grave of Said Hammami. Hammami's widow, Khalida, stood next to Waddad al-Sartawi, and so did the widows of several of the other Palestinian martyrs murdered by Abu Nidal and his masters. Abu Jihad presided over the reception for the mourners. To Maxim Ghilan, who attended, he said, 'The contacts with the Israeli peace forces will go on'.

* * *

To demonstrate this, Yassir Arafat sent his assistant for Israeli affairs, Imad Shakour, to appear with me at the beginning of May in Turin. We were the guests of a small, left-wing, neutralist Italian party, which supports many international fights for peace and justice. During one of the many opulent Italian meals, a curious fact emerged: both Imad's uncle and my brother had been soldiers in the British Army which had fought the Italians in the Second World War.

There was a big group of Palestinian students in the audience at one of the meetings. I was impressed by their thoughtful reactions when I told them: 'You must get used to the fact that no one is going to help you. Not one single Arab regime came to your help in Beirut. The Russians did not lift a finger. The Syrians are out to destroy your independence. The Americans are against you. In the end you'll find out that you have only one real ally: the Israeli peace forces. After we achieve peace, Israel will be the only real ally of Palestine, and Palestine will be the only real ally of Israel.'

In Turin I also met the grand old man of the Italian Communist Party, Giancarlo Payetta. I had met him many times in the early 1970s during the preparatory meetings for the big Bologna conference and at the conference itself. He is a tall, bald, handsome man, vaguely reminiscent of Picasso; he had been a hero of the resistance against Mussolini, and later a staunch defender of Italian communist independence from Moscow.

Over lunch, Payetta told me about a conversation he had had with Abu Bakr, the Iraqi leader. The dictator had told him that the Palestinians are all right but the PLO are traitors. Payetta had answered that he was a friend of both the Palestinians and the PLO, and asked what was the solution envisaged by the Iraqi. Abu Bakr's answer was: 'All the Jews must leave Israel and go home.'

'But it will take hundreds of years!' the Italian communist leader had answered.

The Iraqi was unmoved. 'So what? We shall wait. The main thing is not to compromise on questions of principle.'

Payetta could not restrain himself from saying: 'So why don't you change places with the Palestinians?'

Payetta recounted a similar conversation with the Algerian leader, Houari Boumedienne, who had told him that the Arabs should have continued the fight in 1973. 'But the Israelis would have conquered Cairo!' Payetta had interjected, to which the Algerian had countered: 'So what? Algiers was under French occupation for over 100 years, and we liberated it!'

With friends like these, the Palestinians needed no enemies.

Reviewing the situation with Payetta, I remarked that in my opinion, it was in the best interests of Israel to make peace now when its strength was at its height. To this he answered: 'That's the whole point.'

As Imad Shakour told it, the Abu Nidal people were not resting on their murderous laurels. They were conducting a wild campaign against Abu Iyad, the chief of the Palestinian security services, whose real name is Saleh Khalaf. According to an Abu Nidal pamphlet, his real name was Itzhak Khalafa and he was a Jew.

Imad himself was worried about his family. This is a simple problem, which illustrates the Palestinian condition perhaps more than anything else: the question of where to keep one's family. The very choice of a place of domicile and the school for one's children was a political decision. Abu Jihad had removed his family to Amman before taking up a consistent anti-Syrian line; Imad Shakour had sent his family to Cairo.

One morning, sitting in the lobby of our little hotel, waiting for the security people to take us to the airport, Imad and I found the perfect solution for how to deal with the question of Zionism — a term dear to most Israelis, but which has a satanic ring to all Palestinians. We agreed to postpone the discussion about the nature and history of Zionism until one day after the achievement of peace between our two peoples.

We flew together to Rome, where we met Mahmoud Darwish, an outstanding Palestinian poet who had grown up in Israel, been arrested and allowed to leave. Among the Palestinians, poetry plays a big role. During one of the sessions of the Algiers PNC, Darwish had held his audience spellbound when he recited a new, long poem of his, devoted to the PNC. Cassettes of this reading were devoutly passed around among the Palestinians.

Mahmoud was in Rome to receive a prize for literature. We all attended the ceremony, where we met Nimer Hammad, one of the most talented Palestinian diplomats, who at the time represented the PLO in Rome. In the car after the meeting, Imad, Mahmoud and I talked happily in Hebrew, until Hammad, who was driving and who does not know Hebrew, turned around and complained.

* * *

During the Turin meeting, I had discussed with Imad the question of the six Israeli prisoners held by Fatah in North Lebanon.

These soldiers had been captured in a rather bizarre way. After the evacuation of Beirut, they had been manning an Israeli Army outpost east of the city, where they were captured without a fight.

As Arafat himself told me the story, in Tunis, the eight Israelis had been captured by a Fatah squad composed of green recruits, Palestinian students who had rushed to Lebanon to help in the fight. After the capture, the captives and their captors had begun a long trek on foot. Operating in Syrian-held territory, the Fatah men had no transportation. The Syrians allowed transportation only to those Palestinian forces attached to the Syrian Army and toeing the Syrian line.

On their way back, the group met a car which belonged to the Ahmed Jibril organization, a small group supported by Libya and Syria. They had hitchhiked and, in return, the Fatah commander had turned over two captives to the Jibril group, which was holding them now.

Israelis are extremely sensitive about the fate of their prisoners. This has something to do with ancient Jewish tradition. During medieval times, when Jews were often kidnapped and held for ransom, it was the duty of every Jewish community to pay the ransom and liberate the Jewish prisoner held in its neighbourhood, wherever he came from. This fine example of Jewish solidarity has become a religious imperative.

The parents of the prisoners approached me and asked whether I could do anything to liberate their sons, or at least ameliorate the conditions in which they were held. Before coming to me, they had met with Begin and asked his permission to enlist my help. 'By all means', Begin had said. The parents of two prisoners gave me a written authorization to speak on their behalf.

I went again to Rome to see what I could do in this matter. After consulting with the PLO people there, I sent a letter to Arafat dated 14 July 1983, on the letterhead of the Israeli Council for Israeli-Palestinian Peace.

Mr Chairman,

First I would like to express my strong hope that the Fatah movement overcomes the present crisis, and that your leadership will be even strengthened. I believe that this is essential not only for the cause of Palestine but also for the cause of Israel and peace.

I have been approached by families of the six Israeli prisoners held by Fatah in Lebanon. They officially asked me to represent them and to use my good offices — and the contacts established between the Israeli peace movement and the PLO —in order to help their sons. Mr Begin and other Israeli authorities know about this approach and did not object — it being understood that I act for the families only.

I am doing this for humanitarian reasons. But I also believe that the success of this mission will strengthen the peace movement and improve the climate for a peace solution.

I would divide the problem into two: the present conditions in which the prisoners are held and their eventual release.

As for the first: the families are greatly concerned by the news that their sons are now held in solitary confinement. I would very much ask you to consider my request that they be put together again, or at least in groups. Apart from the immediate humanitarian consideration, this will also be reflected in the stories they will tell upon their return, which will be important for the future development of Israeli public opinion.

If you could make this change and announce it publicly, or inform me about it, my friends and I would be immensely grateful. It would be considered a victory for the Israeli peace movement.

The same goes, of course, for any other improvement in their living conditions, letter writing, etc. I would very much like to get from them letters I could convey to the families, and vice versa. This may be the most urgent first step.

As to the questions concerning release and exchange of prisoners, I would be happy to contribute whatever I can. I am confident that General Matti Peled and I are now acceptable to the Israeli government as go-betweens if there is any chance of success. The parents of the prisoners can exert great pressure in this respect.

I understand that there are great obstacles, but I feel certain that with goodwill they can be overcome. As I have always been active in the effort to improve the conditions of Palestinian prisoners in Israel and Ansar, and to achieve for them prisoner-of-war status, I at least understand the problem.

Dear Mr Chairman, I would very much welcome an early reply, in spite of all your many other obligations. I would come and meet with you in Tunis or anywhere to further this effort. I am also ready to go to Tripoli to meet the prisoners, if you consider this advisable.

May you overcome the present trouble as quickly and successfully as possible.

*In sha Allah.*

A few weeks later, Matti Peled went to Moscow as a member of an Israeli peace delegation. He used this opportunity to see the PLO representative there and approach him on the same matter. On his advice, he sent another memorandum to Tunis through him.

All to no avail. Months later, at the height of the battle of Tripoli, prisoners were returned in exchange for a great number of PLO fighters held in Israeli prisons, as well as all the inmates of the notorious prison camp at Al-Ansar, in South Lebanon. The deal was made with an Israeli right-wing politician, a former Minister of Justice who had become famous for enacting an infamous law under which Palestinians displaying or even possessing a Palestinian flag received a two-year prison sentence. It was a sad and typical example of an opportunity missed.

But at least the prisoners, on their return, during the first flush of excitement, revealed that they had been extremely well treated by their Fatah captors. Needless to say, they and their families were muzzled and not one single story about their experiences during their long capture was published. Also, needless to say, neither the prisoners nor their parents ever thanked me for my humble efforts, which I did at my own expense.

* * *

On 29 August 1983, the United Nations convened, in their Geneva headquarters, an international conference on the question of Palestine. This was a gala gathering, the result of a long string of meetings and resolutions of the United Nations General Assembly, all of which had been boycotted by Israel, the United States and their allies. The United States, under Israeli pressure, boycotted this gathering too. Most of the Western countries bowed to American wishes and sent observers only. The governments of Israel, the United States and West Germany were absent altogether.

Both Matti Peled and I were invited to take part in the conference with the personal status of 'eminent persons', in the company of about a dozen others from different parts of the world who were considered experts on this subject. The Israeli Council was invited as a non-governmental organization.

The decision to attend was not easily reached. We knew that the whole propaganda apparatus of our government would be mobilized against the conference, that any Israeli participating would be branded a dupe of the enemy. The cards in the conference would be stacked against Israel, with the full weight of the Arab and communist world present, and the West silent.

On the other hand, it was important to encourage the moderate mainstream of the PLO, now faced with open rebellion by the hardliners supported by Syria and Libya. A big international conference, expressing worldwide support for the realistic leadership of the PLO, would enable Arafat to demonstrate to his own people that the moderate, responsible line was bearing fruit, while the hardliners' way led to total isolation. Even the symbolic presence of the Israeli peace camp was important in this context.

The Labour doves, who were also invited, declined, of course, with Yossi Sarid publishing his usual condemnation of those who accepted.

The deciding argument for us was practical. After Sartawi's assassination, our connection with the PLO had become tenuous. I had met several times with Nimer Hammad, the Rome representative, but there was no regular contact, and nobody was charged by the PLO with taking over the job left vacant. Even while it was painfully clear that no one could fill the vacuum left by such a unique person as Issam Sartawi, there was an urgent need to create a regular link for the continuation of the dialogue. We hoped that in Geneva, in the halls and corridors of the conference, the regular contact could be re-established.

With this hope, but with no little foreboding, we flew to Geneva.

* * *

The beautiful town on Lake Geneva resembled an armed camp in a state of siege.

The Swiss had been reluctant to host the conference. Initially it was to take place in Paris, but the Americans had exerted intense pressure on the French government to prevent the meeting from being held there. The same had happened in Austria. The Swiss could not refuse, because the Geneva installation of the United Nations, the former seat of the League of Nations, was much too important for Switzerland, and the UN did not need Swiss permission to conduct its own affairs there.

But long before the conference even started, the military preparations cast a pall over it. Perhaps the Swiss, with their usual thoroughness, only took the precautions they deemed necessary. Perhaps, as some believe, the Swiss Army used this opportunity to stage a large-scale military exercise in urban defence. But the most sinister interpretation was that the Swiss, unable to refuse pointblank to have this conference on their soil, tried to sabotage it by creating the derogatory impression that this was a meeting of terrorists and their sympathizers, who were liable at any moment to massacre each other or to be assassinated by the competition. Anti-aircraft guns were mounted in the park of the UN headquarters, gunboats patrolled the lakefront next to it, armoured cars rumbled through the streets. At the Intercontinental Hotel, where I was staying with most of the delegations, security precautions were so tight as to be absurd. I was searched several times a day.

All this was in complete contrast with the conference itself. Endless streams of diplomats made endless speeches, each one starting with elaborate congratulations to each other, most consisting of platitudes betraying a total ignorance, and even indifference, to the problem at hand. Some of the speeches were outrageous, such as one by the Iranian foreign minister, who insinuated that the Zionists had butchered six million Jews with the help of the Nazis in order to create a pretext for the expulsion of the Palestinians from their rightful homeland. With such friends as these, the Palestinians surely did not need any enemies. But some of the speeches were penetrating and thought-provoking. Some of the best friends of the Palestinians called upon them to come forward with an unequivocal statement of their readiness to recognize Israel and live in peace with it, in return for Israel's agremeent to withdraw from the occupied territories and recognize the right of the Palestinians to have a state of their own. Whatever the rhetoric, it was clear that there exists a worldwide consensus as to the solution: the coexistence of Israel and a Palestinian state to be set up in the West Bank and Gaza, with its capital in East Jerusalem, and negotiations between Israel and the PLO. Sitting in the gallery reserved for the 'eminent persons' and listening to speaker after speaker expressing this consensus in the name of his government, the rather immodest thought crossed my mind that I was perhaps the only person in the hall who could claim that he had advocated this solution twenty years ago. The plan had come a long way since then.

But while there was near unanimity about the solution (excluding, of course, the Iranian and Libyan speakers, and some others, but most definitely including the Syrian foreign minister, his belligerent rhetoric notwithstanding), there was also another kind of unanimity. No one knew how to put the solution into action. It was all rather like the mice deciding to bell the cat.

When I was called upon to address the conference, I attacked this problem. There was only one point where a breakthrough could be achieved, I said, and that was in Israeli public opinion. Only by changing Israeli public opinion could the policy of Israel and the United States be changed. And there was only one way to achieve this: direct contact between Israeli peace forces and the PLO, leading towards dramatic initiatives, designed to rout deep-seated fears, stereotypes and prejudices. It was the same message I had given Said Hammami at our first meeting nearly nine years earlier.

The delegates who applauded my speech rather extravagantly turned this into a kind of demonstration. They knew I was hinting at something happening at the conference.

* * *

The PLO was represented at this conference by two of its high-ranking officials: Farouk Kaddumi, head of the political department, acting as head of the delegation, and Yasser Abed Rabbo, a member of the Executive Committee of the PLO, representing the Democratic Front of Nayef Hawatmeh. For us it was the worst possible choice. Kaddumi was our old enemy, a man who had been dedicated to the destruction of Issam Sartawi's initiatives who was still hoping for a reconciliation between Arafat and the Syrians. Rabbo represented an organization closely aligned with Syria and the Soviet Union.

The choice was typical of the PLO. It was a compromise between different tendencies, weighed on apothecary scales. The PLO had discreetly agreed to the participation of the Israeli peace delegates, approving specifically those people present, including the Zionist ones. At the same time, they sent as their own delegates two dignitaries opposed to a dialogue with Israeli Zionists. By sending pro-Syrians, they prevented a Syrian attack on the conference where the Palestinians were sitting together with Israelis. It was all rather complex.

The practical outcome was disastrous. Here we were, Israelis viciously attacked in our own country for taking part in this conference, cut dead by the official representatives of the PLO. When Kaddumi and Rabbo sat next to us in the cafeteria or passed us in the endless corridors, they looked through us as if we were thin air, neither saying good morning nor even nodding in recognition. The place was swarming with Israeli journalists, who were thoroughly briefed by the Israeli Embassy, which was closely monitoring the conference, and they did not fail to note this.

Sometimes the situation became positively ridiculous. The Palestinian delegation included some of our best friends. With Zehdi Terzi, the PLO permanent observer at the United Nations, I had spent evenings in pleasant conversation. Shafiq al Hut, the PLO ambassador in Beirut, had been present at my first dramatic meeting with Arafat. Edward Said, the noted Palestinian scholar, who had been invited like us as an eminent person, is a friend we like and respect. All these were put in a quandary. We exchanged greetings and friendly talks in hotel corners, or quick remarks in the corridors, but the PLO officials could not, of course, flout the directives of their superiors.

One of the most important delegates at the conference was the new Austrian foreign minister, Erwin Lanc, the former minister of the interior with whom I had spent so many hours in consultation with Sartawi, dealing with the Abu Nidal outrages. He invited us to his hotel suite and promised us to arrange a discreet meeting between us and Farouk Kaddumi. He thought that Kaddumi might agree to meet us under the auspices of the Austrian minister, who would guarantee total secrecy. But the next day Lanc had to inform us, rather sadly, that Kaddumi had refused, using the delicate situation between the PLO and Syria as a pretext.

On the first evening of the conference, the PLO representatives used a parliamentary trick in order to gain the floor. They pretended that they were reading a congratulatory telegram from Arafat, which they had concocted on the spot. It was a bad statement, falling back on rejectionist terminology (talking about the Zionist Entity, instead of Israel, etc) and totally negative. We decided to immediately publish a statement expressing regret.

But when Kaddumi's turn came to deliver his speech, which had been carefully worked out in advance in Tunis, it was surprisingly moderate. Setting forth all the peace plans which had been officially endorsed by the PLO, he nearly sounded like Issam Sartawi. He finished his speech by paying tribute to the Israeli peace forces, including a sentence which for him represented a major departure. Even within the Zionist camp, he said, voices were raised against the policy of the Begin government. This was the first time Kaddumi ever had anything good to say about Zionists. It did not, however, induce him to say *ahalan* to the next Zionist he met, a few minutes later. Perhaps he was upset by a photo which had appeared that very day on the front pages of Swiss newspapers. A quick photographer had succeeded in taking a picture of me passing Kaddumi, giving the impression that we were together.

The crisis came to a head when the PLO delegation gave an official reception for the delegates in the UN building. No Israeli was invited. This was a slap in our face which could not be ignored. Several important delegates who heard about it sharply remonstrated with Kaddumi, who promised to reconsider, but, of course, did not.

The Israeli communists crashed the reception, but Matti and I decided that this would be beneath the dignity of the forces in Israel which we represented. We did not attend, and therefore were not hugged by Yassir Arafat.

The PLO chairman made a surprise appearance in Geneva. Unannounced, as usual, he had come to the conference just in time for the reception. When he saw the communists there, he publicly asked: 'Where are Avnery and Peled?' When told by an Israeli journalist, who had also gatecrashed, that we had refused to attend because we had not been officially invited, Arafat exclaimed in mock indignation: 'But I gave instructions to send them invitations. Are they trying to insult me?'

Arafat and his entourage were also quartered in the Intercontinental Hotel, the safest place in Geneva, and perhaps the whole world, that evening. I was just going to sleep, angry and frustrated, when the telephone rang and a Hebrew voice, which I could not quite place at first, asked: 'How are you?' It was Imad Shakour.

I went to his room, where an attractive Arab woman journalist was trying to get information out of him. After she gave up and departed, we sat down to a serious discussion. I explained to him what had happened and brought home to him the seriousness of the situation. We had been snubbed and humiliated under the eyes of hostile Israeli journalists reporting to the Israeli Embassy. If we went back and had to report what had happened, the cause of Israeli-Palestinian peace would be set back by years.

It was nearly two o'clock in the morning, when Imad decided that the situation was so grave that he had to inform Abu Amar immediately. 'If he is not yet in bed, I'll arrange for him to meet you immediately. If he's in bed, I'll wake him and talk with him myself,' he said.

He came back an hour later. While we opened a second bottle of whisky, he told me that everything was arranged. Abu Amar, who had been in bed, had understood the problem. It was agreed that at the end of his speech the next morning, he would demonstratively walk up to us and embrace us. If this was impossible, because of security arrangments, he would call us immediately to a public meeting.

The next morning the whole building was humming. As an old parliamentarian, I know the signs indicating that something unusual and dramatic is in the offing. At such moments there is a subdued air of excitement, the hall fills up before the appointed time, delegates jostle for seats, secretaries and various aides fill the aisles and galleries.

They were not disappointed. Clad in his usual khaki uniform, draped in a red kuffia, Yassir Arafat made a sad and moving speech. To me it recalled a memory from my early youth. I was thirteen years old when Haile Selassie, the Negus of Ethiopia, after being evicted by Italian machine guns and poison gas from his homeland, made his dramatic appearance at the League of Nations in Geneva, on this very spot, vainly appealing to the conscience of the world.

Like Kaddumi before him, Arafat enumerated the many resolutions of the Palestinian National Council welcoming and adopting the various international peace plans. Quoting these plans, all of which at least implicitly recognized the State of Israel, and some of which, like the Brezhnev peace plan, explicitly did so, the Chairman of the PLO practically told the conference that his organization was ready for peace with Israel. But, like so many times before, he did not utter the one, clear, unequivocal direct sentence which is absolutely essential to convince Israelis, who don't give a damn for diplomatic texts.

Nearing the end of his speech, he turned towards the gallery where Matti and I were sitting, and, addressing us directly, said: 'On this occasion, I feel that reference should be made to the democratic and progressive Jewish forces in and outside Israel which have condemned war, condemned the invasion, condemned the massacres of Sabra and Shatilla and condemned expansionist policies and which are firmly advocating the rights of our people. I convey to them my greetings and appreciation for the courageous stand, especially in the face of the terror of the Israeli military authorities. Let us realize, together, our dream of an exemplary peace in the land of peace to be offered as a gift from us all to human civilization. Let us cooperate side by side with all noble-minded, peace, justice and freedom-loving forces the world over.'

While he was saying this, hundreds of delegates turned around to see to whom Arafat was addressing these words.

While the final applause was still ringing, Arafat was whisked away by the security people to some place behind the stage. A few minutes later Imad Shakour appeared in the gallery in great excitement and called upon Matti and me to follow him. The communist leader, Tawfiq Toubi, an old warhorse, immediately realized what was up. Motioning to his associate, the lawyer Felicia Langer, who had made a very strident speech at the conference, he hastened to follow us. We were led through corridors filled with security people, Swiss, Palestinian and United Nations personnel, into a room where Arafat was chatting with some black delegates. Seeing us enter, he came up to us and embraced each of us, making sure that his photographer had time to take the pictures.

It was clear that there was no time for a serious discussion. Under pressure from the Swiss security forces, Arafat had promised to leave the city immediately after his speech. The presence of several people in the room did not allow for any exchange of confidences. This, my third meeting with Arafat, was purely a demonstration, designed by Arafat to prove to the whole world that the contacts between the PLO and the Israeli peace forces, including the Zionist ones, were going on as a part of the PLO effort towards recognition and peace.

This was clearly understood by the enemies, both Israeli and Palestinian. A few hours afterwards the news agencies reported our meeting, the leader of the so-called 'Fatah rebels', Abu Saleh, made a statement in Tripoli, Libya, denouncing the traitor Arafat for meeting with two notorious Zionists like Matti Peled and me. While he was reading this statement, he was standing next to Mahmoud Labadi, the former PLO spokesman who had turned renegade and joined the rebels, after being relieved of his post.

I remembered Labadi well. He had been present at my first meeting with Arafat in Beirut. His obsequious manner towards Arafat, quite different from the manners of other Palestinians present, had impressed me unpleasantly. Throughout the day in West Beirut he had accompanied me, making propaganda speeches, idolizing Arafat. Now he denounced him as a traitor for meeting me again.

* * *

During the meeting with Arafat, I had sensed in him a buoyancy which vaguely reminded me of his mood in Beirut. I had registered it unconsciously.

A few days later I understood its meaning. Immediately after our meeting in Geneva, Arafat had mysteriously found his way into Tripoli, Lebanon. After their onslaught on the Palestinian forces in the Bekaa, the Syrian Army, hiding behind their Palestinian mercenaries which the world called 'rebels', had started a siege of the PLO Army in Tripoli and the neighbouring Palestinian refugee camps. It was a re-enactment of the siege of Beirut, with the Syrians now openly taking the place of the Israeli Army. But the Israeli side of the Syrian-Israeli collusion did not disappear. While the Syrians and their stooges were besieging the Palestinians on land, accusing them of the traitorous design to make peace with Israel, the Israeli Navy was blockading the Palestinians from the sea.

In Israel there was great jubilation. All the media reported that Arafat was now finally finished, the PLO destroyed and nothing left but a handful of extremists devoted to the annihilation of Israel. This was, of course, the picture which successive Israeli governments strove to preserve for years, in the face of all evidence to the contrary, in order to avoid a situation where Israel could be called upon to negotiate for the return of the occupied territories.

Israelis were therefore upset, and even some of my friends amazed, when I wrote an article before the end of the first week of the Tripoli siege, analysing the battle and stating unequivocally that Arafat had won another big victory. Some thought I'd finally lost my senses. But, three or four weeks later, it dawned on most Israelis that something had been wrong with the early predictions. They saw Arafat and Abu Jihad daily on Israeli television, smiling and exuding confidence, in the face of the massive onslaught.

Actually, my analysis was based upon the facts I knew. I had seen the PLO forces in besieged Beirut, and it was easy for me to imagine them in besieged Tripoli. I knew that the Syrian Army would shrink from entering a fortified city and battling from house to house, for the very same reason that even a person like Ariel Sharon had drawn back from entering West Beirut. Attacking a large Arab city, faced with the enmity of the Sunni population, encountering a resolute resistance of a fighting force especially well-suited to streetfighting — these were not prospects a cautious man like Hafez al-Assad would entertain. Having failed to win a surprise victory in the first two or three days, he was bound to be bogged down in inconclusive skirmishes. This was all quite obvious, if one knew the facts (which almost all Western observers did not) and if one's judgment was not clouded by prejudices and wishful thinking (as was the case with all Israeli observers).

The siege of Tripoli, and Arafat's survival and his extrication of his forces intact from what seemed a hopeless trap, had a profound impact on both the Palestinian and Israeli publics. Talking with Palestinians in towns and refugee camps of the West Bank, I found that support for Arafat was now practically unanimous and more intense than ever. Not only had he proved his personal courage by joining his forces in the beleaguered city and staying with them until their honourable retreat, as he had done in Beirut, but the fact that the 'rebels' had taken up arms against their own people for what were obviously Syrian interests had totally discredited them. As Issam Sartawi had predicted, the split with the Syrians and their collaborators had indeed happened.

But the circumstances were such that the vast majority of the Palestinian people rallied around Arafat, who had now become more than ever the symbol and the very personification of the Palestinian condition.

Still, Israelis hoped that Arafat was now so weakened as to become politically insignificant. They hoped that he would just fade away. Learned professors, the very same Israeli 'experts' who had been invariably wrong in the past, expounded this view in solemn talk shows on Israeli television. They were dumbfounded when Arafat sailed straight from Tripoli to Egypt and met with President Hosni Mubarak, Sadat's successor and heir.

In a way, it was a stroke of genius. In one simple act, Arafat put himself in the centre of world attention. Like a jack-in-the-box, a few days after most Western commentators predicted his inevitable demise in Tripoli, he popped up again. By effecting a reconciliation with Egypt, the arch-enemy of Syria, he had slapped al-Assad's face. By helping Mubarak ease his way back into the Arab fold, he demonstrated how important the role of the PLO was in the Arab world. By going to Cairo, he demonstrated that the way to a political solution did not necessarily have to lead through Amman, and thus he somewhat deflated Jordanian pretensions. And, more important than anything, by going to the one Arab capital in which the Israeli flag flew over an Israeli Embassy, he clearly indicated that the PLO, under his leadership, was ready and able to make peace.

Those of us who had been counting lost opportunities for many years could add another one to the list. Neither the Israeli government, nor the opposition, nor even the parts of the peace camp close to the establishment raised its voice to demand an Israeli response.

For me there was a postscript. After the Arafat-Mubarak encounter, Israeli television broadcast live a simulation exercise, with four different 'experts' taking the places of Reagan, Shamir, King Hussein and Arafat, each of whom spoke in the first person singular. I was chosen to play Arafat.

With more than a million Israelis watching, I explained Arafat's position at the moment. Asked whether the PLO has a future, I said: 'As long as there are four and a half million Palestinians alive in this region, the PLO is alive.'

Asked what I (meaning Arafat) had to offer, I imitated Arafat by raising my pen and saying: 'This is the only pen in the world which can recognize the State of Israel as a part of the Middle East and put an end to the conflict.'

## 49

*We are on the plane from Paris to Tunis. Matti and Abu Faisal are in front, Yaacov and I just behind.*

*We are, of course, speaking in English. But at one point, for some reason, we slip into Hebrew.*

*Abu Faisal turns around. 'What kind of English are you speaking?' he queries.*

*'It's Yorkshire English', Matti quips. 'No one understands that.'*

# 50

Abu Faisal had disappeared.

About an hour earlier, while we were sitting in the sun on the verandah of my hotel room, overlooking the Bay of Tunis, the telephone had rung. Abu Faisal had answered and then just disappeared, saying nothing.

After about half an hour we became a little uneasy. After an hour, without any sign of Abu Faisal, we were getting worried.

Earlier in the morning we had heard rumours that the chief of the Tunisian security services had been indicted. Was anything happening in the country which we knew nothing about?

It dawned on us that our situation was highly irregular. Here we were, in an Arab country, without passports, without any connection at all, knowing nobody but Abu Faisal, and Abu Faisal had disappeared.

'Perhaps there's been a *coup d'état*!' Matti ventured, not very reassuringly.

I started to write a story in my head. There had been a *coup d'état*, The Tunisian security officers, who had received us at the airport, had been thrown into prison as traitors. Army officers had taken over the government, accusing the former government of being in the pay of the imperialists and Zionists. Any moment now we would be arrested, confirming with our very presence the perfidy of the former rulers. An Israeli general, an Israeli politician, and an Israeli high functionary, staying illegally on Tunisian soil — was this not the perfect proof of the conspiracy between the traitors, the Israeli Mossad and Yassir Arafat?

Telling this story to Matti and Yaacov, I felt that they failed to appreciate it. So I made up another story, more in the style of Kafka. Abu Faisal had just disappeared. No one comes to contact us. We stay in the hotel, enjoy the meals, stroll on the seashore. No one asks us anything, no one demands anything. We are there and not there, in a country where we know no one, where we can't telephone anyone, where we can't leave the hotel for lack of papers. And this just goes on and on and on.

After another half hour, Abu Faisal reappears, smiling happily, saying: 'Fine, everything is in order', completely oblivious to the worry he had caused. Perhaps he had gone to meet his girlfriend, of whom he had told us, or perhaps he had been in consultation with Abu Maazen, who was waiting for us downstairs.

* * *

We had met Abu Faisal in Paris, in Issam's old office overlooking the river Seine. Nothing had changed there, but everything was different. Without

Issam Sartawi, the apartment was somehow lifeless, like an empty shell. We noticed that Abu Faisal did not sit in the armchair which Issam had always sat on. It had been discreetly put into a corner.

At Orly airport we three had kept at a distance from Abu Faisal, meeting only on the plane. At the Tunis airport we were received by the brother of the PLO ambassador there and Tunisian security officers, who locked our passports in their safe. From there we had gone to an hotel on the Bay of Monkeys, named, we learned, because there had been a wood inhabited by monkeys there, before a modern hotel was built by the government for the tourist trade.

After being ushered to our rooms, the usual game began. We had to fill out the registration forms. Who were we?

On the plane we had travelled under Arabic names, both Matti and I being registered, for some reason, as children. This had not fazed the airline official, who had waved us on, as had the black policeman at the Paris passport control, who saw nothing unusual in three Israeli passport holders travelling to Tunis.

In the hotel, Matti became Mahmoud Baladi, born in Acre. Yaacov became Abd-al-Aziz Yaacub, born in Haifa, far from his native Holland, and I became Daoud Abu Lughud, born, of all places, in Seattle.

I wanted to use the time to make a short trip to the city, but Abu Faisal was not happy about that. 'Matti and Yaacov may pass unnoticed', he said, 'but Uri's face is too well-known. Somebody might recognize him, and this would create unnecessary security problems.' So we stayed in the hotel and enjoyed the sun. Matti drank whisky, neat, as he had learned as a young army officer studying at the British War College. I refused to drink. 'I am angry, and I want to stay angry,' I said. 'Once I start drinking, I become mellow.'

Abu Faisal asked me what I was angry about, and I said that I wanted to criticize the unwillingness of the PLO leadership to let the Palestinians in the occupied territories play a bigger role. I always thought that because the PLO was based mainly on the Palestinian diaspora, and not enough on the 1.5 million Palestinians living in occupied Palestine, these were prevented from conducting an active, nonviolent resistance to the occupation.

'Okay, don't drink and stay angry,' Abu Faisal conceded, 'and tell this to Abu Mazen!'

* * *

During our first meeting in Tunis, fifteen months earlier, Abu Maazen had insisted on speaking Arabic, claiming he was not fluent enough in English. He had relied on Issam to translate. Now it turned out that his English was excellent, and we talked freely for about two hours over the Tunisian meal. A special dining room had been cleared for us. Several bodyguards were waiting outside.

Abu Maazen looks like an Arab schoolteacher. He has a no-nonsense manner and an analytical mind. Over a Tunisian dish called *brick,* the equivalent of an Oriental dish we call *bourrekas* in Israel, he gave us the rundown on the current situation in the PLO, while we talked about the forthcoming elections in Israel. Neither situation was very comforting.

The PLO was preparing for the seventeenth session of the Palestinian National Council, which had been postponed several times. The break with Syria and its stooges was final — but was it? In between there were the organizations which did not want a break with Syria, but which had remained loyal to the PLO — the Popular Front of Habash, the Democratic Front of Hawatmeh and the Palestinian Communist Party which, like Moscow, was betting on both sides. Abu Jihad was at the moment conducting negotiations with them in Algiers, hoping to convince them to stay in the PLO and to take part in the National Council, accepting the role of a loyal position, while decisions were taken by majority vote. This had never happened before.

For Habash and Hawatmeh, this was a delicate situation. During the Tripoli battle, they had not betrayed Arafat, knowing that the Palestinian people was practically unanimous in its support for the leader and in its hatred for those who had taken up arms against the Palestinian leadership. On the other hand, their organizations were based in Syria, their families lived there, they were, in a way, Syrian hostages. They were also sensitive to the Soviet line. The Soviets had, of course, an interest in preventing a split which would compel them to face an impossible choice.

Arafat himself, we understood, was ready for a showdown. Relying on his personal popularity among the Palestinian people, he was ready to convene the council and push through the resolutions which were needed with whatever majority there was. On the basis of these resolutions he would then conduct the unequivocal policy which he had in mind: announce a clear Palestinian peace line, call upon the Americans to start negotiations and try to influence Israeli public opinion in favour of the two-state solution. But other members of Fatah were afraid of a split and felt that another great effort should be made to achieve things by consensus. The postponement and the ongoing negotiations in Algiers were, primarily, designed to convince them that everything possible would be done to achieve agreement.

The tidings we brought them from Israel were not very gladdening either. In fact, they were worse. There was no chance at all of creating a united peace front, which could change the political setup of the country. Public opinion polls showed that an important body of opinion did now support the peace line, but the pattern of Israeli politics prevented this body from expressing itself as an organized political force. Many were going to support the Labour alignment again, believing that the main objective was saving the country from the Likud, disregarding the fact that in practice there was little difference between the two great blocs. Labour Party 'doves' were in fact acting as pied pipers, attracting moderate voters for a party led by hawks or semi-hawks.

What was left was a number of small peace groups, each competing with the others, some led by single leaders who detested each other.

The protest groups played no political role at all. The Peace Now movement, which consists of a small number of activists who were able at certain times to mobilize a great mass of unorganized demonstrators of various persuasions, had become subservient to the Labour alignment, and was inactive in elections. The much smaller Committee Against the War in Lebanon, which had played such an important role in the first stages of that war, had been practically deactivated by the Communist Party.

The Israeli Communist Party, Rakakh (the Hebrew acronym for the New Communist List), is a party totally subservient to Soviet policy, following its every twist and turn. Ninety-five percent of its voters, who constitute about three-and-a-half percent of the Israeli electorate, are Arab citizens. It is universally hated in Israel because of its anti-Zionist and pro-Soviet line, which has expressed itself in the past in justifying Stalin's paranoid ravings about a Jewish Doctors' Plot against his life, and which still denies the right of Soviet Jews to learn Hebrew or to emigrate to Israel. Needless to say, the party supported the Soviet invasion of Afghanistan and the suppression of Solidarity in Poland. There was no chance at all of the party changing its status in Israel without a thorough overhaul of its whole structure and outlook, such as becoming part of a much broader-based peace front. This it refused to do.

We were therefore planning to create a different kind of alignment, an alliance between Arab groups in Israel and Israeli peace groups, led by our own party, called Alternative after the split in Sheli following (and caused by) our first meeting with Arafat in Tunis. In the given circumstances, we were not too optimistic about the chances of this alignment in the 1984 elections, but we hoped to create, for the first time, a real, integrated Jewish-Arab movement in Israel, based on an agreed peace programme, as an investment for the future.

All this interested Abu Maazen very much. From time to time he made some notes, adding: 'You must tell this to Abu Amar.' We were scheduled to meet the Chairman later in the day, but no one quite knew when. Arafat was travelling, as usual, and was expected to arrive at any time.

* * *

It was already late in the evening on Shabbat, 21 April 1984, when the familiar face of Major Fathi, my old Beirut bodyguard, appeared in the doorway of the hotel. A convoy of four cars, two of them loaded with heavily armed bodygaurds, was waiting to conduct us to our meeting with the Chairman.

On the road along the seashore, we were stopped at a Tunisian Army checkpoint, which was set up to intercept possible saboteurs coming from Libya. Our guide said a few words and we were waved on.

At the Palestinian Embassy, another group of heavily-armed bodyguards in civilian clothes received us. We were conducted to a sitting room, similar to the one in which we had met Arafat the year before, and waited for a few minutes.

Upon entering, Abu Amar embraced and kissed all three of us, in his usual way. He was wearing a khaki uniform and the fur hat with the insignia of the commander-in-chief of the Palestinian forces. He took it off upon sitting down at the head of the table. As this was a secret meeting, and no photographer was about to take pictures, he did not put it on again.

During the two-hour-long conversation I watched him constantly, fascinated again by his personality. His famous defiant smile, it seemed to me, was in reality a kind of defence that hid a basically shy and introverted nature. When he took it off, there was a rather sad expression on his face. I was struck again by the thought that in a way Arafat personifies the Palestinian condition — the defiance, the pessimism, the perseverance, the sadness. Often a tone of bitterness crept into his voice, especially when he was speaking about other Arab countries, the Syrians and their Palestinian adherents. 'They are puppets, they are just puppets', he said, more in sorrow than in anger.

I reminded him that we had last met just before he went to Tripoli, and that he had not given us the slightest hint of his intentions. 'I knew that I was going there', he said, smiling. 'I also knew that I was going afterwards to Egypt'.

Tripoli, he told us, was worse than Beirut. In Beirut there were certain areas which were not shelled by the Israeli Army, such as the foreign embassies and the Hamra area. In Tripoli there were no exceptions made. Also, in Tripoli, only a part of the Palestinian forces was present. Yet he had come out victorious.

It seemed that his chief preoccupation at the moment was the situation in Syria. The PLO leadership seemed to be waiting for Hafez al-Assad to vanish from the political scene. In such a situation, there was bound to be competition between the two rival Alawi factions, one led by Assad's brother, Rifaat, and the other by the army group. Rifaat was closer to the PLO, but both factions would be in dire need of support, both in Syria and in the Arab world. The importance of the PLO was bound to increase rapidly should this happen. The darkest period would be over.

In the meantime, Arafat wanted to convene the PNC. He was determined to put an end to the consensus rule and adopt a system of majority decisions.

This gave me an opportunity to cite a historical example which was unknown to him: the Liberum Veto system, which had been the rule in Poland for many centuries. Under this rule, any member of the Polish Sejm, a parliament composed of noblemen, could stand up and say 'I object!' and this was enough to prevent a decision from being adopted. Historians agree that this rule played a great role in destroying the Polish state, which became time and again victim of the evil designs of its powerful neighbours.

We said that without wishing to interfere in the internal affairs of the PLO, we thought that it was of paramount importance for the organization to get rid of this evil practice, which was a travesty of democracy, giving a small minority veto power over the majority, and which had crippled the organization when bold and unequivocal decisions were needed. The dialogue with us was one of the victims of this configuration, which has made it impossible for Arafat to make the dramatic steps which we thought necessary to effect a basic change in Israeli public opinion.

One such decision, we added, could be to set up a Provisional Palestinian Government. To my surprise, Arafat readily agreed, adding 'It's already late, we should have done it long ago.' But there had been obstacles. The Soviet Union, he hinted, did not view such a step favourably. I could understand that. Since the Second World War, the Soviet Union had been loathe to create a precedent, fearing, not without justification, that it might be used by the Americans for dealing with emigré groups from countries annexed by the Soviet Union. Of course there was no sense in setting up a provisonal Palestinian government if it was not assured of official recognition by the Soviet bloc governments.

Our thoughts reverted constantly to the Lebanon War. I mentioned that Israeli military commentators had lauded the Palestinian resistance in the Sidon area during the first week of the war. It was now agreed that this resistance had created a bottleneck, which had held up the Israeli advance on Beirut for several crucial days.

At a recent meeting in Morocco, a Lebanese minister had told Arafat: 'We miss you already. As long as you were in Lebanon, the country was not cantonized.' King Hassan, who had overheard the remark, and, not believing his ears, had asked the Lebanese to explain what he meant. It appeared that the PLO had indeed acted as a unifying factor in the central and southern areas of Lebanon and prevented the different sects from setting up separate, *de facto* autonomous cantons.

Another incident was even more bizarre. After Beirut, when Arafat had come for the first time to Damascus, President Assad had welcomed him with the remark: 'How is it you're alive? You should have all died in Beirut!' To which Abu Jihad (or was it Abu Maazen?) had replied: 'It's not yet too late. If you wish, we can all die together in Damascus'.

Arafat recounted this gleefully. He was also amused by his recent meeting with Zbigniew Brzezinski. He had reminded him of Brzezinski's famous saying: 'Bye, bye PLO!' pointing out the obvious: that the PLO was still there, while Brezinski and Jimmy Carter were out of office. To which I added that the three conspirators of the Lebanon War — Menachem Begin, Alexander Haig and Bashir Gemayel — were all out of office, Bashir dead, Haig fired and Begin out of touch with the world. 'By the way, how is Begin?' Arafat inquired. I provided him with all the clinical details I could muster.

I was impressed by his grasp of the Israeli situation. Indeed, I have been amazed time and again by his astonishing memory for details, as well as by his quick intelligence, two attributes which may help to explain his dominant position. There can be no doubt that he is a consummate politician.

There was no need to impress him with the paramount necessity of changing Israeli public opinion, if any peaceful solution was to be achieved. He was totally set against the attitude of those Palestinian citizens of Israel who preached the gospel of boycotting Israeli elections, out of a misguided Palestinian patriotism. 'They are helping the extremists!' he asserted, echoing our own feelings. He promised to broadcast this message. It went without saying that he thus endorsed the Israeli electoral process. In fact this was a recognition of Israel, inside its pre-1967 borders, more eloquent than any other statement.

Another important point was the attitude towards recent guerrilla attacks in Jerusalem, in which a number of innocent bystanders had been killed. It had been widely published in Israel that the PLO had officially endorsed these acts. Arafat denied this vigorously. 'I have not endorsed the attack on the bus. After the Israeli government asserted that such an endorsement was published, we checked the matter thoroughly and found no such statement. Terzi [the PLO chief observer at the UN] has been asked about it, and has officially denied it.'

As Arafat later told me, this part of our conversation spurred him to publish two important statements, one in the London *Observer*, and the other in the important French left-wing *Le Nouvel Observateur*. In the 4 May issue of *Le Nouvel Observateur*, Arafat was asked about the Jerusalem attack and replied:

> I repeat that I have already often said: I make a great separation between military operations against military targets and military operations against civilian targets. I am against operations which affect civilians, as I have said a thousand times. But it's necessary to look at what is happening. In face of the terrorism that the State of Israel practices against us — the assassinations, and our prisoners in Israeli prisons and the attacks on the Palestinian mayors, such as Bassam Shaqa — there is this counterterrorism.'

In the same interview, Arafat was asked: 'You don't want to give up the war and you say that you want peace — without victors or vanquished. What do you propose to do?' Arafat answered: 'A direct negotiation: the Israelis and us, under the auspices of the United Nations.' The interviewer continued: 'You are for a mutual recognition between Israel and the PLO?' To which Arafat responded: 'I am for a mutual recognition of two states.'

Never before had Arafat endorsed the two-state peace solution in such completely unequivocal terms. Yet this historic statement was only briefly reported in the Israeli press, as routine news, and the Israeli government reacted with a short statement condemning it as another terrorist ploy.

Before this, Arafat was asked in another interview by Radio Monte Carlo who his candidate in the Israeli election was. He answered: 'My candidate is peace, peace, peace!'

* * *

One of the most important questions raised in the conversation concerned the immediate future. The Palestinian National Council had 364 members, most of them appointed by the constituent organizations, while others were independent members. Under its rules, a two-thirds majority was needed for the adoption of resolutions. Arafat and Abu Maazen seemed confident that they could command — barely — such a majority. But the picture could change drastically if the members were joined by another 180 delegates from the occupied territories.

Under the PNC rules, 180 seats were kept open for such delegates from the occupied territories, meaning in fact any personalities from the West Bank and Gaza who could attend. But this had been prevented at all previous sessions of the Council by the Israeli government, which threatened that any person from the West Bank and Gaza attending the Council session would not be allowed to return home. As it was clear that such delegates would almost automatically join the most moderate wing of the PLO, there could be no doubt that the Israeli government wanted to reinforce the PLO radicals and rejectionists, thus preventing the PLO from presenting itself to the world as an organization sincerely striving for a peaceful solution. The rationale was, of course, that in such a situation Israel could expect worldwide pressure for a peace settlement that would compel it to give back the occupied territories.

I had already taken up this subject with Itzhak Rabin, when he was prime minister of the Labour government, and had met with his absolute and total opposition. But now the situation was even clearer. If the 180 West Bank and Gaza delegates could attend the Council, the decisive majority for Arafat's peace line, as well as a decisive rejection of the rejectionists, was assured. But how could they come? There was no chance of the Israeli government changing its stance. Would the delegates dare to come without permission? Could Israeli peace forces exert an influence to make this possible?

Long after midnight we were driven back to our hotel. It had been a fruitful conversation, to use a trite diplomatic phrase. By this time I was ready for a few long drinks, while we compared notes and impressions.

As usual, I did not take notes during the conversation, but reconstructed it later, supplementing my own recollections with those of Matti and Yaacov. Back in Paris, these notes mysteriously disappeared, and I wonder in which archive they rest now. I had to reconstruct them all over again on my flight back to Tel Aviv.

## 51

*I am sitting opposite Yassir Arafat. As usual, he is wearing his khaki trousers. khaki sweater and brown boots. His head is bare. Around his neck he wears an elastic brace.*

*'What's wrong?' I ask.*

*'You know I once had disc troubles,' he answers. 'Lately I've travelled so much and spent so many hours in airplanes, that I need this.'*

*'Why? You're much too young for that. I remember that you're younger than I am', I rib him.*

*'Yes, but you have not gone through what he has gone through', says Abu Maazen, who is sitting next to him*

# 52

Three weeks later I went again to Tunis. This time alone.

Developments in the PLO and in Israel had made another exchange of views desirable.

Arriving at the Palestinian Embassy on the Tunis seashore, the ambassador, Hakam Mal'abi received me at the entrance and showed the way to the same room in which the last meeting had taken place. I walked ahead into the room, expecting it to be empty. During all my former meetings with Arafat, he had come into the room after some time.

Entering, I was therefore surprised to see Abu Maazen sitting on the sofa watching television. I went up to him and we embraced. Only then did I notice that Yassir Arafat was sitting quietly in the corner of the sofa. He came up and we embraced, too.

* * *

Going to Tunis had nearly become routine.

Abu Faisal had asked me to come to Paris. At the airport I was met by the indefatigable Joyce Blau. She told me that Abu Faisal was already waiting for me in Tunis and asked me to continue on by myself. She had booked a flight for me, using the name U. Armeli.

I went to the Air France counter to buy the ticket. There was a problem. I did not want to use the few dollars I had with me, and therefore I handed over my Israeli credit card. The pretty ground hostess made out the ticket, and only when I was on my way to the check-in counter did I realize that she had used my real name, the one that appears on my credit card.

Both Joyce and I were worried. Would somebody recognize my obviously Hebrew name? Would anyone demand to see my passport, or ask me to produce a Tunisian visa? Neither I nor any of my colleagues had ever travelled to an Arab country without being accompanied by either Issam or Abu Faisal.

But Abu Faisal is a travel expert, and he obviously knew all the procedures. At the check-in counter no one asked for a passport. In the departure lounge the reception clerk waved me on.

Waiting for the plane, I put on the earphones of my Walkman. Nothing discourages anyone so much from striking up a conversation with a stranger than this. No one dares disturb a person listening intently to music. I did not take it off on the way to the plane, nor in the plane itself. Beethoven's *Emperor Concerto* stood me in good stead!

I did not ask myself what would happen if Abu Faisal or his friends failed, through some misunderstanding or negligence, to meet me at the plane in

Tunis. I had learned to trust Abu Faisal's efficiency implicitly. And indeed, when I came down the steps of the plane, the brother of the ambassador was already waiting, accompanied by the Tunisian security officer whom I knew well by now. As usual, I was whisked away in a special bus, which I had all to myself, to the VIP lounge, where I again deposited my Israeli passport.

Abu Faisal and I indulged in our usual sport of inventing an identity for me for the hotel registration forms. This time I was endowed with the identity of a gentleman whom I happened to know because I had met him at the Geneva Conference. So I became Fauzi Khouri, a professor born in Bethlehem, now living in Seattle. For somebody who had not quite finished elementary school, this was progress indeed.

We were still laughing when the brother of the ambassador reminded us that this was a sad day for the Palestinian people: May 15. For a moment I did not comprehend and asked: 'What's wrong with May 15?' Only then did I remember the meaning of this date for the Palestinians. We Israelis commemorate the founding of our state according to the Hebrew calendar, which generally precedes the May 15 date by a few days.

On 15 May 1948, I had been staying in the Arab village of al-Qubab, on the highroad between Tel Aviv and Jerusalem, which we had occupied the evening before, finding in many houses unfinished meals, abandoned by the inhabitants a few moments earlier. These were the refugees, the people for whom and for the descendants of whom the PLO was working, the people with whom we Israelis wanted to make peace.

* * *

I had expected to meet with Abu Maazen in Tunis. But now Abu Faisal told me why he had asked me to come urgently that very day. 'The old man is waiting for you. He's leaving tomorrow morning, and he has set aside the time for a long meeting with you.'

I knew by now why Abu Faisal had not received me in Paris. Information had been received that a hit squad had arrived in France to kill him. Prudently, he had not entered that country for some time. But his fate was very much on my mind. Hammami and Sartawi had been killed, as had Curiel. I did not want to write another obituary.

So, during my conversation with Arafat, when the Chairman mentioned that he wanted Abu Faisal to do something for him, I interjected: 'But his first job is to stay alive!' When Arafat asked what I meant, I told him the story about the hit squad. Without hesitation, he decided to detail three of his most trusted personal bodyguards to follow Abu Faisal wherever he went. As Abu Faisal later told me, Issam Sartawi, when offered the same protection, had proudly refused.

* * *

During the intervening three weeks, quite a lot had happened. Arafat had gone to China, where he had been accorded the honours due a head of government. A few days before him, President Reagan had been received in Beijing with a 21-gun salute. Arafat received only a 19-gun salute, and so had the Japanese prime minister a few days earlier. The meticulous Chinese had decided that Arafat was not a head of state — not a king or a president

— but rather, as Chairman of the PLO Executive, ranked as a prime minister. Hence the two salvo difference. But, as if to make up for this, Arafat had stayed in the same palace as Reagan; perhaps he slept in the same bed.

More importantly, the Chinese had been completely won over to the formula proposed by Arafat: an international conference for the solution of the Palestine question, with the participation of all the concerned parties, under the auspices of the United Nations Security Council. Indeed, at the conclusion of the state visit, the official Chinese organ, *Reming Bao*, had put forward this proposal as the official policy of the Chinese government itself.

It was a clever formula, because, by emphasizing the role of the Security Council, Arafat automatically conferred a leading role on all five permanent members of the Council — China, Great Britain, and France, besides the United States and the Soviet Union. The Chinese liked this, as did the West Europeans. This explains why the Chinese had come out for the first time in favour of Israeli–Palestinian peace. Until then, Chinese policy had been more in line with the rejectionist position.

On the way to China, Arafat had been the guest of honour at the congress of the ruling Greek Socialist Party. There he had propounded the same line. In a press conference, he had been asked whether 'all parties' included Israel, to which he replied: '*All* parties', emphasizing the word 'all'.

At the same time, King Hussein, in an interview, put forward the same proposal, also stressing that such a conference must include Israel and the PLO.

This was not surprising. But what was remarkable was that President Assad, in his first interview in the American media after a long silence, put forward the very same proposal — in spite of the fact that the Soviet Union, for obvious reasons, was talking about a new Geneva-style peace conference. At Geneva in 1973, the conference had been chaired jointly by the American and Soviet foreign ministers, as well as by the UN Secretary General. China and the West Europeans had not been there. Syria had also left its seat unoccupied.

All this was great progress — or could have been, if it had not been totally ignored by Israel and the United States. Indeed, the Israeli press hardly mentioned any of these facts.

The only time the famous 'political circles' in Jerusalem (always meaning the foreign office) had reacted to any recent PLO move was when it rejected the Arafat interview in *Le Nouvel Observateur*, pretending that the unequivocal call for mutual recognition between Israel and the future Palestinian state was another example of PLO deviousness.

Arafat seemed hurt by this reaction. 'You see,' he told me, 'I have done what you asked me to do. I have made an unequivocal statement about mutual recognition and I have again roundly condemned guerrilla attacks against civilians. But the answer has been very rude.' And after a short silence he repeated: 'Very rude.'

I told him that there was no cause for surprise here. 'The Likud government wants to annex the occupied territories. They are not afraid of an extremist PLO. They are mortally afraid of a moderate PLO. The more unequivocal your statements in favour of peace, the ruder their answers. The very rudeness should encourage you, because it means that they are frightened. As Yaacov Arnon told you last time, the Likud government has an answer for every move you make, except this one.'

I again urged Arafat to make dramatic gestures, in order to speak directly to the Israeli public. It was my old message all over again: in order to change the government, one had to change public opinion. In order to change public opinion, which had become solidified after four generations of war, dramatic gestures were needed. For example, his *Nouvel Observateur* interview would have had a different impact if it had been made directly to the Israeli media.

To illustrate my point, I told Arafat and Abu Maazen a story. The relaxed atmosphere of our conversation made this possible. I was emboldened by it to do something which I would not have dared to do before — to give Arafat, the master politician, something like a political lesson.

In 1959, I had been on a visit to the States, and a friend had dragged me to a high-class benefit ball. When everybody stood up to dance, I was left alone at the table in the company of a gentleman unknown to me. Drinking vodka together, we introduced ourselves. It appeared that he was the ambassador of the People's Republic of Rumania to Washington. This was, of course, when Rumania was still an integral part of the Soviet bloc.

When he heard that I was an Israeli journalist, but not knowing my views, he sadly exclaimed: 'What has happened to the Jews? You used to be the most clever people in the world, and now you've become plain stupid!'

Rather taken aback, I asked what he meant. 'The way you treat the Arabs,' he said. 'You must make peace with them. You should be clever enough to know how to do that.'

Asking again what he meant, he gave me a lecture which ran like this: 'One day the Soviet Union decided that the continuation of the Cold War was detrimental to its interests, and that it had to get the Americans to change their policy. So what did the Soviets do? They knew that it was useless to send such a request to President Eisenhower or to [John Foster] Dulles [at that time the Secretary of State and renowned for his rigid anti-Sovietism], but they knew that by changing public opinion in America, they could compel the president to change his policy. They started to bombard the American public with initiatives. In the morning American veterans were invited to take part in a meeting with Soviet veterans of the Second World War in Stalingrad commemorating the comradeship that had prevailed then. At noon a Soviet trade mission was sent to Japan to tell the Japanese that a bottomless Soviet market was awaiting their goods, if only there were no Cold War. In the evening the memory of Lincoln was toasted at a reception for American writers in Moscow. And so on and so forth, day after day. Each little initiative got some coverage in the Western media, and bit by bit the American view of the Soviet Union changed. The Soviet Union was de-demonized. In the end the American government had to follow suit.'

I added that after this, the American public elected Kennedy, preferring him to the rabidly anti-communist Nixon, and the nuclear non-proliferation pact was signed, leading eventually to detente. If I wanted to change public opinion in democratic countries like the United States and Israel, this was the way.

Our conversation turned to the upcoming Israeli elections. I told them about our efforts to set up a joint Jewish–Arab peace list. This was a breakthrough in Israeli politics, because it was the first really integrated effort of Jewish and Arab nationalists in Israel to work together. The platform, of course, called for equality between Jewish and Arab citizens of Israel within its 4 June 1967 borders; for the setting up of a Palestinian national state in the Gaza Strip and the West Bank, including East Jerusalem; and for direct negotiations between the Israeli government and the PLO.

I was again astonished by the agility of Arafat's mind in sizing up a political situation. He immediately pointed out that, as the main object was to change Jewish public opinion in Israel, a Jew should head the list. Sadly, our Arab friends in Israel did not grasp this point, and insisted that one of their members be number one on the list. This, among other things, reduced the appeal the list should have had among the Jewish public in Israel. Arafat also characterized as idiotic the call of some Arabs in Israel for a boycott of the elections on nationalistic grounds. 'They are helping the enemies of peace,' he commented.

Moving from our problems to his, we talked about the forthcoming session of the Palestinian National Council. I frankly expressed my worry that this session, if it took place on the eve of our elections, and if the hardliners again unleashed their scurrilous rhetoric, could do us great damage. I mentioned that this had happened in 1977 and in 1981 — this point led to a quick exchange of meaningful glances between Abu Amar and Abu Maazen.

Anyhow, Arafat reassured me, there was no chance of the PNC convening before our elections. The month of Ramadan was coming up, and during the fast no political action could take place. Without much obvious regret, he foresaw that the PNC would take place after July.

* * *

The next day I flew back to Paris. I was again denied the opportunity to see the city of Tunis. My hosts did not wish me to be recognized. The negotiations inside the PLO were still at a delicate stage, and my meeting with Arafat could have been construed as a deliberate provocation by him. For the time being, therefore, secrecy was important. Besides Matti and Yaacov, and of course my wife, no one knew about this journey.

On the plane, sipping champagne, I tried to recapture the excitement I had felt during my first flight to Tunis, my first flight to Rabat, my first meeting with Arafat in Beirut, my first meeting with Hammami. Now our meetings with Arafat had become routine, or nearly so.

This was perhaps the best indicator of how far we had come since my first meeting with Said Hammami in London, more than nine years ago.

## 53

*Abdel Fatah Kalkili, former PLO representative in Rome, says that he loved and admired Issam Sartawi, even though he didn't agree with many of his ideas.*

*Kalkili likes to illustrate all his points with stories, the Arab way. About the Palestinian attitude towards Issam, he tells this story:*

*'A city is beleaguered. Its commander, a famous general, plans treason. He meets with the agents of the enemy, and the two agree that the general will open one of the gates and let the enemy in.*

*'The son of the general overhears this conversation. He does not know what to do. Who would believe him if he told the story to the city fathers? In the end, in desperation, he kills his father.*

*'The enemy, thwarted in its design, departs. The city is saved.*

*'But the city — it is horrified by the crime. It erects a statue to the great general, the saviour. The son is chained to the statue, and every citizen spits in his face while passing.*

*'Only much later does the truth come to light, and the city realizes that it is the son who saved the city, taking it upon himself to do the terrible deed.'*

# 54

General elections were held in Israel on 23 July 1984.

Two months earlier we had set up the *Progressive List for Peace.* It was a revolutionary departure in Israeli politics. For the first time in the history of the state, Jews and Arabs created a joint and fully integrated political force. Our election list was composed of 60 Jews and 60 Arabs, alternating, headed by an Arab, Mohammed Miari, and followed by General Matti Peled. The list adopted a short but far-reaching programme: Coexistence of Israel and a Palestinian state (this to be set up in the occupied territories); complete equality of all Israeli citizens irrespective of nationality, religion, community or sex.

The reaction was speedy. The Minister of Defence, Moshe Arens, declared his intention to outlaw the List, but after a long and acrimonious meeting with us, he gave up this idea. Next, the General Election Committee, composed of party hacks, decided to ban the List. We went to the Supreme Court which, after a lengthy hearing, set the decision aside. Later the Court published its judgement, one of the most important in the constitutional history of Israel, saying that there existed no reasonable grounds for banning this List.

On election day we gained two seats. Miari and Peled both entered parliament.

In the Arab sector of the electorate, our victory was remarkable. Nearly 20% voted for the new list. This was even more impressive in view of the fact that the List was not only attacked by the Labour Party, but also became the object of a ferocious onslaught by the Communists, who had until now enjoyed a virtual monopoly of the Arab Nationalist vote in Israel. Our list was described in daily attacks in the Communist Arab newspaper — the only Arab daily in Israel proper — as the instrument of an American conspiracy. I myself was branded as a CIA agent. These attacks did not stop on election day, but continue with ever growing vehemence to this very day.

* * *

However, our achievement was overshadowed by two other election results.

Rabbi Meir Kahane, running on a straight racist platform, gained entry into the Knesset. Israel, and the whole world, was shocked by the sight of an honest-to-goodness Jewish Nazi sitting in the Knesset, demanding the enactment of the Nuremberg laws, with the Jews taking the place of the Aryans and the Arabs filling in for the Jews. Very soon public opinion polls would show that Kahane would now get five or even more seats.

The other result posed more immediate problems. The new Knesset was exactly evenly divided between the Labour Party and the left wing on the one side, and the Likud bloc and the other right-wing groups on the other. Shimon

Peres, the Labour leader, could have set up a narrow-based government of his own, if he had been ready to rely on the votes of our list and the Communists. In that case he would have needed the votes of two maverick members in order to secure a majority. But nothing was further from his mind. He indignantly turned down this suggestion, even after we told the President, in an obligatory meeting, that we were ready to support such a government without joining it, if it were based on a minimum programme of peace and equality.

Instead Peres set up a government of national unity, in which he became a virtual prisoner of the need for unanimity. Even the slightest move towards peace became impossible. The Likud had a veto over any action by the government, at a time when the party, now thoroughly alarmed by the success of Kahane and the near-fascist Tehiya Party, moved even more to the right in order to compete.

This was even more unfortunate in view of the dramatic developments on the other side.

***

In November Arafat convened the Palestinian National Council in Amman. This location was dictated by necessity. Virtually no other Arab state would agree to have the Congress convene on its soil, in face of Syrian and Libyan threats. At no other time was the isolation of the Palestinians in the Arab world so apparent. But the choice of Amman for the Council meeting had an importance of its own. It showed that Arafat had now reached the point of no return. He was committed to cooperation with Jordan and to the peace process.

The fact that more than two-thirds of the Council members — the necessary quorum — showed up proved that the vast majority of the Palestinian people had rallied behind the leadership of Arafat and disavowed the so-called rebels and their Syrian masters.

At my previous meeting with Arafat I had strongly advocated convening the Council in Amman for quite a different reason. Jordanian television is widely viewed in Israel. When the Jordanian station broadcast the proceedings live day after day, the effect was electrifying. Life in the occupied territories and the Arab towns and villages in Israel proper practically stopped, and everybody was glued to their sets. For the first time they saw the whole spectrum of Palestinian leaders. Arafat and his colleagues were in people's living rooms, talking directly to two million Palestinians under Israeli rule, giving them a new pride and sense of identity.

Not less important was the effect on Jewish Israelis, many of whom also saw the proceedings on Jordanian TV or saw those parts broadcast by the Israeli station. For the first time they saw the dreaded 'terrorist gang' as real people, arguing, debating, voting. And they looked like very ordinary people, rather bourgeois — indeed the general appearance was much like the familiar sight of a Zionist Congress. Surprising to Israelis was the obvious democratic character of the Council. Arafat himself was told by the Chairman to sit down when he tried to speak out of turn; debates were real; votes far from unanimous. The boast of the Palestinians, that their parliament-in-exile was the only democratic institution in the Arab world, seemed well founded.

The political result was no less important. The Council adopted the idea of a peace conference under the auspices of the five permanent members of the UN Security Council. In such a conference the PLO was to take its seat alongside Israel, which meant in practice that the PLO was ready for direct, face-to-face negotiations with Israel.

Three months later Arafat took the next logical step on the road to peace. He signed an agreement with King Hussein, endorsing again the idea of an international peace conference, the aim being the establishment of a Palestinian state in the West Bank and the Gaza Strip within the framework of a confederation with Jordan. The first step was to be the opening of a dialogue with the United States. A joint Jordanian–Palestinian delegation was to be set up for this purpose in order to overcome the US commitment to Israel not to negotiate with the PLO unless that body recognized Israel's right to exist as well as Security Council Resolution 242. As the Palestinians object to doing this prior to negotiations, instead of as a result of the negotiations themselves and in return for Israel's recognition of the Palestinians' right to self-determination, a way had to be found to circumvent this obstacle.

* * *

A few days before Arafat went to Jordan to sign this agreement, he received in Tunis a delegation of the Progressive List for Peace, consisting of Mohammed Miari, the Anglican Arab priest Riah Abu-Al-Assal and the Arab advocate Kamel Daher, a descendant of the legendary 18th Century King of Galilee, Daher Omar; the Three Musketeers — Arnon, Peled and I — constituted the other half of the delegation.

Sipping tea sweetened with honey, Arafat listened attentively. We told him about our List, its purpose and struggle. His first reaction was: 'This is extremely important because Jews and Arabs are fighting together. That's good!'

Arafat did not pin many hopes on Shimon Peres and the new government — a scepticism which proved only too well founded. He did not believe that the US would budge from its negative stand until it found it expedient during negotiations with the Russians. He was cautiously hopeful that this would eventually happen, but did not believe that it would be very soon.

One of the main problems on our mind was the escalating violence. We cautiously aired the idea of an armistice or cease-fire, perhaps in the context of a new political initiative. Arafat did not reject the idea out of hand, but made it clear that the Palestinians would discuss it only if Israel accepted in principle the plan for an international peace conference.

Of more immediate concern to us was an idea which was very close to our hearts. During the war in Lebanon several Israeli soldiers had disappeared. Their bodies had not been found, and they were not known to have been captured. Their families were, of course, in a terrible state of uncertainty, hoping against hope that their sons might turn up in captivity. We asked Arafat to give us information about their fate, both as a humanitarian gesture and as a political act.

Without the slightest hestitation Arafat assented, adding that he would need a few days to assemble the relevant information.

We discussed our problems for several hours, had lunch together, adjourned for a few hours so as to enable Arafat to rest, and reconvened late in the evening. Arafat had visited about a dozen countries in as many days, sleeping on the plane, and obviously needed some sleep. So did his photographer, who did not show up at all. I had taken up photography only a few days before, following my wife, and had a small amateur camera with me. So I took the necessary official pictures myself. During the intermission we visited the ruins of Carthage. By coincidence the Mayor of Rome had come to Tunis on the very same day to sign a symbolic Peace Treaty with Carthage. 'If Rome makes peace with Carthage, Israel can make peace with the Palestinians!' joked one of the PLO people who accompanied us. 'I hope it will take less than 2,500 years,' I quipped.

We also went to see the Souk of Tunis — the first time, after so many visits, that I saw the town itself. Being accompanied by a Muslim like Miari, I was even allowed to enter the beautiful mosque, famous throughout the Muslim world.

In the evening I read to Arafat the draft of a communique we had prepared. With minor changes Arafat approved it, but not as a joint declaration; it was to be a unilateral statement which we were allowed to read out at home.

It read as follows:

> 1. A delegation of the Progressive List for Peace (PLP) met with Yassir Arafat, chairman of the executive committee of the Palestine Liberation Organization (PLO). The delegation included Knesset Members Muhammed Miari and Mattityahu Peled, and the Rev. Riah Abu-Al-Assal, Mr. Uri Avnery, Dr Yaacov Arnon and Adv. Kamel Daher, members of the PLP executive.
>
> 2. In the meeting there took place a frank and open exchange of views on recent developments in the region, and both sides presented their views and positions.
>
> 3. The delegation presented a request to obtain the names and other information concerning Israeli soldiers missing in the Lebanon war. Chairman Arafat promised to transmit that information to the PLP within a few days.
>
> 4. Chairman Arafat expressed his appreciation of the Israeli peace forces, who support the principle of self-determination for the Palestinian people, and emphasized the interest of the PLO in an ever-widening dialogue with all these forces, in order to further the endeavours for a just peace.
>
> 5. Both sides expressed their view that the best way to achieve a just peace is through an international peace conference, under UN auspices, with the participation of all parties concerned, principally Israel and the PLO — as proposed by the UN secretary-general, on the basis of U.N. resolutions. The willingness of the PLO to participate in such a conference is based on the resolutions of the 17th session of the Palestinian National Council (PNC), held in Amman. The opposition by the Israeli and US governments to the convening of this conference is the cause of the present deadlock in the peace process, and of the deteriorating situation in the occupied territories.

6. The PLP delegation submitted proposals for a mutual cessation of violence in the context of such an international peace conference.

Before coming back to Israel, we alerted our friends who called a press conference at Ben Gurion airport. But when the journalists arrived, a police officer prevented them from entering the hall. The Inspector-General of the Israeli Police later apologized for this, but in the meantime we had to talk with the journalists outside the airport building. In no time at all, a crowd of hooligans surrounded us, shouting fascist slogans and threatening violence. In the tumult, the poor journalists had to write down our statement, fearing for their own safety. The police looked on, taking no action.

The Tunis meeting had an extremely unfortunate aftermath. All Israel waited for us to produce the information about the missing soldiers within a few days. It did not arrive. We could only guess that Arafat was overruled by his colleagues, who did not want to give away something for nothing. To us it was a terrible blow, discrediting our whole enterprise.

* * *

During the following months the situation worsened. Throughout 1985 violent action in Israel multiplied. On top of the usual bombings by clandestine cells of the various Fedayeen organizations, expressing the growing frustration of their members at the virtual standstill of the peace process, a sinister new element appeared. Spontaneous groups of young Palestinians in the occupied territories committed random acts of violence, generally killing Jewish couples looking for privacy in remote parts of the country. This poured oil on the flames of hatred, assiduously fanned by Meir Kahane and his gang. There were pogrom-like outrages against Arabs in several places. Racist incitement flourished.

Trying to compete with Kahane, the Likud element in the governing coalition introduced a Bill which was a kind of legal coup d'état. One day, when the Members took their seats in the Knesset, they found on the tables a piece of blue paper signifying a draft law proposed by the government. The Labour ministers were completely taken by surprise. It appeared that the Bill had been prepared by the Minister of Justice, a Likud functionary, and that his Labour colleagues had not noticed it — an act of omission which was itself significant.

The Bill completely changed the legal status of our peace talks with the PLO. It simply said that any meeting with officials of a 'terrorist organization' (as the PLO is officially defined by law in Israel) constitutes a crime, punishable by three years imprisonment, irrespective of the reason for the meeting. The two defence clauses in the existing law which had made our contacts legally possible — namely, that there were 'reasonable grounds' for the meeting and that there was no intent to harm the security of the State — were simply abolished.

There was an outcry in some circles, in Israel and abroad, and a row ensued between the Likud and the Labour Party which felt that it had been tricked. Both sides looked for a face-saving device, meaning that the new law would be enacted after only slight semantic changes.

* * *

Faced with increasing acts of violence and growing racist reactions the Israeli government struck a new and sinister note. All the fault lay supposedly with King Hussein, who had allowed the 'terrorist bases' to be set up in his kingdom. Peres and his colleagues meant, of course, the political offices of the PLO which had started to function again in Amman as a part of the joint Jordanian–Palestinian effort to get the peace process going.

This was exactly what the Israeli government was out to prevent. An understanding between Hussein, Arafat and the Americans could only lead towards a process that would eventually compel Israel to relinquish the West Bank and Gaza in return for peace. This was anathema to the Likud and unacceptable to the Labour Party too, as Yitzhak Rabin had explained to me nine years before. Better stop the process right at the beginning.

I now met Shimon Peres in the very same room in which Rabin had told me this. He was much more circumspect in his utterances, blaming Hussein and Arafat for not being accommodating enough. He expected them to give away all their cards before the game had even started.

I tried to explain to him the intricacies of the Palestinian situation and voiced my fears that if Israel or the Americans would not budge an inch, after all the progress made by the PLO, sooner or later the moderate leadership would fall and be replaced with Khomeini-type leaders. 'And then,' I added, 'God have mercy on us all.'

Peres remained unmoved. During the days that followed he continued to threaten King Hussein, saying that Israel would strike at the terrorists 'wherever they were to be found' — even in Amman.

This was an ominous statement. Much the same words had been used before the Israeli attack on Egypt in 1956, and before the Israeli attack on Lebanon in 1982.

## 55

*We are sitting in Tunis, talking about conditions which would put an end to the acts of violence, which Israelis call terrorism and the Palestinians a war of liberation.*

*'We don't fight because we like fighting!' Arafat exclaims. 'Military action serves a political end. We want to achieve our freedom, our State. But what do you expect us to do when all our political signals remain unanswered, by both the Americans and Israel?'*

# 56

I have to stop the narrative here. Not because it has come to an end. On the contrary, looking back over the last ten and a half years, since my first meeting with Said Hammami in London, I realize that we are still only at the first section of a long road.

I have tried to tell this story as truthfully as I could. Perhaps it is a sad story, perhaps an encouraging one. We have suffered a host of defeats and setbacks. But we have also encountered human perseverance, dedication to an ideal, courage in the face of adversity. People have given their lives, many have faced daily danger for years. Not for war, but for peace.

* * *

What have we achieved? Has anything been won at all? Were all these sacrifices justified? Those who gave their lives, those who sacrificed political careers and material benefits, those who have suffered unspeakable calumny, who have been branded by their peoples as traitors and fools — have their endeavours been in vain?

To me, the answer is self-evident. This long effort, this adventure for peace is of historic significance.

I often feel like a boy playing a game from my childhood. You face a blank wall and hide your face. A group of other boys is trying to reach you, starting some way away. Whenever you turn round you see no movement, but the other boys are not standing where they stood before.

The thousands of hours we have spent in argument with our Palestinian counterparts, trying to explain to them Israeli problems, Israeli traumas, Israeli realities, have had a profound impact — not only on the people with whom we spoke, but on an ever-widening circle of PLO leaders and officials.

During these ten years the PLO had advanced an immense distance towards peace. This has been hidden behind a smokescreen of propaganda, both Palestinian and Israeli. But ten years ago Hammami seemed a solitary figure, with his patrons only vaguely discernible in the fog. Today the governing bodies of the PLO have openly adopted resolutions designed to lead to an international peace conference, which means a readiness to recognize Israel and to make peace with it.

This is not enough. Many more steps have to be taken before peace becomes possible. But the present stance of the PLO leadership is sufficient for the negotiations to start, provided Israel and the US are ready for them.

It is my deep conviction that nothing can take the place of direct, face-to-face dialogue. Dialogue has become a cult phrase, a cliché, an empty slogan on pamphlets. But in reality dialogue is one of the most profound human and political instruments. One does not only exchange words, one exchanges looks, involuntary facial expressions, unconscious gestures. One persuades and is persuaded in many ways, conscious and unconscious. One detects truth and mendacity. One uses one's intuition.

This is true between friends and lovers. It is even truer between enemies. One does not make peace except with enemies, and one does not make peace with enemies who are despised or who are conceived of as inhuman monsters. After four generations of war between the Jews and the Palestinians, the enemy — the PLO and its leaders — are regarded by Jewish Israelis as demons, as abominations. In exactly the same way Palestinians regard the hated Zionists, not as normal people with their everyday hopes and cares, but as the new Nazis, beyond the pale of humanity. Our dialogue had helped to shatter these diabolical images. It has de-demonized each side in the eyes of the other. Arafat sitting between an Israeli General and an Israeli Member of Parliament is not the same 'captain of murderers' he was before; and Zionists cannot all be devils if they sit next to Arafat.

Political decisions are made by people. People's actions are shaped by their perceptions. Mere politicians do not understand the underlying psychological realities of the world in which they move. Our job is to change these realities on both sides in order to change the course of events from war to peace.

* * *

The Palestinians have changed, and I believe that our action has had some bearing on this.

Can the same be said about the Israelis?

A Palestinian diplomat once told me: 'The gap between the two sides remains unchanged. The more we become moderate, the more the Israelis become extreme.' He was not wrong.

At this very moment, the intransigence of the Israeli government is reaching new heights. There is a total Israeli veto on any negotiations with the real representatives of the Palestinian people, not only by Israel but also by the US. The peace process, so much talked about, has come to a total standstill. Fearing, not without justification, that the peace process will lead to a Palestinian State in the territories now being Judaized by the government of national unity, the government is trying to stop this process right at the beginning.

Realizing the importance of our dialogue, the government is paying us a dangerous compliment. A new law, making everything we have done during the past ten years a crime, will probably bring us to prison. Meeting for peace is now a crime. Meeting for war remains a virtue.

At the same time the Knesset has enacted another law, designed to prevent Arabs from taking part in Israeli democracy. Under the guise of combating racism, this law says that no list of candidates will be allowed to stand for election if it denies that 'Israel is the State of the Jewish people'. A philosophical and historical question — Who are the Jews? Is there a Jewish people? — has been turned by law into the demand for an ideological declaration, reminding one of mediaeval times. The law does not mention the existence of 700,000 Palestinians who are full Israeli citizens. It simply demands that they abjure their stake in the State.

At the moment of concluding this narrative the chances of peace are at their lowest ebb. Both in Israel and amongst the Palestinians, powerful forces are arrayed against it. Both super-powers seem indifferent. The prospect of another war, with its dead and maimed, looms on the horizon. This time the target may be Amman.

* * *

This book does not try to apportion blame, even if I sometimes find it difficult to refrain from this. After all, with so many opportunities missed, so many people killed — surely someone must be responsible.

But we are dealing here with an historical process. Both sides are prisoners of their history, of their traumas. The Jews, with their long history of persecution, their memories of the Holocaust, their ensuing craving for absolute security, their unresolved relationship to the Gentiles, and their own religion, find it as difficult to face reality rationally as do the Palestinians with their grievances, humiliations and fathomless feeling of the injustice done to them. This creates a vicious circle. Frustrated in all their endeavours, offered no chance of freedom and independence, Palestinians resort to violence. Israelis in turn see this as proof that only war will safeguard their future. Arab violence and Jewish racism feed on each other.

We are trying to break this deadly circle. Sometimes it seems that we are losing the race against time. Only our optimism, totally unfounded, keeps us going. But perhaps we are right after all. There is no solution but the one we are advocating. The alternative is too terrible to contemplate.

Without a solution, sooner or later, and perhaps sooner rather than later, the Middle East is going to blow up. Moderate rational leaders will be replaced by religious fanatics, Islamic and Jewish. There will be no one to talk to. Both sides will explode in a cataclysmic, joint, nuclear holocaust.

* * *

Many people realize this today, but none as clearly as did Issam Sartawi.

De Gaulle once remarked ironically that the world's graveyards are filled with people who are irreplaceable. But Issam really is irreplaceable — a man of vision, who dared to speak up and say the things which needed to be said. How few are the Issams of this world!

In February 1979 I made a bet with him that within seven years a Palestinian State would come into being and peace would reign in our common homeland. I am going to lose that bet. I shall empty the bottle of whisky alone, in his memory.

# Index